Library Service

LEISURE SERVICES

Please remember that this item will attract overdue charges if not returned by the latest date stamped above. You may renew it by personal call, telephone or by post quoting the bar code number and your personal number. I hope you enjoy all of your library services.

Peter Herring, Head of Arts and Libraries

INCARNATIONS

Also by Clive Barker

INCARNATIONS

THREE PLAYS

BY

CLIVE BARKER

HarperCollins*Publishers*

HarperCollins*Publishers*
77–85 Fulham Palace Road,
Hammersmith, London W6 8JB

Published by HarperCollins*Publishers* 1996
1 3 5 7 9 8 6 4 2

First published in the USA by
HarperPrism 1995

A catalogue record for this book is
available from the British Library

ISBN 0 00 225404 2

Set in Berkeley

Printed in Great Britain by
HarperCollinsManufacturing Glasgow

Contents

FOR BILL HENRY,
MY FRIEND

Notwithstanding the notice posted on the copyright page of this book, alerting potential producers to the fact that the plays in this volume are fully protected under the Copyright Laws and thus subject to a royalty, it is my intention that any <u>amateur</u> or <u>non-profit</u> organization that wishes to mount a theatrical production (this does not apply to any other medium) do so with the minimum of contractual or financial burden. Plainly, if a company or a producer seeks to profit by one of these plays, then a royalty rate must be agreed and paid. If, however, an amateur or non-profit company is interested in mounting a production, write to me or my representatives at the address below, and let's see if we can make it work. Please note: the above does not mean I am offering a blanket sanction to any and all. I reserve the right to veto any production (if, for instance, a professional version is planned in the vicinity) but plays are written to be produced, and I will certainly entertain any reasonable approach from any organized source.

Please write to my agent: Adam Krentzman, Creative Artists Agency, 9830 Wilshire Blvd., Beverly Hills, CA, 90212, (310) 288-4545.

The Painter, The Creature and The Father of Lies: an Introduction

The dictionary defines *incarnation* variously as the action of being made flesh, the assumption of a bodily form (particularly of Christ, or of God in Christ) and as the creation of new flesh upon or in a wound or sore: thus, a healing. I cannot imagine an apter title for this collection of plays. Story-telling has always been for me a process of putting on skins; of living lives and dying deaths that belong to somebody else. And the more unlike me I look with these borrowed faces the more interested I am to see the world through their eyes. The thrill of living for a little time as a visionary painter like Goya, or as the Devil, or—as in *Frankenstein in Love*—a murdered fan-dancer blithely awaiting the end of the world, brings me back to my desk in the certain knowledge that I am venturing where my daily life would never take me. I am, if you will, addicted to incarnation.

Let me say here and now that reading these plays does not require a degree in theatre arts or a burning ambition to tread the boards. The words are laid out a little differently from a novel or a short story, but the three tales that unfold in the pages that follow are fueled by many of the same passions that shaped *Imajica,* or *The Damnation Game* or *The Books of Blood*. More of that later. First, I would like to offer a brief history of how these dramas, and this edition, came into existence.

The earliest of the plays, *The History of the Devil,* was written in 1980, for a theatre troupe I had co-formed along with a group of friends in London: The Dog Company. *Frankenstein in Love* was written two years later, and performed by the same company in both Britain and Europe. *Colossus* has different origins. It was commissioned in 1983, and became a project for a large and eclectic group of young people brought together to create an original theatre work. It has been my intention to set about collating versions and editing all three texts for several years, but somehow the time has never been there to do so. With hindsight, I think this wasn't simply a question of opportunity. There was in me a certain reluctance to go back and examine work I'd done before the publication of the books—pieces I'd been proud of at the time—in case I discovered I hated them.

My anxieties misled me. The experience has not only been pleasurable but positively enlightening. It's aroused memories not only of the first productions of the plays but of my earliest encounter with the theatre, which was that most English of entertainments: the pantomime. For those of you not familiar with this extraordinary ritual, let me offer you a thumb-nail sketch. Panto is a Christmas entertainment, usually based on some bastardized fairy-tale, in which the ugly old woman, the Dame, is traditionally played by a man (often a well-known comedian) and the hero is played by a long-legged, thigh-slapping girl. Add a few music numbers, a couple of specialty acts, some smutty double-entendre for the adults and a singalong (complete with song-sheet) for the kids, and you have the mix. It is not, needless to say, the most coherent form of entertainment, but to a child born and raised in drab, post-war Liverpool as I was, Panto offered a glimpse of magic and spectacle that would fuel my dreams for weeks before and after my visit. And in truth there is much in the form I admire. Its artlessness, for one; its riotous indifference to any rules of drama but its own; its guileless desire to delight. And of course beneath all its tartish ways there is buried a story of primal simplicity: good against evil, love triumphing over hate and envy.

This was one of the two formative theatrical experiences of my childhood. The other—and in some senses more influential experience—was that of the puppet theatre. Like so many imaginative kids whose lives would take them into the theatre, my first taste of working behind the footlights was as a puppeteer. I made a cast of hand, rod and marionette puppets, and then proceeded to write elaborate vehicles for them. My father, who is a fine carpenter, built a stage and painted a variety of backdrops. One I remember with special clarity: a quay-side, with tall ships at anchor, sails unfurled or unfurling in preparation for a voyage.

And voyages I took. My cast was fairly generic, if memory serves. A sword-welding hero, a princess, a skeleton, a Devil, a hag-witch, a dragon. But they were all I needed to create exotic tales of midnight crimes and magic rituals, of horrendous jeopardies and last-minute escapes. There was a good deal of cruelty in the stories I created. This isn't so surprising, given that my earliest exposure to the world of puppets was Punch and Judy shows: short, brutal tales of how the devious and unrepentant Mister Punch kills his own child, beats his wife to death and then inexorably murders the rest of the cast (one at a time; the Punch and Judy man only has two hands) with his truncheon. My puppet tales also contained a measure of supernatural stuff, the appetite for which I trace to my paternal grandmother, who had a healthy nineteenth century appetite for the macabre.

This was, please remember, at a time and place when only a few of the neighbors owned television sets (we didn't) and comics were rare treasures. It isn't so surprising then that I found an audience of local kids for my entertainments. They would gather in the alley behind our house to watch my one-man epics, and though I'm sure time has improved the reviews, the shows seemed to find favor.

So, the years passed. I got myself an education, and courtesy of one great English teacher in particular, Norman Russell, was exposed to real drama. Conventional wisdom holds that force-feeding children Shakespeare, Webster and Moliere does both young minds and the classics a disservice, but I question this. First, it assumes that if kids weren't obliged to read *The Tempest* at school they'd discover it as adults and fall upon it with far greater appetite. This I doubt. It further assumes that putting these complex dramas into minds that are not experienced enough to fully understand them is an error. Again, I beg to differ. I didn't grasp more than a quarter of what I was being taught but by God that quarter made me ache to understand all that escaped me. Not because of the poetry or the aesthetics, but because of the raw human stuff that I knew was bedded in the fine language.

At University, drowning in words and theory, I almost lost sight of that root stuff. No great surprise. I was taught Poe by a man who scrupulously avoided Edgar's interest in bodily corruption and Whitman by a fellow who would not tolerate talk of Walt's queerness. I escaped to London, and to a self-created world, where I painted and wrote a number of experimental pieces for the theatre. They were mime-pieces to begin with (three years of English and Philosophy had silenced me), and then, once my faith in language had returned, plays.

The first substantial piece was called *Dog,* from which our company took its name: a highly stylized tale of sex, transformation and apocalypse which drew on Commedia dell 'Arte (one of the sources of Punch and Judy), pantomine, personal psychosis, the Bible and werewolf movies. It was not a success. But its fantastical nature, its philosophical pretensions and its use of effects, violence and low comedy began to define my approach to theatre work.

Given that Old Nick, the Father of Lies, had been a member of my stock puppet company, it was not perhaps so strange that the next substantial piece I penned was *The History of the Devil.* The trial format allowed for a range of short, sharp episodes, some of them serious, some comedic, each allowing the Devil—who has the best collection of personae of any character in Western culture—to try on another skin. (Until, finally, he loses them all.) It was written with the limitations of our production budget in mind, relying on verbal description to create scenes, and on the skill of the performers to evoke period detail rather than fine costumes and expensive props. It is story-telling theatre (this should be a tautology; regrettably, it's not) and was originally played, though this is too tight for comfort, by a company of six. They fell in and out of character at the drop of an accent, one moment portraying an officer of the court, the next a character in one of the Devil's tales, the speed of the changes keeping the audience in a state of dizzied admiration even when the drama faltered. The metaphysics of the piece is not particularly original, but the characters are lively, I think, and what the play lacks in profundity it makes up for in audacity. One of the critics, reviewing the first production, described it as: " . . . a mixture of *Decline and Fall, Paradise Lost, Perry Mason* and *Flash Gordon.*"

Lord, I loved that description! Why? Because it evokes a stew of high art and low, of intellect and spectacle, pretension and fun.

None of these plays are *nouvelle cuisine:* two warmed over subjects aesthetically arranged on a perfectly proportioned, but otherwise vacant, plate. They are pots full to brimming with plots and possibilities, and unapologetic about it. *Devil* is perhaps more plainly a stew than the other two, but history's like that, isn't it?

On, then, to the creature.

Studying *Frankenstein In Love* with fresh eyes, I was taken aback by how unrelentingly grim it is. There are some dark journeys taken in *The Books Of Blood,* to be sure, but I can't think of a tale even there that so obsessively circles on images of death and taboo. I don't remember my state of mind when I wrote the play (perhaps that's for the best) but plainly I was in pursuit of an experience that would push the audience to its limits.

I have very seldom used other creators' mythologies for inspiration—*New Murders In the Rue Morgue,* a homage to Poe's detective tale is a rare example—but there are certain ideas that exercise such fascination that I want to put my own spin on them. The Faust story, for instance, which I have explored several times (*The Damnation Game, Hellraiser, The Last Illusion*) and of course Mary Shelley's extraordinary creation, which is the starting place for *Frankenstein In Love.* In his extremely thorough study of how the Frankenstein story has been interpreted for the stage, *Hideous Progenies,* Steven Earl Forry describes the play thus:

"Clive Barker's "Frankenstein In Love" is arguably the most challenging adaptation ever written. The play, set in a banana rebublic undergoing a state of siege, captures the plight of humankind caught is a dystopic, godless universe . . . Driven by such diverse forces as the Grand Guignol, the theatre of Artaud and of the Absurd, Jacobean masques and Welles' "The Island of Dr. Moreau," Barker's play is unrelenting in its pessimistic view of the sordid acts to which humans somehow aspire."

I quote at length because Mr Forry's observations seem to me so acute, both in terms of my influences and the intentions of the play. In fact as far as the last part of his description is concerned, it seems to me the play is a virtual catalogue of atrocities (though I don't recall consciously constructing it as such). Cannibalism, necrophilia, vivisection, human experiment, torture, violent murder—the piece is as exhaustive as a report from a war-zone.

I don't believe such excesses need defending or explaining. It's what I chose to write, and there it is. I will, however, remark upon the dramatic consequences of these excesses. Plainly, when a piece of drama is too extreme there are certain safety-valves which an audience seeks (and will find, whether they are supplied or not), the most obvious being laughter.

It is a commonplace that the horror-response (gasps, screams, and tears) is close in nature to the comedy-response (giggles, laughter, and tears), and that one can very easily slide into the other. In *Frankenstein In Love* I tried to sew the triggers for these disparate responses together, so that the audience is never quite sure which is appropriate. Everything is pressed to a state of decadence—the violence, the gallows humor, the perversity of the romantic elements, the bitter poetry—none of it offering any relief from the general miasma of the piece. The humor doesn't lance the boil of our anxiety because its imagery is rooted in the very source of that anxiety. The romance doesn't offer any salve because it is tied to the horrific elements. In short, we are prisoners of the play's despair, stuck with its heat, its bloat and its decay.

Surprisingly perhaps, there proved to be a sizable audience for the experience. While I certainly met people who, having seen the play, considered me a minor felon, I've also encountered audience members who years later still called it the single most intense experience they've ever had in the theatre. It's a hot-house bloom, to be sure, but for those who have a taste for such specialized forms it remains, I think, a potent example of a relatively rare species.

Finally, to *Colossus*. Unlike the other two, it has at its heart an historical figure: that of Francisco Jose Goya y Lucientes, the supreme genius of Spanish painting. His work is an extraordinary interweaving of almost documentary realism—*Yo Lo Vi*, he titles one of his prints: *I Saw This*—with a visionary imagination that is in my opinion without parallel. There are of course countless books and essays devoted to his life and works, many of them relevatory, but however copiously a critic sweats to attach readily summarized meanings to Goya's images they constantly outwit interpretation. This is most particularly true of the so called Black Paintings, the troubled works of his last years, which more closely approximate the vast distressing landscapes of nightmare than any art I know.

In writing the play my central challenge was how to create a portrait of Goya and his world without falling prey to the clichés of biographical fiction: scenes of famous folks meeting more famous folks at historically significant events. The solution, I decided, was to create a drama in which Goya was effectively invisible much of the time, a situation which would allow me to explore the idea of the painter as a witness to events he could do little or nothing to influence.

The play begins with the destruction of a country house a short distance from Madrid. Goya has been painting a portrait in one of its rooms until moments before the play begins, when a barrage of French cannon fire reduces the house to rubble. It is in the midst of this chaos that the action of the play takes place: a succession of tragedies and unexpected epiphanies that spring from the characters' response to this disaster. Plainly, revolution is in the air, represented metaphorically by the image of this treasure-house blown open from attic to cellar, *"its hierarchies a continuum of heaped rubble . . . unexplored and unpredictable."* As the ruling classes steadily restore order, all manner of betrayals, seductions, caprices, discoveries, griefs, and revelations occur, many of them presented in fragments—pieces of storylines emerging for a brief time then disappearing again to be resolved later in the play. And watching these dramas, unseen because he is assumed dead, is the stone-deaf genius himself, sketch-book in hand. He has plenty to draw. Many of the tableaux in the play are inspired by Goya's paintings and prints: a case of art imitating life in order to evoke a life that inspired art.

The play was written for a large cast and needs numbers to make it work. This is not a piece that can be mounted by a cast of ten, however hard-working. But for the right ensemble, driven by the desire to create an ambitious piece of environmental theatre, and immerse themselves in Goya along the way, the piece is quite an adventure.

These are all plays that deal in some fashion with apocalyptic events: with order overturned and reason gone to hell, leaving the incarnations of our darker selves to stalk the shambles. And yet am

I utterly self-deluding if I see optimism in these stories? It is not, to be sure, the kind of optimism a studio executive here in my adopted city would recognize (though come to think of it all three plays finish with lovers re-united). Perhaps it is the unruly abundance of characters and ideas in the texts that gives them a hopeful feeling; an abundance which ends with the hope of continuance. At the close of *The History Of The Devil* and *Colossus* the world is returned—in all its frailty—into human care. And at the end of *Frankenstein In Love,* the wandering fan-dancer Maria, free of her responsibilities now that she's told her story, is embraced by a loving Death, leaving the monsters to court, dance and prepare for a new and better world. None of these, I think, are grim conclusions.

Some final thoughts. While I have gone back to the original texts and filled out the stage directions somewhat in order to make the plays more accessible to the casual reader, I have deliberately not tried to turn them into pseudo novels. They remain dramatic pieces; practical (and, I hope tempting) blueprints for producers, directors, actors, and designers to use to mount productions of their own. That said I trust that readers of my other fiction will also find interesting material here, and that the plays will reward the challenge of an unfamiliar format.

Speak these stories aloud, by all means; read them with friends, play out scenes for the simple pleasure of inhabiting other skins. If the origins of theatre lie, as some claim, in religious ritual, then these incarnations are visits with household gods. Inhabit them freely: see how they feel. That's what skins, and divinities, are for.

Clive Barker—Los Angeles, 1995

INCARNATIONS

COLOSSUS

Production Notes

Colossus is the closest I have ever come to writing a naturalistic play. The world it describes contains no supernatural manifestations, but teeters instead on the brink of collapse. That state, however, induces its own visions. Like a man *in extremis,* the play constantly glimpses hints of heaven and hell. A sub-structure of dream images lurks beneath the surface of the piece, haunting it as surely as any ghost or demon. We live, the play suggests, in more than one world. It's only when events shatter our simple constructs—when the order we have imposed on reality falters—that we sense this multiplicity. The revelation may drive us crazy, or help us better understand ourselves. The choice is ours.

To Goya, whose paintings and prints are the starting place for many of these images, this subversion of singularity was a given. He effortlessly married a vivid record of observable reality with forms from his own imaginings; recorded events with a documentarian's eyes, but froze them at the moment when something grander—and more profound—appeared; described the midnight life of the world—a Black Mass, beasts behaving as men (and vice versa)—with the casual strokes of an artist who knew them better than his own face.

The visionary layer of *Colossus* must, however, be approached through the naturalism, not the other way about. The more believable the wreckage and rubble in which the action is set, the better. The audience should feel like sight-seers in a disaster zone, voyeristically watching the dramas as they unfold. All that can be done by way of set design and lighting to make them believe they are witnessing the aftermath of a genuine act of destruction, the better. No symbolic rocks here. No mime; no dance. The air should be thick with dirt and smoke; the sunlight should be painfully bright and the darkness dreadful. The dead, dragged from the rubble, should be unbearable to look at. In short, the play must be as urgent and mesmeric as a news bulletin.

So often "historical" drama is comforting. We watch events unfold in the knowledge that they are past, and cannot significantly impinge on our lives. That is, of course, the antithesis of Goya's work. Part of his genius lies in his power to find ageless application in the particulars of his time. The vocabulary of social hierarchies may have changed, but the cruelty and hypocrisy of the ruling classes is still in place. The uniforms may be different, but the war-crimes are all too recognizable. Even his more fantastical visions move us with unalloyed power, because he has drawn them from a well of primal images, shaping them to his own particular needs but never sacrificing their universality. That achievement could serve as a touchstone for a production of the play.

The language of *Colossus* is on occasion poetic—even oblique—but it can fly if the rhythms are discovered and followed. The rest of the exchanges, the bulk of them in fact, are short and sharp, fragments of feeling rather than complete statements. The audience is obliged to fit the emotional jigsaw of the piece together for itself, drawn along by the threads of mystery (who did what to whom, when and why) that run through the narrative. They serve to keep the audience tracking the characters, connecting one piece of action with another, making sense of the patterns that exist within what at first seems to be chaos. When not involved in an audible exchange, the characters should always be active. We should have the sense that what we hear is merely a portion of the puzzle. That in every unheard whisper, every look, every touch lie clues to the nature of things.

For research purposes I simply say: go to Goya; to his paintings, drawings and prints. They are a creative and historical resource second to none, full of faces, poses, costume details and sheer imaginative power that can help fuel every element of the production. That said, the play is not a Goya pageant or a series of tableaux. See the paintings, study the prints and then close the books and go back to the play. If *Colossus* is to have the force of truth then it will not be because the production runs in Goya's shadow, but because the characters are quirky, oblique and difficult, the images they create as they go about their grim business momentarily reminding us of a picture Goya might have made but the next moment moving on, becoming something that could only be found on the living stage.

Clive Barker—Los Angeles, 1995

The Cast:

MELCHOR: a dead servant
NOVICK: a silver thief
LUISA: one of the Duchess Sofia's maids
JOLY: a theology student, employed as secretary to
SANTIAGO: the Duke's major-domo
RAFAEL: a gardener, husband of Daniella
ESTELLA: a celestina, the Duchess Sofia's confidante and some-
    time procuress
DONA PASCUALA: the Duke Damaso's insane mother
FELIPE FALCO: a laborer on the Duke's estate
NATANIEL FALCO: Felipe's brother, also a laborer
FRANCISCO GOYA Y LUCIENTES: a painter
JULIA COURCEL: a young French noblewoman
LEANOR COURCEL: her cousin
FOUCHE: a maidservant
SURZUR: an effete French gentleman
GENERAL NICHOLAS GUYE: General with Napoleon's Armee
    d'Espagne
MADAME DELVAUX: a French matron, and close friend of
    General Guye
SHATTERELL: a blind guitarist
THE DUKE
CAXA: the Duke's Horse-master
CASTROPOL: an actor
REUBELL: (the 1st Soldier) a fusilier
2nd Soldier: a fusilier
1st Woman
2nd Woman
3rd Woman
THE DUCHESS
THE COFFIN MAKER
BARBARA: the coffin-maker's daughter

SISTER MAGDALENA ⎱
SISTER ISOBEL: ⎰ Daughters of Jerusalem
ST PIERRE: a drummer with the 44th Line Infantry Regiment, Armee d'Espagne
GREGORIO: a trumpeter with the 44th Line Infantry Regiment, Armee d'Espagne
XAVIER GOYA: Goya's son
GUMERSINDA: Xavier's wife
MOREL: a critic
SERGEANT GRIS: with the 44th
CAPTAIN VERON-REVILLE
EVA: an actress
HOLY JOE NAVARRO: a playwright and actor
TUNG: a clown
SEREPHINA: an actress
GERONIMO: an actor ⎱
VIOLANTE: an actress ⎰ Twins
JOSEFA BAYEU: Goya's wife
A PRIEST

Act 1

IN A WARM DARKNESS, THE REASSURING SOUNDS OF AN EARLY SUMMER DAY. A GUITAR IS BEING PLAYED SOMEWHERE; WOMEN ARE LAUGHING LIGHTLY, NEARBY DOVES FLUTTER AND COO; CICADAS RASP IN THE GRASS. A VOICE, THAT OF DANIELLA, CALLS 'RAFAEL!' AND LAUGHS.

SUDDENLY THE BOOM OF A CANNON, FOLLOWED BY THE WHISTLE OF A CANNON-BALL THROUGH THE AIR. BEFORE THE FIRST SHOT HAS LANDED, THE ATTACK INTENSIFIES: ANOTHER BOOM, ANOTHER. THE SHOTS HIT HOME; THE SOUND OF A HOUSE BEING DEMOLISHED BY THIS BOMBARDMENT BLANKETS OUT THE MUSIC, THE DOVES, THE LAUGHTER. WE HEAR SCREAMS; THE RUSH OF WALLS COLLAPSING, ROOFS AND FLOORS THUNDERING DOWN. THE BARRAGE IS STILL GOING ON; THE ROAR IS GETTING LOUDER—GUNS, DESTRUCTION—A STOMACH-TREMBLING DIN. IT PEAKS AND THEN SLIDES AWAY INTO SILENCE.

NOW THERE IS ONLY A DOG BARKING IN THE HOT AFTERNOON AND A DISTANT BELL TOLLING A TARDY ALERT.

SLOWLY, THE LIGHTS, YELLOW-WHITE, COME UP ON THE SCENE. IT IS JUNE, 1811, THE COUNTRYSIDE A FEW MILES OUTSIDE MADRID. THE SPECTACLE OF DEMOLITION THAT CONFRONTS US IS THE REMAINS OF A LARGE COUNTRY HOUSE. THE BOMBARDMENT HAS BLOWN IT OPEN, REVEALING THE ENTRAILS OF THE HOUSE IN DETAIL. WE CAN SEE CLEARLY ITS SYSTEM OF ROOMS, PASSAGES AND STAIRWAYS, ONCE SO CAREFULLY ORGANIZED, AND NOW CHAOS, ITS HIERARCHIES A CONTINUUM OF HEAPED RUBBLE AND COLLAPSED ROOF TIMBERS.

*THE INTERIOR WALLS THAT STILL SURVIVE ARE TESTA-
MENT TO THE ONCE SUMPTUOUS DECORATION OF THE
HOUSE. ITS OWNER, THE DUKE, IS A LOVER OF ALL THINGS
FRENCH, AND THIS HOUSE WAS, UNTIL A MOMENT AGO, A
TREASURE-TROVE, LAID OUT WITH THE CALCULATED TASTE-
FULNESS OF THE FRENCH STYLE.*

*NOW THE SPANISH SUN, BRILLIANT AND RELENTLESS,
BEATS DOWN ON THIS CONFUSION OF FURNITURE, CARPET
AND OBJETS D'ART, ALL THROWN IN AMONGST THE RUBBLE.
ON ONE STANDING WALL, PICTURES STILL HANG, PORTRAITS,
CAPRICE PICTURES AND LANDSCAPES IN ORNATE FRAMES.
TAPESTRIES, SCORCHED AND TORN, HANG IN THE AIR LIKE
TATTERED FLAGS. THERE ARE GLINTS OF GLASS AND GOLD
AMONGST THE SMOKING STONE; THE THICK DUST WHICH IS
SETTLING AS WE WATCH CANNOT QUITE DISGUISE THE
RICHES EVERYWHERE.*

*BUT FOR ANYONE WHO WISHES TO MINE HERE, THE RUINS
ARE DANGEROUS. A BACK WALL REARS UP, TOP-HEAVY NOW
THAT A CANNON-BALL HAS TAKEN A BITE OUT OF THE FOUN-
DATIONS; THERE IS PERHAPS A TOTTERING PILLAR WHICH
BARELY SUPPORTS A GROANING BEAM, A WALKWAY, A BALCONY.*

*IN A MOMENT, THE HOUSE HAS BEEN TRANSFORMED
FROM AN ELEGANT STRUCTURE, ITS FORMS CALCULATED,
TO A SCENE OF PIRANESIAN DEPTHS AND HEIGHTS, UNEX-
PLORED AND UNPREDICTABLE.*

*STRANGE JUXTAPOSITIONS ABOUND. PERHAPS A STAIRWAY
THAT ENDS IN THE AIR; A DOOR THAT LIES HORIZONTAL,
OPENING INTO THE EARTH; A CHANDELIER, TWINKLING IN
THE SUNLIGHT. AND EVERYWHERE THERE ARE SMALL
REMINDERS OF THE WAY THIS WORLD WAS AN INSTANT AGO:
ORANGES STILL SITTING ON A WINDOWSILL, UNDISTURBED
BY CATASTROPHE; A BIRDCAGE, ITS OCCUPANT DEAD, SUS-
PENDED IN THE AIR; AN EASEL, STILL BEARING A PAINTING,
ITS FACE AWAY FROM US, STANDING ON AN ISLAND OF SUR-
VIVING FLOOR. THE MODEL HAS GONE. SO HAS THE PAINTER.
THERE ARE PEOPLE, BOTH ALIVE AND DEAD, IN THE RUINS.
THE DEAD ARE: MELCHOR, A SERVING BOY, WHOSE BODY LIES
ON THE SURFACE OF THE RUBBLE ALONG WITH THE SCAT-
TERED LIMBS AND BLOOD OF OTHER SERVANTS CAUGHT IN
THE BLAST. BURIED MUCH DEEPER, AND OUT OF SIGHT, IS*

*TEODORO, A THIEF, DRESSED IN GOYA'S CLOTHES. THE SUR-
VIVORS ARE: GOYA, HIDDEN BENEATH THE DUST AND BRICK;
DONA PASCUALA, THE DUKE'S MAD MOTHER, WHO SITS,
COVERED BY A CLOTH THAT HAS FALLEN OVER HER, UNNO-
TICED FOR THE FIRST FEW MINUTES OF THE ACTION; A SEC-
OND THIEF, CALLED NOVICK, LIES DOWN STAGE, PARTIALLY
COVERED BY RUBBLE, AND TRAPPED BENEATH A BEAM, HIS
BONES BROKEN. ELSEWHERE A YOUNG STUDENT CALLED
JOLY, SECRETARY TO THE DUKE'S MAJOR-DOMO, IS IN THE
ACT OF DISROBING LUISA, A MAID. HE STANDS, TROUSERS
AROUND HIS ANKLES, KISSING HER ON THE NECK WHILE SHE
SOBS.*

*SMOKE ISSUES FROM SEVERAL PLACES AMONGST THE
RUINS; ROPES, CHANDELIERS, CURTAINS OF CLOTH, SWING
BACKWARDS AND FORWARD.*

LUISA: Oh Jesus in Heaven!

SHE PUSHES JOLY BACK; HE LOOKS AROUND.

JOLY: Damnation. Earthquake! Earthquake!

HE STARTS TO PULL UP HIS TROUSERS.

JOLY: There may be more shock-waves. We should get into the
open.

*CICADAS, INTERRUPTED IN THEIR MUSIC BY THE
BARRAGE, BEGIN AGAIN ALL AROUND.*

LUISA: I heard whistling just before the explosion.
JOLY: Cover yourself up.
LUISA: I thought it was Melchor in the hall; I thought he'd found
    us together.

A CREAKING NOISE. JOLY LOOKS UP; SOMETHING

*FALLS FROM THE BEAMS ABOVE, AND CRASHES
DOWN IN A WELTER OF DUST.*

LUISA: Everything gone in the space of a prayer.
JOLY: It's impossible.
LUISA: Is it real?

SHE CROSSES TO HIM.

LUISA: Touch me.

JOLY TURNS OVER THE BODY OF MELCHOR.

JOLY: Melchor.
LUISA: (*Looking*) Ask him was he whistling?
JOLY: If God had wanted to prevent me making love to you, there
    must have been an easier way.

*RAFAEL APPEARS; HE IS ONE OF THE DUKE'S GAR-
DENERS, A LARGE, CLUMSY MAN, HIS FACE CON-
TORTED WITH HORROR.*

RAFAEL: Oh Jesus in Heaven. Where's my Daniella? Daniella.

*HE STARTS TO DIG IN THE DEBRIS, THROWING IT
ASIDE IN HIS PANIC.*

RAFAEL: Daniella! It's me! It's Rafael! Where is she?
JOLY: She could be anywhere.
RAFAEL: She waved to me from the window. Which window was
    she at?

HE LOOKS AROUND, STUPEFIED.

RAFAEL: Somebody tell me!

*ESTELLA, THE CELESTINA WHO ATTENDS ON THE
DUCHESS SOFIA, HAS APPEARED AT THE EDGE OF
THE RUINS. SHE IS DRESSED IN BLACK, A MIDDLE-*

AGED WOMAN OF CONSIDERABLE UGLINESS, WHO HAS A MUSTACHE AND SMOKES A SMALL, DARK CIGAR.

ESTELLA: It came down like a pack of cards, did you see it?

LUISA: We were in it.

JOLY: What about the Lodge and the stable. Are they flattened too?

ESTELLA: No; they were only interested in the house.

JOLY: They?

ESTELLA: The gunners. I saw the smoke on the hill; then the noise. Looked around, the house coming down—

JOLY: Cannon?

ESTELLA: Where's the Duchess?

JOLY: Cannon? Are you certain?

LUISA: That was the whistling. Not Melchor at all.

ESTELLA: She was in the library with Goya. (*She crosses to the easel*) He was painting her. (*She picks the painting off the easel, looks at it, and puts it back*) Where is she now? Sofia!

RAFAEL: The Duchess is in the garden.

ESTELLA: But I left her with the painter.

RAFAEL: Fetch help will you? My wife's under here somewhere.

JOLY: And God knows who else.

RAFAEL: We have to dig.

JOLY: With our bare hands?

LUISA: I'll find Nataniel and Felipe.

JOLY: They'll come of their own accord.

RAFAEL: No time to waste—

JOLY: You get the Falcos. I'll stay. Wait for Santiago.

RAFAEL: Tell them to bring pick-axes.

LUISA EXITS.

RAFAEL: Run!

RAFAEL SETS TO DIGGING AT THE RUBBLE. JOLY JUST STANDS, STARING AT THE WALLS. ESTELLA IS SEARCHING AMONGST THE RUINS, PICKING THINGS UP AND QUIETLY POCKETING THEM. SHE COMES ACROSS NOVICK IN HER SEARCH.

ESTELLA: Joly. You know this man?

*JOLY PULLS A CLOTH OFF HIM. NOVICK MOANS AS
LIGHT HITS HIM.*

NOVICK: Ah, Holy Mother . . .
JOLY: No.
NOVICK: Help me . . .
ESTELLA: Was he with the painter maybe? A bum-boy?
NOVICK: Castropol. Where are you?
ESTELLA: Castropol?
NOVICK: Where's he gone?
JOLY: I don't know anyone of that name. (*To Estella*) Do you?
ESTELLA: Yes: the name rings a bell.

*ESTELLA HAS MOVED BACK TO RAFAEL, AND TAKES
HOLD OF HIS ARM.*

ESTELLA: Was the Duchess alone in the garden?
RAFAEL: I'm not certain.
ESTELLA: Don't be discreet with me; I'm the one who'll have to
    wipe the grass-stains off her backside.
RAFAEL: She wasn't alone.
ESTELLA: And what did he look like?
RAFAEL: I could only see his buttocks.

*DURING THIS EXCHANGE, JOLY HAS UNBUTTONED
NOVICK'S SHIRT; HE GROANS, AND HIS BROKEN FIN-
GERS SCRAMBLE TO PROTECT HIS SECRET, BUT IT IS
REVEALED. SILVER, STOLEN FROM THE HOUSE, FILLS
HIS SHIRT. JOLY LIFTS SOME OF IT UP, BLOOD-STAINED.*

JOLY: A thief.
ESTELLA: Thief?
JOLY: He was stealing silver. There's a spoon punctured his chest;
    that's why he's bleeding.
ESTELLA: Now she keeps company with thieves.

*SOMEBODY HAS STARTED SINGING A SOFT LILTING
SONG.*

JOLY: What's that?
ESTELLA: What's what?
RAFAEL: Daniella?
JOLY: (*Points to the cloth covering Dona Pascuala*) It's coming from
over there!
RAFAEL: Daniella!

*HE PULLS THE CLOTH OFF IN A CLOUD OF DUST
REVEALING THE ANCIENT DONA PASCUALA, WHO
IS SITTING ON AN ORNATE CHAIR WITH A DEAD
DOG ON HER LAP; THE DOG HAS BLED COPIOUSLY
DOWN HER FINE DRESS; HER FACE IS COVERED
WITH AN IMPASTO OF POWDER AND GREASE. SHE
HAS FEW TEETH; A PREPOSTEROUS WIG.*

DONA PASCUALA: Draw the blinds!
ESTELLA: So she survived.
JOLY: What in God's name is that?
ESTELLA: Dona Pascuala; the Duke's mother. She will survive the
Apocalypse.
DONA PASCUALA: Draw the blinds, boy!
ESTELLA: She's speaking to you. Do as she says or she'll throw a
fit.

JOLY CROSSES TO HER.

JOLY: There are no blinds.
DONA PASCUALA: You come closer.

DONA PASCUALA GRABS HOLD OF JOLY'S LEG.

JOLY: She smells.
DONA PASCUALA: That's a fine thigh. Are you a bull-fighter?
JOLY: I'm a theology student.
DONA PASCUALA: (*Pushes him off*) Where have all the bull-fighters
gone? All eaten.
JOLY: She's insane.
ESTELLA: It's a family weakness. After a certain age their brains
start to ooze from their ears.
NOVICK: (*Laughing*) Bravo! Castropol! Bravo!

HE TRIES TO APPLAUD.

JOLY: (*Pulling himself away*) Let go of me.
DONA PASCUALA: Where have all my lovers gone? All eaten?
NOVICK: (*Quietly now*) Castropol . . .
JOLY: (*To Estella, who is watching Novick rave*) Who is this Castropol?
ESTELLA: Why shouldn't you know: everyone else will soon
    enough. He's an actor.
JOLY: (*With disgust*) Actor?
NOVICK: Bravo! Bravo!
JOLY: How do you know him?
ESTELLA: I don't. The Duchess does.

*DONA PASCUALA HAS BEEN TRYING TO WAKE HER
DOG.*

DONA PASCUALA: I can't wake the dog. What a lazy dog! Have
    you ever seen a lazier animal?
ESTELLA: Listen to her rave. Go and calm her down.
JOLY: I'm not going near her.
ESTELLA: Scared?
DONA PASCUALA: Is that Estella?
ESTELLA: Yes.
DONA PASCUALA: Haven't you died of the clap yet? Draw the
    blinds woman!
JOLY: What's she saying about you?
DONA PASCUALA: Greatest brothel-keeper in Madrid, that one.
ESTELLA: Will you be quiet?
JOLY: You?
ESTELLA: (*To Rafael*) Which part of the garden was the Duchess in?
RAFAEL: At the end of the promenade. In the hyacinths.
DONA PASCUALA: Take my dog for a walk, woman.
ESTELLA: The dog is dead!
DONA PASCUALA: Then walk it to its grave.

LUISA ENTERS

LUISA: The Falcos are coming.
JOLY: Where's Santiago? He'll know what to do.

HE GOES TO STAND AT THE WINDOW

DONA PASCUALA: The dog, whore.

*RELUCTANTLY ESTELLA TAKES THE DOG FROM
DONA PASCUALA'S LAP.*

DONA PASCUALA: Look; it's pissed on my lap. (*Slaps the dog's
nose*) Naughty thing!

*FELIPE AND NATANIEL FALCO APPEAR, CARRYING
SPADES AND PICK-AXES. THEY ARE GENERAL
LABORERS ON THE ESTATE, AND BROTHERS.
THOUGH THEY ARE SIMILARLY DRESSED, THERE
ARE DISTINCT DIFFERENCES BETWEEN THE WAY
THEY PRESENT THEMSELVES. FELIPE HAS A BRU-
TALLY SHORT HAIR-CUT, NATANIEL WEARS HIS
LONG; NATANIEL IS SHAVED, FELIPE IS NOT.
ESTELLA EXITS WITH THE DEAD DOG.*

NATANIEL: Christ alive, will you look at this? What a mess.
RAFAEL: Felipe.
FELIPE: I'm here.
NATANIEL: Where do we start?
FELIPE: Any sign of Daniella?
RAFAEL: No. I'm digging blind. What else can we do?
NATANIEL: You sure she's under here?
RAFAEL: The child is almost due. The heat makes her tired so I
told her to stay inside.
LUISA: It's not your fault.
RAFAEL: She wanted to sit in the orchard. I said there were too
many bees.
FELIPE: Who did this?
JOLY: It was cannon fire, apparently.
FELIPE: That's not our business.
JOLY: Your brother's right.

*NATANIEL HAS FOUND A SHOE. HE PULLS ON IT;
THERE IS A FOOT IN THE SHOE AND A LEG
ATTACHED.*

NATANIEL: Jesus.
DONA PASCUALA: That's a fine leg somebody had. Bring it here.
JOLY: Humor her. She smells but she's well connected.

NATANIEL TAKES THE LEG TO DONA PASCUALA, WHO IS OBVIOUSLY IMPRESSED BY HIM.

DONA PASCUALA: Put it here, in my lap.
FELIPE: Who else is missing, besides Daniella? Santiago will know.

A LOOK OF DISTASTE COMES ACROSS FELIPE'S FACE.

JOLY: If they're under this lot, they're dead for certain.
RAFAEL: No.
JOLY: Face it.
RAFAEL: She's alive. If she were dead, I'd be dead too, or at least a part of me would have died. But I'm whole. Tell him Felipe.
FELIPE: We'll find her. Take no notice of him.
NATANIEL: You don't usually trust providence.
DONA PASCUALA: What a fine piece of flesh it is.

FELIPE IGNORES NATANIEL, AND WORKS ON THE RUINS. JOLY GOES UP TO THE WALL THAT STILL HAS THE PAINTINGS HANGING ON IT, AND TAKES ONE DOWN. BEHIND IT, A HOLE IN THE WALL, WHICH HE EXAMINES. DONA PASCUALA IS HAPPY WITH HER THIGH, SINGING. NATANIEL IS PROBING BETWEEN THE STONES FOR BODIES, USING A STICK. LUISA HAS FOUND A CLOTH TO COVER MELCHOR'S BODY WITH, AND HAS FOUND A CUSHION FOR NOVICK'S HEAD. SHE NOW KNEELS BESIDE THE DYING THIEF.

ALL ARE ABOUT THEIR BUSINESS.

UNSEEN BY EVERYONE, THE SOUND OF HIS MOVE-MENT MASKED BY NOVICK'S GROANS, DONA PAS-CUALA'S SINGING, AND THE GRUNTS OF THE WORKMEN, GOYA GETS UP FROM THE DEBRIS. HE IS BLOODIED AND DAZED, WEARING ONLY HIS UNDERCLOTHES. HE TRIES TO ORIENTATE HIM-

*SELF; HIS HEAD WHINES AND THUNDERS: WE
HEAR, FOR A MOMENT, THE SOUNDS OF THE
WORLD HE LIVES IN; THEN, ALMOST UNNOTICED,
HE STAGGERS AWAY. DONA PASCUALA, UNOCCU-
PIED EXCEPT BY SONG, SEES HIM.*

DONA PASCUALA: Ah! I see a ghost.
JOLY: What did she say?
DONA PASCUALA: Goya! There!
JOLY: Goya?

> *SHE POINTS: JOLY LOOKS ROUND, BUT GOYA HAS
> SLIPPED AWAY.*

DONA PASCUALA: There! see him? Look how he sprints!
JOLY: There's nothing, madam.
DONA PASCUALA: Call him back: I'd like to talk with a ghost!
    Go on! Call him!
JOLY: There's nobody!
DONA PASCUALA: Behind the wall! Follow my finger! He's run-
    ning towards the fountains! Quickly! (*She laughs*)

> *JOLY RELUCTANTLY FOLLOWS WHERE DONA PAS-
> CUALA IS POINTING AND EXITS.*

LUISA: What will happen to us now with the house gone?
FELIPE: The Duke will take refuge in Madrid, and we'll be dismissed.
LUISA: There's a famine in Madrid.
FELIPE: Not for Dukes.
NATANIEL: For everyone.

> *SANTIAGO HAS ENTERED, UNSEEN. A WAN MAN
> DRESSED IN BLACK, WHOSE EYES ARE PERPETU-
> ALLY RIMMED WITH ROSE-RAW FLESH, AS THOUGH
> FROM SOME INFLAMMATORY DISEASE. HE CARRIES
> A LARGE BUNDLE OF KEYS CONSTANTLY. HE
> WATCHES AND LISTENS.*

FELIPE: He won't starve. And he'll be safe from rebels in Madrid.
    They shoot on sight.

LUISA: Rebels?

FELIPE: Who else did this?

LUISA: But why?

FELIPE: Because the house was filled with French carpets and French furniture, and the gardens are laid out like Fountainbleau.

NATANIEL: You're suddenly very interested in Politics and Gardening.

FELIPE: If I'm going to be thrown on the shit-heap and told to die quietly, I want to know why.

NATANIEL: You, die quietly? All you do is gab.

FELIPE: And you take whatever they give you. If they spit on you, you lick it up like you'll get fat on it.

LUISA: Don't let Santiago hear you talking like this.

FELIPE: He's not God.

SANTIAGO STEPS INTO PROMINENCE.

SANTIAGO: No but I'm an adequate substitute.

FELIPE: Shit.

SANTIAGO: Nataniel?

NATANIEL: Sir?

SANTIAGO: If I gave you needle and thread would you sew up your brother's lips? I really advise it, for his own good.

NATANIEL: He didn't mean it, sir. Did you?

SANTIAGO: (*To Felipe*) Well? Did you?

A BEAT.

FELIPE: I think I must have done. I said it.

SANTIAGO: We won't call you Felipe from now on. We'll call you Hunger. You're dismissed.

FELIPE: Thank You.

SANTIAGO: You will never work again, not in this vicinity. You'll have to walk to England; they like talkers there.

FELIPE HAS A STONE IN HIS HAND, WHICH HE IS WEIGHING UP IN AN AMBIGUOUS MANNER.

SANTIAGO: The stone you hold in your hand is Ducal property. Put it down.

FELIPE DROPS THE STONE AT SANTIAGO'S FEET.

SANTIAGO: Leave the estate now. If you're still here by noon you will be beaten as a trespasser. Flogged skinless.

FELIPE NODS; EXTENDS A HAND TO NATANIEL

FELIPE: Nat . . .

NATANIEL SHAKES HIS HEAD AND TURNS AWAY.

NATANIEL: Stupid.
FELIPE: Rafael . . . ?

FELIPE AND RAFAEL EXCHANGE HANDSHAKES.

FELIPE: When you find her, kiss her for me, the place she likes to be kissed.

FELIPE EXITS.

SANTIAGO: Where's Joly?
DONA PASCUALA: He went chasing the ghost.
SANTIAGO: Ma'am: how well you look.
DONA PASCUALA: The slut was in the garden I hear.
SANTIAGO: The Duchess you mean? Yes. She has been violated.
DONA PASCUALA: Impaling herself on saplings?
SANTIAGO: Raped; brutally raped. Joly! What ghost was this you saw?
DONA PASCUALA: I forget. Some man I knew, had between my legs once.

JOLY APPEARS.

JOLY: Santiago. Sir. You're here.
SANTIAGO: (*He gives Joly a book*) This is the house inventory. A complete list of contents. Furniture, pictures, bed-linen, servants, down to the last mechanical bird. As each item is exhumed, you mark it down. If it's broken or burnt mark that down too. Find a clear place, collect up whatever can be salvaged and restored, and keep it safe. I'll deal with the guests myself.

JOLY TAKES THE BOOK. THROUGH THE SCENE THAT FOLLOWS HE IS OCCUPIED WITH THE TASK SANTIAGO HAS GIVEN HIM. HE FINDS A TABLE. ON IT HE LAYS OBJECTS THAT ARE UNCOVERED OR THAT HE UNCOVERS, FROM THE DEBRIS; A COLLECTION OF PITIFUL REMNANTS GATHER ON THIS TABLE AS THE ACTION PROGRESSES.

SANTIAGO: (*Pointing to the leg in Dona Pascuala's lap*) Whose limb is that? Does anybody recognize the shoe?
LUISA: It's Carballo's shoe.
SANTIAGO: And the rest of him?

LUISA SHRUGS.

SANTIAGO: We must assume he's smithereens then. And what about the rest? Madame Delvaux's party is all at the stables, viewing the stallion. General Guye is with them. The Duchess is amongst the hyacinths, ravished but alive. Which leaves Goya.

A BEAT.

SANTIAGO: Oh dear.
JOLY: There's somebody coming! The Duke!

SANTIAGO'S PACE CHANGES. HE SPITS OUT ORDERS.

SANTIAGO: (*To Rafael*) You! A chair! (*To Luisa*) There's wine on the window sill. Bring it. Did you hear me? Chair!
JOLY: He lost his wife.
SANTIAGO: Priorities are everything. First the chair! (*To Joly*) Find a glass!
JOLY: A glass, in this?
SANTIAGO: Catastrophes are unpredictable: they can wipe away mountains and leave mice untrammelled in their nests. A glass!
JOLY: Yes sir!

SANTIAGO IS SUDDENLY VERY NERVOUS. HE DABS AT HIS UPPER LIP WITH HIS HANDKERCHIEF.

SANTIAGO: (*To himself*) Show no fear. There's nothing he can blame you for.

THE FIRST OF GENERAL GUYE'S PARTY ARRIVE AT THE RUINS. THEY PRESENT A STARTLING CONTRAST TO THE GRIM WORKERS AND THE SHATTERED BODIES BELOW.

TWO YOUNG WOMEN LEAD: LEANOR AND JULIA. THEY ARE BOTH ABOUT TWENTY, JULIA THE MORE CONVENTIONALLY PRETTY OF THE TWO, LEANOR'S FACE A HAUNTED, IMPENETRABLE FORTRESS. SHE CARRIES A BOOK; JULIA A PARASOL. A VERY EFFETE YOUNG MAN FOLLOWS THEM, HIS NAME IS SURZUR, CARRYING ANOTHER PARASOL, WHICH HE ATTEMPTS TO KEEP OVER LEANOR'S HEAD. SHE REPEATEDLY MOVES IT AWAY, PREFERRING THE SUN ON HER FACE. BOTH WOMEN ARE MADE-UP ALMOST LIKE DOLLS AND DRESSED IN A FRENCH STYLE, PASTEL COLORS. JULIA HAS HAY-FEVER. SHE SNEEZES CONSTANTLY. THEY ARE FOLLOWED BY FOUCHE, MADAME DELVAUX'S MAID, WHO CARRIES A BASKET WHICH CONTAINS A PICNIC.

JULIA: (*Sneezing*) Oh the dust.
LEANOR: (*Entranced*) Have you ever seen such a spectacle?
FOUCHE: (*Dropping the basket*) Oh my God!

SHE BACKS OFF.

LEANOR: What's wrong with you?
FOUCHE: I hate the sight of blood.

SHE RUNS AWAY.

LEANOR: Fouche! Come back.
JULIA: If she can't look . . .
LEANOR: (*To Surzur*) Fetch her! Tell her it's not real; just Signor Goya, spilling the paint.
SURZUR: Ma'am?

LEANOR: Go on.

EXIT SURZUR.

SANTIAGO: Mademoiselles, I suggest you retire to a safe distance.
LEANOR: We will not.
JULIA: Leanor—
LEANOR: We will not, Julia. Just because he wants to prevent us from seeing it all with our own eyes.
SANTIAGO: The house isn't safe.
LEANOR: It must be safe, you're standing in it.
JULIA: Must you insult everyone?
LEANOR: No, just the chosen few. (*Looking at Dona Pascuala*) Who's the mad woman?

THE VOICES OF GENERAL GUYE AND MADAME DELVAUX, OFFSTAGE, OVERLAP WITH THIS LAST EXCHANGE.

GENERAL GUYE: Here. Step up here. Give me your hand.
MADAME DELVAUX: You're courtesy itself.
GENERAL GUYE: Take care.
MADAME DELVAUX: My ankle is weak. I broke it skating last winter.
JOLY: Somebody else is coming.
JULIA: It's the General. (*To Leanor*) And Madame Delvaux! Come away Leanor. She'll forbid you, you know she will.
LEANOR: (*Ignoring Julia and speaking to Dona Pascuala*) Who are you?
DONA PASCUALA: Are those legs your own?
LEANOR: Yes.
DONA PASCUALA: One of mine is wooden. I can unscrew it. You want to see?

SHE HITCHES UP HER SKIRT. ONE OF HER LEGS IS INDEED WOODEN.

DONA PASCUALA: It rotted; so I had them saw it off.

MADAME DELVAUX AND GENERAL NICHOLAS GUYE APPEAR. THE FORMER IS A FRENCH MATRON IN

STURDY MIDDLE AGE. THE GENERAL, WHO ESCORTS HER, IS AN IMPRESSIVELY HANDSOME MAN A FEW YEARS OLDER THAN GOYA'S PORTRAIT OF HIM.

MADAME DELVAUX: Oh, how terrible this is. We were standing on this very spot an hour ago. Now look. I could weep. To think.

LEANOR: It's only bricks and mortar.

GENERAL GUYE: He loved this house. I fear for his sanity with it gone.

MADAME DELVAUX: Don't say that.

JULIA HAS BEEN OVERTAKEN BY ANOTHER FIT OF SNEEZING.

MADAME DELVAUX: Julia. Go back to the garden. Take her back Leanor; the dust is too much for her.

LEANOR: The flowers make her sneeze just as much.

JULIA: I don't want to go.

MADAME DELVAUX: Well, as you like. Where's Fouche?

LEANOR: Sick. Surzur has gone after her.

MADAME DELVAUX: And the guitarist? Has he run off too?

LEANOR: He's blind Madam.

MADAME DELVAUX: Is he? You know I hadn't noticed.

LEANOR: He can't get over the rubble without help.

JULIA: I'll fetch him.

MADAME DELVAUX: You do that.

JULIA EXITS.

MADAME DELVAUX: (*Fanning herself*) This heat is so debilitating. I think we should find a shady spot and have a glass of lemonade.

SURZUR BRINGS FOUCHE BACK ON, SOBBING.

FOUCHE: No; I can't . . . it's horrible.

MADAME DELVAUX: Oh for pity's sake, girl, your monthlies are bloodier than this. Surzur?

SURZUR: Madam?

MADAME DELVAUX: We'll have a picnic here.

SURZUR: Here?

MADAME DELVAUX: Shatterell can play something soothing while we watch the rescue operations. Will you join us, General?

GENERAL GUYE: Presently.

LEANOR: You know how the guitarist lost his eyes?

GENERAL GUYE: How?

MADAME DELVAUX: Please don't be morbid Leanor.

LEANOR: He blinded himself.

MADAME DELVAUX: Now, now.

LEANOR: He did! He told me! He was at Saragrossa, and he blinded himself because he'd seen too much for a man to bear. Do you believe that?

GENERAL GUYE: It's possible.

LEANOR: Were you at Saragrossa?

MADAME DELVAUX: (*Breaking in*) General, could you ask that man to have somebody clear a place for us?

GENERAL GUYE: Yes. Of course.

THE GENERAL CROSSES TO SANTIAGO.

GENERAL GUYE: Santiago?

SANTIAGO: General Guye.

GENERAL GUYE: The ladies insist on watching. Would you have one of your men clear a space for them to sit?

SANTIAGO: My pleasure.

GENERAL GUYE: Your keys are redundant now.

SANTIAGO: So it seems. Falco?

NATANIEL: Yes sir.

SANTIAGO: With the General.

NATANIEL MOVES UPSTAGE, LEAVING THE SERIOUS DIGGING TO RAFAEL. DURING THE NEXT FEW MIN-UTES CHAIRS ARE FOUND AND A TABLE LAID WITH THE PICNIC, AN APPETIZING ABUNDANCE OF MEAT, BREAD, WINE AND FRUIT.

THE GENERAL GOES AROUND THE RUINS, CHECK-ING THE WALLS FOR SAFETY.

JULIA: (*Guiding Shatterell in*) This way.

SHATTERELL: There's a smell. Burning.

JULIA: It's all right, really.
LEANOR: Nothing to be frightened of.

*SHATTERELL ENTERS; AN EMACIATED MAN WITH A
BLINDFOLD COVERING HIS SIGHTLESS EYES.*

SHATTERELL: Sit down where it's cool.

*MADAME DELVAUX IS ALSO EXPLORING THE
RUINS; SHE PICKS UP A PAIR OF SPECTACLES.*

MADAME DELVAUX: Whose are these?

*SANTIAGO CROSSES TO HER AND TAKES THEM
FROM HER.*

SANTIAGO: May I?
MADAME DELVAUX: Yours?
SANTIAGO: No. The painter's. Where did you find them?
MADAME DELVAUX: Just here.

*SANTIAGO DIGS AROUND A LITTLE MORE, AND
PULLS OUT A BOOK.*

SANTIAGO: So . . .
MADAME DELVAUX: It looks as though the ground just swal-
lowed him up.
SANTIAGO: Joly. Take the sketch-book.

JOLY TAKES THE BOOK.

MADAME DELVAUX: (*Points to Melchor*) Who's this?
JOLY: A servant.
LEANOR: Can we see?
MADAME DELVAUX: It's just a corpse.
LEANOR: Then there's no harm is there?

JOLY LIFTS THE CLOTH ON MELCHOR.

LEANOR: He looks surprised.

THE DUKE APPEARS, FOLLOWED BY CAXA, THE HORSE MASTER. THE DUKE IS IN HIS MIDDLE-SIX-TIES, A VACANT-EYED, INBRED NOBLEMAN WHOSE DESOLATE LOOK IS EXACERBATED BY THE GREY CLOTHES HE FAVORS. HE ENTERS SO QUIETLY NOBODY NOTICES HIM.

MADAME DELVAUX: You'd look surprised if the roof fell on you.

LEANOR: And his mouth, so full of blood. Has he bitten off his tongue?

DUKE: Where is Goya?

EVERYTHING STOPS WHILE THE DUKE ENTERS.

SANTIAGO: (*Dropping the cloth back down on Melchor*) Lordship. We haven't found him yet.

GENERAL GUYE: Damaso: we'll find the men who did this. I swear this obscenity will be revenged.

DUKE: (*Without feeling*) Thank you, Nicholas. That gives me comfort.

GENERAL GUYE: Sofia's unharmed?

DUKE: She says thieves broke in; one of them took to torturing the painter, another dragged her outside and raped her.

GENERAL GUYE: We're none of us safe, even in our own houses.

DUKE: Where were you Santiago, when the cannon hit?

SANTIAGO: I was emptying my bowels.

DUKE: Somebody inside the house let these thieves, these rapists in.

GENERAL GUYE: There's time for detection later.

DUKE: Yes. For now, we must find Goya. (*He looks at Rafael*) In God's name. Is this all? One man digging with a spade and his bare hands? Falco! Get to it! Where's your brother?

NATANIEL: Gone, Lordship.

DUKE: Gone where?

SANTIAGO: He was talking subversion.

DUKE: Indeed.

MADAME DELVAUX: Perhaps he was the one who let the intruders in.

SANTIAGO: Very possible.

DUKE: So just two men to dig for Goya?

GENERAL GUYE: We'll round up some workers in the field.

DUKE: Caxa lend a hand here.
GENERAL GUYE: Lordship.

CAXA HELPS RAFAEL.

DUKE: He could be anywhere.
GENERAL GUYE: It's a question of organization, that's all.
DUKE: Nicholas, oblige me.
GENERAL GUYE: Yes. I'll find some fusiliers. Veron-Reville has a bat-
　　talion on maneuvers within a mile of here. Leave it with me.

EXIT GENERAL.

DUKE: I built this house with such love. Filled it with the finest
　　treasures Europe could produce. I dreamt of it when I was
　　away. When death seemed close I prayed to come back here,
　　a ghost, and haunt it for all eternity.
DONA PASCUALA: I saw a ghost. Oh yes. Sprinting away.

THE DUKE SEES DONA PASCUALA.

DUKE: So.
DONA PASCUALA: Who are you?
DUKE: Mother—
DONA PASCUALA: You're never my mother.
DUKE: Is that your blood?
DONA PASCUALA: No. My blood is blue.
DUKE: Get her out of the sunlight. She'll cook sitting there.
DONA PASCUALA: Just draw the blinds. I'll sleep awhile.
DUKE: You do that.
DONA PASCUALA: You look familiar. Did I sleep with you once?

*THE DUKE TURNS HIS BACK ON HIS MOTHER,
DISGUSTED.*

DUKE: Am I never to be rid of her?
DONA PASCUALA: I remember your skinny thighs.
SANTIAGO: (*To Dona Pascuala*) Ssh! Ssh! (*He gestures to Nataniel
　　and they move Dona Pascuala out of the sun, into the shade.*)
DONA PASCUALA: What are you doing? Murder! murder!

SANTIAGO: It's all right.

DONA PASCUALA: (*To Santiago, about Nataniel*) Have this one stay by me. Fan me awhile.

SANTIAGO NODS AND LEAVES NATANIEL WITH DONA PASCUALA. THE DUKE HAS CROSSED TO WHERE NOVICK, WHO HAS HIS HEAD IN LUISA'S LAP, IS LYING. LEANOR IS WATCHING HIM. HE TALKS QUIETLY TO HIMSELF.

DUKE: I don't recognize this man.

JOLY: He's one of the thieves.

DUKE: Are you sure?

JOLY: His shirt was full of silver.

DUKE: Really? Caxa!

LUISA: The flies won't let him alone.

DUKE: You've done your best for him. Let him be now.

LEANOR: What are you going to do?

SANTIAGO: (*To Leanor*) This isn't for you to watch.

LEANOR: (*To Delvaux*) What are they going to do?

DUKE: (*To Caxa*) Pick him up.

LUISA: His bones are broken.

DUKE: *Pick him up!*

CAXA PICKS NOVICK UP. THE THIEF GROANS.

DUKE: Santiago!

SANTIAGO: Lordship.

DUKE: Ask him will you?

SANTIAGO: Ask him what?

DUKE: Concerning my Duchess—

MADAME DELVAUX HAS COME DOWN TO COLLECT LEANOR.

MADAME DELVAUX: Come away. Shatterell.

SHATTERELL: Ma'am?

MADAME DELVAUX: Play!

SHATTERELL: Anything in particular?

MADAME DELVAUX: Yes. Loudly.

DUKE: (*To Santiago*) Ask him first who he came with.

SANTIGO: (*To Novick*) Can you hear me?

NOVICK: Castropol . . .

DUKE: Was that a name?

CAXA: He said Castropol.

SANTIAGO: Is he your associate?

NOVICK: Bravo! Castropol.

SANTIAGO: You broke in, why?

NOVICK: You know . . . he knows . . .

SANTIAGO: No.

NOVICK: The lady, for the lady.

DUKE: Sofia?

SANTIAGO: Do you mean the Duchess?

NOVICK: He took her into the garden. I went for the silver.

DUKE: Goya. Ask him about Goya.

NOVICK: Who?

SANTIAGO: The painter.

NOVICK: Teodoro.

SANTIAGO: Another thief?

NOVICK: Like his coat; good coat. Where are you? I can't see
   you. Castropol!

DUKE: Ask him—

SANTIAGO: What?

NOVICK HAS SLUMPED.

DUKE: Did she go willingly?

SANTIAGO: Do you hear the question?

DUKE: Is he dead?

CAXA: Almost.

DUKE: (*Pressing past Santiago to peer into Novick's face*) You've
   done me wrong thief. But just answer me one question, and
   it's forgiven. Does he hear me?

NOVICK: My balls itch. Scratch them will you?

DUKE: Tell me! My Duchess? Did she go smiling into the garden?
   Just answer me. Please.

NOVICK: (*A pause; then he laughs*) Yes. She was smiling.

THE DUKE TURNS AWAY, MORTIFIED.

DUKE: Everything. Gone.
SANTIAGO: Sir?
DUKE: Shreds and scraps.

> SANTIAGO GESTURES TO THE HORSE-MASTER TO
> DROP NOVICK. HE DOES SO AND NOVICK SCREAMS.
> SHATTERELL, STARTED, STOPS PLAYING. IN THE SUD-
> DEN SILENCE THE DUKE CAN BE HEARD SOBBING,
> HIS BACK TURNED TO THE ASSEMBLED COMPANY.

MADAME DELVAUX: Anyone for quail?

> THE GUITARIST STARTS AGAIN. LUISA HAS GONE
> BACK TO NOVICK TO COMFORT HIM. THE DUKE
> SITS DOWN. CAXA RETURNS TO HELPING RAFAEL
> DIG.

JOLY: Goya painted a portrait of me when I was five or six. Every-
one said it was the perfect likeness.
MADAME DELVAUX: That was his problem: too many likenesses.
Some of his portraits were so true they were slanderous.
That picture of the queen: like a constipated toad.
LEANOR: That's the way she was.
MADAME DELVAUX: He had no business painting her the way
she was. His job was to improve on what nature had done to
her, not report it.

> WHILE THIS CONVERSATION IS GOING ON CAS-
> TROPOL, AN ACTOR, HAS ENTERED. HE IS HEAVILY
> DISGUISED AS A DOCTOR. THIS IS NOT A
> RESPECTED PROFESSION, AND HIS IMPERSON-
> ATION PLAYS UP THIS IMAGE. HE WEARS A BLOOD-
> STAINED WAISTCOAT, A GRUBBY COAT, A SMALL
> FALSE BEARD, GLASSES, A WIDE-BRIMMED HAT,
> AND CARRIES A LARGE BAG.

CASTROPOL: Anyone in need of a doctor? I am Clot. Doctor
Clot. Believe it or not it's the name I was born with.
SANTIAGO: Are you qualified?

CASTROPOL: Enemas, amputations: anything in that line. I also make wills, and I'm a passable barber.

JULIA SNEEZES.

CASTROPOL: Touch of consumption?
MADAME DELVAUX: Stay away from her.
CASTROPOL: Bathe in milk; it's what they're doing in Vienna. I saw the smoke and came directly. Can I be of use?
SANTIAGO: You know Vienna?
CASTROPOL: I've been all over. (*Lifts the cloth on Melchor*) Bit late for this one. What happened? Lightning out of the clear blue sky?
SANTIAGO: In a matter of speaking.

JULIA SNEEZES AGAIN.

CASTROPOL: Bless you. (*Points to Novick*) What about this one?
LUISA: He's dying. He wants a priest.
CASTROPOL: I like a challenge.
SANTIAGO: Where's the harm?
CASTROPOL: You took the words out of my mouth.
SANTIAGO: Do your worst.

CASTROPOL CROSSES TO NOVICK.

LEANOR HAS LEFT THE PICNIC AND IS WATCHING CAXA AND RAFAEL WORK, BARE-BACKED, AMONGST THE WRECKAGE. JULIA SITS, SNIFFING AND SNEEZ-ING. MADAME DELVAUX CROSSES TO THE DUKE, WITH FOUCHE IN TOW, CARRYING A PLATE OF FOOD.

MADAME DELVAUX: Now you must eat something.
DUKE: Thank you, but I have no stomach for it.
MADAME DELVAUX: Grief always makes me ravenous.
DUKE: Yes?
MADAME DELVAUX: I've gorged over all my husbands' funerals.
DUKE: Well perhaps I'll be a glutton when my Duchess dies.
MADAME DELVAUX: Do you intend to outlive her?
DUKE: I know. You laugh at me. She's eighteen, I'm old enough to be her grandfather.

MADAME DELVAUX: I never laughed. But having married her for her tiny ankles and her enormous eyes, knowing she was a quarter your age, should you be surprised if you're betrayed by her? Isn't that what you suspect? And if it's true, what are you betrayed by? Eyes and ankles. She's not real to you.

DUKE: Show me how to forgive her and I will. For my . . . sanity's . . . sake.

MADAME DELVAUX: You suffer so much. You should be made a saint.

SHE LEAVES HIM TO IT.

CASTROPOL: (*To Luisa*) Would you leave me alone with the patient? I don't work well when I'm watched.

LUISA: Oh. I'm sorry.

LUISA WITHDRAWS; CASTROPOL PUTS HIS HAND ON NOVICK'S FACE. NOVICK TWITCHES.

NOVICK: Castropol . . . you're here.

CASTROPOL: Ssh! How did you know it was me?

NOVICK: The scent on your hand.

CASTROPOL: I came to say good-bye.

NOVICK REACHES UP, RUNS HIS HANDS OVER CASTROPOL'S CLOTHES.

NOVICK: What are you wearing?

CASTROPOL: It's one of the costumes from "Don Juan." They think I'm a doctor. Where's Teodoro?

NOVICK: I said there was something terrible in the air didn't I?

CASTROPOL: Nothing terrible happened to me; I made love to a Duchess under a tree. Blossom fell in my hair. Heaven can be no sweeter.

NOVICK: Can you find me a priest?

CASTROPOL: I'll play the priest for you.

NOVICK: I need a real Priest to hear my confessions.

CASTROPOL: I can be real. What kind of Priest do you want? Consoling? Demanding?

NOVICK: Don't joke.

CASTROPOL: I can play anything you ask me. I can be a doctor, a priest, a lover. I can be death itself if it seems appropriate.

HE PUTS HIS HAND ON NOVICK'S THROAT.

NOVICK: What are you doing?
CASTROPOL: Don't be afraid. Nothing to be afraid of.
NOVICK: Castropol—
CASTROPOL: You'll get crazy in this sun and start to babble. Who knows what you might let slip then, eh?
NOVICK: (*Raising his hand to Castropol's face*) I beg you.
CASTROPOL: And so you should.
NOVICK: Don't! Don't!

NOVICK CLAWS AT CASTROPOL'S CHEEK. CASTROPOL STRANGLES HIM ONE-HANDED, WHILE HE PULLS THE ATTACKING HAND AWAY. NOVICK DIES.

CASTROPOL: Oh dear. This man is dead.
LUISA: Are you sure?
CASTROPOL: He just slipped through my fingers.

LUISA KNEELS BY THE BODY AND PRAYS.

THE GENERAL ENTERS, FOLLOWED BY A GROUP OF WORKERS. TWO ARE SOLDIERS, DRESSED IN WORK-ING CLOTHES, WITH ONLY A FEW REMINDERS OF THEIR PROFESSION ABOUT THEIR PERSON. THE OTHER THREE ARE WOMEN WHO, TO JUDGE BY THEIR STRAW-COVERED CLOTHES, HAVE BEEN WORKING IN THE FIELD. THESE THREE WOMEN WILL REAPPEAR THROUGHOUT THE REST OF THE PLAY. THEIR SECRET SMILES, THEIR INDECIPHER-ABLE LOOKS MAY AT PRESENT SEEM DELIGHTFUL. LATER, THESE SAME LOOKS BECOME SIGNS OF A CONSPIRACY BETWEEN THEM.

GENERAL GUYE: I've brought some help with the digging.
SANTIAGO: Good.
MADAME DELVAUX: Seems to me the sun's getting hotter.

GENERAL GUYE: I've sent word to the Captain of the 44th. Do you know him? Veron-Reville.

LEANOR: Oh, yes. The handsome one.

MADAME DELVAUX: All French Captains are handsome.

GENERAL GUYE: He's sending a patrol to watch the house tonight.

SANTIAGO: Thank you.

MADAME DELVAUX: I wonder where Sofia got to?

JULIA: Maybe she's resting after her ordeal.

SANTIAGO: Luisa. Find the Duchess. (*Luisa exits*)

JULIA: The thief died; look, they've covered him up.

MADAME DELVAUX: We went to Saragrossa after the siege, Frederick and myself. The terrible things.

LEANOR: What kind of terrible things?

MADAME DELVAUX: Atrocities.

JULIA: Is this an atrocity?

LEANOR: No.

THE GENERAL IS ORGANIZING THE DIGGING.

GENERAL GUYE: You're not excavating with any system behind the work, so you're moving muck from one spot and piling it somewhere you'll want to dig in an hour. Make a chain, and remove the bricks out of the house altogether, so we can see what's what. Do you understand?

1ST SOLDIER: Yes sir.

GENERAL GUYE: All of you!

NODS OF AGREEMENT, MURMURS. RAFAEL HAS IGNORED THIS PEP-TALK, AND IS STILL DIGGING.

GENERAL GUYE: (*To Nataniel*) Who's he? He'll break his back.

NATANIEL: He believes his wife is buried alive.

GENERAL GUYE: Well help him then. Take a lesson from his passion. Minutes are of the essence. If there is anyone left alive under here they may be wounded, suffocating. Think as you dig that you hear somebody's voice beneath the stones, calling your name. Go to it. (*He sees Santiago staring at him*) Yes?

SANTIAGO: You talk like a poet, General.

GENERAL GUYE: Scarcely. (*Back to the workers*) Remember, lives depend on you.

THE GENERAL WATCHES THE CONVEYOR BELT
ESTABLISH ITSELF. MADAME DELVAUX GIVES HIM
THE BENEFIT OF HER OPINION, OVERLAPPED WITH
OTHER TALK.

MADAME DELVAUX: You know I think the women are better at this than the men; they're more methodical, don't you think? I never had a husband who didn't leave his clothes lying all over the bedroom, and never thought once about picking them up.

SANTIAGO: Have you finished, Doctor?

CASTROPOL: He died in my arms.

SANTIAGO: For which service you'll want a fee presumably—Joly!

JOLY IS STILL MARKING HIS INVENTORY, SOMETHING
HE'S BEEN DOING THROUGHOUT THE SCENE.

JOLY: Sir?

SANTIAGO: Will you pay the leech?

JOLY LOOKS AFTER PAYING THE DOCTOR.

GENERAL GUYE: (*To Santiago*) A coffin-maker is on his way. We're going to need several before the afternoon's out.

SANTIAGO: Well at least somebody will profit by this.

GENERAL GUYE: You've responded well to the disaster, Santiago. The man who can keep his head at times like these is a man of destiny.

SANTIAGO: (*Deeply pleased*) General.

GENERAL GUYE: But such a man must await his hour; pressing for honor is a dishonorable business. Wait.

SANTIAGO: I'm patient.

THE GENERAL MOVES ACROSS TO THE PICNICKERS.
JOLY, THE PERFECT PETTY BUREAUCRAT, IS MAK-
ING CALCULATIONS AND NOTES BEFORE HANDING
OVER THE CASH. CASTROPOL IS VISIBLY EDGY.

GENERAL GUYE: And how are you ladies?

MADAME DELVAUX: Fine.

LEANOR: Except for the flies.

GENERAL GUYE: Julia?

JULIA: I don't mind the flies. It's wasps I can't bear.

LEANOR: I don't think wasps like carcasses do they? That's bees.

JULIA: Bees?

LEANOR: Making honey in dead lions.

JULIA: How horrible.

2ND SOLDIER: Sir! General Guye! We've found something! I don't know what it is—

GENERAL GUYE: A palette.

SANTIAGO: It must be Goya's.

DUKE: Is he there?

MADAME DELVAUX: At last, some action. I was falling asleep.

JULIA: Are they going to find him?

LEANOR: It's not that exciting.

JULIA: You were excited before.

DUKE: Is he there . . . ? Nicholas?

> THE DUKE HAS CROSSED TO THE HOLE THAT IS
> BEING DUG BY THE WORK-PARTY; HE LOOKS
> DOWN INTO IT.

GENERAL GUYE: We'll soon find him if he is.

DUKE: Is there any noise? Any sound of breathing?

1ST SOLDIER: Not that I can hear.

GENERAL GUYE: He many be much deeper.

DUKE: Hurry them. Don't they understand? What's that? Is that paint or blood?

> LUISA AND ESTELLA ASSIST THE DUCHESS SOFIA
> ON STAGE. HER HAIR IS CRUMPLED, HER FINGERS
> BLOODY; HER BEAUTY, HOWEVER, IS EXTRAORDI-
> NARY. SHE IS EIGHTEEN. SHE WILL NEVER BE MORE
> SUMPTUOUS.

DUCHESS: Damaso? Oh Damaso.

DUKE: (Dryly) Sofia. Are you finally dazzling us with your presence?

DUCHESS: Hello Julia—

JULIA: Are you all right?

DUCHESS: No, not really.

MADAME DELVAUX: Poor child. Poor child.

JULIA: Sit down. Did you have to fight?
DUCHESS: Tooth and nail.
LEANOR: But he overcame you?
DUCHESS: I feel as though I've been torn apart.
ESTELLA: She's ruptured.
DUKE: Is she?
DUCHESS: Yes. I am. (*Shows her fingers*) See?

THE DUKE LOOKS AT THE BLOODY FINGERS, AND
SEEMS TO SOFTEN A LITTLE.

DUKE: Oh. I didn't realize . . .
DUCHESS: Please don't touch me.
DUKE: At least let the Doctor examine you.
DUCHESS: No Doctors!
DUKE: Sofia.
DUCHESS: No doctors. You know how I hate doctors!

CASTROPOL APPROACHES.

CASTROPOL: If I may intrude a moment, Ladyship. There is
   some wisdom in my examining you. I realize how tender
   you may be after such a violation, but I swear, on my Moth-
   er's grave, I will be gentility itself.
DUCHESS: This . . . is . . . the . . . Doctor?
DUKE: Yes.
CASTROPOL: Of course if you would prefer not—
DUCHESS: Would it please you, Damaso?
DUKE: It would please me, yes.
DUCHESS: Then I must. Let nobody say I am a disobedient wife.
1ST WOMAN: (From the hole) A hand!
DUCHESS: What?
DUKE: Is it him?

HE RUSHES TO THE EDGE OF THE HOLE.

DUCHESS: What's going on? Damaso! You see how much he cares?
ESTELLA: They're digging for Goya.
DUKE: What's to be seen?
1ST WOMAN: Just fingers poking up.

SANTIAGO: Dig!

2ND WOMAN: We're doing our best.

GENERAL GUYE: Don't stand so close to the work, Damaso; you're impeding progress.

DUKE: Pray he's alive! For my sake, Pray.

THE BUZZ OF INSTRUCTION AND CHATTER ROUND THE HOLE COVERS THE FOLLOWING CONVERSATION. ONLY SANTIAGO WATCHES IT, EYES BURNING.

DUCHESS: (*To Castropol*) Castropol?

CASTROPOL: Yes.

DUCHESS: I thought you'd gone.

CASTROPOL: Believe in me.

DUCHESS: I do.

CASTROPOL: What's on your fingers?

DUCHESS: Dog's blood.

CASTROPOL: Ha!

DUCHESS: (*Smiles*) Estella's idea. To add credibility.

CASTROPOL: She should be writing plays.

THE DUKE TURNS AWAY FROM THE HOLE, STUMBLING, SWEATING.

DUKE: Christ save me; I feel strange.

SANTIAGO: Lordship—

DUKE: It's nothing. Just giddiness from looking into the hole. Sun on back of my head.

SANTIAGO: Sit down—

DUKE: No. I have to watch. He was my guest.

HE TURNS BACK TO THE WORK.

DUCHESS: Pathetic old man.

CASTROPOL: Where's your charity?

DUCHESS: When's he ever shown me charity? It was clever, coming as a doctor. Estella? Find some pillows for the examination will you?

CASTROPOL: And wine.

ESTELLA: Do you ever cool down?

DUCHESS: Not with him. He's an actor: never the same from hour to hour. Like having a regiment in between my legs.

THE DUKE ALMOST COLLAPSES; DELVAUX TRIES TO SUPPORT HIM.

DUKE: Oh! Oh!
MADAME DELVAUX: Oh Damaso. Help me someone. He's too heavy.
SANTIAGO: Stand aside! Joly!

MADAME DELVAUX AND SANTIAGO, ASSISTED BY JOLY, HELP HIM AWAY FROM THE PIT.

DUCHESS: See how weak he is?

THE DUKE SITS DOWN; HE IS SHAKING.

ESTELLA: He's going the way of his Mother.
DUCHESS: God help me if he does.
DUKE: Where is the Doctor?
CASTROPOL: Oh Christ. I hope he doesn't want medication.
ESTELLA: What's in your bag?
CASTROPOL: A change of costume.
DUKE: Doctor!
CASTROPOL: Yes. Yes.
DUKE: A private word.
SANTIAGO: Joly . . .

JOLY WITHDRAWS.

DUKE: All of you.

SANTIAGO AND DELVAUX WITHDRAW TOO.

DUKE: Doctor, if my wife has not been raped I want to know, do you understand? If there is hemorrhage, I will be a happy man. If not, at least I want the truth.
CASTROPOL: Of course. But I shall need privacy for the examination.
DUKE: The Dovecote. It's large and has no windows.
CASTROPOL: Where is that?

DUKE: The ugly one knows. She'll lead you. I'm grateful.

CASTROPOL: Really, the honor's mine.

DUCHESS: He never finished my portrait.

LEANOR: Goya's last gasp.

JULIA: Was it good? He painted me, when I was a child, everyone said—

LEANOR: It doesn't matter if it's good; it's his last work; it will be worth a fortune.

DUKE: He isn't dead yet! Why do they take so long?

SANTIAGO: Each stone they move shifts another; and the foundations are collapsing; it's not easy work.

DUCHESS: It will be well, Damaso, one way or the other.

ESTELLA: The Doctor's waiting.

DUCHESS: Have you told him to be tender with me?

DUKE: Of course.

THE DUCHESS, ESTELLA AND CASTROPOL EXIT.

THE DUKE GOES BACK TO THE HOLE.

SANTIAGO: (*To Joly*) Where are Goya's family?

JOLY: In Madrid. Calle de los Reyes.

SANTIAGO: If this body is his, go fetch them. There's a wife?

JOLY: Yes. And a son: Xavier.

SANTIAGO: Bring the son at least, to identify him. There'll presumably be a state funeral.

1ST SOLDIER: Sir!

GENERAL GUYE: Almost there! Careful now!

DUKE: Is he alive?

GENERAL GUYE: Stay back a moment. Everybody stay back.

JULIA: (*Delighted*) Oh, this is awful.

LEANOR: I think it's like a fish-market. Flies everywhere, and people peering around.

JULIA: Are you never satisfied?

DUKE: Is it him?

THE BABBLE CEASES.

GENERAL GUYE: Yes it's Goya.

DUKE: And dead?

GENERAL GUYE: Dead.

THE BABBLE ERUPTS AGAIN.

JULIA: You hear that? It was Goya, and he's dead, and we were here. Isn't it tragic? He painted me once and now he's dead.
DUKE: Haul him up into the light where we can see him, for God's sake.

LEANOR CROSSES TO NOVICK'S BODY, AND UNCOVERS IT, STARES AT IT, WHILE THE CHAOS GOES ON BEHIND HER.

1ST SOLDIER: He's crushed. The head . . .
1ST WOMAN: The state of him.
MADAME DELVAUX: What's he saying?
JULIA: Something about the head.
FOUCHE: Oh God.

FOUCHE STUMBLES AWAY TO BE SICK. SURZUR COMFORTS HER.

MADAME DELVAUX: What about the head?
1ST WOMAN: It's crushed.
GENERAL GUYE: The face is destroyed. The wounds are terrible.
DUKE: If the corpse has no face, how can you know it's him?
GENERAL GUYE: There's no doubt, Damaso. The coat is his, I recognize it. The paint on it, the lace on the sleeves. It's him for certain.
DUKE: Why? Why in heaven's name here, in my house?
MADAME DELVAUX: Oh, how horrible. What terrible mutilation.
JULIA: You can see all his workings.
GENERAL GUYE: Make a sling, haul him up that way.
MADAME DELVAUX: I think I've seen enough.

SHE TURNS AWAY FROM THE HOLE TO SEE LEANOR AT NOVICK'S BODY.

MADAME DELVAUX: The flies are getting insistent, aren't they? Leanor?

LEANOR: What?

MADAME DELVAUX: What are you doing?

LEANOR: I thought I was going to see something that would change me, but I'm just the same.

MADAME DELVAUX: Why should you want to change? People live and people die, and that's all there is to it. Now stop being morbid.

LEANOR: You're the one who said we should go and watch the exhumations.

MADAME DELVAUX: I didn't think you were going to take on this way. This hysteria.

LEANOR: I'm not hysterical.

MADAME DELVAUX: Julia!

JULIA: What?

MADAME DELVAUX: Take Leanor into the garden, she's too hot.

LEANOR: I'm not a child.

MADAME DELVAUX: You're behaving like one.

JULIA: I'm watching.

SANTIAGO: Allow me to suggest Luisa escort the mademoiselle. Luisa!

MADAME DELVAUX: It's all these books.

LEANOR: Yes! Yes, that's what it must be! Books!

SHE THROWS HER BOOK DOWN.

LUISA: Sir?

SANTIAGO: Would you take mademoiselle Courcel into the orchard—

LUISA: Of course.

LEANOR REFUSES LUISA'S ARM, AND EXITS WITH LUISA FOLLOWING.

MADAME DELVAUX: She takes things very badly, but will not admit it. Julia on the other hand, bawls like a baby and feels nothing at all.

GENERAL GUYE: (To *those hauling up the body*) Gently! Gently! Good. Lay him out.

THE BODY IS BROUGHT TO THE SURFACE, PAR-

*TIALLY HIDDEN BY THE SLING THAT HAS BEEN
USED TO RAISE IT. IT IS LAID ON THE GROUND;
THE DEGREE OF MUTILATION CAN ONLY BE
GLIMPSED, BUT IT IS COMPREHENSIVE. THE SOL-
DIERS, TRANSFORMED TOTALLY BY GRIME AND
BLOOD, CLIMB OUT OF THE PIT, EXHAUSTED.
EVERYTHING HAS STOPPED; EVEN RAFAEL HAS
CEASED HIS DIGGING. FLIES WHINE AROUND. DEL-
VAUX FLITS ONE FROM HER FACE.*

DUKE: History will say of me: he built the house that fell on
    Goya.
MADAME DELVAUX: Well it's better than being forgotten.
DONA PASCUALA: (*Having woken*) What's the hush about?
SANTIAGO: It's nothing to concern you.
DONA PASCUALA: I smell something rotting. Let me see!
SANTIAGO: Sir?
DUKE: You heard her.
DONA PASCUALA: I want to see! Send that one across. You! With
    the fat thighs. (*She points to Nataniel*) Lift me up!
SANTIAGO: Go on. (*To Caxa*) Caxa. You can go back to the sta-
    bles. My thanks.

CAXA EXITS.

NATANIEL CROSSES TO DONA PASCUALA.

DUKE: What now?
GENERAL GUYE: There will have to be a state inquiry. A major
    figure like Goya. There may be claims of assassination. He
    was a controversial figure.
DUKE: All I wanted was a portrait of my Duchess.
GENERAL GUYE: You are entirely guiltless in this. Everyone
    knows that. Just a victim of circumstance.
DUKE: Santiago? I feel unwell. Will you watch over my guests,
    while I walk?
GENERAL GUYE: No alone, Damaso.
DUKE: Where's the harm?
GENERAL GUYE: They meant to kill you with their cannon-fire.
    They left you alive—

DUKE: Did they?

GENERAL GUYE: They may come back; try again. I beg you, go with an escort. Reubell?

1ST SOLDIER: Sir?

GENERAL GUYE: Wash yourself; then attend the Duke.

1ST SOLDIER: General.

REUBELL EXITS.

DONA PASCUALA HAS ARRIVED AT THE BODY, ON NATANIEL'S BACK.

DONA PASCUALA: Well there's a pretty thing. Dead is he?

NATANIEL: Yes Ma'am.

DONA PASCUALA: Closer. Flick back the cloth woman, let's see it properly.

1ST WOMAN PULLS BACK THE CLOTH.

DONA PASCUALA: He looks flayed, don't you think? You know, you should doll him up before the widow arrives. Powder his face.

DUKE: He has no face.

DONA PASCUALA: At least cut his nails. Her grief will be bad enough without seeing such ugly hands.

SANTIAGO: I hardly think—

DUKE: Why not? My mother's right.

SANTIAGO: His nails?

GENERAL GUYE: The Duke . . . has made his feelings known, Santiago.

SANTIAGO: Of course.

JULIA: I have scissors. (*She takes them from her bag*) Give them back, mind you, so I can show them off.

SANTIAGO: I'm obliged.

GENERAL GUYE: I think we should go back into the fresh air, don't you?

SANTIAGO: The orchard perhaps.

MADAME DELVAUX: Fouche. Bring the wine.

GENERAL GUYE: (*To Santiago*) Will you pay the women, and have them lay the bodies out away from the house? Except

Goya; we don't want his corpse to become a curiosity. Have him left here, for the coffin-maker.

SANTIAGO GOES TO PAY THE WOMEN. THE SOLDIER WATCHES, EXPECTING PAY, AND MOVES OFF, DISGUSTED, WHEN HE DOESN'T GET ANYTHING.

MADAME DELVAUX: Will you not come to the orchard, Damaso?
DUKE: Poor Goya.
MADAME DELVAUX: He was flesh and blood, the same as the rest of us. It happens to us all.
DONA PASCUALA: Take me to the orchard! I want you to stay with me. Understand? I'll find a silk shirt for you, eh?
NATANIEL: Yes Ma'am.
DONA PASCUALA: And some ribbon for your hair. I like your thighs.

NATANIEL TAKES DONA PASCUALA OFF.

DONA PASCUALA: (*As she exits*) If you see my dog, call after it.
DUKE: Goya was more than flesh and blood. He was a great man.
MADAME DELVAUX: (*Looking at the corpse*) Not so great.

JULIA HAS PICKED UP HIS SPECTACLES, AND GIVES THEM TO THE FIRST WOMAN.

JULIA: Put his spectacles on. His face looks naked.

THE FIRST WOMAN PUTS THEM ON, WINCING A LITTLE AT THE DUTY.

JULIA: That's better.
MADAME DELVAUX: You are the strangest creature. Shall we go?

DELVAUX AND JULIA EXIT, TAKING HELP FROM SANTIAGO TO GET OVER THE RUBBLE. FOUCHE, SURZUR AND SHATTERELL FOLLOW.

DUKE: Where's it gone, Nicholas?

GENERAL GUYE: Where's what gone?
DUKE: His greatness.
GENERAL GUYE: Into history, I suppose.
DUKE: Perhaps that's the safest place to be.

REUBELL HAS RE-ENTERED. AS THE DUKE EXITS, HE FOLLOWS, AT A DISCREET DISTANCE, STILL WIPING HIS FACE WITH A CLOTH.

THE GENERAL LOOKS AT THE CORPSE, THEN LEAVES.

THE THREE WOMEN ARE LAUGHING QUIETLY.

THE CICADAS MAKE THEIR INCESSANT DIN IN THE GRASS AS THE LIGHTS CHANGE.

END OF PART ONE.

INTERLUDE.

MUSIC PLAYS.

THE WOMEN MOVE THE BODIES OF NOVICK AND MELCHOR OUT OF THE RUINS.

BIRDS SING.

THE LIGHT CHANGES, SLOWLY, AS THE AFTER-NOON ADVANCES.

AS THE REMOVAL OF THE BODIES NEARS ITS END, ACT TWO BEGINS.

Act 2

ENTER CASTROPOL, WHO IS NO LONGER DRESSED AS THE DOCTOR, THOUGH HE CARRIES HIS BAG AND HIS COAT AND WEARS HIS FALSE BEARD. HE'S IN THE MIDDLE OF TELLING A STORY TO THE DUCHESS AND ESTELLA.

CASTROPOL: And I'm so infatuated with this woman I have to make love to her, so I break into her house by night, I kill two dogs—

DUCHESS: There are dogs in this play?

ESTELLA: I hate dogs.

CASTROPOL: Not real dogs. Actors dressed as dogs.

ESTELLA: That's even worse.

CASTROPOL: I enter her room and I rape her.

DUCHESS: She doesn't give herself to you?

CASTROPOL: Oh no. This is a highly moral play. If we're going to have sex in it, it's rape or nothing. That way we can claim we disapprove, however pornographic the content.

DUCHESS: So you rape her.

CASTROPOL: Three times. But on the third occasion her father, the Commander, comes running.

ESTELLA: Conveniently late.

CASTROPOL: And I murder him. Stab him in the eye. It's a brutal scene.

DUCHESS: Through the eye?

CASTROPOL: And dangerous to play. So I escape and I go on living my debauched life, until . . . one night . . . I chance to be in a graveyard in which the Commander is buried.

ESTELLA: More convenience.

CASTROPOL: Is she a critic?

DUCHESS: Finish the story.

CASTROPOL: Well the statue on the Commander's grave comes to life, takes hold of me and drags me down to hell.

ESTELLA: Is there a scene in hell?

CASTROPOL: Oh certainly. A vast devil emerges from the pit, there are fireworks. Terrible scenes of punishment. Some surreptitious buggery amongst the lesser fiends. It's a crowd-pleaser. They lap it up.

DUCHESS: I wish I could have seen you in it.

CASTROPOL: Modesty forbids me to tell you how I sparkle in the role.

ESTELLA: Why don't you go back then; I'm sure they're pining for you.

CASTROPOL: Never.

ESTELLA: You've had what you wanted.

DUCHESS: Estella!

ESTELLA: Twice to my knowledge.

DUCHESS: We are in love. (*She kisses Castropol. The kisses escalate.*)

ESTELLA: All in an afternoon? Will you leave him alone? It's two hours since you went to the Dovecote. (*To Castropol*) You should go to the Duke, tell him how badly hurt Sofia is.

CASTROPOL: I suppose I ought.

ESTELLA: He already suspects.

DUCHESS: He does not.

ESTELLA: If he doesn't then Santiago does.

DUCHESS: He's always polite to me. And I like the way his breath smells of peppermint.

ESTELLA: You stupid girl.

DUCHESS: Don't you call me that.

ESTELLA: Just because you caught the eyes of an elder man, doesn't mean you instantly rise in the ways of the world. I was a whore once, (*To Castropol*) did you know that? And I made enough money to buy myself a brothel by marrying a man who was dying of a belly-disease. I had eight months of watching him sick up his stomach, then he died, and I was the richest Madame in miles, 'til the French burnt my establishment down. Now you play the loving wife, be cautious, give him no cause to fault you, and you'll have years to play with his fortune when he's gone.

DUCHESS: I can't stay here 'til he dies. It could be a lifetime yet, putting up with his little demands. I'll go mad before he does.

CASTROPOL: No.

DUCHESS: I will. (*She's close to tears*) I will: thinking about all my wasted opportunities. All the world—

ESTELLA: It's not that good, believe me.

DUCHESS: Easy for you to say: you're almost dead, and the ugliest woman in Spain.

CASTROPOL: That is true.

ESTELLA: Oh yes; it's true. Men who hired me used to say it didn't matter which end up I was in bed, both looked like a mule's backside. It made my fortune, this face. My reputation went before me, the mule-faced woman.

CASTROPOL: You're proud of it.

ESTELLA: No. But not ashamed either.

ENTER LUISA WITH NAIL-SCISSORS.

LUISA: Excuse me, ma'am?

CASTROPOL HURRIEDLY FINDS THE SPECTACLES AND THE JACKET THAT WILL RE-ESTABLISH HIS DISGUISE, BACK TO LUISA.

DUCHESS: Luisa?

LUISA: I have instructions to—

SHE STOPS, WATCHING CASTROPOL DRESS.

DUCHESS: To do what?

LUISA: Cut the nails off the painter.

ESTELLA: Cut his nails?

ESTELLA CROSSES TO LUISA, DISTRACTING HER FROM THE TRANSFORMATION CASTROPOL IS UNDERGOING.

ESTELLA: Why cut a corpse's nails?

LUISA: I don't know; that is what I was told to do.

ESTELLA: Well you'd better get on with it then.

LUISA: Yes.

ESTELLA: Don't stare girl: your eyes will start to water.

DUCHESS: (*To Castropol*) Where are you going now?

CASTROPOL: To tell your husband I've examined every inch and that your body is covered in bites and scratches, as though your rapist were a tiger.

ESTELLA: Don't overdo the story in praise of yourself.

DUCHESS: Then you'll come back?

CASTROPOL: First I have to find myself a new suit. And I'll need money—

DUCHESS: I can get money; a jacket; whatever you need.

CASTROPOL: Will you?

ESTELLA: You know she will. You're so transparent.

DUCHESS: Don't be clever with Damaso. He's unpredictable.

CASTROPOL: I'll be subtle.

ESTELLA: Ha!

DUCHESS: In the Dovecote? Later?

CASTROPOL: At your command. (*He kisses her hand*) Ladyship. (*To Estella, kissing her hand*) Mule.

HE EXITS.

DUCHESS: I'm so hot.

ESTELLA: He makes you hot with his foolishness.

FELIPE HAS ENTERED; HE WATCHES; ALMOST HIDDEN.

ESTELLA: The General has gone to the orchard, with Madame Delvaux and the others. I suggest we join them.

DUCHESS: I couldn't. I'd start smiling without any reason. People will see his face in my eyes. We'll go to the stables; watch the horses coupling.

SHE EXITS. ESTELLA FOLLOWS. FELIPE WATCHES THEM GO.

FELIPE: Luisa.

LUISA: You're a trespasser. He'll have you flogged to death.

FELIPE: Have they found Daniella?

LUISA: No.

FELIPE: Where's Rafael?

LUISA: He's sleeping somewhere.

FELIPE: Sleeping?

LUISA: It's useless. He knows.

FELIPE: I loved her too. The three of us had fine times together, in bed and out of it.

LUISA: She's dead.

FELIPE HAS FOUND RAFAEL.

FELIPE: Hey, bollocks, rouse yourself! What are you doing lying there! Lump of shit, get up and dig—

RAFAEL: Felipe.

FELIPE DRAGS HIM TO HIS FEET.

FELIPE: Up I say!

RAFAEL: She's run away that's all.

RAFAEL HAS HOLD OF FELIPE, EMBRACING HIM.

FELIPE: If she'd run off, she'd have come back by now.

RAFAEL: No. She's sleeping in a field, waiting 'til it gets cooler. The baby makes walking such a chore.

FELIPE: Don't have so much faith, man. Dig! I'll help you! We'll both dig!

LUISA: You should go—

FELIPE: If she's not here, then all we've done is put blisters on our hands.

RAFAEL: I don't want to find her if she has no face. I couldn't bear that.

THE COFFIN-MAKER ENTERS; A SMALL, BEARDED MAN WITH A CIGARETTE IN HIS MOUTH. HE IS CARRYING A COFFIN STRAPPED TO HIS BACK, AND SMILING. HIS DAUGHTER, BARBARA, FOLLOWS, CARRYING TOOLS.

FELIPE: (*Contemptuous of Rafael's lassitude*) So leave her lying where she is; she'll sprout some spring, eh? We'll crop Daniella flowers from the rubble, red and white. What the hell does it matter? Give in to it all. Circumstance is tearing off our balls, so we say we didn't want children anyhow.

RAFAEL: Children?

FELIPE: Children, Rafael. In her belly, remember?

RAFAEL: They must be kept safe.

FELIPE: Then we have to dig, you and I.

RAFAEL: Dig.

FELIPE: Yes.

COFFIN MAKER: Did somebody say dig?

LUISA: Who are you?

COFFIN MAKER: The coffin-maker; I was sent for. This is my daughter, Barbara. (*Crosses to Goya*) I was told there was a disaster, but pickings look thin.

LUISA: The other bodies have been laid on the lawn.

COFFIN MAKER: Covered, I hope, in this heat.

LUISA: Wrapped in cloth.

COFFIN MAKER: Won't do much good to keep the flies out.

BARBARA HELPS COFFIN MAKER PUT DOWN THE COFFIN HE CARRIES, THEN SHE GOES TO LOOK AT GOYA.

BARBARA: He must be the important one; he's wearing the lace.

LUISA: His name was Goya.

COFFIN MAKER: Never heard of him.

BARBARA: The painter?

FELIPE: So they found him.

LUISA: What's left of him.

BARBARA: There are others here though.

FELIPE: What did she say?

BARBARA: Buried in the wreckage. Didn't you know?

COFFIN MAKER: Barbara can sense where the dead lie. It's a peculiar skill she has; and useful in our profession.

FELIPE: And you smell others here?

BARBARA: Not smell. But, yes.

RAFAEL IS WATCHING HER.

FELIPE: Alive?

COFFIN MAKER: She has no skill with the living; just the dead.

RAFAEL: How many?

BARBARA IS WALKING AROUND THE RUIN, SENS-ING OUT THE PLACE.

COFFIN MAKER: More than one, but not quite two.

RAFAEL: (*A strangled sound*) No.

FELIPE: A child?

BARBARA: Not born.

FELIPE: Where?

COFFIN MAKER: Ssh!

RAFAEL: Tell her no.

FELIPE: Where?

BARBARA: Here. Under my feet.

COFFIN MAKER: Uncanny isn't it?

LUISA: Horrible.

FELIPE: Deep?

BARBARA: I don't know.

RAFAEL FALLS TO THE GROUND, TALKS TO THE EARTH.

RAFAEL: Daniella!

BARBARA: They're already dead, I'm afraid.

RAFAEL: Daniella!

HE STARTS TO DIG WITH RENEWED FURY.

LUISA: Keep his voice down! He'll have Santiago over here!

FELIPE: Let him come!

COFFIN MAKER: Is the VIP's manicure finished?

LUISA: Yes.

COFFIN MAKER: We may as well get him to bed. Barbara?

BARBARA HAS TAKEN THE LID OFF THE COFFIN HER FATHER BROUGHT IN, WHILE THE COFFIN-MAKER TIDIES THE CORPSE OF GOYA.

LUISA: You came back for Santiago?

FELIPE: Why else? Nataniel has always hated him. We'll do the job together.

HE CROSSES TO RAFAEL, WHO IS STILL DIGGING FRANTICALLY.

FELIPE: Let me help.

RAFAEL: No!

FELIPE: Four hands—

RAFAEL: No, I said!

LUISA WATCHES THE COFFIN MAKER AND BAR-BARA PUT THE BODY INTO THE COFFIN.

LUISA: What if the box had been too small?

COFFIN MAKER: We'd have waited an hour until he began to get mushy and squashed him in. *(To Barbara)* Brush his hair; see if you can get his teeth in some kind of order. I'll measure up the others, if someone will lead the way.

LUISA: I'll show you.

COFFIN MAKER: Obliged.

COFFIN MAKER EXITS WITH LUISA LEADING.

FELIPE: Strange profession for a woman.

BARBARA: My father had no sons.

FELIPE: Ever seen a ghost?

BARBARA: That's French nonsense.

FELIPE: Is that so?

BARBARA: They're superstitious.

FELIPE: That's true. I was at Saragrossa, after the sieges. At night we'd creep amongst them, and hear them murmuring Hail Marys if a dog barked. Everything made them afraid. We had no ammuni-tion left, no food left but we had something they didn't.

BARBARA: What was that?

FELIPE: Disbelief. It made us strong. Rafael was best at scaring them. He had so many tricks. He could set fire to his own farts; that always had them praying, seeing this madman running around with his buttocks flaming.

BARBARA: And now. You still so disbelieving?

FELIPE: When I start to fear devils I remember us howling down the moon, and I think I'm worse than any devil could ever be. Like you, familiar with the dead, and not fearing them.

RAFAEL: Ah!

RAFAEL HAS FOUND A DOOR LYING FLAT IN THE GROUND.

RAFAEL: Felipe!

FELIPE: I'm here.

RAFAEL: Help me!

FELIPE HELPS RAFAEL TO OPEN THE DOOR. STONES PATTER DOWN INTO THE DARKNESS; THEIR VOICES ECHO AS THEY SPEAK INTO THE PIT.

RAFAEL: It smells dark.

FELIPE: Did you ever go beneath the house?

RAFAEL: Never.

FELIPE: The cellars are huge.

RAFAEL: She's expecting me.

FELIPE: Let me lead. At least I've been down.

RAFAEL: No! (*He holds Felipe back*) Felipe. She and I . . . we need some privacy. To discuss the child.

FELIPE: She's dead, Rafael.

RAFAEL: (*Almost insulted*) I know that. Close the door behind me.

HE DISAPPEARS INTO THE EARTH.

FELIPE: Wait! Let me find you a lamp; something to light your way.

BARBARA: Don't stop him if he wants to go.

FELIPE: He'll get lost: he could die down there.

BARBARA: If he can smell the dark, he can smell sunlight too. Don't shake.

FELIPE: So much lost.

BARBARA: And to gain.

FELIPE: What?

HE LOOKS AT HER; SHE DOES NOT LOOK AWAY.

FELIPE: On such a day?

BARBARA TOUCHES HIS FACE.

BARBARA: On any day.

*ENTER THE NUNS, SISTER MAGDALENA, AND SIS-
TER ISOBEL, DAUGHTERS OF JERUSALEM. SISTER
MAGDALENA HAS HOLD OF A RAGGED MAN
WRAPPED IN A CLOTH. IT IS GOYA. HIS FACE HAS
BEEN CLEANED OF BLOOD; HIS EYES ARE DEEP-SET,
SUSPICIOUS, ESPECIALLY AS HE HAS LOST HIS
GLASSES. HIS SHORT, AWKWARD BODY IS SLUMPED
WITH FATIGUE, AND HE NIBBLES HIS NAILS INCES-
SANTLY. HE CLEARLY LOATHES THESE WOMEN
WHO HAVE BROUGHT HIM HERE.*

SISTER MAGDALENA: God be with you.
BARBARA: (*Standing up*) And with you. Have you come to bless
    the bodies?
SISTER MAGDALENA: We found a man.
FELIPE: Are you boasting, Sister?
SISTER MAGDALENA: (*To Barbara, ignoring Felipe*) He was wan-
    dering along the road; reeling.
SISTER ISOBEL: Blood on him.
SISTER MAGDALENA: We heard there'd been an attack.
BARBARA: And you assumed—
SISTER MAGDALENA: That he came from here. We think he's
    suffered some damage to his head.
SISTER ISOBEL: He won't answer any of our questions.
SISTER MAGDALENA: Except his name. He keeps saying his
    name is—
GOYA: (*Seeing the word on Barbara's lips*) Goya! I am Francisco
    Goya y Lucientes, the painter.
SISTER MAGDALENA: Is it possible he is this man?
BARBARA: No. Goya's dead.
FELIPE: Look how he watches your lips.
BARBARA: (*To Goya*) Goya is dead.
GOYA: Oh? Nobody told me.
BARBARA: He's here, in a coffin.

GOYA: He's here, in bare feet!

SISTER MAGDALENA: We guessed as much. Insane. (*She peers at Goya*) Casualty of war.

GOYA: Casualty of Christ, Sister, same as you.

SISTER ISOBEL: Let him see the corpse. It may shock him into understanding his error.

FELIPE: She's right.

SISTER MAGDALENA: Is there anything left to drink?

FELIPE: Try the table.

SISTER MAGDALENA: Only the heat—

BARBARA: (*To Goya*) Do you want to see your body?

GOYA: Why not? It can only be an improvement.

HE GOES TO THE COFFIN. BARBARA BRUSHES THE FLIES AWAY.

GOYA: (*Recognition*) Ah!

SISTER ISOBEL: I think he understands.

GOYA: There you are!

BARBARA: He does.

HE REACHES INTO THE COFFIN.

BARBARA: Wait!

SISTER ISOBEL: What's he doing?

GOYA PULLS THE GLASSES OFF THE CORPSE BEFORE THE SISTER CAN PREVENT HIM. HE PUTS THEM ON.

GOYA: Dead men's eyes; still, they're better than nothing. I can see you now. (*Looks at Sister Isobel*) Oh, God, you do have a mustache, I thought it was my eyes.

SISTER ISOBEL: Put them back. They're not yours.

GOYA: He won't mind. (*Talks to the corpse*) Do you mind? See, the man's speechless with joy. Poor Goya. He never was pretty. Too short, too fat, too deaf. Oh God, they used to say, here comes Goya and cross over the road to avoid having to shout in his ear. (*A beat; the tone changes*) I am dead. It seems I am actually dead, which comes, to be honest, as a slap in the face.

FELIPE: I don't think he understands at all.

GOYA: What did you say? Enunciate.

FELIPE: You are not Goya. Goya is dead.

GOYA: Oh yes: I concede the point. That is me lying there, any fool can see that.

SISTER ISOBEL SITS DOWN BESIDE THE DOOR RAFAEL DISAPPEARED INTO. SISTER MAGDALENA HAS FOUND AN ALMOST EMPTY BOTTLE OF WINE.

SISTER MAGDALENA: There's no time to rest.

SISTER ISOBEL: I feel sick with the heat.

FELIPE: Rip all your clothes off.

SISTER ISOBEL: What?

FELIPE: God doesn't expect you to wear woolly underwear on a day like this.

SISTER MAGDALENA: Young man—

GOYA: (*To Felipe*) Now you're for it.

SISTER MAGDALENA: We brought the lost sheep home; at least be polite.

FELIPE: He's not our sheep.

SISTER MAGDALENA: Well whose is he then?

A YELL IN THE EARTH.

SISTER ISOBEL: (*Standing up*) I heard a noise.

FELIPE: Rafael.

SISTER MAGDALENA: Is it an animal, trapped somewhere?

BARBARA: No animal.

FELIPE: (*Pushing Sister Isobel aside*) Out of the way, Sister.

HE FLINGS OPEN THE DOOR.

SISTER MAGDALENA: You might be thankful for God's mercy one of these days.

FELIPE: God's mercy does not smell of red wine. Rafael! Can you hear me? Barbara? A lamp?

BARBARA: Yes. (*She goes to her bag*) I have one.

SISTER MAGDALENA: Can't face the dark?

FELIPE DOESN'T REPLY.

SISTER ISOBEL: I'm not staying here. We've done our duty.

*GOYA HAS FOUND THE PLACE WHERE JOLY HAS
COLLECTED THE SALVAGE FROM THE DEBRIS.
WITH JOY HIS HANDS ALIGHT ON HIS SKETCH-
BOOK AND A HANDFUL OF DRAWING IMPLE-
MENTS: BRUSHES, CHARCOAL ETC. HE SITS DOWN
AMONGST THE RUBBLE AND STARTS TO DRAW.
FROM NOW ON THE SKETCHBOOK IS SELDOM OUT
OF HIS HANDS.*

BARBARA: Will you bless the body?
SISTER ISOBEL: I suppose I must.

*THE NUN STARTS TO SAY A BLESSING OVER THE
BODY. BARBARA HAS FOUND THE LAMP, AND LIT IT.*

BARBARA: Here.

*FELIPE CROSSES TO TAKE IT FROM HER. SISTER
MAGDALENA HAS APPROACHED THE HOLE. SUD-
DENLY RAFAEL EMERGES. HE IS COVERED IN
BLOOD; HIS BABY, TORN FROM DANIELLA, IS IN HIS
ARMS. HE GRABS AT THE SISTER, WHO BACKS OFF.*

SISTER MAGDALENA: Christ in heaven preserve us!
FELIPE: Rafael!
SISTER MAGDALENA: What's that in his arms?
BARBARA: Oh no. No!
RAFAEL: I found them. See? The child was there.
GOYA: There's a sight for sore eyes.
SISTER MAGDALENA: The baby's been eaten. There's bite-marks
     in it.
RAFAEL: It's not safe.
SISTER MAGDALENA: Eaten!
FELIPE: Shut up! (*To Rafael*) What do you mean; not safe?
RAFAEL: Better he be in me, safe in me, and wrapped up, than in
     the ground.

GOYA: The man talks perfect sense.

SISTER MAGDALENA: He's eaten his own child, is that what he's saying? Torn it from its mother's womb and cannibalised it!

FELIPE: He has his reasons.

SISTER ISOBEL: He has no reason at all. (*She has brought a gun out, and levels it*)

BARBARA: No!

SISTER MAGDALENA: (*To Rafael*) The Lord forgive you.

FELIPE: Stop!

BARBARA RUSHES AT SISTER ISOBEL AND WRESTLES THE GUN OUT OF HER HAND.

BARBARA: Are you too stupid to see? Grief did this to him. His wife is dead.

SISTER MAGDALENA: He's eaten human flesh.

GOYA: Is that a sin of gluttony, or lust?

SISTER MAGDALENA: You're lunatics, all of you.

SISTER ISOBEL: She's broken my fingers.

SISTER MAGDALENA: We'll find someone in charge. Let them deal with this.

THEY GO TO EXIT.

GOYA: (*Shouting after them*) Thank you, Sisters, from the heart of my bottom!

THEY EXIT. BARBARA HAS PICKED UP THE GUN THE SISTER DROPPED, AND POCKETED IT. RAFAEL HAS COLLAPSED TO HIS KNEES.

BARBARA: If they bring soldiers, he'll be shot, and questions asked.

FELIPE: True.

BARBARA: You must get him away from here.

RAFAEL: Why did they die?

GOYA: What did he say?

BARBARA: He asks why they died.

RAFAEL: What did they ever do? (*Nuzzling the baby, he falls to his knees*)

FELIPE: If only we knew the crime. Just once to be told what we're punished for.

BARBARA: Is that your disbelief speaking?

GOYA: Somebody should hide him. In a tree; under a stone. Where they can't find him, and try to torture some sanity back into him.

FELIPE TAKES A STEP TOWARDS RAFAEL.

FELIPE: Remember, Rafael? Us on the walls, Howling?

RAFAEL LOOKS UP DANGEROUSLY, HIS TEETH AT THE BODY OF THE CHILD.

FELIPE: Didn't we say we were friends for life? Remember? Say you remember.

RAFAEL: She's dead. She'll never speak to me again. Never be three of us laughing.

FELIPE: I know.

RAFAEL: What am I to do?

FELIPE: We have to go before the Frenchmen arrive.

RAFAEL: I'll howl at them.

FELIPE: They won't be afraid, not in the daylight. They'll shoot us, and then who's to look after the baby?

RAFAEL NODS; STANDS UP.

FELIPE: We'll go to the river; you can wash.

RAFAEL NODS AGAIN.

BARBARA: Quickly.

FELIPE: (*To Barbara, as he exits*) Look for me.

FELIPE EXITS. RAFAEL FOLLOWS. GOYA WATCHES THEM GO, BACK TO BARBARA.

BARBARA: Who are you?

HE DOESN'T SEE SO HE DOESN'T HEAR. SHE TOUCHES HIS SHOULDER. HE JUMPS.

GOYA: Ah!

BARBARA: Who are you?

GOYA: Me? (*A beat before he decides to trust Barbara*) I am Goya.

BARBARA SHAKES HER HEAD.

BARBARA: No.

GOYA: The man in the coffin is a thief. He stole my clothes; just as his companion stole the subject of this very painting. (*He takes the painting off the easel*) Believe me or not, it's of no consequence. Am I the only significant corpse?

BARBARA: Yes.

GOYA: Pity.

BARBARA: Weren't you fond of your hosts?

GOYA: I have a weakness common to many under-educated men; I am pitifully impressed by conspicuous wealth, at the same time as finding it repulsive.

BARBARA: I think you are Goya.

GOYA: Yes; I think I am too.

BARBARA: I'll go and tell the Duke.

GOYA: (*Taking hold of her arm to halt her*) They'll find me soon enough. Let me enjoy a few minutes of your company, and my anonymity. What's your name?

BARBARA: Barbara.

GOYA: I'm stone deaf, Barbara. Struck down by a disease twenty odd years ago. Will you be my interpreter for a while?

BARBARA: If you want.

GOYA: (*Staring into the coffin*) I think perhaps the dead see more than we do. I envy that.

BARBARA: Envy?

GOYA: If they can see more, yes. Other men have to fill their mouths all day, I have to cram my eyes. Looking's a vice with me. I have to devour everything I so much as glance at, what the angels and the fallen angels made, it's the same to me. And when I've got the sights in here I want to make them all over again, in paint, and sign them, yes sign the world and say: 'Goya saw this!'

BARBARA: Very humble.

GOYA: I don't believe in modesty; the English invented it to disguise their lack of talent.

OFF-STAGE, THE SOUND OF MARCHING AND VOICES.

SISTER MAGDALENA: (*Off*) And the child was still screaming.
GENERAL GUYE: (*Off*) Allow me, Sister, to see for myself.
SISTER MAGDALENA: I can't go there again.
GENERAL GUYE: (*Off*) Sister, you're safe now.

OVERLAPPING WITH THIS EXCHANGE IS ONE BETWEEN GOYA AND BARBARA.

BARBARA: Voices! Soldiers! It's General Guye.
GOYA: Guye? He knows me. I painted him.
BARBARA: Then you can show yourself to him.
GOYA: No! Not yet. Not yet—

HE HIDES, AND GENERAL GUYE, SISTER MAG-DALENA AND TWO SOLDIERS IN UNIFORM APPEAR. THE SOLDIERS WILL APPEAR AGAIN. THEY ARE ST. PIERRE AND GREGORIO, BOTH FUSILIERS IN THE 44TH LINE INFANTRY REGIMENT.

GENERAL GUYE: Well?
SISTER MAGDALENA: He emerged out of the ground over there. The look on his face.
GENERAL GUYE: Calm, Sister. St. Pierre!
ST. PIERRE: Sir?
GENERAL GUYE: Are you shaking?
ST. PIERRE: No sir.
GENERAL GUYE: I can distinctly hear your buttons jangling.

GREGORIO LAUGHS.

GENERAL GUYE: You're not afraid are you, Gregorio?
GREGORIO: No sir.
GENERAL GUYE: Then you can go down the hole and bring the man up.
SISTER MAGDALENA: This was no man.
GENERAL GUYE: Please Sister; you're frightening the fusilier. Go on; down you go.
GREGORIO: Yes General.

GREGORIO APPROACHES THE HOLE, RIFLE READY.

GENERAL GUYE: Fetch him into the light.

SISTER MAGDALENA: He may have run off. He was foaming at the mouth.

GENERAL GUYE: We'll see. Soldier . . .

GREGORIO GOES DOWN INTO THE HOLE.

GENERAL GUYE: (*To Barbara*) Did you see the cannibal?

SISTER MAGDALENA: She's the one who stopped Sister Isobel shooting it.

GENERAL GUYE: Is this true?

BARBARA: No.

GENERAL GUYE: Are you calling the Daughter of Jerusalem a liar?

BARBARA: Why not?

GENERAL GUYE: But there was a man here?

BARBARA: There was.

GENERAL GUYE: And where did he go?

BARBARA: Back underground.

GENERAL GUYE: Then we'll need to be patient. St. Pierre? When you report back to the Captain volunteer yourself for the night watch.

ST. PIERRE: With respect sir.

GENERAL GUYE: Yes?

ST. PIERRE: I'm a drummer sir.

GENERAL GUYE: Oh you're a drummer.

ST. PIERRE: That's right, and Gregorio—

GENERAL GUYE: Don't tell me, violin.

ST. PIERRE: Trumpet.

GENERAL GUYE: Well, no wonder we're sweeping Europe before us. They loathe our politics, but they love our music. You will stand guard here all night, fusilier, and if you get nervous, I suggest you beat your drum. Hard.

ST. PIERRE: Yes sir. Thank you sir.

GREGORIO EMERGES, SHAKEN. HIS ARM IS COVERED IN BLOOD.

GENERAL GUYE: What's this?

GREGORIO: There's something down there, I put my hand in its mouth.

GENERAL GUYE: You didn't lose your fingers.

GREGORIO: I pulled it out sir, before it could snap them off. It was hot, and sticky, sucking on me.

GENERAL GUYE: You put your hand in a wound, soldier.

GREGORIO: Oh Christ.

GENERAL GUYE: There are still bodies under here to be dug out. That's all it was. Very well; we won't flush him out this way. If he has a taste for human flesh he'll come back to where he knows he can get it easily. We'll watch, and wait.

SISTER MAGDALENA: *(Re: Barbara)* She knows.

GENERAL GUYE: Knows what?

SISTER MAGDALENA: More than she's saying. She's protecting him.

GENERAL GUYE: Thank you Sister.

SISTER MAGDALENA: Look at her eyes; she knows where he went. Don't you see?

GENERAL GUYE: No.

SISTER MAGDALENA: Slut.

ANGERED, THE SISTER LEAVES.

GENERAL GUYE: *(To Barbara)* If this unfortunate is a friend of yours, don't consort with him again. My loyal fusiliers have had three years in your country, and they think it crawls with bogeymen. No amount of common sense will wash the prejudice out. It makes them jumpy, and dangerous. If you are seen near this man, you'll be shot in your tracks, though you may be entirely innocent.

BARBARA: He's no friend of mine.

GENERAL GUYE: I'm pleased. St. Pierre, my respects to Veron-Reville. Tell him I expect to see him here in a while.

ST. PIERRE: *(Saluting)* Sir!

THE GENERAL EXITS. GOYA WATCHES HIM GO.

GOYA: He's a good man.

GREGORIO: Look at my hand.

ST. PIERRE: Was it a wound?

GREGORIO: How the fuck should I know?

ST. PIERRE: What did it feel like? Look, the lady'd like to hear.

GREGORIO: It was hot and wet.

ST. PIERRE: Well that gets me sweaty, it does really. (*Turns to Barbara, looking at her*) How deep did you get in?

GREGORIO: You can see for yourself; up to my wrist.

ST. PIERRE: Doesn't sound so deep to me. I'm sure I could get in deeper with not much problem.

IT'S CLEAR THAT ST. PIERRE IS ABOUT TO MAKE A MOVE ON BARBARA; GOYA STEPS IN.

GOYA: Why don't you go home and wash his hand for him?

ST. PIERRE: Who are you?

GOYA: Her husband.

ST. PIERRE: (*To Barbara*) Christ: what'd you marry a rat like that for? Come with me, love, I'll see you all right.

BARBARA: No thank you.

ST. PIERRE: Maybe later.

BARBARA: Only if you stop your buttons jangling.

ST. PIERRE'S SMILE FADES; HE EXITS. GREGORIO FOLLOWS.

BARBARA: I hope Felipe's sensible, and stays with Rafael. There'll be soldiers everywhere now. It's time you made yourself known, before you get shot too.

GOYA: I was watching the General—I've painted his son, you know, a most winning child—and a part of me itched to stand up and say: "Nicholas! I'm here! I'm alive!" and another part said: "Watch. Be invisible. You may find you like being dead."

HE STARTS TO GO.

BARBARA: Are you leaving?

GOYA: No. I'm going to find myself a change of clothes.

BARBARA: Steal them?

GOYA: Painters never steal. We may pay homage to, we are influenced by, but we never steal. I am now going to pay homage to somebody else's coat.

HE EXITS.

BARBARA: (*Calls after him*) Goya—

*ENTER FROM ANOTHER DIRECTION, THE COFFIN-
MAKER.*

COFFIN MAKER: Barbara?
BARBARA: Father.
COFFIN MAKER: There's wood to be cut; two coffins. What took
   you so long?
BARBARA: I'm sorry.
COFFIN MAKER: This heat! We should have brought some
   incense. Stupid.

*HE EXITS. BARBARA GATHERS UP HER TOOLS. SANTI-
AGO ENTERS AS SHE WORKS. SHE SINGS, A WORD-
LESS SONG. HE STANDS LOOKING AT THE RUINS.*

BARBARA: (*Startled by him*) Oh.
SANTIAGO: Have you cleaned up the body?
BARBARA: Yes.
SANTIAGO: It's fit to be seen by his family?
BARBARA: As fit as I can make it.
SANTIAGO: I don't know how you can bear to touch him. I can't
   even touch uncooked meat. (*He gives her money*) There. In
   addition to your father's fee.
BARBARA: Thank you.

BARBARA EXITS. SANTIAGO CROSSES TO THE COFFIN.

SANTIAGO: Wise to be dead.

*HE STARTS TO SEARCH THE RUBBLE, STILL ADDRESS-
ING HIS CONVERSATION TO THE BODY.*

SANTIAGO: Of course, you never liked me, am I right? I was
   always indifferent to your conspicuous shows of suffering on
   behalf of humanity. Well yes. I thought it undignified to be
   frank, a man your age, sweating and wringing his hands about

the facts of life. Tomorrow, you see, things will be different: we won't waste time agonizing over how to save our vile souls.

HE HAS FOUND SOMETHING IN THE RUBBLE; A PIECE OF CLOTH. HE PULLS IT OUT.

SANTIAGO: Anger will be a thing of the past.

HE PUTS THE PIECE OF CLOTH, WHICH IS PASTEL-COLORED, TO HIS NOSE AND INHALES ITS SCENT.

SANTIAGO: (*Very quietly, as an article of faith*) Perhaps we will not even be human.

ENTER THE DUCHESS, WITH ESTELLA.

DUCHESS: Santiago?
SANTIAGO: Ma'am.
DUCHESS: I want to ask a favor of you.
SANTIAGO: Anything I can do.
DUCHESS: What's that in your hand? Mine I think.
SANTIAGO: Is it?
DUCHESS: (*Crosses to him; extends her hand*) Thank you.
SANTIAGO: (*Giving it to her*) Such a color.

THE DUCHESS GIVES THE CLOTH TO ESTELLA, THEN TURNS BACK TO SANTIAGO.

DUCHESS: I need money. A significant amount.
SANTIAGO: Ladyship . . .
DUCHESS: I hope I've always been kind.
SANTIAGO: Kindness itself.
DUCHESS: Help me now.
SANTIAGO: I'm sure his Lordship will be more than happy—
DUCHESS: The Duke mustn't know. That's why I've come straight to you. You can organize something without his knowing. Can't you?
SANTIAGO: I suppose—
DUCHESS: Can't you?

SANTIAGO: It's difficult.

DUCHESS: (*She produces jewelry*) Look; he gave me these last Christmas, God alone knows what they are worth. Take them, sell them, do whatever you need to do with them— I'm relying on you.

SANTIAGO: (*Taking the jewelry*) May I ask . . . are you planning to leave?

DUCHESS: I know how respectable a man you are; how loyal to the estate. That's why I can't tell you very much. I don't want to burden you with secrets, do you understand?

SANTIAGO: I understand.

GOYA HAS ENTERED RE-DRESSED. HE WATCHES FROM A DISTANCE.

DUCHESS: I need money, a set of clothes, horses and a carriage. Is it possible?

SANTIAGO: Certainly. With time.

DUCHESS: How soon?

SANTIAGO: By dawn.

DUCHESS: So long?

SANTIAGO: You're asking a great deal. But I'll work as speedily as I can.

DUCHESS: Thank you.

LUISA ENTERS.

LUISA: Ladyship?

ESTELLA: What do you want?

LUISA: The General asks after the Duchess; invites her to join his party.

DUCHESS: I should go . . .

SANTIAGO: Leave this with me.

DUCHESS: (*Offering her hand to him to be kissed*) I'm obliged.

SANTIAGO: (*Kisses her hand*) To serve is everything.

HE EXITS.

LUISA: What shall I say?

ESTELLA: Say we're coming.

LUISA EXITS.

DUCHESS: Must I?

ESTELLA: Be guided for once. You've composed yourself, now go and show your face, before the guests get suspicious.

DUCHESS: (*Looking after Santiago*) You know I think every man on earth would love me, given the chance.

ESTELLA: Santiago?

DUCHESS: Perhaps even him.

ESTELLA: Whatever he feels, it isn't love.

DUCHESS: And the painter too.

ESTELLA: Well that was entirely different. He was a lunatic.

DUCHESS: They all love me.

ESTELLA: Do you think for one moment your beauty makes lambs of them? They hate you, don't you see that, they all hate you for the power you have over them, even your actor—

ENTER CASTROPOL.

CASTROPOL: What about me?

DUCHESS: She's insulting you.

CASTROPOL: Just because I'm famous.

DUCHESS: She wants me to stay, but I'm not going to.

CASTROPOL: Have you arranged our getaway?

DUCHESS: It's all in hand. Santiago will see to everything.

CASTROPOL: (*Uncomfortably*) Santiago.

DUCHESS: He's the Duke's Major-domo.

CASTROPOL: You can trust him?

DUCHESS: He's clay in my hands.

CASTROPOL: I don't like being here.

DUCHESS: Be patient.

CASTROPOL: I love you.

DUCHESS: And so you should.

CASTROPOL: When you're gone, I'm like Lazarus, with his Savior in another city—

ESTELLA: What's that from?

THE DUCHESS AND CASTROPOL KISS. HE FUMBLES UNDER HER DRESS.

ESTELLA: In God's name stop this! (*Pulls the Duchess*) Did you go to the Duke and play the Doctor?

CASTROPOL: Poor man. He's distracted. He was sitting under a tree; I thought he was a laborer.

ESTELLA: And you made your report?

CASTROPOL: (*Staring at the Duchess all the time*) I told him what he wanted to hear. I know my audience. I've got the popular touch.

ESTELLA: I'm sure you have.

CASTROPOL: Quicksilver tongue.

DUCHESS: Oh yes.

CASTROPOL: Yes.

DUCHESS: Yes.

ESTELLA: Now come on . . .

CASTROPOL: I wonder—

ESTELLA: What?

CASTROPOL: Before you desert me. I'm penniless.

DUCHESS: Oh. Estella.

ESTELLA: Yes; yes. (*She finds some money and gives it to him*)

CASTROPOL: To bide the time—

DUCHESS: Be careful. Hide yourself.

SHE KISSES HIM. ESTELLA PULLS HER AWAY.

ESTELLA: No more kisses!

ESTELLA AND THE DUCHESS EXIT. CASTROPOL POCKETS THE MONEY, BACK TO GOYA; THEN TAKES OUT A KNIFE.

CASTROPOL: Now . . . Who the fuck are you?

NO ANSWER. HE TURNS, RUSHES ACROSS TO GOYA AND PULLS HIM OUT OF HIS HIDING PLACE.

CASTROPOL: A spy!

GOYA: What?

CASTROPOL: You think I didn't feel your eyes on me? I'm an actor! I know when I've got an audience! Who are you?

GOYA: Talk more slowly. I can't follow your lips.

CASTROPOL: Deaf?
GOYA: Yes, I'm deaf.

CASTROPOL DROPS HIM.

CASTROPOL: So you heard nothing?
GOYA: What?
CASTROPOL: You heard nothing?
GOYA: Nothing.
CASTROPOL: What were you doing then, if you weren't spying?
GOYA: Drawing.

CASTROPOL PULLS THE SKETCHBOOK OUT OF GOYA'S HAND.

CASTROPOL: Drawing me were you? (*He looks*) It's not much of a
    likeness. My nose is finer than this.
GOYA: I'm an amateur.
CASTROPOL: Still, it's not bad.
GOYA: Take it.
CASTROPOL: Finish it first.
GOYA: It is finished.
CASTROPOL: I have no substance. It's just an outline.
GOYA: Yes.
CASTROPOL: (*Angry*) Oh I see, it's a portrait of my soul, is that it?
GOYA: How should I know? I just draw it.
CASTROPOL: (*A moment of recognition*) You know who I am.
GOYA: The thief who came for the Duchess.
CASTROPOL: And you are . . . her portrait painter, am I right?
    You're Goya.
GOYA: Yes.
CASTROPOL: Playing dead? It's a difficult role. Requires patience.
    Stillness.

HE TOYS WITH THE KNIFE.

CASTROPOL: Are you afraid of me?
GOYA: No; because you're not afraid of me, and as there is no fear
    between us, there need be no violence.
CASTROPOL: You could reveal me.

GOYA: I would have to reveal myself.

CASTROPOL: Still . . . I don't like the element of doubt . . .

BARBARA ENTERS, AS CASTROPOL POINTS THE KNIFE TOWARD GOYA.

BARBARA: Quickly!

CASTROPOL: What?

BARBARA SEES THE KNIFE AND PULLS OUT THE NUN'S GUN. POINTS IT AT CASTROPOL.

BARBARA: Leave him alone.

CASTROPOL: Really, you misunderstand.

GOYA: Put your knife away.

BARBARA: Or I'll fire.

GOYA: That pistol belonged to a nun: it's trained to blow off balls. I warn you.

CASTROPOL PUTS THE KNIFE AWAY.

BARBARA: Who is he?

GOYA: I don't know. He doesn't recognize me, and I don't recognize him. Isn't that right?

CASTROPOL NODS.

GOYA: He's harmless. Let him go.

BARBARA DROPS HER ARM. CASTROPOL EXITS.

BARBARA: They've come. Your family.

GOYA: Josefa.

BARBARA: Is that your wife? No, she's not with them. Your son, a young woman, and a man.

GOYA: I'm embarrassed. I feel foolish, like a child. They'll laugh at my game.

BARBARA: No they won't.

GOYA: Josefa would understand. Why didn't Josefa come? She'd think it was a good joke, she's got a sense of humor. But

Xavier: no. He'll look at me askance and show his little teeth. Ah! Why did I let you talk me into this?

BARBARA: Me?

GOYA: I'm a grown man. Playing hide and seek.

VOICES OFF.

BARBARA: They're coming.

GOYA: I can't face them.

BARBARA: But they're in mourning.

GOYA: It'll do them no harm.

HE RUNS FOR COVER.

BARBARA: (*Following him into hiding.*) What are you doing?

GOYA: Hiding my head.

SANTIAGO APPEARS, FOLLOWED BY XAVIER GOYA, HIS WIFE GUMERSINDA, AND THE CRITIC, MOREL. JOLY BRINGS UP THE REAR. XAVIER IS A THIN UNREMARKABLE YOUNG MAN WHOSE PARENTAGE LENDS HIM UNDESERVED AUTHORITY; HIS WIFE HAS A DISTRACTED, UNFOCUSED MANNER.

EVENING IS BEGINNING TO DRAW IN AS THEY APPEAR. DOGS BARK IN THE DISTANCE. THEY ALL SPEAK QUIETLY.

XAVIER: He's here?

SANTIAGO: Yes, sir.

XAVIER: In this plain box? My father?

SANTIAGO: We were awaiting instructions.

XAVIER NODS.

GUMERSINDA: How grim.

XAVIER: I'd like a moment with him alone. Would somebody open the coffin?

SANTIAGO: Joly.

XAVIER AND JOLY STEP FORWARD.

GUMERSINDA: (*To Morel*) I've never seen him so glacial. It's almost frightening.
MOREL: We each deal with grief differently.
GUMERSINDA: So sudden too.
MOREL: A great loss.
JOLY: (*To Xavier*) Sir . . . you know he's not recognisable.
XAVIER: I'm prepared for that.

GUMERSINDA STARTS TO CRY, QUIETLY.

GUMERSINDA: It's so sordid.
GOYA: (*To Barbara*) That's my son. Doesn't he look fine?
BARBARA: Show yourself.
GOYA: I'm ashamed.
BARBARA: Don't make them suffer more than they have.

GOYA NODS. HE IS ABOUT TO STAND UP WHEN XAVIER SPEAKS.

XAVIER: Why is he lying here . . . in the ruins? I take it very badly.
GOYA: (*Moved*) Oh, child.
JOLY: Do you want us to move the coffin?
XAVIER: Yes.

JOLY STOPS UNSCREWING THE LID.

XAVIER: No. No, don't bother. Come to think of it he's probably quite happy here.
GOYA: Happy, did he say?
XAVIER: He always loved dirt and desolation.
GOYA: Is he talking about me?
BARBARA: Yes.
GOYA: No. Don't say that, even if it's true.

JOLY SLIDES BACK THE COFFIN LID.

XAVIER: So.

MOREL: Is it definitely him?

XAVIER: Yes.

MOREL: No doubt.

XAVIER: He's my own flesh and blood; I loved him beyond words. I know when I'm in his presence.

GUMERSINDA: May I see him too?

MOREL: He'd have liked to have painted this scene, I think.

XAVIER: I daresay he would.

MOREL: The ruins. The sky darkening.

XAVIER: If he could he would have painted the smell in the air.

MOREL: That was part of his genius, of course; beauty out of degradation.

XAVIER: There was no beauty. Not that I saw. He had a nose for smells, you know. His deafness sharpened his other faculties. Liked the smell of ashes, thunder, rancid milk. I caught him sniffing at Gumersinda once or twice. He always knew her time of the month—from the change in her smell. (*He mouths the words almost silently, to the body*) Filthy old man.

BARBARA: What did he say?

GOYA: No.

MOREL: But a genius.

GUMERSINDA: Oh yes. A genius.

XAVIER: Most of the work he's left us at the house is unsaleable. Unsavory stuff: nobody will want it. He did them for his own pleasure; flying dogs and witless satires, we'll never get them off our hands.

MOREL: Hang on to them for a few months: the price will inflate. My obituary of him will transform the market.

GUMERSINDA: Are there no priests? We should get a priest for when Josefa comes, you know.

MOREL: The Bishop perhaps.

SANTIAGO: Is your mother devout?

XAVIER: Hellishly so. Well, I'm done here. Morel, Gummy, he's all yours. I warn you, not a pleasant sight.

MOREL: Are you up to it my dear?

GUMERSINDA: I'm not sure.

THEY APPROACH THE COFFIN. THEY BOTH LOOK IN. GUMERSINDA STARES, MOREL FAINTS.

MOREL: Ah!
JOLY: Oh God.

XAVIER LAUGHS, A COARSE, EASY LAUGH.

XAVIER: Poor man.
GUMERSINDA: Look at those wounds.
JOLY: Oh dear . . .

*JOLY FUSSES WITH MOREL. BARBARA LEAVES GOYA
AND STANDS CLOSE TO THE COFFIN.*

XAVIER: Close the lid for Christ's sake, we've seen enough of him.
     Really, I don't think Mother has to see this, does she?
GUMERSINDA: She'll come whatever we say. You know how she
     is.
XAVIER: Well it's her look out if she gets exhausted.
SANTIAGO: Is she following on?
XAVIER: She won't arrive for hours, by the time she's instructed
     the servants, and spent an hour locking up the house. She's
     afraid somebody will break in or burn it down while she's
     away, and all his masterpieces will be lost to posterity.
SANTIAGO: Barbara. Replace the lid.

BARBARA REPLACES THE LID.

XAVIER: There's nothing more to do here is there? We'll just have
     to wait 'til mother arrives.
SANTIAGO: The Duke has opened the lodge; he and his guests
     are staying there. He invites you to join him.
GUMERSINDA: Gladly. Isn't that nice Xavier?
XAVIER: His house fell on Father. He owes us a dinner.

MOREL GROANS, AS JOLY LIFTS HIM UP.

MOREL: Oh I'm sorry, I spoiled the moment. I feel crass.
XAVIER: That's what we love you for, Morel. Don't flap about it.
MOREL: You're too kind.

MOREL SMILES WEAKLY.

XAVIER: I wonder, Santiago, if you could lend a little more dignity to the proceedings? Silk around his head; a change of jacket; and get the coffin on trestles. Maybe even a flag.

GUMERSINDA: A flag would be nice.

MOREL: I wrote of him: he is the bee in the carcass of the lion of Spain.

JOLY: That's a fine turn of the phrase.

MOREL: I thought so.

GUMERSINDA: I'm thirsty.

MOREL: Do you know my work at all?

JOLY: I don't think I do.

SANTIAGO: Shall we go to the lodge then?

XAVIER: Anywhere, away from here.

> *GUMERSINDA AND XAVIER MOVE OFF, LED BY SANTIAGO. AS THEY DISAPPEAR, AND MOREL, ASSISTED BY JOLY, ARE ABOUT TO EXIT, GOYA'S GRIEF AND RAGE FIND VENT. HE MAKES A ROAR OF AGONY.*

MOREL: What was that?

JOLY: Some drunkard probably.

MOREL: Horrible noise. Hold on tighter, young man, my knees are weak.

> *OFF-STAGE XAVIER STARTS LAUGHING AGAIN AS MOREL AND JOLY EXIT. BEFORE THE VOICES FADE, GOYA ROARS A SECOND TIME: A TERRIBLE SOUND. HE STAGGERS, SHAKING, FROM THE RUINS.*

GOYA: I'm not simply deaf. I'm completely senseless, not to have known. They never loved me!

BARBARA: Grief makes people strange.

GOYA: If that was grief, I'm an Englishman! Christ in Heaven I'd bear that misfortune if I thought they shed a single tear for me. What a weight I am to them, even dead. How cumbersome! The truly loving father would dig his grave himself, lie in it and heap the earth on top of his own head, rather than inconvenience his children. How they hated me! (*Anger becomes tears*) How they hated me!

BARBARA CRADLES THE SOBBING GOYA.

BARBARA: Ssh! Ssh!
GOYA: Oh . . . watching them . . . I never felt a horror like it . . .
BARBARA: Never mind.
GOYA: I want to die.
BARBARA: Remember your wife.
GOYA: Josefa . . .
BARBARA: Don't despair. She's coming; and you can reveal that you are alive.
GOYA: I will. But not before I watch her come to the coffin, and see for myself whether she loved me.
BARBARA: And if she fails the test?

HE SITS UP; TEARS STILL FALL.

GOYA: When I lost my hearing, I thought I'd lost the world, forever. I learnt to read lips, and hands, anything to have the world back, close to. If she deserts me, I'll let go again. Willingly. Let it go.

ENTER FELIPE.

FELIPE: Did you ever see such a night?
BARBARA: Never.
FELIPE: What's wrong with him?
BARBARA: Let him alone.
FELIPE: I washed Rafael in the river, and buried the child. He didn't want to give it up, but I persuaded him.
BARBARA: Where is he now?
FELIPE: Asleep, in the field. Thumb in his mouth.
BARBARA: Are you going back to him?
FELIPE: Not tonight. Tonight I'm here, with you. Do you want to go away, old man?

GOYA DOESN'T RESPOND.

BARBARA: He's deaf.
FELIPE: Like the painter.
BARBARA: He is the painter.

FELIPE: Are you sure?
BARBARA: Certain.

*GOYA IS DRAWING AGAIN. FELIPE PEERS OVER HIS
SHOULDER.*

FELIPE: He cries and draws at the same time. (*Looks at the draw-
ing*) A funeral?
GOYA: It's called *How Shall They Bear Their Grief?*
FELIPE: The mourners have holes through their middles.
GOYA: It's where their hearts used to be.
FELIPE: What use is it?
GOYA: It's a comfort.
FELIPE: That all?
BARBARA: Don't bully him.
FELIPE: It doesn't change anything, does it?
GOYA: No. No, it changes nothing, nothing at all. I despair of it. I
am become a commodity, for my son to profit by. The hero
is right! (*He throws his sketchbook down*) I don't want to see
anymore. It's a sickness.

*HE CROSSES TO THE DOOR IN THE GROUND;
LOOKS IN; SIGHS.*

BARBARA: (*To Felipe*) You're too rough.
FELIPE: I said what I felt.
GOYA: (*Turns back from the hole*) When I was a child, I thought
our town was built on the back of a giant. In the night, I was
certain I heard this colossus breathe, and I fretted that someone in their ignorance would wake him, and he'd rise up,
not knowing what he did, and the hills, the town, our
house, my bed, would fall off his back and roll away into the
dark. Now I'm sixty-five, and still I think maybe he's there,
underground. Maybe I could wake him, if I only could find
his face, and there'd be an end to us all.

HE WALKS BACK TOWARD THE HOLE.

BARBARA: Don't go. You'll get lost.
GOYA: An end. Oh yes.

FELIPE: Let him go.
BARBARA: He's too old to go underground.
FELIPE: He's dead isn't he? Let him go.
GOYA: Do you have a light? I'm suddenly afraid.
BARBARA: There's a lamp, there . . .

THE LAMP SHE GAVE TO FELIPE IS STILL BURNING.

GOYA: Thank you.
BARBARA: Be careful . . .

HE LOOKS INTO THE HOLE. FELIPE TAKES HOLD OF BARBARA.

FELIPE: You're the sweetest woman I ever met.
BARBARA: Flatterer.
FELIPE: But then my experience is limited.
BARBARA: I'm overwhelmed.

THE LIGHTS HAVE GONE DOWN A GREAT DEAL. STARS SHOW THROUGH THE RUINS.

FELIPE: May I kiss you?
BARBARA: Don't be polite.

FELIPE KISSES HER.

BARBARA: No need to be polite.

THEY KISS AGAIN. NOW THE SCENE IS IN DARK-NESS. THE LAMP LIGHT IS THROWN UP ON GOYA'S FACE, AS HE GOES UNDERGROUND.

IN THE EARTH THERE IS A ROAR OF FALLING MASONRY, AS IF SOMETHING IS SHIFTING ITS POSI-TION. GOYA, THOUGH HE DOESN'T HEAR THE SOUND, FEELS ITS THUNDER IN HIS BODY.

GOYA: I hear you Colossus! I'm coming.

MORE THUNDER; THE LIGHT OUT OF THE GROUND SEEMS TO BE BRIGHTER.

GOYA: Wait for me!

HE DISAPPEARS, PULLING THE DOOR CLOSED OVER HIS YELLING HEAD WITH A SLAM THAT EXTINGUISHES ALL LIGHT.

END OF ACT TWO.

Act 3

THE SET IS SUBSTANTIALLY THE SAME AS PARTS ONE AND TWO, THOUGH THERE ARE A FEW MINOR ALTERATIONS TO IT. THE FIRST AND MOST SIGNIFICANT, IS THAT IT IS NOW NIGHT. DARKNESS HAS CHANGED THE RUINS: UNILLUMINATED, ITS UPPER FLOORS HANG THREATENINGLY OVER THE ACTION, THE FEW STARS THAT BURN BEYOND THE LOOMING BULK OF THE WALLS AND RUBBLE ONLY EMPHASIZE THE VASTNESS OF THE RUIN ITSELF. SOME RUDIMENTARY ORDER HAS BEEN MADE IN THE WRECKAGE, AND IN THE SHELTER OF THE RUBBLE A FIRE HAS BEEN LIT. THE FLAMES CAN-NOT BE SEEN, JUST THE SMOKE, FLICKERINGLY LIT, SPIRALLING UP, AND THE TWO FIGURES OF ST. PIERRE, THE DRUMMER, AND SERGEANT GRIS, A

SURLY, BAD TEMPERED MAN WHOSE ONE PRIDE IN LIFE IS HIS MUSTACHE, WHICH HE IS TRYING TO TRIM.

THE COFFIN SUPPOSEDLY CONTAINING GOYA'S CORPSE HAS BEEN RAISED, AS XAVIER REQUESTED, ON TRESTLES. THERE ARE FLOWERS AROUND IT NOW, A FLAG DRAPED ACROSS IT.

ST. PIERRE IS PRACTICING A DRUM-ROLL. EVERY TIME GRIS GETS CLOSE TO HIS MUSTACHE WITH HIS SCISSORS, ST. PIERRE TRIES A NEW ROLL. GRIS JUMPS, GROWLS TO HIMSELF, TRIES AGAIN. AGAIN, THE ROLL MAKES HIM JUMP.

SERGEANT GRIS: Pierre?

ST. PIERRE: Sergeant.

SERGEANT GRIS: Shut your drum up.

ST. PIERRE: Seargeant.

SERGEANT GRIS: I know you're nervous.

ST. PIERRE: I'm not.

SERGEANT GRIS: Then you're a damn fool.

ST. PIERRE: They never found the cannibal, did they?

SERGEANT GRIS: No.

ST. PIERRE: I don't think they looked very hard. I wouldn't have looked very hard. Not for a cannibal.

SERGEANT GRIS: Apparently, it was his own baby he was eating. One of the sappers heard tell.

ST. PIERRE: It's all gossip. We're worse than women, the way we talk, aren't we?

SERGEANT GRIS: It's the way an army gets news.

ST. PIERRE: That's true. That's how I'll find out I got killed. (*Two voices*) Eh Pierre? Yes? You know what they're saying down the second battalion. What? They're saying you've had your head blown off! (*Feeling around on his shoulders*) Fucking hell, so I have.

SERGEANT LAUGHS.

ST. PIERRE: I say, give it to the Spanish.

SERGEANT GRIS: Your head?

ST. PIERRE: Spain. It's too hot, too greasy, and the women grow mustaches at sixteen.

SERGEANT GRIS: I thought you liked kissing mustaches. And I've gone to all this trouble.

ST. PIERRE LAUGHS THIS TIME.

SOMEBODY MOVES IN THE DARKNESS OUTSIDE THE RING OF FIRE-LIGHT. IT IS GREGORIO. HE HAS A DEAD SNAKE, WHICH HE IS HOLDING AT GROIN-HEIGHT. HE IS BARELY DISTINGUISHABLE AT THE MOMENT HOWEVER.

ST. PIERRE: What was that?

SERGEANT GRIS: Challenge, soldier.

ST. PIERRE: (*Pointing rifle into the darkness*) Who goes there?

GREGORIO: Me!

ST. PIERRE: Me who?

GREGORIO: Me, you bloody fool.

ST. PIERRE: It's Gregorio. Password?

GREGORIO: I've brought some food.

ST. PIERRE: That'll do.

ENTER GREGORIO.

ST. PIERRE: (*Looking at the snake*) What is that?

GREGORIO: Dinner.

ST. PIERRE: Fuck you.

GREGORIO: It's a snake.

ST. PIERRE: I can see what it is. I'm not eating it!

GREGORIO: It's very nutritious.

ST. PIERRE: I'm not eating it I said!

GREGORIO: Sergeant?

SERGEANT GRIS: Yeah, I'm game.

ST. PIERRE: Is that what we're reduced to?

GREGORIO: It tastes like chicken.

ST. PIERRE: I don't care if it tastes of fucking suckling pig, it's a bloody snake. I'm a drummer, me. Takes muscle, takes an immaculate sense of rhythm, all of which I have. And here I am, in the middle of God knows where, being offered a plate of fried snake for my dinner. Where did I go wrong?

GREGORIO: You joined the fusiliers.

SERGEANT GRIS: Listen, I know men—

ST. PIERRE: Don't say it. Who'd give their right arms to be in this army. Cause I know men who have. And their left arms, and their balls.

SERGEANT GRIS: Why do I give him these openings?

GREGORIO: It must be love sarge.

SERGEANT GRIS: Shut it.

GREGORIO: Yes, Sarge.

GREGORIO HAS PUT THE SNAKE IN A PAN, AND IS FRYING IT. THERE IS A MUMBLE IN THE DARKNESS. THE SERGEANT STANDS UP, GUN AT THE READY.

SERGEANT GRIS: What was that?

ST. PIERRE: It's the debris: every few minutes there's an avalanche.

SERGEANT GRIS: No: there's noises under us. In the ground.

GREGORIO: Don't say that.

SERGEANT GRIS: Didn't you hear it?

GREGORIO: Yes, but don't say that.

ST. PIERRE: It's all right. They're just dead people. No problem. They're just lying there; may be they're a bit hot—

GREGORIO: Maybe they're a bit pissed off—

ST. PIERRE: Maybe they're a bit pissed off, and they're fanning themselves. That's all. No problem.

SERGEANT GRIS: You know what I'd really like to do?

ST. PIERRE: No.

SERGEANT GRIS: Shoot somebody.

GREGORIO: Anyone in particular?

SERGEANT GRIS: I'm not fussy. I'd just like to blast a hole in someone's head.

ANOTHER RUMBLE IN THE EARTH.

GREGORIO: There is something down there.

ST. PIERRE: Maybe you should stop cooking. Maybe the smell's making them hungry.

ENTER CAPTAIN VERON-REVILLE, IMMACULATELY FITTED OUT. THE SERGEANT SWINGS HIS RIFLE TOWARD THE CAPTAIN.

SERGEANT GRIS: Stand!

CAPTAIN REVILLE: Sergeant Gris.

SERGEANT GRIS: Captain.

CAPTAIN REVILLE: Well done! Nobody's going to get past you tonight.

SERGEANT GRIS: Sir!

CAPTAIN REVILLE: At ease. This isn't an inspection; please get on with your meal. (*He peers in the pan*) What in God's name is that?

SERGEANT GRIS: Snake, sir.

CAPTAIN REVILLE: Local delicacy?

SEARGEANT GRIS: Yes sir.

GREGORIO: Want some sir?

CAPTAIN REVILLE: No. But here's something to wash it down.

HE PRODUCES A FLAGON OF WINE. DELIGHT ON THE SOLDIERS' FACES.

ST. PIERRE: Wine!

GREGORIO: Fucking fantastic.

SERGEANT GRIS: Gregorio.

GREGORIO: I mean that's really very kind of you sir.

CAPTAIN REVILLE: From the Duke's own vineyard. It's good stuff so don't dab it behind your ears.

SERGEANT GRIS: It's much appreciated sir.

CAPTAIN REVILLE: Not the most illuminating of duties, watching bodies. I'm aware of your impatience. I share it myself.

SERGEANT GRIS: Any news of the advance sir?

CAPTAIN REVILLE: It's confidential, Sergeant, but rest assured your Emperor's sense of direction is as infallible as ever!

ST. PIERRE, WHO HAS OPENED THE WINE, TAKES A SWIG OF IT.

ST. PIERRE: (*A toast*) Napoleon!

ALL: Napoleon!

CAPTAIN REVILLE: And the 44th!
ALL: The 44th!

THE SERGEANT TAKES A DRINK AND THEN OFFERS IT TO THE CAPTAIN, WHO SHAKES HIS HEAD. THERE IS ANOTHER SOUND, SO QUIET AS TO BE ALMOST INAUDIBLE; THE SOUND OF DRUMBEATS, AND OF TINKLING BELLS.

ST. PIERRE: I keep hearing noises.
GREGORIO: Another avalanche.
CAPTAIN REVILLE: Sounds are deceptive in ruins, don't you find? Echoes . . .

SOMEONE IS SINGING NOW, AGAIN, VERY QUIETLY.

ST. PIERRE: I thought I heard a voice.
SERGEANT GRIS: The captain knows best.
CAPTAIN REVILLE: I had a man at Wortosa; he saw little children everywhere; or thought he did. Playing in the ruins he kept telling us, naked children. Eventually he went into a house to catch one of these phantoms and the place fell on him.
GREGORIO: Did you dig him out?
CAPTAIN REVILLE: Oh yes.
GREGORIO: And was there a child?
CAPTAIN REVILLE: Of course not. He was fatigued, and maybe sentimental and his mind conjured these infants out of thin air, and it killed him. It was a kind of suicide, by imagination.

THE STAGE IS DARK; ONLY THE FIRELIGHT AND THE STARS. SUDDENLY, WE ARE AWARE THAT THERE ARE PEOPLE IN THE SHADOWS, AND MORE; A VAST HUMAN HEAD, APPROACHING FROM BEHIND A CURTAIN OF CLOTH. IT HAS EMPTY EYE-SOCKETS, BUT OTHERWISE IT IS AN EXCELLENT PAPER-MACHE AND WOOD REPRESENTATION OF A MAN WITH A WIDE LEERING SMILE, OR IS IT A GRI-MACE, ON HIS FACE? IT HAS A BEARD, AND LONG HAIR, PERHAPS RUDIMENTARY SHOULDERS. THE

ACTORS WHO STAND WATCHING THE SOLDIERS ARE CLOAKED AND MASKED. THEY CARRY SMALL BELLS AND DRUMS, IT IS THESE THAT PROVIDE THE EERIE, GENTLE RHYTHM THAT ST. PIERRE FIRST HEARD. IT CONTINUES EVEN NOW.

GREGORIO: Jesus wept.

HE PASSES THE PAN ACROSS TO ST. PIERRE, EYES ON THE ACTORS ALL THE TIME.

SERGEANT GRIS: What's wrong?
GREGORIO: Look.
ST. PIERRE: *(Re: pan)* I don't want this.
GREGORIO: Look! (*He is backing away*)
ST. PIERRE: Bloody snake.
GREGORIO: I'm just . . . going . . . to . . . take a piss.
CAPTAIN REVILLE: Hold your ground soldier!

GREGORIO IS STILL BACKING OFF.

ST. PIERRE: I don't want your bloody dinner.

GREGORIO TURNS TO RUN.

CAPTAIN REVILLE: Fetch that man back sergeant.
SERGEANT GRIS: Gregorio! You heard the captain; Gregorio!

SERGEANT GRIS FOLLOWS GREGORIO, AND CATCHES HOLD OF HIM.

GREGORIO: I've had enough!
SERGEANT GRIS: Come back here!

THE CAPTAIN HAS TAKEN OUT HIS GUN; AND IS RAISING IT.

GREGORIO: I'm a trumpeter.

THE SERGEANT HAS HOLD OF GREGORIO. THEY

WRESTLE, TRADING BLOWS.

ST. PIERRE HAS NOW SEEN THE FIGURES TOO.

ST. PIERRE: Oh . . . God.
CAPTAIN REVILLE: Identify yourselves . . .
ST. PIERRE: Please.

> *THE LAST EXCHANGE IS ALMOST DROWNED BY THE FIGHTING BETWEEN THE SERGEANT AND THE PANICKING GREGORIO, WHO DELIVERS ONE PARTICULARLY EFFECTIVE BLOW, THEN MAKES HIS ESCAPE.*

SERGEANT GRIS: Come back here you bloody scab!
ST. PIERRE: Sergeant Gris!
SERGEANT GRIS: I'll beat you bloody for this!

> *HE CHASES AFTER ST. PIERRE, STILL SHOUTING. THEY EXIT.*

SERGEANT GRIS: Come back you fucking coward! You piece of shit!

> *THE VOICES FADE. THE DRUMMING AND THE BELL-RINGING HAVE CEASED. NOW THERE IS ONLY THE SILENT CONFRONTATION OF ACTORS AND SOLDIERS.*

ST. PIERRE: (*Weakly, knowing Gris has gone*) Sergeant . . . ?
CAPTAIN REVILLE: It seems we're outnumbered.
ST. PIERRE: Shit . . .

> *A LONG SILENCE.*

ST. PIERRE: (*Proffering the frying pan*) Anyone hungry?
EVA: (*Under one of the masks*) Food!

> *SUDDENLY THERE IS AN ERUPTION OF VOICES, ALL THE ACTORS SPEAKING AT ONCE AS THEY TAKE OFF THEIR MASKS.*

EVA: He's actually offering his food!

HOLY JOE: God love us!

GERONIMO: My legs have gone to water! I couldn't have walked another foot, you know. I would have collapsed.

VIOLANTE: I just wish he'd stop pointing his gun at us like that.

The actors are:

> *EVA, WHO WAS WEARING THE MASK OF A CON-VENTIONALLY BEAUTIFUL YOUNG WOMAN, AND NOW TAKES IT OFF TO REVEAL A ONCE BEAUTIFUL, NOW STRIKING, BUT HEAVILY MADE UP MIDDLE-AGED WOMAN. HER HUSBAND, HOLY JOE NAVARRO, A PLAYWRIGHT WHO IS DRESSED AS THE COM-MANDER IN DON JUAN. SEREPHINA, AN ACTRESS, WHO WEARS A DOG'S HEAD AS A MASK. GERON-IMO, WHO EMERGES FROM THE HEAD. VIOLANTE, HIS SISTER, WHO HAS LED THE HEAD AROUND THE STAGE AND FINALLY TUNG, THE CLOWN IN THIS TROUPE, WHO WEARS A RIDICULOUS MASK ON THE BACK OF HIS HEAD, AND HAS MOST OF HIS CLOTHES PAINTED ONTO HIS BODY. NOW THAT THEY ARE UNMASKED THESE FEARFUL CREATURES ARE SEEN FOR WHAT THEY ARE. A RAG-BAG OF OVER-ENTHUSIASTIC INNOCENTS, THEIR FACES GLEAMING WITH DELIGHT AS THEY DESCEND LIKE VULTURES ON THE FRYING-PAN. ONLY SEREPHINA DOES NOT EAT. SHE IS STARING AT THE CAPTAIN, WHO HAS PUT AWAY HIS GUN.*

CAPTAIN REVILLE: Actors!

VIOLANTE: What is this? It's swimming in grease.

GERONIMO: It's chicken.

EVA: Any salt soldier?

HOLY JOE: Maybe some bread.

GERONIMO: Bread would do the job!

VIOLANTE: Yes! Bread!

> *ST. PIERRE IS RELIEVED OF THE FRYING PAN, AND BACKS OFF TOWARD HIS PACK.*

ST. PIERRE: No . . . I . . . don't think—
VIOLANTE: I see it!

SHE CROSSES TO THE PACK.

ST. PIERRE: It's my bread.
VIOLANTE: You asked if we were hungry. Well we are! We're
    starving artists aren't we?

THEY ALL SAY, 'YES!', THEIR MOUTHS CRAMMED.

EVA: Eh . . . What's this?

SHE PICKS UP THE FLAGON OF WINE.

TUNG: This is our lucky day.
GERONIMO: Where's the bread?
VIOLANTE: Coming.
EVA: You wouldn't have shot us would you?
CAPTAIN REVILLE: It was foolish, coming on us like that.
EVA: We didn't expect soldiers. We thought we'd make an entrance.
HOLY JOE: What is this we're eating?
ST. PIERRE: Snake—meat.
TUNG: It's good.
HOLY JOE: Were the eggs in the nest?
TUNG: Bread!

> *TUNG TAKES THE BREAD FROM VIOLANTE AND IT
> IS DIVIDED UP WITH AS MUCH RELISH AS THE
> SNAKE. THE GREASE IN THE PAN IS MOPPED UP.
> VIOLANTE SEIZES THE PAN AND WIPES IT CLEAN;
> THE CHATTER STILL GOES ON.*

EVA: People!

THE ACTORS STOP TALKING.

EVA: We have not said good evening to the captain.
ALL: (*Bowing their heads, mouths wide, bread poised*) Good evening
    captain.

THEY START TO TALK AGAIN, SQUABBLING OVER THE WINE THIS TIME, PASSING IT ROUND UNTIL IT'S EMPTY.

EVA: People!
HOLY JOE: Yes?
EVA: Leave some for Serephina.
TUNG: Oh yes.
HOLY JOE: Too late. We ate it all.
VIOLANTE: She should have fought for her slice, same as we all did.

THEY GO BACK TO THEIR TALK, MORE QUIETLY.

SEREPHINA: I'm not hungry anyway.
EVA: *(To Reville)* I'm Eva Navarro. This is my husband, Holy Joe. We are actors.
TUNG: Tung!
GERONIMO: Geronimo!
SEREPHINA: Serephina!
VIOLANTE: Violante!
EVA: We offer you and your men entertainment of every shape and size, all morally uplifting fables inspired by—
TUNG: Stolen from—
EVA: Inspired by the great Spanish poets—Calderon, Quevedo.
CAPTAIN REVILLE: No.
EVA: No?
CAPTAIN REVILLE: We don't want your fables. Thank you. But no.
EVA: We have a telling of Don Juan—
CAPTAIN REVILLE: I said no.
HOLY JOE: There's a fine rape in the first act. Show them Serephina.

SEREPHINA STEPS FORWARD; TUNG PUTS HIS ARM AROUND HER, FROM BEHIND, RUNNING HIS HANDS UP AND DOWN HER BODY.

SEREPHINA: Help me! Rape! Rape!

SHE WATCHES THE CAPTAIN ALL THROUGH THIS PERFORMANCE, EYES BURNING.

HOLY JOE: There is murder too.

VIOLANTE: Terrible, bloody murder.

EVA: Your men would lap it up.

CAPTAIN REVILLE: I don't like fiction.

EVA: Why not?

CAPTAIN REVILLE: Like Plato, I think it's disruptive to the equilibrium of the state.

EVA: Well, you're quite happy performing.

CAPTAIN REVILLE: What?

TUNG: Lovely costume, is it not?

CAPTAIN REVILLE: Go to hell.

HOLY JOE: We do sir. At every performance. Don Juan is taken down, into the underworld, to suffer penance for his crimes.

CAPTAIN REVILLE: Your fictions are redundant: they don't touch upon life as it is lived. Find another audience. Good night.

SEREPHINA: You're Captain Veron-Reville.

THE CAPTAIN STOPS. DOESN'T TURN

SEREPHINA: Aren't you? You were one of the heroes of Saragrossa.

EVA: Serephina, be careful.

SEREPHINA: I remember him, on his horse. You rode into the convent. I was a nun, captain, I was fifteen, and your men followed you into the chapel, and you watched while they fell upon us like wolves. That's why I can play rape so well. Is that your real life, captain? What a fine thing it must be.

CAPTAIN REVILLE: Pick up your paper devils and leave.

SEREPHINA: (*As he exits quietly*) Are you incapable of shame?

SHE STARTS TO CRY.

TUNG: Nice one. Very clever. Now we don't eat for another week. Couldn't you have told him you enjoyed it just a little?

SEREPHINA: You weren't there.

VIOLANTE: You stupid bitch, we'll starve.

GERONIMO: (*To Violante*) Let her alone. She had every right—

TUNG: This is the end.

GERONIMO COMFORTS SEREPHINA.

EVA: Not if we can find Castropol.

HOLY JOE: The man's a thief and a womanizer, he's more trouble than he's worth.

HOLY JOE: We need him.

VIOLANTE: You need him.

EVA: He has a popular touch, you know that as well as I do.

TUNG: He stole our takings, all the best costumes, a horse—

EVA: All right. He's a shit. One of the lowest creatures that God created. But when he plays Don Juan we have full houses every day, and we eat. That's the choice, bread and shit, or nothing at all.

HOLY JOE: Not a very palatable dilemma.

VIOLANTE: Of course she has her own reasons, but she's right.

TUNG: He's not going to be here . . .

EVA: Where else would he come, but to find the Duchess?

TUNG: He said she was inept.

HOLY JOE: Soldier?

ST. PIERRE: What?

HOLY JOE: We're looking for a pretty boy by the name of Castropol.

ST. PIERRE: You could try the lodge . . . there's people down there. There's people all over. Eating, drinking.

HOLY JOE: And you?

ST. PIERRE: I'm thinking about onion soup.

EVA HAS COVERED HER HEAD WITH A CLOTH.

EVA: All right, let's spread out and find him. We'll meet back here in a few minutes.

ST. PIERRE: Take care, wandering around; you'll get yourselves hurt.

THE ACTORS DISPERSE, LEAVING SEREPHINA, WHO IS STANDING, GLASSY-EYED WITH MEMORIES OF GRIEF.

ST. PIERRE: Are you all right?

SEREPHINA: I was a virgin.

ST. PIERRE: So was I once.

SEREPHINA: I'd given my life to Jesus.

ST. PIERRE: Listen. It was wasted on him . . .

HE REACHES OUT AND TOUCHES HER BREAST.

ST. PIERRE: (*Almost in awe*) God.

SHE MAKES NO MOVE TO RESIST, SO HE PRESSES HARDER ON HER.

ST. PIERRE: Mind if I take a look?

SHE DOESN'T REPLY.

ST. PIERRE: I won't hurt you.

GERONIMO COMES BACK.

GERONIMO: Eh!
ST. PIERRE: What?
GERONIMO: Hands off!
ST. PIERRE: She said I could.
GERONIMO: Hands off unless you pay.
ST. PIERRE: You ate my snake.
GERONIMO: Then you should be satisfied.

HE TAKES HOLD OF SEREPHINA'S HAND.

GERONIMO: Come along, Serephina.

EXIT GERONIMO AND SEREPHINA.

ST. PIERRE: (*Relishing the word*) Ser-reph-ina.

THE FIRE IS GUTTERING. HE SQUATS BY IT.

ST. PIERRE: Don't ever leave me.

A LIGHT MOVES IN THE GROUND. GOYA IS EMERG-ING, UNSEEN BY ST. PIERRE.

ST. PIERRE: Why don't you just lie down there . . . by the fire . . . and I'll make passionate love to you, eh?

HE KISSES HIS RIFLE, PRETENDING IT'S A WOMAN.

ST. PIERRE: Serephina.

HE HAS HIS EYES CLOSED. GOYA HAS EMERGED, AND IS WATCHING.

ST. PIERRE: (*His hand between his legs*) Feel that? That's for you.
GOYA: I'd watch it doesn't go off in your hand.
ST. PIERRE: (*Opening his eyes*) What? Oh shit!

GOYA COMES TO SIT BY THE FIRE.

GOYA: It's cold eh?
ST. PIERRE: Where did you come from?
GOYA: It was magic.
ST. PIERRE: You haven't seen a sergeant have you?
GOYA: Why, have you lost one?
ST. PIERRE: I tell you, I've lost everything.
GOYA: I know the feeling.
ST. PIERRE: I had a woman here, a few minutes ago. Even lost her.
GOYA: The pity of it.
ST. PIERRE: Had a bottle of wine, bread. All gone. (*He picks up his rifle*) I hope nothing's happened to the sergeant.
GOYA: Like what?
ST. PIERRE: The captain said something about ghost-children, playing in the ruins.
GOYA: Children now.

ST. PIERRE GETS UP.

GOYA: I'd go look for him if I were you.
ST. PIERRE: Watch the fire.

ST. PIERRE EXITS.

ST. PIERRE: (*Off*) Sarge . . . ?

GOYA BLOWS ON THE FIRE. IT FLARES A LITTLE. HE LOOKS UP AT THE STARS, AND SIGHS.

ENTER FELIPE AND BARBARA.

FELIPE: Did you find your Colossus?
BARBARA: He doesn't hear. Be careful, you'll make him jump.

BARBARA WALKS INTO GOYA'S LINE OF VISION.

BARBARA: Are you all right?
GOYA: It's filthy down there.
FELIPE: And the Colossus?
GOYA: I found something else entirely.
BARBARA: What?
GOYA: A few yards down I stumbled across the body of Rafael's wife.
FELIPE: Daniella.
GOYA: Daniella. The shock made me drop the lamp. It went out. I was in absolute darkness; and for the first time since I went deaf I heard something other than the whines and moans that fill my head. I heard my heart.
BARBARA: Your heart?
GOYA: The hot darkness, the smell of a woman's blood, the heart-beat, suddenly I was a baby again, wanting to be born. There was no Colossus underground, just this memory, so strong I remembered how it felt, being spat into the world. The ache of separation and the beginning of love. Mourning begins there, doesn't it? It's the dawn of grief.
FELIPE: Do you understand what he's saying?
BARBARA: Some of it.
FELIPE: I preferred his Colossus. Now that would have been a sight and a half.
GOYA: Oh he's there. He's that baby, grown fat on sorrow, grown angry and monstrous like you.

FELIPE SHAKES HIS HEAD.

FELIPE: I'm not monstrous.
GOYA: You will be given half the chance.
FELIPE: I'm going to find Santiago. When I'm finished with him will you go with me?
BARBARA: I don't think so.

FELIPE STARES AT HER A MOMENT, AS IF READYING A REPLY. THEN, WITHOUT SAYING ANYTHING, HE EXITS.

GOYA: He's not so bad, is he?

GOYA GETS UP.

BARBARA: I don't know, advise me.
GOYA: Go with him.
BARBARA: And you?
GOYA: I'll wait for my wife.

HE HAS SEEN THE HEAD, COVERED WITH THE CLOTH.

HE APPROACHES IT, TURNING TO READ BARBARA'S LIPS.

BARBARA: You look so weary.
GOYA: She'll come. She's not strong, but she's determined. Has to be, living with an arrogant bugger like me.
BARBARA: I'm thinking of Felipe all the time, can't help myself. I thought I was past this confusion.
GOYA: How old are you?
BARBARA: Nineteen.

HE PULLS THE CLOTH OFF THE HEAD.

GOYA: I'm three times your age, and the confusion is still there. Anticipating new love every moment. What is this?
BARBARA: A mask.
GOYA: Actors?
BARBARA: I don't know.
GOYA: Well go find out!
BARBARA: Why?
GOYA: It'll take your mind off the hero.

BARBARA SMILES, AND EXITS. GOYA SITS BESIDE THE HEAD.

GOYA: Oh, Josefa . . .

ENTER, AT A RUN, GREGORIO.

GREGORIO: Oh Christ . . . (*He stops, breathless, to himself*) I'm a trumpeter. That's all.

HE HIDES HIMSELF. SERGEANT GRIS RUNS ON.

SERGEANT GRIS: Where are you soldier? First thing in the morning you go before the Captain; and if he doesn't string you up by the balls I will! (*He looks around*) Where's St. Pierre? Fucking hell, what kind of sodding army is this?

HE EXITS.

GREGORIO: (*Emerging*) I never wanted to be a fucking hero.

ENTER, ALMOST DISGUISED BY THE DARKNESS, SANTIAGO. GOYA HAS SLIPPED INTO HIDING WHEN THE SOLDIER HAS COME ON, HE NOW SEES SANTIAGO.

GREGORIO: (*Searching through his belongings by the fire*) Where's my baby? Daddy's here, baby. Come to Daddy! (*He pulls his trumpet out*) Ah! Got you.

HE STROKES IT; AND HURRIES OFF IN THE OPPO-SITE DIRECTION TO THE SERGEANT.

SANTIAGO STEPS FORWARD AND CROSSES TO THE COFFIN ON THE TRESTLES. HE CARRIES A LAMP, WHICH HE SETS DOWN ON THE COFFIN. HE TAKES OUT A PEPPERMINT AND SUCKS ON IT. CASTROPOL ENTERS, AND COUGHS.

SANTIAGO TURNS AROUND.

SANTIAGO: Castropol?

CASTROPOL EMERGES FROM THE DARKNESS. HE IS IN HEAVY DISGUISE AGAIN. A CLOAK AND HAT, A FALSE MUSTACHE.

SANTIAGO: Another performance?

CASTROPOL: Things are getting dangerous. Why are you so damned slow? I think you want to see me killed.

SANTIAGO: Don't be so melodramatic.

CASTROPOL: Where's my money? My horse?

SANTIAGO: I can't raise the sums you want easily. I'm making a deal with Goya's son, for the Duke's collection.

CASTROPOL: Isn't that premature?

SANTIAGO: The Duke has disappeared. I doubt he'll be sane when he's found.

CASTROPOL: And Sofia?

SANTIAGO: You leave her with me.

CASTROPOL: Oh don't fret; I have no intention of stealing her away. We have a deal, and I'll honor it. But you have to hurry.

SANTIAGO: Is that what you called me here to say?

SANTIAGO STARTS TO EXIT, LEAVING THE LAMP ON THE COFFIN.

CASTROPOL: And I'm hungry! I can't eat fresh air!

SANTIAGO: You're an actor. Imagine you're full.

SANTIAGO EXITS. CASTROPOL IS ANGRY; HE BEATS HIS HAND ON THE COFFIN, THEN PICKS UP THE LAMP AND TURNS. THE LIGHT FALLS ON THE HEAD.

CASTROPOL: Oh Christ, I'm dreaming.

HE CROSSES TO IT.

CASTROPOL: I can't bear it.

ENTER EVA, WITH TUNG.

TUNG: Then the information was wrong, it's as simple as that.

EVA: Excuse me.

CASTROPOL TURNS.

CASTROPOL: (*In thick accent*) Eh?
TUNG: We're looking for a man called Castropol.
CASTROPOL: Ridiculous name. Never heard such a ridiculous name.
EVA: And I've never heard such a ridiculous accent.

SHE CROSSES TO HIM.

EVA: It's him.
CASTROPOL: (*Still in accent*) I don't understand. Please?
EVA: Castropol.
TUNG: Give it up.
CASTROPOL: Shit. (*He takes off hat*)
EVA: Character roles never were your strong suit.
CASTROPOL: Look, I can explain.
TUNG: Bastard!
EVA: Round up the others.

TUNG EXITS.

EVA: You are the lowest of the low.
CASTROPOL: You're right. I don't know what came over me—
EVA: Contrition now.
CASTROPOL: I get these blinding headaches, and I have to steal things.
EVA: You might have taken me.
CASTROPOL: Eva . . .
EVA: You came here to meet your Duchess, didn't you?
CASTROPOL: Yes.
EVA: Damn you! Don't you give a shit about leaving us in a lurch?
CASTROPOL: I signed a contract with the Major-domo here. He had me over a barrel; knew about some past indelicacies of mine. He blackmailed me; I had no choice.
EVA: What sort of contract?
CASTROPOL: To come here, seduce the Duchess and break the poor child's heart.

EVA: Why?

CASTROPOL: So that he can pick up the pieces presumably. I was going to come back, but there were complications. For one thing, the house was blown apart. I could have been killed, except that she wanted to screw in the garden.

EVA: And do you love her?

CASTROPOL: (*Laughing*) Love? Her? Oh Eva . . .

ENTER VIOLANTE, FOLLOWED BY HOLY JOE.

VIOLANTE: Ah ha!

CASTROPOL: How good to see your smiling face.

VIOLANTE: Scum bag.

ENTER TUNG, SEREPHINA AND GERONIMO.

GERONIMO: We've damn well starved because of you!

GERONIMO GETS HOLD OF CASTROPOL.

CASTROPOL: Take your hands off me!

HOLY JOE: You're not above the law you know. We could have you in prison for theft.

SEREPHINA: A madhouse would be more appropriate.

CASTROPOL: (*To Serephina*) You too? Oh Serephina . . .

TUNG: What happened to the money?

CASTROPOL: Well, . . . I . . . I had to buy new shoes. And a haircut.

SEREPHINA: That was all we had in the world.

VIOLANTE: How could you? The time it took us to earn that, and you fritter it away on shoes!

CASTROPOL: Look, I'll earn it back for us. We'll do a tour of Don Juan. We'll play every two mule village in the country. I'll work my buttocks off and take no payment for it. (*As if he has been contradicted*) No! really! I insist!

TUNG: You think you're so much better than us don't you?

CASTROPOL: Me?

TUNG: You're just shit like the rest of us, except you're shit with a haircut.

VIOLANTE: We can see through you, Castropol. The game's up.

CASTROPOL SIGHS, DEFEATED. THEN, AN IDEA. HE THINKS IT THROUGH FOR A MOMENT, AND THEN TURNS BACK TO THE ACTORS.

CASTROPOL: Suppose I were to arrange a performance here, for the infantry. There's battalions of them: We could clean up.

EVA: We already tried; no dice.

CASTROPOL: I'm a personal friend of the captain. He owes me a favor.

HOLY JOE: Really?

VIOLANTE: He turned up his nose at Don Juan.

CASTROPOL: We could perform the Bandit play: There's more action in that, less romance. The soldiers would take to it.

EVA: You think so?

CASTROPOL: I don't know much, but I know audiences. Trust me.

VIOLANTE: Never.

CASTROPOL: All right, give me a chance at least. You play a few scenes for the captain, and see what he thinks.

GERONIMO: Tonight?

CASTROPOL: Why not tonight? You get yourselves changed. Dig out the swords, the guns. They like meticulous realism, so don't make a farce of it.

EVA: This is your last chance.

CASTROPOL: I'm aware of that.

EVA: Well people?

VIOLANTE: It's worth a try.

CASTROPOL: You come back here when you're ready and I'll find the captain. Deal?

EVA: Deal. Back to the wagon—

THE ACTORS START TO LEAVE, TALKING EXCITEDLY.

GERONIMO: Where are the swords?

VIOLANTE: They need a lick of paint.

HOLY JOE: Maybe I should write a speech about Napoleon.

TUNG: Why not?

THEY EXIT.

EVA: (*To Castropol*) Thank you.

SHE KISSES HIM, AND FOLLOWS THE REST.

CASTROPOL: (*To himself*) So I'm shit, am I?

HE EXITS. GOYA EMERGES AND WATCHES HIM GO.

GOYA: Something is wrong here, can't quite grasp it. Something terrible. Go to the Duke, eh? Forget this playing dead. Oh Josefa. I have to see you. (*A beat*) There's nothing. It's just hunger, making my head go round.

HE EXITS. DOGS BARK IN THE DISTANCE. THE WIND COMES UP, FOR THE FIRST TIME; IT WHISTLES AROUND THE RUINS. ENTER SANTIAGO AND CAXA, THE HORSE-MASTER, WHO CARRIES A WHIP AND A FLAGON OF WINE, FROM WHICH HE DRINKS DEEP. SANTIAGO IS IN A HIGHLY CHARGED STATE, THERE'S NERVOUS EXCITEMENT IN HIS MANNER WE HAVEN'T SEEN HITHERTO.

SANTIAGO: No need to be gentle tonight Caxa. I've won.

HE STARTS TO UNBUTTON HIS SHIRT.

SANTIAGO: So easily I scarcely believe myself. It's only right I pay the price of that ease-in pain.

HE TAKES OFF HIS SHIRT.

SANTIAGO: So don't be kind.

HE LAYS OUT A CLOTH HE HAS BROUGHT WITH HIM, KNEELS DOWN AND CROSSES HIMSELF.

FELIPE APPEARS, AND WATCHES, UNSEEN.

SANTIAGO: After this, I won't ask you again Caxa. I know how distasteful you find it.

CAXA SAYS NOTHING.

SANTIAGO: But I take no pleasure in it.

CAXA: No.

SANTIAGO: Show God I take no pleasure. Show God I am willing to mortify myself in payment for his generosity. Don't spare me, I won't thank you for it.

HE BOWS HIS HEAD, AND SPREADS HIS ARMS. CAXA WIPES HIS FACE. HE LOATHES THIS RITUAL, BUT HE'S BEING PAID WELL FOR IT. HE STARTS TO FLOG SANTIAGO WHO, THOUGH HIS FACE REGISTERS THE PAIN OF EACH BLOW, DOES NOT MURMUR.

SANTIAGO: (*Eyes turned heavenward*) See . . . how . . . I bleed?

SANTIAGO HAS STARTED BREATHING HEAVILY. FELIPE COMES UP BEHIND CAXA AND DRAGS HIM BACK, BEATING HIM INTO UNCONSCIOUSNESS WITH A BLOW.

SANTIAGO: Why have you stopped? Go on. Go on 'til I tell you to stop.

FELIPE PICKS UP THE WHIP.

SANTIAGO: I beg you—

FELIPE LANDS A VICIOUS BLOW. SANTIAGO TAKES A SHARP INTAKE OF BREATH.

SANTIAGO: Better.

FELIPE LANDS ANOTHER BLOW, HARDER, AND ANOTHER.

SANTIAGO: God Almighty, hear my agony . . .

THE FLOGGING GOES ON. SANTIAGO STARTS TO REEL.

SANTIAGO: . . . and forgive my trespasses . . .

FELIPE IS WORKING UP A SWEAT. HIS EYES GLITTER.

SANTIAGO: Enough!

FELIPE DOESN'T STOP.

SANTIAGO: Enough, Caxa! I said enough!

FELIPE LAYS THE WHIP HARDER THAN EVER.

SANTIAGO: Caxa! You're killing me!

HE TRIES TO GET UP. THE BLOW FORCES HIM DOWN AGAIN.

SANTIAGO: Have you gone mad? Stop! Stop!
FELIPE: Pray, Santiago!
SANTIAGO: Falco!

SANTIAGO AGAIN TRIES TO GET UP AND CRAWL AWAY. HIS BODY IS RUNNING WITH BLOOD AND SWEAT. WHEREVER HE TRIES TO CRAWL, FELIPE FOLLOWS, HIS FACE TRANSFORMED.

SANTIAGO: Stop! In God's name, stop!

CAXA IS STIRRING, UNSEEN BY FELIPE. FELIPE STOPS BEATING SANTIAGO. HE IS BREATHLESS.

FELIPE: Had enough?
SANTIAGO: A little mercy.
FELIPE: When were you ever merciful?

CAXA STANDS UP.

FELIPE: I'm going to kill you.
SANTIAGO: I won't beg.
FELIPE: Useless to try.

CAXA STRUGGLES TO THE EDGE OF THE RUIN.

SANTIAGO: But forgive me.
FELIPE: Do you beg?
SANTIAGO: I'm asking you to prove your humanity. That's all.
    Forgive me.

FELIPE STARES DOWN AT SANTIAGO, PERPLEXED.

CAXA: Help! Murder! Help!
FELIPE: (*Turns*) Christ!

*SANTIAGO ALL BUT COLLAPSES, FELIPE CROSSES
TOWARD CAXA.*

FELIPE: Shut up!
CAXA: Murder! Over here! Quickly!
FELIPE: (*Looks back to Santiago*) Maybe God's on your side after all.
SANTIAGO: (*To Caxa*) Don't let him get away!

CAXA MOVES ON FELIPE.

CAXA: You stupid asshole!
SERGEANT GRIS: (*Off*) This way! You ! You! (*Off*) Yes sir!
SERGEANT GRIS: (*Off*) Move it!
CAXA: Here! Over here!

*HE CLOSES IN. FELIPE DODGES HIM, AND MAKES
HIS ESCAPE. HE RUNS STRAIGHT INTO SERGEANT
GRIS, WHO IS FOLLOWED BY ST. PIERRE AND A SEC-
OND SOLDIER. HE ABOUT TURNS AND RUNS IN
THE OPPOSITE DIRECTION.*

*THE RUINS ARE SHADOWY, AND THE CHASE THAT
FOLLOWS IS DIFFICULT TO SEE PROPERLY.*

SERGEANT GRIS: Halt or we fire!

ENTER CAPTAIN VERON-REVILLE, WITH CASTROPOL.

CAPTAIN REVILLE: Sergeant!
SERGEANT GRIS: Sir!

CAPTAIN REVILLE: What's going on?

FELIPE MAKES A DASH FOR IT, KNOCKING ST. PIERRE TO THE GROUND WITH A BLOW TO THE GROIN. FELIPE EXITS.

ST. PIERRE: Ah!

ST. PIERRE IS DOUBLED UP, WINCING.

SERGEANT GRIS: (*To the soldier*) Shoot him!

THE SOLDIER EXITS.

CAPTAIN REVILLE: This man reports seeing rebels around.
SERGEANT GRIS: That's all we need.
CAPTAIN REVILLE: Where are your men?
SERGEANT GRIS: I haven't found Gregorio. Reubell is with the Duke, where ever he is. St. Pierre?

ST. PIERRE TRIES TO STAND UP.

CAXA: (*At Santiago's body*) Can I have a hand here?

THE CAPTAIN CROSSES TO THE SPOT.

CAPTAIN REVILLE: Who did this?
CAXA: His name's Falco. Felipe Falco.

OFFSTAGE, AND SOME DISTANCE AWAY, TWO SHOTS ARE FIRED. ST. PIERRE HELPS CAXA PICK SANTIAGO UP.

SERGEANT GRIS: We'll find him.
CAPTAIN REVILLE: Is he one of the rebels?
SANTIAGO: It's possible. It's more than possible.
CAPTAIN REVILLE: (*To Castropol*) It seems your information may be right.
CASTROPOL: What will you do? Arrest them?
SERGEANT GRIS: Arrest them be damned. String the fuckers up.

CASTROPOL: Well, I can't be certain—

ENTER THE DUCHESS, WITH ESTELLA, AND LUISA, WHO CARRIES A LAMP.

CASTROPOL EXITS.

DUCHESS: Captain! What's going on?
CAPTAIN REVILLE: Ma'am. There are insurgents in the vicinity.
DUCHESS: Thank you for your concern.

SHE SEES SANTIAGO, WHO HAS HIS BACK TO HER.

DUCHESS: Who is this bloody thing?
SANTIAGO: (*Very quietly*) Don't look at me.
DUCHESS: Santiago?

SANTIAGO TURNS AND BOWS, MAKING A PATHETIC ATTEMPT TO KEEP HIS DIGNITY DESPITE HIS CONDITION. HE STANDS UPRIGHT; ALMOST FALLS. CAXA OFFERS A HAND TO SUPPORT HIM. HE PUSHES THE HORSE-MASTER AWAY. STRAIGHTENS HIMSELF.

SANTIAGO: (*To the Duchess*) If you would excuse me . . . ?

HE EXITS, UNWILLING TO BE HELPED. CAXA FOLLOWS.

DUCHESS: The look on his face.

ENTER THE SOLDIER.

SOLDIER: I think I injured him, but I lost him again in the darkness.
CAPTAIN REVILLE: Sergeant.
SERGEANT GRIS: St. Pierre, come with me.
CAPTAIN REVILLE: Be careful. There may be more of them. (*Looks around*). Where did the informer go? We must make every effort to find the Duke. When you've located Falco, come back here. I'll get a patrol together.

SERGEANT GRIS: Sir! (*The Sergeant exits*)
CAPTAIN REVILLE: (*To the Duchess*) Please. Go back to the
     lodge.

THE CAPTAIN EXITS.

ESTELLA: He's right. This is dangerous.

ESTELLA STARTS TO EXIT.

*GOYA APPEARS. HE CARRIES THE PORTRAIT OF THE
DUCHESS UNDER HIS ARM.*

ESTELLA: Goya?
DUCHESS: Dead or alive?
GOYA: It's open to debate. I . . . I brought you your portrait.
DUCHESS: (*Pleased*) Oh!
GOYA: I finished it in the half-light, but it's my first posthumous
     work so it has curiosity value.
DUCHESS: (*Looks at it*) Is this me?
GOYA: Yes.
DUCHESS: And the monster leaning over me, with its claws in
     my breast, what's that?

GOYA SHRUGS.

DUCHESS: Tell me.
GOYA: It's the future.
ESTELLA: Moralist.
GOYA: It may kill you.
ESTELLA: She's just a girl.
DUCHESS: I don't understand what you're saying.
GOYA: Forget I spoke.
DUCHESS: What do you see in me?
GOYA: Oh the old lie. Beauty as truth.

DUCHESS LOOKS AT THE PICTURE, FROWNING.

GOYA: As if in your perfection there might be some signal from
     the far side of Hell.

ESTELLA: Take the painting back.
DUCHESS: No.
GOYA: It's only a metaphor.
ESTELLA: Then I'll burn it.

ESTELLA TAKES THE DUCHESS AWAY. BARBARA, WHO HAS BEEN WATCHING THIS SCENE, STEPS FORWARD.

BARBARA: You are so cruel.
GOYA: Put it down to indigestion. Did you find the actors?
BARBARA: Oh yes.

SUDDENLY, WITH A BURST OF CHATTER, THE ACTORS ENTER. ONE IS JUGGLING, ONE IS PARRY-ING AND THRUSTING A PATENTLY WOODEN SWORD. LAMPS ARE HELD HIGH; THEIR FACES HAVE BEEN MADE UP; MUSTACHES DRAWN ON PALE FACES. SEREPHINA, WHO HAS A MUSTACHE LIKE THE OTHERS, STEPS FORWARD, DECLAIMING.

SEREPHINA: And yes I am that daughter—
HOLY JOE: (*Also declaiming*) Daughter?
SEREPHINA: Whom so long ago you lost and thought was dead—
HOLY JOE: My heart is mended and these many tears I shed for you
       are dried. Dearest Laura, though you see I am a Bandit-King,
       before your beauty I'm a lamb. Forgive my crimes. I pray that
       henceforth we may love as child and Sire until Heaven we see.

A ROUND OF APPLAUSE FROM THE ACTORS, AND FROM BARBARA.

BARBARA: It's wonderful.
HOLY JOE: It's mine.
EVA: And you sir?
GOYA: Unfortunately I'm deaf; so I have difficulty following the
       argument. But I like your looks. What are you?
GERONIMO: Bandits.
EVA: Show the man!

THEY START TO DON THE LAST OF THEIR COS-

TUMES; COVERING THEIR FACES WITH HALF-MASKS,
AND DONNING CLOAKS.

EVA: We're performing for the troops, for an exorbitant fee.
GOYA: Oh . . .
HOLY JOE: Lay the lamps amongst the rubble. Let's get some
   drama going here.

THE ACTORS PLACE THE LIGHTS SO THAT THEY
SHINE UP, ALMOST LIKE FOOTLIGHTS. GOYA
WATCHES THE PREPARATION WITH EXCITEMENT.

GOYA: Is there dancing?
HOLY JOE: There is.
GOYA: I love dancing. Once I've got the rhythm I'm away. It
   doesn't matter that I can't hear the tune.
GERONIMO: Where's Castropol?
GOYA: (*To Barbara*) What did he say?
BARBARA: Something about Castropol.
HOLY JOE: He's our agent in this.

GOYA SUDDENLY BECOMES UNEASY.

GOYA: No.
EVA: What's wrong with him?
BARBARA: What is it?
GOYA: Make them stop.
EVA: Stop?
TUNG: What's he foaming at?
GOYA: It's a trick! (*He starts to try and pull the costume from Eva*)
   Take it off!
EVA: Get away.
GOYA: There's going to be blood spilt.
VIOLANTE: (*Producing the false human head from a bag*) Indeed
   there is!

WHOOPS AND HOWLS OF DELIGHT FROM THE ACTORS.

GOYA: (*To Barbara*) Make them understand!
BARBARA: Understand what?

TUNG: (*Hits Goya, who has been dragging at his costume*) Find you
    own stuff.
GOYA: Take them off!
GERONIMO: He's rabid.
GOYA: Go naked! It's safer!
TUNG: (*Gets ready to hit Goya again*) I'm warning you!
BARBARA: Leave them be!

    BARBARA DRAGS HIM OFF. THE PANIC HAS SUD-
    DENLY EXHAUSTED HIM, HE CAN'T RESIST HER,
    AND IS PULLED AWAY FROM THE ACTORS.

BARBARA: You'll get your head broken.
SEREPHINA: There's somebody coming!
GOYA: Stop them!
EVA: Positions everyone!
BARBARA: Now just watch!
GOYA: No! No! No!

    GOYA IS PULLED OUT OF SIGHT BY BARBARA. THE
    SERGEANT ENTERS, FOLLOWED BY ST. PIERRE AND
    THE SOLDIER.

SERGEANT GRIS: Round in fucking circles—
GOYA: (*Hidden*) No!
SERGEANT GRIS: What?
ST. PIERRE: We're surrounded!
SERGEANT GRIS: Rebels! Fucking rebels!
VIOLANTE: Wait!

    ST. PIERRE FIRES AT VIOLANTE, WHO COLLAPSES.

HOLY JOE: What are you doing?
EVA: Oh Jesus in Heaven!
ST. PIERRE: The bastards are everywhere!
HOLY JOE: Don't shoot . . .
ST. PIERRE: Bloody lice!

    HE AIMS HIS RIFLE. HOLY JOE APPROACHES THE
    SERGEANT, WOODEN SWORD IN HAND.

HOLY JOE: Look, you bastard—

SERGEANT GRIS BAYONETS HIM.

SERGEANT GRIS: Ha!

HOLY JOE IS IMPALED ON THE BAYONET. HE PULLS HIMSELF OFF THE POINT; LOOKS AT HIS HANDS.

HOLY JOE: Real . . . blood.

SUDDENLY, ALL HELL BREAKS LOOSE.

EVA: Run!

THE ACTORS TURN TO RUN. GOYA BREAKS FREE FROM BARBARA AND CROSSES TOWARD THE SERGEANT. ANOTHER SHOT IS FIRED, BY THE SOLDIER, WHICH WOUNDS GERONIMO, WHO HAS GONE TO HELP VIOLANTE. BARBARA JUST MANAGES TO PULL GOYA OUT OF THE LINE OF ATTACK AS THE SERGEANT FOLLOWS THROUGH, WITH A BLOOD CURDLING SCREAM ON HIS FIRST BAYONETING, WOUNDING EVA, WHO HAS GONE TO THE ASSISTANCE OF HOLY JOE. EVA FIGHTS BACK, THOUGH WOUNDED. HOLY JOE SCREAMS AS HE DIES. THE CAPTAIN ENTERS, SWORD AT THE READY.

CAPTAIN REVILLE: Sergeant!
SERGEANT GRIS: They're everywhere!
CAPTAIN REVILLE: Back to back!
SOLDIER: (*Joyful*) Kill! Kill! Kill!
SERGEANT GRIS: (*Bayoneting Eva again*) We're getting the best of
    them!

TUNG ATTACKS THE SERGEANT, IN A FRENZY OF ANGER.

TUNG: You stupid bastards! Stop! Stop!
SERGEANT GRIS: Help me!

*THE CAPTAIN PULLS TUNG OFF. THE SERGEANT DIS-
EMBOWELS HIM WITH BAYONET. SEREPHINA, WHO
HAS BEEN WOUNDED, IS TRYING TO STAGGER AWAY.*

CAPTAIN REVILLE: Don't let them escape!
ST. PIERRE: I see him!

*ST. PIERRE FOLLOWS SEREPHINA. GERONIMO IS
NOW FIGHTING THE CAPTAIN, WOODEN SWORD
AGAINST STEEL.*

GERONIMO: Wait! Listen! For God's sake listen! It's not real! It's not—

*THE CAPTAIN RUNS GERONIMO THROUGH. THE
SOLDIER IS FINISHING OFF HOLY JOE WITH BAYO-
NET STABS. ST. PIERRE HAS CORNERED SEREPHINA,
WHO HAS COLLAPSED. VIOLANTE HAS DIED OF
HER WOUND; EVA, ON TOP OF HOLY JOE, IS DIS-
PATCHED BY THE SERGEANT.*

GERONIMO: It's a wooden sword!

HE FALLS TO HIS KNEES, AND BREAKS THE SWORD.

GERONIMO: See?

SEREPHINA PULLS OFF HER MASK.

SEREPHINA: Soldier! Please . . .
ST. PIERRE: Oh mother of God.

*THE FIGHTING HAS STOPPED. ALL ARE DEAD,
EXCEPT GERONIMO, WHO IS ON HIS KNEES, AND
SEREPHINA.*

ST. PIERRE: (*Drops the sword*) No.
SOLDIER: It's a woman.
SERGEANT GRIS: Fanatics.
CAPTAIN REVILLE: A woman?
ST. PIERRE: What have we done?

SERGEANT GRIS: Came at us out of nowhere.
CAPTAIN REVILLE: The actors.

A TERRIBLE SILENCE.

SERGEANT GRIS: Actors?
SOLDIER: (*Still not realizing*) We showed them, didn't we? No trouble.
CAPTAIN REVILLE: (*Horrified*) This is more than my career's worth.
SERGEANT GRIS: Rebels . . .
CAPTAIN REVILLE: No.
SOLDIER: No trouble.
CAPTAIN REVILLE: Shut up!
ST. PIERRE: (*Cradling Serephina*) Please for God's sake. Breathe.

SEREPHINA DRAWS ONE TINY BREATH AND DIES.

ST. PIERRE: Breathe.
SERGEANT GRIS: Impossible.
SOLDIER: It's true?
SERGEANT GRIS: Wooden sword.
SOLDIER: Fuck.
SERGEANT GRIS: Heat of the moment. Error in the dark.

ENTER GREGORIO.

GREGORIO: Sergeant . . . ?

HIS PRESENCE SEEMS TO WAKE THE CAPTAIN.

CAPTAIN REVILLE: We must . . . make a report.
GREGORIO: What happened?
CAPTAIN REVILLE: You saw nothing.
GREGORIO: No.
CAPTAIN REVILLE: Rebels.
GREGORIO: Are they?
CAPTAIN REVILLE: Certainly.
ST. PIERRE: (*He points to Geronimo, still kneeling upright*) He'll tell if we don't. Somebody has to tell! I'm weak and terrified and I'm a barbarian.

CAPTAIN REVILLE: We shall admit to no such thing.

HE CROSSES TO GERONIMO, AND NUDGES HIM.
THE BODY TOPPLES OVER.

CAPTAIN REVILLE: Nor will he.
SOLDIER: There were others here. They saw.
CAPTAIN REVILLE: No one will question our actions, as long as
    we're in uniform. We'll substitute real weapons for these
    shams. We'll tell what they want to hear; that we're just
    men. They pay our wages. We owe them the lie.

HE PICKS UP THE WOODEN SWORD GERONIMO
HELD, AND THROWS DOWN HIS DAGGER.

CAPTAIN REVILLE: (*Looking at the sword*) Brings back my child-
    hood. Follow on.

HE EXITS. THERE IS A BUSTLE OF ACTION, AS THE
SOLDIER AND THE SERGEANT DOCTOR THE EVI-
DENCE, CLEARING AWAY THE PROPS.

SERGEANT GRIS: Gregorio? A hand here.

GREGORIO NODS, AND HELPS.

SERGEANT GRIS: If you want to avoid a court-martial concern-
    ing your cowardice, I suggest you agree with the Captain's
    account of this fracas. Raise yourself, St. Pierre.

THE SERGEANT, THE SOLDIER, AND GREGORIO
EXIT. ST. PIERRE SITS AMONGST THE BODIES. THE
WIND BLOWS. GOYA EMERGES FROM HIDING.

GOYA: What a world of wonders.
BARBARA: I didn't understand.
GOYA: Where's my sketchbook?
BARBARA: I thought you'd thrown it away.
GOYA: It's the only way I can stop my hand shaking.

BARBARA GOES TO LOOK FOR THE SKETCHBOOK. CASTROPOL, IN SILHOUETTE, APPEARS, AND LOOKS DOWN ON THE BODIES. HE TAKES OFF HIS HAT, AND HIS BEARD, AND WATCHES, FACE IMPAS- SIVE, THEN MOVES OFF. ST. PIERRE STARTS TO PULL OFF HIS BOOTS.

ST. PIERRE: You shouted.
GOYA: What?
ST. PIERRE: The old man. He shouted.

BARBARA GIVES HIM THE SKETCHBOOK. HE BRINGS CHARCOAL FROM HIS POCKET, AND CROSSES TO WHERE SEREPHINA IS LYING.

GOYA: If I hadn't wanted my privacy she'd be alive. All alive.

ST. PIERRE IS STRIPPING OFF HIS UNIFORM NOW.

ST. PIERRE: You said: It's only safe to go naked. Is that true?
GOYA: What's true? (*Looks at the body*) Maybe this is truth.
ST. PIERRE: Don't tell me that.

ST. PIERRE, HALF-UNDRESSED, STAGGERS AWAY INTO THE DARKNESS.

BARBARA PUTS A LAMP BESIDE THE BODY OF SEREPHINA. GOYA IS SQUATTED BESIDE IT, DRAWING.

BARBARA: They'll need more coffins.

SHE EXITS.

GOYA: (*To Serephina*) Don't worry. I'll make it a good likeness.

THE LIGHTS FADE.

END OF PART THREE.

INTERLUDE

MUSIC PLAYS.

*THE THREE WOMEN MOVE THE BODIES OF THE
ACTORS OUT OF THE RUINS.*

DOGS BARK.

*THE LIGHT CHANGES, DARKENING AS THE NIGHT
DEEPENS BEFORE DAWN. AS THE REMOVAL OF THE
BODIES NEARS ITS END, ACT FOUR BEGINS.*

Act 4

*THE SAME SCENE, BUT BY FIRELIGHT. THE LAST OF
THE BODIES ARE STILL BEING PUT IN BAGS AND
REMOVED AS PART FOUR OPENS. GOYA HAS GONE.*

*ENTER NATANIEL, HIS COSTUME NOW ENTIRELY
CHANGED; IT IS SMART, HE'S NO LONGER THE
LABORER. HE WEARS A COAT, LACE CUFFS, A WIG.
HE STILL CARRIES DONA PASCUALA ON HIS BACK
HOWEVER, AND THE BURDEN IS MORE WEIGHTY
NOW. SHE IS WITHOUT HER WIG AND ENTIRELY
BALD.*

DONA PASCUALA: I did smell fire.
NATANIEL: You did.
DONA PASCUALA: Put me down.

NATANIEL: The ground is slippery.

DONA PASCUALA: Put me down; I've walked in blood before.

HE PUTS HER DOWN.

DONA PASCUALA: What are they doing? (*She gets hold of one of the women who is removing the bodies*) You! What's going on?

WOMAN: Rebels. They attacked the soldiers. The soldiers were outnumbered; just two against a horde. The rebels were killed. We're burning them on a mass pyre.

DONA PASCUALA: Are they much mutilated?

WOMAN: One or two.

DONA PASCUALA: Kept any of the teeth?

THE OTHER WOMEN HAVE GATHERED AROUND.

2nd WOMAN: Why?

DONA PASCUALA: They're good as an aphrodisiac, the teeth of those who died by violence.

3rd WOMAN: Is that right?

DONA PASCUALA: Gives a man a hard-on just like that.

1ST WOMAN OPENS ONE OF THE SACKS.

DONA PASCUALA: They need help once in a while, don't you find? My stud Nataniel—even he needs help, don't you? Come over here, don't be shy. Let the ladies see your thighs.

NATANIEL CROSSES TO THE WOMEN; THEY LOOK AT HIM BALEFULLY.

DONA PASCUALA: You can touch him if you want, he won't shy away. He may not look like much, but he goes like the clappers if you scratch him in the right places.

THE WOMEN START TO FEEL HIS BODY.

NATANIEL DOESN'T MOVE; HE IS COMPLETELY PASSIVE.

THE 3RD WOMAN IS DIGGING IN THE CORPSE'S
MOUTH, TO PULL AT THE TEETH.

3rd WOMAN: I can't get the tooth out.
DONA PASCUALA: Let me! Let me!

SHE PUTS HER HAND IN THE CORPSE'S MOUTH,
AND PULLS. SHE PRODUCES A TOOTH.

DONA PASCUALA: There! Grind it down, put it in his bread with
    some rosemary and some cattle-spit.
3rd WOMAN: (*Taking the tooth*) Thank you.
1st WOMAN: What about me?
2nd WOMAN: There's plenty for all of us.
DONA PASCUALA: The trick is to yank hard, and twist as you do it.

2ND WOMAN DOES AS INSTRUCTED.

DONA PASCUALA: Harder! Harder! (*To Nataniel*) Go graze for a
    while, this is women's work.

NATANIEL MOVES AWAY. THE ARGUMENT, THE
SQUEALS OF DELIGHT ETC. GO ON.

NATANIEL STANDS BESIDE A WALL, OR A PILLAR. A
BLOODY HAND GRIPS THE BRICK.

FELIPE APPEARS. HE IS WOUNDED IN THE SIDE.

NATANIEL: Oh God.
FELIPE: Ssh!!
NATANIEL: Felipe!
FELIPE: Brother of mine . . . lucky you chanced by.
NATANIEL: What's wrong with you?
FELIPE: I've been shot.
NATANIEL: It was you beat Santiago, I suppose.
FELIPE: You suppose right. Help me, for the love of God, I'm
    bleeding to death here.
NATANIEL: Stay away from me.
FELIPE: I need your help, brother.

NATANIEL: You're getting blood on my coat, brother. You got yourself into this. I'm not responsible. Just go away. Things are going well for me.

FELIPE: Oh yes? Servicing the grande dame? How in God's name can you go near her?

NATANIEL: You used to share a bed with Rafael and his wife. That's worse.

FELIPE: Don't lecture me, give me a hand—

ENTER THE GENERAL, WITH THE CAPTAIN AND SERGEANT GRIS.

GENERAL GUYE: —and finished by morning?

CAPTAIN REVILLE: Oh certainly.

GENERAL GUYE: I don't like mass cremations. They have the feel of an atrocity.

CAPTAIN REVILLE: They were rebels, sir.

GENERAL GUYE: I know. I know.

SERGEANT GRIS: You women! Break this up! Break this up! (*Sees Dona Pascuala*) Oh.

DONA PASCUALA: Come to take me, Lieutenant?

SERGEANT GRIS: Sergeant.

DONA PASCUALA: Beautiful mustaches. Do you wax them?

SHE GETS HOLD OF HIM.

SERGEANT GRIS: Let go of me.

GENERAL GUYE: What's going on?

SERGEANT GRIS: It's just an old bitch. She—

DONA PASCUALA: Oh, General.

GENERAL GUYE: (*Bowing deeply*) Dona Pascuala. Out so late?

DONA PASCUALA: I was strolling. We ladies got to talking about love.

GENERAL GUYE: Why don't you let the sergeant go?

DONA PASCUALA: Oh yes. (*She does so; the Sergeant, whom she had by the thigh, staggers back*)

GENERAL GUYE: Perhaps it's time you went to bed.

DONA PASCUALA: With my mad son still to be found? Oh yes, I heard everybody saying it. The Duke is missing. Well, you know what I think? I think he inserted his head in his own backside and disappeared up it. (*She laughs*) That's my opinion.

BARBARA ENTERS.

BARBARA: Are there more bodies yet?
CAPTAIN REVILLE: Yes. Here, and in the orchard.
GENERAL GUYE: Are you cremating those killed in the bombardment?
CAPTAIN REVILLE: I thought it best.
GENERAL GUYE: I suppose so.

THE WOMEN PICK UP THE BODY THEY WERE REMOVING THE TEETH FROM AND TAKE IT OFF TO THE FIRE.

BARBARA DOES NOT LEAVE. SHE SITS DOWN AND WIPES HER FACE.

GENERAL GUYE: Why don't you just go back to the lodge?
DONA PASCUALA: No; I want to see the bodies burn.

SHE ACCIDENTALLY DROPS THE TEETH.

DONA PASCUALA: Oh, now look what I've done.
CAPTAIN REVILLE: Teeth?
DONA PASCUALA: Will you ask mustache to pick them up for me?
CAPTAIN REVILLE: Sergeant.
SERGEANT GRIS: Teeth. What does she want with teeth?

SERGEANT GRIS GROVELS AROUND TRYING TO PICK UP TEETH.

DONA PASCUALA: There were six. Nataniel?

NATANIEL COMES FORWARD.

DONA PASCUALA: Doesn't he look fine? The coat belonged to a lover of mine. Died of leprosy.

THE CAPTAIN RESPONDS, SO DOES NATANIEL.

DONA PASCUALA: Not in the coat.
GENERAL GUYE: (*To Nataniel*) You have blood on your cheek.

NATANIEL IS VERY NERVOUS.

DONA PASCUALA: What's wrong with you?
NATANIEL: Nothing.
DONA PASCUALA: Is that your blood?
GENERAL GUYE: Answer.
NATANIEL: Yes.
GENERAL GUYE: I see no wound.
NATANIEL: Please. It's not me. I don't know him! I don't know him!

NATANIEL MAKES A BREAK TO RUN.

DONA PASCUALA: What's he talking about?

FELIPE BREAKS IN THE OPPOSITE DIRECTION.

CAPTAIN REVILLE: There! You! Halt!

FELIPE STUMBLES.

GENERAL GUYE: Gris!

*THE SERGEANT LOOKS UP, SEES FELIPE. THROWS
AWAY TEETH AS HE DIVES AFTER FELIPE.*

DONA PASCUALA: The teeth!

*THE WOMEN, WHO HAVE COME BACK FOR THE
NEXT BODY, SCRABBLE AFTER THEM.*

DONA PASCUALA: Let them alone! They're mine, you thieving
bitches.

*BARBARA STOPS NATANIEL, WHO'S TRYING TO RUN
OFF.*

BARBARA: What's going on?
NATANIEL: Felipe!
BARBARA: Felipe?

BARBARA LETS NATANIEL GO; HE DASHES OFF.

DONA PASCUALA: Come back boy! Boy! My legs won't work!

THE CAPTAIN AND SERGEANT GRIS HAVE CAUGHT FELIPE.

SERGEANT GRIS: Got you!
GENERAL GUYE: Who is he?
CAPTAIN REVILLE: Falco. The man who made such a mess of the major-domo.
FELIPE: He got what he deserved.
GENERAL GUYE: That was a foul and cowardly act.
CAPTAIN REVILLE: He's wounded.
GENERAL GUYE: Find the doctor; get the hole dressed.
SERGEANT GRIS: Why bother? Why don't we just string him up on the spot? Attempted murder.
GENERAL GUYE: There's been enough impromptu slaughter tonight, Sergeant.
FELIPE: Get it over with.
GENERAL GUYE: You confess to this crime?
FELIPE: I do.
GENERAL GUYE: Very well. (*To Captain*) Have the appropriate papers drawn up; I'll sign them.
CAPTAIN REVILLE: Sir.

FELIPE, TOO WEAK TO MOVE, IS KNEELING ON THE FLOOR.

ENTER JOLY.

JOLY: General! Sir! General Guye!
GENERAL GUYE: Yes?
JOLY: There's a body been found, sir. In one of the trees.
GENERAL GUYE: And?
JOLY: It's the Duke; he's hanged himself.
GENERAL GUYE: Good God. Take me to him.
JOLY: Yes sir.

GENERAL EXITS WITH JOLY.

CAPTAIN REVILLE: (*To Barbara, who is staring at Felipe*) Do you know the prisoner?

FELIPE LOOKS UP AT HER.

FELIPE: No. She doesn't.
CAPTAIN REVILLE: Then stop staring.

BARBARA CROSSES TO "GOYA'S" COFFIN, AND BUS-IES HERSELF WITH THAT.

SERGEANT GRIS: (*To Felipe*) You've caused me no end of trouble tonight. You panicked my men, and that's had some serious repercussions. Seems to me . . . you're getting off lightly with an execution.
CAPTAIN REVILLE: Do you want to interrogate him?
SERGEANT GRIS: May I sir?
CAPTAIN REVILLE: Seems a reasonable request to me, Sergeant.
SERGEANT GRIS: (*Grinning*) Thank you, sir.
CAPTAIN REVILLE: Just make sure he stays alive long enough to be shot.
SERGEANT GRIS: (*To the soldier*) Want to lend a hand?
SOLDIER: My pleasure.

THE SERGEANT AND THE SOLDIER DRAG FELIPE OUT OF SIGHT.

CAPTAIN REVILLE: (*To Barbara, who is looking*) Spoils of war.

LAUGHTER FROM THE SERGEANT. A MOAN OF PAIN FROM FELIPE. BARBARA COVERS HER EARS. THE MOAN BECOMES A CRY. THE WOMEN HAVE COME BACK IN FOR ANOTHER BODY.

1st WOMAN: What was that?
2nd WOMAN: A baby.
DONA PASCUALA: I like babies; cooked in brine till the flesh floats off the bone. Did you see where my Nataniel went?
3rd WOMAN: He ran off.
DONA PASCUALA: They're such cowards.

ANOTHER CRY, AND MORE LAUGHTER.

DONA PASCUALA: I mean listen to them.

*RAFAEL ENTERS, AND WATCHES THE WOMAN
BUNDLING UP ONE OF THE BODIES.*

DONA PASCUALA SEES HIM.

DONA PASCUALA: Ah! An able-bodied man.
BARBARA: (*Sees*) Rafael.
DONA PASCUALA: I know your face. Did you work here?
RAFAEL: What's the noise?
BARBARA: Felipe.
DONA PASCUALA: You can carry me. Come here.
1st WOMAN: No. Not him.
DONA PASCUALA: Why not?
1st WOMAN: He's dangerous. Let me carry you.
DONA PASCUALA: I'm too heavy.
2nd WOMAN: We'll take turns.
DONA PASCUALA: (*Hobbles toward Rafael*) But . . . I want . . . this
    one. (She stumbles) Oh! Oh! My leg . . . (*To Rafael*) Help me.

*ONE OF THE WOMEN COMES FORWARD AND PICKS
HER UP. GOYA HAS COME ON, AND WATCHES THIS.*

DONA PASCUALA: At least kiss me, handsome.
1st WOMAN: Go on.
DONA PASCUALA: It's not much to ask.
2nd WOMAN: Kiss her.
DONA PASCUALA: Or I'll think you don't love me.

*VERY GENTLY, RAFAEL LEANS FORWARD AND
KISSES HER. LIKE A SHOT AN ARM REACHES
ROUND AND HOLDS HIM THERE. HE PULLS AWAY.*

DONA PASCUALA LAUGHS.

DONA PASCUALA: Yes! Oh yes? Such love! Take me to the fire!
    The fire!

SHE CLIMBS ON THE BACK OF THE 1ST WOMAN AND THEY EXIT.

THE WOMEN FOLLOW ON WITH ANOTHER BODY.

GOYA: You're not much of a lover, are you?
RAFAEL: Never was.

BARBARA CROSSES TO RAFAEL.

BARBARA: Help him.

ANOTHER CRY. BARBARA COVERS HER EARS.

BARBARA: Please help him.
GOYA: Are you sick?
BARBARA: They have Felipe.
GOYA: Oh . . .
BARBARA: That's his scream.
GOYA: Sometimes it's good to be deaf.

RAFAEL HAS CROSSED TO WHERE THE TORTURING IS GOING ON.

THE SERGEANT EMERGES, BLOOD ON HIS HANDS.

SERGEANT GRIS: What are you peering at?
RAFAEL: Nothing.
SERGEANT GRIS: This is official business, all right? National security. You keep your nose out.

HE PUSHES RAFAEL BACK, LEAVING A BLOODY HAND-PRINT ON RAFAEL'S CHEST.

THE SERGEANT RETURNS TO HIS WORK.

BARBARA: I don't want him to die like that.
RAFAEL: We can't do anything.
BARBARA: He helped you keep your sanity. Help him.

RAFAEL: Show me how.

BARBARA: Are you all so harmless now, when you need to do something? They're going to execute him when they're done playing games. He was prepared for that. But this . . .

ANOTHER CRY. BARBARA CAN'T BEAR IT ANY LONGER. SHE TAKES OUT THE GUN SHE TOOK FROM THE NUN.

RAFAEL: No!

BARBARA: I will.

RAFAEL: They'll cut you down, for Christ's sake.

RAFAEL TRIES TO TAKE HOLD OF HER.

THE CRIES HAVE STOPPED FOR THE MOMENT.

BARBARA PUSHES RAFAEL AWAY.

GOYA: Turn your back.

BARBARA: No.

GOYA: You can see, when it's over.

BARBARA CLOSES HER EYES TIGHT, AND WAITS, THEN SHE EXITS.

GOYA: *(To Rafael)* Keep her from harm.

RAFAEL EXITS.

GOYA: Is he screaming now?

ENTER GENERAL GUYE, WITH SANTIAGO, WHO IS VERY PALE.

JOLY FOLLOWS.

GENERAL GUYE: Where is Sofia?

SANTIAGO: (*Sitting down, back to Goya, a bottle of morphine in his hand*) I've sent for her.

GENERAL GUYE: Shall I break the news, or you?

ANOTHER CRY FROM FELIPE. SANTIAGO FLINCHES.

GOYA: He screamed then—
JOLY: Who?

*AFTER A MOMENT OF AGONIZED INDECISION,
GOYA CROSSES TO GENERAL GUYE.*

GOYA: Nicholas . . .
GENERAL GUYE: Do I know you?
GOYA: Save him this unnecessary agony.
SANTIAGO: Is it Falco?
GENERAL GUYE: The condemned man.
GOYA: Stop this barbarity for me.

GENERAL RECOGNIZES HIM.

GENERAL GUYE: Goya? My God! You're alive!
GOYA: Yes. God help me.

ANOTHER CRY. THE GENERAL CROSSES TO THE PLACE.

GENERAL GUYE: Sergeant!

THE SERGEANT EMERGES.

SERGEANT GRIS: General?
GENERAL GUYE: What is this?
SERGEANT GRIS: The Captain invited us to interrogate the pris-
    oner, sir.

*THE GENERAL PUSHES PAST THE SERGEANT TO SEE
FELIPE, THEN TURNS BACK AND DELIVERS A BLOW
TO THE SERGEANT WHICH SENDS HIM SPRAWLING.*

GENERAL GUYE: If there is any justice in the war we wage, you
    betray it.
SERGEANT GRIS: I was just following orders.

GENERAL GUYE: Find a doctor for this man. You lose your
    stripes for this, Gris.
SERGEANT GRIS: Yes Sir.

THE SERGEANT STANDS UP AND EXITS.

GOYA CROSSES TO THE GENERAL.

GOYA: Thank you.
GENERAL GUYE: Why?
GOYA: He's got a taste for it; that's the worst of it. You see the
    glitter in his eyes? It's not ignorance, it's appetite.
GENERAL GUYE: Not him. You. This deception. We thought . . .
GOYA: Oh yes. Francisco dead, Francisco mourned, Francisco sit-
    ting in future history, watching life go on, unnoticed. What a
    terror it is.
GENERAL GUYE: My dear man.
GOYA: Will you forgive me?
GENERAL GUYE: What's to forgive?

ENTER THE DUCHESS, WITH ESTELLA, AND LUISA.

GOYA DOESN'T HIDE ANY LONGER.

DUCHESS: What news?
GENERAL GUYE: Ma'am . . .
DUCHESS: Spare me your delicacy. Just tell me. He's dead?
GENERAL GUYE: Yes.
ESTELLA: How?
GENERAL GUYE: He hanged himself in an orange tree. I suppose the
    loss of the house was too much for him. The last person to see
    him was that doctor; he sent the soldier I left with him away. He
    must have brooded a while, then found a rope and done it.
GOYA: Who are you talking about?
SANTIAGO: The Duke, Goya. Your patron. Even art couldn't save
    his soul apparently.

GOYA GOES TO SIT DOWN.

DUCHESS: Was it easy?

GENERAL GUYE: Let us hope so. Shall I make the arrangements for the body to be taken to Madrid?

DUCHESS: Yes. Please.

SERGEANT GRIS APPEARS, WITH CASTROPOL.

CASTROPOL: Who needs a doctor?

GENERAL GUYE: The prisoner. Make him as comfortable as you can.

CASTROPOL: I'll do my best.

GENERAL GUYE: And when you're done, I'd like to talk to you about the Duke.

CASTROPOL: As you wish.

SANTIAGO: Are you giving aid to Falco?

GENERAL GUYE: I am.

SANTIAGO: After what he's done?

GENERAL GUYE: I have his death warrant. He'll be shot at dawn. But I will not have him cut to ribbons in the meanwhile for the entertainment of . . . *(To Sergeant)* What do you call yourself? Human, was it? *(To Duchess)* If you'll excuse me?

DUCHESS: Yes. of course.

GENERAL GUYE: Anything you need . . .

DUCHESS: I'm obliged.

GENERAL GUYE: Francisco?

GOYA: Yes?

GENERAL GUYE: *(Points to coffin)* Who is he?

GOYA: A thief with a taste for my coats.

GENERAL GUYE: No need for this ceremony then—

GOYA: Let it stay, say nothing to Xavier, or to Morel, or any of my loved ones. I can't face their questions tonight.

THE GENERAL NODS, AND EXITS.

CASTROPOL HAS GONE TO LOOK AT THE PRISONER.

THE SERGEANT NOTICES THE GENERAL GO.

SERGEANT GRIS: It was just a bit of fun.

SERGEANT WANDERS OFF.

SANTIAGO: Ma'am, I beg a word. (*He gets up, with evident pain*) Alone.

ESTELLA, LUISA AND JOLY WITHDRAW.

DUCHESS: This isn't the time for business, Santiago.
SANTIAGO: I have a confession to make.
DUCHESS: Make it.
SANTIAGO: The morphine makes my head spin.
DUCHESS: Say whatever you have to say.
SANTIAGO: Castropol . . .
DUCHESS: Who?
SANTIAGO: It was I let him into the house.
DUCHESS: I don't know who . . .
SANTIAGO: I've watched over your affairs from the beginning; on
    occasion I prevented the Duke from discovering you. Estella
    was always crude. A dozen times her plots would have been
    uncovered but for me.
DUCHESS: Why?
SANTIAGO: I love you.
DUCHESS: And?
SANTIAGO: I watched you.
DUCHESS: Watched?
SANTIAGO: To share a little of what you gave them. To prepare
    for giving you love in my turn.
DUCHESS: Not Castropol!
SANTIAGO: I paid him to come to you. I confess that, and I ask
    to be forgiven. I ask more than that. Marry me.
DUCHESS: Castropol loves me.
SANTIAGO: My words, on his lips.
DUCHESS: (*In shock*) In my stupidity . . . I thought circumstance
    was very accommodating. Lovers came to me easily. My
    indiscretions were never discovered. Even in winter I had
    only to smell my skin to sense spring. But you were there—
SANTIAGO: Always.
DUCHESS: Arranging it all. Eyes on me.
SANTIAGO: You are a widow at eighteen. Because I was there,
    your reputation is flawless.
DUCHESS: Go away.
SANTIAGO: Without me, you are a whore.
DUCHESS: (*To Estella*) Tell him to go away!

SANTIAGO EXITS.

THE DUCHESS TURNS TO GOYA.

DUCHESS: Is that the beast you painted, Signor Goya? You didn't tell me it would be so subtle.

CASTROPOL APPEARS.

CASTROPOL: I've done what I can for him.
DUCHESS: Oh doctor?
CASTROPOL: Ladyship?
DUCHESS: Will you attend on me a moment?
CASTROPOL: What can I do?
DUCHESS: I have this appalling wound. I've had it since a child. It bleeds without the least provocation, and I hate it so much. So very much. It's here, between my legs.
CASTROPOL: (*Under his breath*) Sofia, stop this.
DUCHESS: I wonder; would you like to sew it up?
CASTROPOL: Are you out of your mind?
DUCHESS: Wouldn't you like to revenge yourself on me that way?
CASTROPOL: Please! Stop this!
DUCHESS: Say something pretty to me. Call me by the names love uses. Call me lamb, call me chick. Make a meat-market of me, I won't cry.
CASTROPOL: What have I done to deserve this?
DUCHESS: You told him I hadn't been raped, didn't you?
CASTROPOL: Why would I say that?
DUCHESS: For the chaos it would cause.
CASTROPOL: No!
DUCHESS: And he hanged himself. He hanged himself!
CASTROPOL: You can't blame me!
DUCHESS: (*Announcing*) This is Castropol! This is not a doctor at all! (*She pulls off the hat*) This is an actor! Look, that mouth never told the truth in its life.
CASTROPOL: The woman's gone mad!
DUCHESS: I believed you! I believed you!

CASTROPOL DROPS HIS BAG AND EXITS.

ESTELLA: Don't break your heart!
DUCHESS: Let me be.
ESTELLA: It's all right.
DUCHESS: Away! Both of you!

ESTELLA AND LUISA EXIT. THE DUCHESS IS EXHAUSTED AFTER THIS EXPLOSION OF FEELING. SHE SITS DOWN. GOYA CROSSES TO HER, AND TOUCHES HER FACE. THERE IS A MOMENT OF TENDERNESS BETWEEN THEM.

DUCHESS: You know what you told me?
GOYA: What was that?
DUCHESS: About my beauty being a . . . what was it? A signal from the far side of hell?
GOYA: Did I say that?
DUCHESS: It seems to me I'm full of flaws. One of my eyes turns in, slightly, my throat gets blotchy in the heat.
GOYA: I said you were beautiful, not divine.
DUCHESS: Santiago has proposed marriage. He's going to be very powerful; all those years, working on Damaso so he could secure himself a fortune.
GOYA: There's beast called a Basilisk, ever heard of it?

THE DUCHESS SHAKES HER HEAD.

GOYA: This thing is supposedly so unspeakable that if you see it, you turn to stone. But nobody can tell if it exists or not, because if you've seen it, you're dead.
DUCHESS: Do you believe in it?
GOYA: I think maybe the worst monsters are almost invisible, just seen out of the corner of the eye. And I think the future will be full of them. Don't marry him.

ENTER THE CAPTAIN, WITH GREGORIO AND REUBELL, CARRYING THEIR RIFLES.

DUCHESS: What's this?
CAPTAIN REVILLE: Execution party, ma'am.

*CAPTAIN CROSSES TO WHERE FELIPE IS LYING, AND
SPEAKS TO THE SOLDIER.*

GOYA: Is it dawn already?

DUCHESS: Soon.

GOYA: I don't think the sun will come up. I think if it's got any
sense it'll hide until the ashes have been raked, and the bodies all boxed. Shall I escort you back to the lodge?

DUCHESS: I'm going to watch.

GOYA: No.

DUCHESS: I think I could learn to look at the worst thing in the
world with practice. Even your Basilisk. Wouldn't that defeat
it? To look with open eyes at it and see it clearly, in all its
detail, and know it utterly?

GOYA: It might . . .

DUCHESS: We mustn't hide.

*THE SOLDIERS BRING FELIPE OUT. HE LOOKS UTTERLY
BROKEN. RAFAEL APPEARS. HE SLIPS AROUND THE
BACK OF THE RUIN, CARRYING SOMETHING. HE THEN
DISAPPEARS INTO THE HOLE IN THE GROUND.*

CAPTAIN REVILLE: (*Reads*) Felipe Falco, having confessed to the
attempted murder of Louis Santiago, you are condemned to
death by firing squad at dawn on this the twenty-second day
of June 1811, by order of General Guye.

*FELIPE IS BEING BLINDFOLDED. HE IS PULLED
AGAINST THE PILLAR AND SLUMPS THERE.*

CAPTAIN REVILLE: Do you have anything to say?

GOYA: Isn't this a little premature? It's always darkest at this
moment, the moon down, the sun not yet up. The lamp-
light is confusing.

CAPTAIN REVILLE: Keep out of the way.

GOYA: I shall report this to General Guye.

BARBARA HAS ENTERED.

CAPTAIN REVILLE: A few minutes either way makes no odds.

GOYA: It might to him!

SUDDENLY, A TERRIBLE SOUND, OUT OF THE GROUND.

CAPTAIN REVILLE: What in Christ's name is that?

BARBARA CROSSES TO THE LAMP, AND THROWS IT DOWN. IT GOES OUT. THE ROARING GETS LOUDER AND THE SOLDIERS ARE ALL SHOUTING. RAFAEL APPEARS FROM THE EARTH. HE HAS LIT A FIRE IN THE GROUND. SMOKE AND LIGHT POUR OUT OF IT. HE HAS COVERED HIMSELF IN MUCK. IN EITHER HAND HE HOLDS PIECES OF HUMAN FLESH.

GREGORIO: No? No! No! No!
CAPTAIN REVILLE: Hold your ground.
DUCHESS: What's happening?
REUBELL: Holy Mary, Mother of God—

REUBELL HAS FALLEN TO HIS KNEES, PRAYING.

GOYA IS WHOOPING, AND APPLAUDING.

GOYA: I knew it! Hell itself! About time too.

RAFAEL EMERGES FROM THE HOLE.

SOLDIER: Light! Light!
CAPTAIN REVILLE: Stand and fire! Stand and fire!

RAFAEL RUNS TOWARD THE SOLDIERS, HOWLING, AND SCATTERING THEM. HE RUNS OFF.

SOLDIER: Light! Oh God, somebody, light!

BARBARA LIGHTS THE LAMP, AND HOLDS IT UP. A CIRCLE OF LIGHT AROUND HER. IN THE SUR-ROUNDING DARKNESS THE SOLDIERS ARE CRAWL-ING AROUND, WHISPERING. ONE IS PRAYING. GRE-GORIO IS CURLED UP INTO A LITTLE BALL.

BARBARA: All gone.
GREGORIO: No more. No more.

FELIPE HAS GONE. SO HAS GOYA.

DUCHESS: Where's the prisoner?
CAPTAIN REVILLE: Get up! Find him!

CAPTAIN GOES AMONGST THE SOLDIERS, KICKING THEM.

CAPTAIN REVILLE: Up, you bastards, up! He can't have gone far. He's wounded! Find him!

THE SOLDIERS GET UP, AND LOOK FOR THEIR WEAPONS. GREGORIO REMAINS, WHIMPERING, ON THE GROUND.

CAPTAIN REVILLE: Gregorio.

HE DOESN'T RESPOND.

DUCHESS: Like children.
CAPTAIN REVILLE: I beg your pardon?
DUCHESS: To judge by the smell I think one even filled his pants. Was it you Captain?
CAPTAIN REVILLE: (*Profoundly offended*) Have you women no decency left?
DUCHESS: It was you.
CAPTAIN REVILLE: Gregorio!

THE CAPTAIN EXITS. GREGORIO GETS UP, AND STAGGERS AFTER HIM. THERE ARE SHOTS BEING FIRED. SHOUTS IN THE DARKNESS.

DUCHESS: Was Felipe your lover? Please tell me.
BARBARA: Yes. We felt something . . .
DUCHESS: I envy you.

ENTER GOYA, WITH A HAMMER.

GOYA: They're after him. I don't think he's got much chance, frankly. Not with dawn coming.

BARBARA STARTS TO LEAVE.

GOYA: Where are you going?
BARBARA: To help him.
GOYA: With a lamp? Very clever. Why not just point them to him?
BARBARA: He can barely walk.
GOYA: Well maybe he'll lie down.
BARBARA: What?
GOYA: There may be safety in lying down for a while. Somewhere dark. Go and watch the fire, you can't do anything for him now.

ENTER RAFAEL.

DUCHESS: Ah!
GOYA: It's all right. He's quite human.
RAFAEL: Did it work?
GOYA: Who knows?
DUCHESS: This was a conspiracy, was it?

A BELL HAS STARTED TOLLING, VERY SLOWLY.

RAFAEL: Goya? A bell has started to ring.
GOYA: Really.
RAFAEL: Perhaps your wife has arrived.
GOYA: Josefa . . . but I haven't shaved.

HE GOES OFF TO LOOK.

RAFAEL: I'm going to the river to wash.

BARBARA EXITS TOWARD THE FIRE.

DUCHESS: You make a fine monster.
RAFAEL: Thank you.
DUCHESS: Maybe . . . You'll perform for me?

RAFAEL BOWS DEEPLY. CASTROPOL COMES ON, AT

*A RUSH. THERE ARE MORE SHOTS IN THE DARK-
NESS. HE IS TERRIFIED OF THEM.*

CASTROPOL: What's going on? What have you told them?
DUCHESS: Afraid?
CASTROPOL: Terrified, if that gives you any satisfaction. You've made
     up some lie about me, isn't that it? Look at you. Oh Sofia! You
     condemn me to death and I still want to cover you in kisses.
DUCHESS: Am I perfect?
CASTROPOL: Flawless.
DUCHESS: If you're not careful, you're going to get shot.
CASTROPOL: Protect me then.

HE KISSES HER.

CASTROPOL: In the name of love.

HE KISSES HER AGAIN. MORE SHOTS.

CASTROPOL: I can't run any further.
DUCHESS: Hide yourself away.

*HE LOOKS AROUND AND HIS EYES ALIGHT ON THE
HEAD.*

CASTROPOL: I'm watching you.

HE KISSES HER AGAIN. SHOUTS OFF.

REUBELL: (*Off*) I saw him! This way!
SERGEANT GRIS: (*Off*) Are you sure?

*CASTROPOL HIDES HIMSELF IN THE HEAD. THE
DUCHESS STAYS SITTING DOWN.*

REUBELL: (*Off*) Here!

ENTER REUBELL, WITH THE SOLDIER.

REUBELL: He came this way. I saw him running.

DUCHESS: What do you want?
REUBELL: Where is he?
DUCHESS: Where is who?
SERGEANT GRIS: (*Entering*) The escaped prisoner. Felipe Falco.
SOLDIER: He's dangerous.
DUCHESS: Is he?

SHE STANDS UP.

DUCHESS: So many pursuits tonight. Mistakes can be made in the dark.
SERGEANT GRIS: It's a risk you take.
DUCHESS: Your quarry?
SERGEANT GRIS: Yes?
DUCHESS: He's watching me.

THE SERGEANT GLANCES ROUND, SEES THE HEAD.
HE EXCHANGES A GLANCE WITH THE DUCHESS.

SERGEANT GRIS: Thank you.
DUCHESS: No, Sergeant. Thank you.

SERGEANT GRIS GESTURES TO REUBELL, WHO
MOVES AROUND THE SIDE OF THE HEAD. GRIS
FEIGNS DISINTEREST, AND WANDERS TO THE
OTHER SIDE. THEY READY THEMSELVES.

SERGEANT GRIS: Strike!

THEY DRIVE THEIR BAYONETS INTO THE EARS OF
THE HEAD. INSIDE, CASTROPOL SCREAMS. THE
DUCHESS PUTS HER HAND TO HER MOUTH. CAS-
TROPOL'S HANDS REACH FROM THE EYE-HOLES OF
THE HEAD, THEY SLIP BACK AS THE SOLDIERS
TWIST THEIR BAYONETS. HE DIES. THE DUCHESS
TURNS AND LOOKS AT THE HEAD.

DUCHESS: Blind.

SHE EXITS.

SERGEANT GRIS: Nice one. Nice one. I'll get my fucking stripes back for this. I'll find the captain eh? You get this thing hauled up, get him out of here!

SOLDIER: Haul it up? Why?

SERGEANT GRIS: It's a trophy, right?

ENTER BARBARA.

BARBARA: Are there any more bodies for the fire?

SERGEANT GRIS: Over here!

BARBARA: Who?

SERGEANT GRIS: Your pretty boy, Falco.

SERGEANT GRIS EXITS. THE SOLDIER BUSIES HIM-SELF WITH FINDING A ROPE TO HAUL THE HEAD UP ON; REUBELL WATCHES.

REUBELL: *(To Barbara)* Don't look at me. I don't much like it either.

SOLDIER: Give us a hand here.

A ROPE IS TIED TO THE HEAD.

REUBELL: All right; up we go.

THE HEAD IS HAULED UP. CASTROPOL'S BODY DAN-GLES FROM IT, BLEEDING, THEN FALLS.

SOLDIER: It's not him!

REUBELL: What?

SOLDIER: It's not him!

REUBELL: Well who the fuck is it?

CASTROPOL IS DRAGGED INTO THE LIGHT.

SOLDIER: God knows.

REUBELL BENDS OVER AND TUGS AT THE BEARD.

REUBELL: It's false.

HE PULLS IT OFF.

SOLDIER: Another actor. Fuck!
REUBELL: Give me a hand; let's get him to the fire.
SOLDIER: I should tell the Sergeant before he makes a fool of himself.

ENTER GOYA.

GOYA: It is her. She's coming! It's Josefa! How do I look? Alive?

BARBARA NODS.

GOYA: Listen. They're going to be moving the last of the coffins from the lawn onto the fire.
BARBARA: So?
GOYA: Don't let them.
BARBARA: Why not?
GOYA: They're such fine pieces of carpentry.
BARBARA: They're just boxes.
GOYA: Trust me. Don't let them move the coffins.

ENTER XAVIER, FOLLOWED BY A SLEEPY AND IRRITABLE MOREL, AND GUMERSINDA. GOYA DOESN'T HIDE. HE JUST SITS IN A CHAIR, WITH HIS BACK TO THE NEWCOMERS. A GREY LIGHT HAS STARTED TO INFILTRATE. THE FIRE HAS GONE DOWN: DAWN IS IMMINENT.

GUMERSINDA: Why now? Why can't she wait 'til morning?
MOREL: You didn't have to come.
XAVIER: You know what she's like.
MOREL: I couldn't sleep. Not with that terrible smell of burning.
GUMERSINDA: I've got quite used to it.
MOREL: I kept dreaming about houses on fire.
GUMERSINDA: (*Giggles*) How perfectly stupid.

JOLY HAS ENTERED.

JOLY: (*To people following, but as yet out of sight*) This way . . .
MOREL: Pity there's no flowers.

XAVIER: He didn't much care for them. Too normal.

*JOSEFA ENTERS, FOLLOWED BY A PRIEST. SHE IS A
FRAIL LOOKING WOMAN, BUT HER FACE IS STRONG
AND DETERMINED. LUISA IS WITH HER, ESCORTING
HER OVER THE RUBBLE. JOLY CROSSES TO THE COF-
FIN, PULLS THE FLAP OFF AND SLIDES BACK THE LID.*

XAVIER: Now Mama—
JOSEFA: No more Xavier. I will see him.
GUMERSINDA: There's no need.
JOSEFA: There's every need.
XAVIER: Sleep a little. Come back tomorrow when you've rested.
JOSEFA: Show me his face!
GUMERSINDA: He has none.
XAVIER: Ssh!

*GUMERSINDA, SILENCED, MOVES AWAY; MOREL
MOVES AWAY TOO. BARBARA STANDS A LITTLE WAY
OFF, WATCHING. GOYA, SITTING IN HIS CHAIR, IS
BARELY ABLE TO BREATHE WITH THE AGONY OF
THIS MOMENT.*

*THE PRIEST READS FROM THE BIBLE, A MUMBLED
FLOW OF LATIN WHICH IS INDECIPHERABLE.*

*JOSEFA STEPS TO THE COFFIN AND LOOKS IN.
GOYA WATCHES HER FACE. IT REGISTERS A MILD
DISGUST, NOTHING MORE.*

GOYA: (*Very quietly*) Weep, woman. Please weep.

SHE TURNS AWAY, UNTOUCHED BY THE SIGHT.

XAVIER: No tears?
GUMERSINDA: Do you feel sick?
JOSEFA: No tears.
XAVIER: You surprise me, Mama.
JOSEFA: That's not worth crying for.
GOYA: (*Destroyed*) Oh God in Heaven.

JOSEFA: You see it's not him.

GOYA LOOKS UP.

JOSEFA: *(To Xavier)* You careless child. That's not your father. He
  bites his nails down to the quick. This man's nails are cut as
  neatly as a hairdresser's. It isn't him. *(She smiles, tears begin-
  ning)* He's alive. I know he's alive.
GOYA: My sweetest lady.
JOSEFA: Goya?
GOYA: Your servant.
JOSEFA: My husband.
GOYA: Here. Here. Into my arms where you belong.

*THEY EMBRACE. XAVIER, GUMERSINDA AND MOREL
DON'T KNOW WHAT TO MAKE OF IT. THEY STAND,
OPEN-MOUTHED. THE PRIEST, TOO INVOLVED IN HIS
WORDS TO SEE THE RESURRECTION, BABBLES ON.*

XAVIER: Shut up!

THE PRIEST LOOKS UP; SEES; STOPS.

GUMERSINDA: How dare he? He's made fools of us.
XAVIER: Why?
MOREL: It's unbelievable.
JOLY: Shall we . . . ? I mean, I wonder . . . if we should leave?
GUMERSINDA: He's lost his mind.
MOREL: A genius of course.
JOLY: But scarcely civilized.

*MOREL EXITS. GUMERSINDA, OUTRAGED, FOLLOWS
HIM. JOLY GOES TOO, FOLLOWED BY THE PRIEST.*

GOYA HAS SEPARATED FROM JOSEFA.

GOYA: Am I unforgivable?
JOSEFA: Almost.

SHE SMILES.

XAVIER: You don't know the grief you caused, Papa.
GOYA: Oh I do. I saw it with my own two eyes.
XAVIER: I'm your son.
GOYA: God help me, you are.

XAVIER STARTS TO EXIT.

JOSEFA: He feels cheated.
GOYA: Tell him I won't write him out of the will. That'll salve his
    disappointments.
JOSEFA: You'll come too. Away from this terrible place.
GOYA: In a moment.
JOSEFA: Have you slept?
GOYA: For a while, underground.

*THE WOMEN BRING A COFFIN ON, TO TAKE TO
THE FIRE.*

GOYA: What's this?
1st WOMAN: From the lawn.
GOYA: Put it down.
2nd WOMAN: But it's to go to the fire.
GOYA: Let me . . . draw it.
JOSEFA: Goya. You don't want to be drawing coffins.
GOYA: (*Kisses her*) Xavier's waiting. I won't be long; and I'll tell
    you everything I've seen.
XAVIER: (*To Josefa*) What did you marry?
JOSEFA: Nobody you know.

*JOSEFA EXITS WITH XAVIER. THE WOMEN HAVE
PUT THE COFFIN DOWN.*

GOYA: (*To the women*) Go along. Leave me in peace.

THE WOMEN EXIT. GOYA WATCHES THEM GO.

GOYA: Quickly! Stones!
BARBARA: What for?
GOYA: Plenty of stones. Move yourself! And something for the
    lid! Damn you! The lid; there's not much air in these things!

BARBARA OFFERS A KNIFE WHICH GOYA USES TO LEVER THE LID OFF THE COFFIN. INSIDE IS FELIPE. HE GASPS FOR AIR.

BARBARA: Felipe!
FELIPE: *(To Goya)* I thought you'd forgotten me.
GOYA: Oh ye of little faith.
BARBARA: You hid him.
GOYA: I told you he'd lie down in the dark— Didn't I?
BARBARA: Is the wound bad?
GOYA: Bad enough.
FELIPE: I'll live. I swear . . . I will live.
GOYA: Get out of there, and put stones in his place. They can put the coffin on the fire then, and no one's the wiser.

BARBARA HELPS FELIPE OUT OF THE COFFIN.

GOYA: Look at the light. I thought it would never come. Ribbons of it; just look.

BARBARA CRADLES FELIPE.

GOYA: Coming through the smoke like that. Coming down on all this ruin. So confident, as though it's never heard of night. As if it's here forever.

BIRDS BEGIN TO SING. GOYA WATCHES THE LIGHT IN AMAZED SILENCE, WHILE BARBARA STROKES FELIPE'S FACE.

GOYA: What kind of world is this?

AFTER A MOMENT, BARBARA REPLIES WITH CERTAINTY.

BARBARA: Ours.

THE BIRDS SING. THE LIGHTS GO DOWN.

THE PLAY ENDS

FRANKENSTEIN IN LOVE

OR

THE LIFE OF DEATH

A Grand Guignol Romance
Inspired by Mary Shelley's Frankenstein

Production Notes

We can keep this simple. *Frankenstein in Love* is a play designed to disturb and scare its audience; to take them by their clammy hands and lead them into distressing spaces, there to show them sights that they will not readily forget. It is no more realistic, of course, than *The History of the Devil* (in some ways it is less so), but whereas *Devil* presents us with a constantly moving panorama, and despite its often grim subject matter has a kind of perverse lightness about it, *Frankenstein in Love* is a play of dark, airless places that have been long sealed from any hope of sanity. This claustrophobia is, of course, a common device in horror fiction, allowing the readers or spectators no escape from the source of their anxiety, and the theatre is arguably the easiest place to evoke it.

Though the stage instructions at the beginning of the play propose a relatively open, symbolic space—decorated with hanging lights and carnival banners—I now think that may not be the best solution. Doubtless it was the most financially feasible at the time of writing the play—and for some companies might well remain so (hence my leaving the description in place)—but with the benefit of hindsight I wonder if a more confined and solid rendering of the palace and the barrio might not serve the drama better. If I sound tentative about this, it's because I see my function in these notes not as a proscriber but as a guide. Solutions to the challenges of staging are a function of aesthetics, pragmatism and finances (rarely in that order). One space will lend itself to a symbolic solution, another to something more literal. Just as long as the audience feels trapped in an asylum with a cast of wicked, and occasionally inspired, poet psychotics, then the endeavor will be off in the right direction.

In the original production the costumes, which were a particular obsession of the director, were either severe—even puritanical—or fetishistic and sexual. I thought the contrast interesting and pertinent, though I would have liked to have seen more modernity in the designs. They gave off a whiff of the nineteenth century, which distance made the production more reasurringly remote, and reassurance is not what this piece is about. As to the props—which in the Grand Guignol tradition are of no little importance—we did what we could with relatively crude techniques. Clearly the ever greater sophistication of special effects in the cinema makes audiences more critical when judging such illusions, but the stage is far more forgiving than the camera, and the very presence of a distressing sight—right in front of you, where it's not going to be snatched away at the next edit—makes it all the more powerful. Several audience members were driven from their seats by the intensity of it all—a sampling of an experience I'd become familiar with later; there was seldom a screening of *Hellraiser, Candyman,* or *Lord of Illusions* that didn't drive somebody out.

But for all the trickery and effects in the piece, its strength must finally reside in its efficacy as a story. That means discovering a style of performance that services the characters; that makes them understandable, even in their most extreme forms and behaviors. Though the play is subtitled a "Grand Guignol Romance", don't be fooled into thinking that the piece is best mounted as dark "kitsch." It can be a good deal more than that if the project is approached with sufficient seriousness of intention. In its obsessive way, the play creates a kind of alternative world, where everybody is corrupted or corrupt, dead or dying; monstrous in form, deed, or both. A fantasia, if you will, on taboo themes, which refuses to offer much in the way of comfort to its audience. In that singularity of intention lies both its limitation and its potential for theatrical power.

Clive Barker—Los Angeles, 1995

The Cast:

MARIA REINA DURAN: a dead fan dancer
PRESIDENT GARCIA HELIODORO PEREZ: a failed autocrat
COCKATOO: a revolutionary
CESAR GUERRERO; EL COCO: a visionary
VERONIQUE FLECKER: one of Frankenstein's victims
CARDINAL ARMITANO: a Christian
FOLLEZOU ⎱ Two creatures
MALTOS ⎰
LAZARO: a half-wilted friend of Maria's
DR. JOSEPH FRANKENSTEIN: a monster
CAMILO BOZUFFI: a homosexual tailor
DOCTOR FOOK: a cross-dressing pathologist

Act 1:

<u>Scene One</u>

THE PERFORMANCE SPACE IS PART ABATTOIR, PART CARNIVAL, DECORATED WITH BANNERS ILLUS-TRATING VIOLENT SCENES FROM HISTORY AND FICTION. LOOPS OF COLORED LIGHTS HANG OVER THE SPACE, MINGLING WITH BLOODY CHAINS AND BUTCHERS HOOKS.

SMOKE IN THE AIR, FROM A SMOLDERING BUCKET. DISTANTLY, THE SOUND OF EXPLOSIONS AND GUNFIRE. CLOSER, ROMANTIC MUSIC.

ON STAGE, FOR THE FIRST SCENE, TWO NECESSI-TIES: THE HEAD OF A MAN, IMPALED ON A POLE AND COVERED WITH STAINED CLOTH. A COLLEC-TION OF SURGICAL SAWS, DRILLS AND SCALPELS, LAID OUT AS IF FOR AN INTERRUPTED OPERATION.

IDEALLY THERE SHOULD BE OTHER LITTER ON THE STAGE, SUGGESTING A PANICKED DEPARTURE FROM THIS VAULT, AND A FAILED ATTEMPT TO DESTROY EVIDENCE. HYPODERMICS, HALF-BURNED NOTES, BLOODY SHEETS.

*THE MUSIC HAS FADED. THE NOISE OF THE DIS-
TANT BATTLE CONTINUES. BLACKOUT.*

IN THE DARKNESS, EXPLOSIONS, SCREAMS, HOWLS.

*A LIGHT ON MARIA REINA DURAN, A FAN-DANCER.
SHE LOOKS DEAD. SHE WEARS HER SHROUD,
ROUGHLY COVERING HER SEXY DRESS.*

MARIA: It is the last, long night of the world. The last, the very last.
Tomorrow . . . (*Shrugs*). Expect an apocalypse. How should I
know this? Well, my name is Maria Reina Duran. I was, until
recently, a palm reader, a fan-dancer, and alive. I'm now none
of those. I came here tonight a walking corpse, to show you
the story I read on my murderer's palms. I call it *Frankenstein
In Love*, or *The Life of Death*. Some of this story has already
happened, but the worst is yet to come. I can see the future. I
know there are monsters out there tonight, roaming around,
looking for love. And when they find it . . . endless night.

I must be quick. My brain's turning to mush. Flies find
me increasingly attractive.

You are buried alive in a nameless city, in the vault
beneath the palace of President Garcia Heliodoro Perez. It is
yesterday. (*Takes off her shroud*) I was alive yesterday.

The walls here are slimy with human grease, for this was the
operating room of Dr. Joseph Frankenstein, surgeon. Atrocities
were committed here in the name of God and Science, acts so
obscene they beggar words. So we must show you—(*Crosses to
the shrouded head and goes to pull off the cloth*) But no. You don't
want to see the appalling sight beneath this cloth. Do you?
You're not sick, like some I could mention. The author for one.
I won't offend you with it. You look disappointed.

*ENTER PRESIDENT GARCIA HELIODORO PEREZ, IN
HIS ONCE-SPLENDID UNIFORM. HIS FACE IS A BALL
OF GREASE, AND YELLOWISH. HIS CRUDELY APPLIED
ROUGE AND MASCARA IS RUNNING. HE CARRIES, IN
A GLOVED HAND, A REVOLVER. HE SEES MARIA. HE
LEVELS THE GUN AT HER.*

PEREZ: Who are you?

MARIA: (*Laughs*) This is President Garcia Heliodoro Perez. Last night he ruled the world. This morning he can barely control his own bladder.

PEREZ: Are you with the rebels?

MARIA: No. I'm just a ghost.

PEREZ: Ghosts can be Marxist. (*He fires—click*) No bullets!

MARIA: You've been busy.

PEREZ: They won't catch me.

MARIA: You should have kept a bullet for yourself.

PEREZ: I had to shoot my stallions. I couldn't let the rebels take them, they would have ridden them to death. I had to be compassionate.

MARIA: (*To audience*) They say he ate babies. Now don't look so shocked. Eating babies is least of tonight's entertainments.

PEREZ: What is this place?

MARIA: Dr. Frankenstein's workshop.

PEREZ PEERS IN A BUCKET.

MARIA: They'll blame you for this.

PEREZ: Am I my doctor's keeper? If there were crimes, let him answer for them.

MARIA: Didn't you sniff the stench?

PEREZ: I thought it was the sewers. Or the kitchens. (*Goes to the sheet as if to pluck it off, then thinks better of it*) Human experiments, were they?

MARIA: Pray you die before you see them.

PEREZ: I won't die. Oh no, no. I have friends, phantasma. In Washington. Here, a letter from the American President of Vice.

MARIA: Vice President.

PEREZ: (*Reads*) "The administration recognizes your invaluable services to the cause of democracy . . . your regime is"—here it's torn. They'll maybe send an eagle for me, in a day or two. I'll be snatched away. If I can escape from the city. Get into the mountains.

MARIA: There are beasts in the mountains.

PEREZ: There are beasts here, with machine guns. (*Goes to leave*)

MARIA: Not that way. That's his funeral parlor.

PEREZ: I'm not scared of the dead.

MARIA: The dead don't stay dead down here. What's a mortuary to some was a cradle to him. He used to take them in his arms and sing them lullabies.

PEREZ: He sang to cadavers? Would nobody else listen?

MARIA: He was their mother; he kissed them into life, he suckled them, rocked them—

PEREZ: Impossible. If you could raise the dead, life wouldn't be worth living.

MARIA: He didn't just raise them—he cut them up, made new children—endless combinations. Day old babies with horses' heads.

PEREZ: He did violence to horses? Shame on him.

MARIA: Have you ever seen a man turned inside out? Wearing his entrails as a skirt?

PEREZ: I don't want to know.

MARIA: Go look for yourself. He tried to cremate the worst of them before he escaped, but I'm sure there'll be some putrefying thing left crawling around.

PEREZ: I can't, I have ulcers. My stomach's weak.

MARIA: Wise man. It would turn your hair white.

PEREZ: Is there no other way out?

MARIA: (*Picks up a knife*) Slit your wrists.

PEREZ: I meant a door.

MARIA: They'll make you suffer if they catch you. The poor in the Barrios, they want your hide. You bled them dry.

PEREZ: Ingrates! I built them an opera house.

MARIA: Let them eat Verdi.

PEREZ: I love Verdi. What will they do to me?

MARIA: What's the worst you can imagine?

PEREZ: No, not that.

MARIA: It'll be worse, I guarantee it. Slit your wrists.

PEREZ: Give me a scalpel. Ah, it's sticky. Ave Maria Purisima—(*He is about to slit his wrists*) Who's breathing? There's something alive in here.

MARIA: Not guilty.

HE REALIZES THE BREATHING COMES FROM BENEATH THE SHEET. HE CROSSES TO IT AND PULLS IT OFF, REVEALING THE SCREAMING HEAD OF A MIDDLE-AGED MAN. CICERO, IMPALED ON A

POLE. HE IS STILL ALIVE, THOUGH THE TOP OF HIS SKULL HAS BEEN SAWN OFF TO EXPOSE HIS BRAIN, FROM WHICH WIRES EMANATE. THE SEVERED NECK IS FED WITH BLOOD-FILLED PIPES. HE SHRIEKS AS THE LIGHT HITS HIM.

PEREZ: No! Not Cicero!

MARIA: You know him?

PEREZ: Know him? He was my dearest friend. I had him shot. He was planning a coup. I saw his body myself. Frankenstein did the autopsy. Was he responsible?

MARIA: Ask your friend.

PEREZ: Do you hear me Cicero?

THE HEAD MOANS.

PEREZ: Can you speak?

THE HEAD MAKES INCOHERENT NOISES.

PEREZ: Why did he do this?

MARIA: Maybe he wanted company?

PEREZ: Cicero was always well-read. That's what made him dangerous. Do you hear me Cicero?

MORE MOANS.

PEREZ: Do you know me? It's Garcia. Cicero, remember me? I want to know who did this, Cicero. Who was responsible for this? Was it Frankenstein?

THE HEAD BEGINS A KEENING SOUND, WHICH BECOMES A SCREECH OF FRUSTRATED FURY.

PEREZ: It *was* Frankenstein! Thank you.

THE SCREAMING CONTINUES.

PEREZ: I said thank you. You may be quiet a while my friend. My friend! Quiet, I said. There's some people upstairs that mean me harm, so hush your row. Rebels, burning the palace, shooting the cooks. Please be quiet, Cicero. I can't hear myself think. (*Covers the mouth with his hand*) Ssh! Ssh! You've got no right to make a noise, amigo, because you've got no hands. And those who can't do should keep their mouth shut. Ah! (*Removes his hand, bloodied*) He bit me, the bastard bit me! He's mad—

MARIA: Well, I wouldn't be very pleased.

PEREZ: Shut up! I command you! Shut up!

COCKATOO: (*Off*) Cesar—there's somebody down here.

PEREZ: Now see what you've done.

COCKATOO: Cesar! This way! Voices! This way!

PEREZ: (*Picking up the scalpel*) Shut your mouth, damn you. (*Drives the knife into Cicero's exposed brain—blood pours down the face and out of the mouth*) Hush, damn you, hush!

HE HACKS AT THE HEAD, DEMANDING THAT IT KEEP QUIET, UNTIL THE SCREECHING FALTERS AND DIES AWAY. HE IS EXHAUSTED BY HIS EFFORTS. HE DROPS THE SCALPEL, BREATHLESS, AND FALLS TO HIS KNEES.

PEREZ: Hush, Cicero . . . hush, my friend, or they'll find us. And we don't want that do we? (*Starts to cry*)

MARIA: What's the matter?

PEREZ: (*Looks at his hand*) Brain-tissue, mostly.

MARIA: Are you always so good to your friends?

PEREZ: I had to do it. I mean, the poor man was suffering the torments of the damned. You'll tell them, won't you, that I did it out of compassion?

MARIA: I can't tell them. I'm just a visitor.

PEREZ: You must. They're coming for me. You must! Phantasma, I beg you.

MARIA: They won't even see me. I'm dead and visiting from the future.

PEREZ: I see you!

MARIA: That's because you're almost dead yourself.

EXIT MARIA.

PEREZ: No! Don't say that! No! Don't leave me woman. I demand you stay.

ENTER COCKATOO. HE IS A REVOLUTIONARY AND A DANDY. HE IS DRESSED IN A BRILLIANTLY COLORED SELECTION OF LOOTED CLOTHES. HE WEARS COCKATOO FEATHERS IN HIS CAP AND A BROAD GRIN ON HIS FACE. HE HAS A MOUSTACHE AND BEARD A LA FRANK ZAPPA. HE CARRIES A MACHINE GUN, WHICH HE POINTS AT PEREZ.

COCKATOO: Well, well—

PEREZ: No, not at all. I'm feeling very sick.

COCKATOO: We've been looking for you.

PEREZ: Welcome, a thousand welcomes. My Government and I . . . and I . . .

COCKATOO: (*Sees the head*) Dios mio, who's this?

PEREZ: I'm not responsible. It was Frankenstein—

COCKATOO: Still warm.

PEREZ: It's unsupportable. I'm losing my mind.

COCKATOO: That makes two of you.

PEREZ: Who do I have . . . the honor . . . of addressing.

COCKATOO: Juan Thomas Navarro of the People's Revolutionary Militia. Also called Cockatoo.

PEREZ: I can see why. Very fetching.

COCKATOO: We found your horses. They're all dead. You?

PEREZ: Yes.

COCKATOO: Just to stop us from having them?

PEREZ: They were thoroughbreds. You couldn't treat them properly. You've no idea of dignity, honor—

COCKATOO: Honor? Pig features. I'll give you honor.

PEREZ: Shoot me then.

COCKATOO: Oh no.

PEREZ: You wouldn't dare, would you?

COCKATOO: If I was in charge, you'd be slow roasted, with a spit up your middle. But Cesar, El Coco, he wants you tried.

PEREZ: El Coco, ha! The Bogey-Man. Was that the best you could manage, to terrify the people into submission? You're innocents aren't you? You won't hold power for more than a week. El Coco! Ha!

COCKATOO: Don't anger me.

PEREZ: What'll you do? Scare me to death?

HE GOES TO STRIKE PEREZ, WHO COWERS.

ENTER CESAR GUERRERO, EL COCO. HIS FLESH IS A PATCH-WORK—PART RED, PART BLACK, PART WHITE, AND BADLY SCARRED. HIS LONG, BLACK HAIR IS KNOTTED. HE WEARS CLOTHES ALL OF ONE COLOR, IN AN ATTEMPT TO UNIFY A BODY THAT SEEMS AT WAR WITH ITSELF. HIS GAIT IS UNEASY, HIS TORSO CROOKED. HIS ARMS AND FINGERS TWITCH; ONLY HIS FACE IS STILL.

HE CARRIES A BOTTLE OF SALT WATER, FROM WHICH HE DRINKS. HE IS NOT ARMED.

EL COCO: If it pleases you to strike, strike. If it pleases you not, then not. But don't torment him, Cockatoo. He may look like a slug, but he's some mother's child.

COCKATOO: Cesar. I—

EL COCO: No matter.

COCKATOO: I thought you'd lost your way.

EL COCO: I had to prepare myself. (*He drinks*)

COCKATOO: It's not so bad.

PEREZ: This is El Coco? This is the hero of the people?

EL COCO: Cesar Guerrero, of the People's Revolutionary Militia. Garcia Perez, I arrest you for crimes against humanity.

PEREZ: What crimes?

COCKATOO: You pig.

PEREZ: That's not a crime, it's a description.

EL COCO: You will be tried.

PEREZ: Under what law?

EL COCO: New laws.

PEREZ: Yours?

EL COCO: Mine, and the people's.

PEREZ: It's the same game with a different ball. You're no different to me except you're frightened.

COCKATOO: Eh?

EL COCO: Let him be.

PEREZ: Shaking.

COCKATOO: You shut your mouth—

EL COCO: No, he's right, Cockatoo. He's got eyes in his head. This place makes me want to puke. (*He drinks again*)

PEREZ: What's your poison? Brandy?

EL COCO: You want some?

PEREZ: My mouth's full of sawdust. Thank you. (*He drinks and spits it out*)

PEREZ: Brine.

EL COCO: Salt water.

PEREZ: It drives you mad.

EL COCO: Then be polite.

PEREZ: You've destroyed half of my city, and you ask me to be polite.

EL COCO: The army ran riot.

PEREZ: The army?

EL COCO: Your men, not mine.

COCKATOO: They were with us within two hours.

EL COCO: Except for the Generals.

COCKATOO: Who are now with God.

PEREZ: Lynched?

EL COCO: Publicly executed.

PEREZ: Excrement!

EL COCO: If I'm excrement, and you're less than me, what does that make you? Better your mother never made you, never suckled you, never called you Garcia Perez. Better you were nothing than to be less than shit.

PEREZ: I'm sorry. Don't hurt me.

EL COCO: I don't want to hurt you.

PEREZ: And I don't want to be hurt. So we have some common policies. I can help you. I was only saying to your parrot how many problems there are to power. Twists and turns.

EL COCO: Would you follow me?

PEREZ: Of course. At your heel.

EL COCO: I walk barefoot on white-hot coals, had you heard that?

PEREZ: There were rumors of your performances. They might have deceived the people in the mountains, but here we're too sophisticated. You need a speech writer . . .

EL COCO: I bathe in fire; I wash by standing in the burning heart of furnaces. Would you follow me there?

PEREZ: Come now—

EL COCO: Would you?

PEREZ: If you taught me the trick of it.

EL COCO: There is no trick. I do it.

COCKATOO: I've seen him.

PEREZ: Then perhaps you were . . . deceived.

EL COCO: Cockatoo. Take the dead man's head and bury it, will you?

PEREZ: His mortuary is—(*He points*) if you have the stomach for it.

COCKATOO REMOVES THE HEAD AND WRAPS IT IN THE SHEET THAT COVERED IT.

PEREZ: Alas poor Cicero—I knew him well.

COCKATOO EXITS WITH THE HEAD

EL COCO: Where is Frankenstein?

PEREZ: I don't know.

EL COCO: He was your creature.

PEREZ: He went his own way. I fed him my enemies. He had his business, I left him to it. Truly, I don't know. He frightened me. I never asked questions of him.

EL COCO: I won't torment you Perez, though by God they want me to. But if you once lie to me, I'll let Cockatoo have you and he'll castrate you with his teeth. And then while you're bleeding to death he'll feed you like a child, fill your mouth up with your own meat. I trust I appall you.

PEREZ: You appall me.

EL COCO: Where is he?

PEREZ: He had secret places. A whore-house in the Barrios. He was fond of the mortuary of the Hospital of the Innocents, and the Cathedral to make confession. He could be anywhere.

EL COCO: That's sufficient.

PEREZ: I never understood, Guerrero, for my soul's sake believe me. I'm greedy maybe, stupid even, but this . . .

EL COCO: I believe you.

PEREZ: It's profane.

EL COCO: No. Quite the contrary. I think God probably approves.

OFF STAGE, COCKATOO YELLS.

EL COCO: Cockatoo!
PEREZ: Is that one of his lullabies?

ENTER COCKATOO, HIS FACE SCRATCHED.

COCKATOO: Ah! It nearly took off my face.
PEREZ: Is there something left alive down there? Shoot it! Shoot it!
COCKATOO: It nearly killed me—
EL COCO: No, Cockatoo.
COCKATOO: If you won't, I will. (*He picks up his machine gun*)
PEREZ: Something's missing.
COCKATOO: Bastard!
EL COCO: Wait!

ENTER VERONIQUE FLECKER, HER HANDS BLOODY, HER EYES WILD. SHE HAS BEEN A PRISONER OF FRANKENSTEIN'S FOR A YEAR, THE SUBJECT OF HIS RAPES AND EXPERIMENTS.

COCKATOO: A woman!
PEREZ: Shoot her! She's wild. Shoot her.
EL COCO: Come no closer.
PEREZ: She's insane. Look at her eyes.

SHE STOPS AND STARES AT COCKATOO, WHO LOWERS HIS GUN.

COCKATOO: I won't shoot a woman.
VERONIQUE: I thought you were Frankenstein.
EL COCO: He's gone.
VERONIQUE: You let him escape. Imbecile. Don't you know what he's done?
COCKATOO: There's bodies in there, burned to hell.
VERONIQUE: I would have killed you, but you don't wear his perfume.
EL COCO: What are you doing down here?
VERONIQUE: Perez.

PEREZ: I don't know this woman.

VERONIQUE: Have you forgotten? It's a year since we met.

PEREZ: I don't recall the face.

VERONIQUE: I've changed. He's worked on me. I came to you appealing for my husband's life. Do you remember now? Veronique Flecker? My husband was arrested as a spy—

PEREZ: I don't—

VERONIQUE: —and tortured to death.

PEREZ: No!

VERONIQUE: I found his arm down here, grafted onto another man's belly. I recognized his ring.

EL COCO: And you?

VERONIQUE: Given to Frankenstein to play with, to silence me.

EL COCO: But you've survived.

VERONIQUE: He thought I was dead. Buried me alive in his slaughter-house, under a heap of human debris.

EL COCO: Are there any other survivors?

VERONIQUE: He burned them all in their cages. What's left isn't worth pitying.

EL COCO: Cockatoo, fetch some men and have the place scoured.

VERONIQUE: No! Leave them be. They don't want to be stared at and puked over any longer.

COCKATOO: Don't talk to him like that.

VERONIQUE: So shoot me for it. You're El Coco, aren't you?

EL COCO: How did you know?

VERONIQUE: My husband talked about you. That appalling face, he knew your face. Said you were like a salamander. Live in fire.

EL COCO: That's right.

VERONIQUE: Well, we have no need of you here. This is hell. Fire-walking's common knowledge.

EL COCO: Will you give evidence to the People's Courts?

VERONIQUE: There are no words. We had a Cardinal down here. He used to come and bless the scalpels, and then watch Frankenstein at work. He liked vivisections best. (*Points to Perez*) And him too—

PEREZ: I knew nothing.

VERONIQUE: He came, once only. A little slop of bile stained his cuff. He never came again. But he knew—

PEREZ: I didn't understand.

VERONIQUE: If I had a knife—

PEREZ: There was no help for it. They were traitors anyway—the children of traitors—human trash.

VERONIQUE: Yes, I've learned that lesson. Flesh is trash. Its natural state is meat. Everybody is just meat. The rest is the will to be more than meat.

EL COCO: Give her a knife, Cockatoo.

COCKATOO: You must be kidding.

EL COCO: You heard her. She wants a knife.

PEREZ: No. She'll slit me—

COCKATOO: We need him, Cesar.

EL COCO: She needs him more than we do. Give her a knife and let her do her work.

COCKATOO TAKES A KNIFE FROM HIS BELT AND OFFERS IT.

EL COCO: Use it, or never dare call for justice again.

PEREZ: No, no—anything; not death. Have my balls—you want my balls? Have my balls.

EL COCO WALKS AWAY AND PLAYS DICE WITH HIS LEFT HAND.

PEREZ: He doesn't mean it.

COCKATOO: Cesar. She'll do it.

VERONIQUE STABS PEREZ. HE SCREAMS.

PEREZ: Bad cut! Bad cut!

EL COCO: Instruct her then.

PEREZ: Deeper!

VERONIQUE PRESSES THE KNIFE HOME.

PEREZ: Now up! Up!

SHE DRAWS THE KNIFE UPWARDS AND THE PRESIDENT HOWLS.

PEREZ: Enough.

SHE PULLS IT OUT. THE PRESIDENT COLLAPSES TO THE GROUND.

PEREZ: (*Choking*) Better . . . Better . . .
EL COCO: You'd do well in an abbatoir.
PEREZ: Confess me—
VERONIQUE: Ha!
PEREZ: Confess me—

EL COCO GOES TO HIM.

EL COCO: Padre Nuestro que estas en los cielos, santificado su hu nombre venga en tuerinio—

THE PRESIDENT DIES.

EL COCO: And so to bed.
COCKATOO: We could have had a show-trial. You wanted him alive.
EL COCO: We can still judge him, Cockatoo. As long as we don't find him innocent.
COCKATOO: Stupid waste, stupid. Just to indulge a woman.
EL COCO: Take him away, Cockatoo, and show him to the crowd. They'll be pleased to see him—alive or dead.

COCKATOO, UNSMILING, REMOVES THE BODY.

VERONIQUE: It was easy.
EL COCO: He wanted to die.
VERONIQUE: You comforted him, as though he was a child.
EL COCO: You wanted justice, not to torture his soul.
VERONIQUE: Soul? That?
EL COCO: Yes, even that.
VERONIQUE: Well, what do we have here? A pious Marxist?
EL COCO: Where are you going?
VERONIQUE: I have business with friends. And with the Cardinal.
EL COCO: Won't you testify? Accuse the Cardinal publicly?
VERONIQUE: There's no pleasure in that. I want him to go God-less in the night with his heart in his mouth. Literally.
EL COCO: Listen to me. Tonight, tomorrow maybe, you're safe to commit murder. After that, there will be law, my law, and

you'll be judged by it. So do your justice quickly, before it
becomes a crime.

VERONIQUE: Do you really walk on fire?

EL COCO: Only when I'm cold.

VERONIQUE: And now?

EL COCO: Freezing.

*EXIT VERONIQUE. AS SHE GOES EL COCO, NOW
ALONE, ROLLS UP HIS SLEEVE AND TAKES OUT A
HYPODERMIC. HE INJECTS HIMSELF WITH HEROIN.*

EL COCO: . . . Father . . .

*BELLS RING OUT IN CELEBRATION. AS THE LIGHTS
GO DOWN, EL COCO IS IN ECSTACY, BROUGHT ON
BY THE HEROIN.*

Scene Two

*OUT OF THE DARKNESS, A CHORD, FOLLOWED BY
A BRASH MUSIC. A LIGHT ON MARIA, WHO PER-
FORMS HER FAN-DANCE FOR COCKATOO, WHO IS
SITTING, WATCHING HER. SHE FINISHES, AND HE
EMBRACES HER.*

COCKATOO: God you're good. You should be in Rio. They'd love
an act like that in Rio. You wouldn't get out alive. (*Kisses her*)

DISTANT SHOUTING, THEN SHOTS, AND CHEERING.

MARIA: What are they doing?

COCKATOO: Executing the old Presidential Guard.

MARIA: Who's doing it?

COCKATOO: The new Presidential Guard.

MARIA: I want to go out and see.

COCKATOO: We'll look at the bodies tomorrow. They'll be on display at the Opera House.

MARIA: Are they blindfolded?

COCKATOO: How should I know?

MARIA: Do you think they see it coming? The bullet, I mean.

COCKATOO: I don't know. I don't think about it. They're geeks, and they're getting what they deserve.

MARIA: What's a geek?

COCKATOO: It's a thing, it's a freak. They have them in Mexico, in the Carnivals. You pay money to watch them bite the heads off live chickens.

MARIA: Really?

COCKATOO: And then you watch the chickens running around with no heads wondering who put the lights out. Are you a whore?

MARIA: What's it to you?

COCKATOO: I just want to know whether I have to pay for it.

MARIA: It comes free to the heroes of the revolution.

COCKATOO: You are a whore.

MARIA: It's my body, I'll do what I like with it.

COCKATOO: Better make the most of it.

MARIA: Oh, I've got other skills.

COCKATOO: Nobody will want a forty year old fan-dancer.

MARIA: I read palms.

COCKATOO: Shit.

MARIA: I can read the past and the future in hands.

COCKATOO: We're not having any more of that—no more superstitious stuff like that. It's one of the first articles of the Revolutionary Manifesto: liberation of the people from all sources of metaphysical conditioning. Everything from palm readers to the Pope.

MARIA: The Church? You wouldn't dare.

COCKATOO: Cesar would dare. How do you think we lived in the jungle? How do you think we bought guns? We killed priests and we raided churches. There's money in churches.

MARIA: Really?

COCKATOO: Easy.

MARIA: You're not scared?

COCKATOO: Nothing scares me. I'm too stupid to get scared.

MARIA: So I can't even read palms?

COCKATOO: It's magic. It'll be forbidden by law.

MARIA: Cesar Guerrero calls himself El Coco, the Bogey-Man. That's a superstition, isn't it? He'll have to forbid himself, won't he?

COCKATOO: He doesn't believe in magic any more than I do. It's a trick for peasants. He'll become a man of state like a proper President. He'll go to the U.N., tell them our demands. I'm going to be Minister of Football.

MARIA: Ask him to make me Minister of Brothels then. We'll turn the Presidential Palace into a whore-house. Women in the upper rooms, boys on this floor, and donkeys in the vaults, for the Cubans.

COCKATOO: And the Yankees.

MARIA: I'll be the madam, fat as a cat, dripping with gold. And I'll entertain the National Football Team, once a week, at a reduced rate. Maybe we'll have a geek too, in the very deepest hole, and for a special price you get lowered into this hole and it's yours for the night.

COCKATOO: If you can last out that long. Geeks don't have much of a clue about sex, you know.

MARIA: No?

COCKATOO: They've got no brains. They just slobber. (*He crawls after her*) With their tongues hanging out. (*He creeps under her dress*) But they like to be thrown a fish once in a while. Once they get their hands on a wet, sloppy fish, there's no stopping them. They just go berserk. Start pulling off its skin, licking it all over—(*He is stripping her, she is stripping him*) then they start eating them, snaffling away like there's no tomorrow—

MARIA: Go on, go on—

COCKATOO: —biting and slashing and ripping it up, pulling it open, wide open, putting its nose, putting its tongue in, putting its head in—

MARIA: Yes. Yes. Yes. Yes. Yes. Yes.

COCKATOO: Wild. Wild—

MARIA: Come on—

COCKATOO: No stopping it.

MARIA: Go on—

AS THEY MAKE LOVE, A FIGURE APPEARS IN THE

SHADOWS. IT IS EL COCO. HE WATCHES THEM, ENTRANCED. HIS STARE IS LUNATIC.

MARIA: Go on—go on—please—please—STOP!
COCKATOO: Stop?
MARIA: There's somebody there.
COCKATOO: Let them watch.
MARIA: No!

EL COCO DISAPPEARS.

COCKATOO: Damn you.
MARIA: Eyes on fire. God, the eyes on him.
COCKATOO: Some drunken soldier—
MARIA: I feel sick.
COCKATOO: Don't be stupid.
MARIA: It was staring at us, like a—
COCKATOO: Like what?
MARIA: Like your precious geek.
COCKATOO: I tell you, you'd better be a good palm-reader, 'cos you're a lousy lay—
MARIA: What's that smell?
COCKATOO: They're burning bodies in the courtyard. I'm going to take a look. A damn sight more fun than you—
MARIA: I'm frightened. Don't leave me here.
COCKATOO: I don't want you.
MARIA: I saw someone—
COCKATOO: Don't tell me you've never done it in public before.
MARIA: Bastard.
COCKATOO: I love you too.

EXIT COCKATOO, LEAVING MARIA, PARTIALLY UN-DRESSED, SITTING ON THE FLOOR, SHE WANTS TO CRY. SHE SNIFFS, SHE CURSES, THEN SHE STARTS TO DRESS. EL COCO IS STILL THERE, IN THE DARK.

MARIA: Who's there?

SILENCE

MARIA: Please answer. Who are you?

EL COCO: Nobody.

MARIA: Well, it's been very nice not to meet you. Will you leave me alone, please? I don't like being watched.

EL COCO: I like to watch you. I'm not going to hurt you.

MARIA: Cockatoo—

EL COCO: He's gone.

MARIA: Why were you staring at us?

EL COCO: Curiosity.

MARIA: Never done it?

EL COCO: No.

MARIA: Want to try?

SILENCE

MARIA: Is that it?

SILENCE

MARIA: Do you want to try?

EL COCO: No.

MARIA: Who are you?

EL COCO: Nobody.

MARIA: Tell me. I'm not going to spread it around. If you just want to watch, that's all right. Just tell me who you are.

EL COCO: Go away.

MARIA: What!

EL COCO: Go away now, quickly.

MARIA: I'm not a dog, you can't kick me out. This is the People's Palace.

EL COCO: You're not people, you're a whore. Go. Quickly

MARIA: Are you all right?

EL COCO: Go—

MARIA: Yes.

SHE TURNS TO GO. SUDDENLY HE'S ON HER, HIS RIGHT HAND HAS HOLD OF HER.

MARIA: Ah!

EL COCO: Go on!

MARIA: I can't—you've got hold of me—
EL COCO: Break free.
MARIA: What—
EL COCO: Fight me off—
MARIA: Is that what you want? Who are you?
EL COCO: Cesar Guerrero.
MARIA: No you're not. You're with his rebels, is that it?
EL COCO: I'm not going to kill you.
MARIA: Are you trying to frighten me? Is that it? Well you're suc-
    ceeding. I'm frightened. You've no reason to hurt me.
EL COCO: Don't need a reason.
MARIA: I'm just a fan-dancer and—
EL COCO: And—
MARIA: I read palms.
EL COCO: Mine? Read mine.
MARIA: Show me your palms then.

HE SHOWS HIS LEFT.

MARIA: Both of them.

*HE LOOSES HER, BUT THE RIGHT HAND AUTOMAT-
ICALLY MAKES A FIST.*

MARIA: Open your hand. (*He does so*) That's better.
EL COCO: I could catch you if you ran.
MARIA: I know. Let me look at your hands. (*She looks at them, back
    and forth; the realization of what she's seeing dawns on her*) Dios
    mio.
EL COCO: What do you see?
MARIA: Your hands—
EL COCO: Yes?
MARIA: Your hands, they're odd. They don't match. Why don't
    your hands match?
EL COCO: Poor workmanship. Read!
MARIA: It frightens me.
EL COCO: Read!
MARIA: I can't make sense of two futures. They're different.
EL COCO: Tell me what's there. Please . . .
MARIA: (*She looks at the left hand*) Gentle. (*Right hand*) Murderer.

(*Left hand*) No children. (*Right hand*) No father. (*Left hand*)
Long life. (*Right hand*) Short life, dead, already over. It makes
no sense. (*Left hand*) Old. (*Right hand*) Young. It's all contra-
dictions. It's nonsense.

EL COCO: Read. The future.

MARIA: There's no future for dead men. Wait. The life line stops
and starts again. (*Left hand*) Success. (*Right hand*) Violent
death. (*Left hand*) And yet success. (*Right hand*) Horrors,
pain, murder. You commit murder. Many murders. (*Left
hand*) Joy, marriage, love forever.

EL COCO: Love?

MARIA: Happy now?

EL COCO: You wouldn't lie?

MARIA: There's no pattern to it. Just chaos.

EL COCO: I'll make sense of it.

MARIA: Which hand is yours?

EL COCO: Neither.

MARIA: If those aren't your hands, then that's not your future.

EL COCO: They don't belong to me, but I belong to them. What
else did you see?

MARIA: Power. A crown. Who are you?

EL COCO: I can tell you who my hands are. This (*The left*) is a
writer's hand. He died old and blind. He wants nothing better
than to hold a pen and write fictions. He obeys me, sometimes.

MARIA: And the other one?

EL COCO: A dice-player. He shot his children, then himself.

MARIA: A young man?

EL COCO: Twenty-three. Impulsive, proud, angry. He wants freedom.
He wants to be away, off like a spider to find a grave. Sometimes
I see him smiling at me with his creases and his tucks. They hate
each other—the writer and the dice-player. And you know
what's worst about that? I can't pray (*Brings his hands together,
they fight*) because they hate each other so much. (*Pulls them
apart*) Is there salvation for a man whose hands won't pray?

MARIA: I suggest you see a doctor.

EL COCO: A doctor did it.

MARIA: Then cut them off.

EL COCO: How can I cut off my own hands? The dice-player
would know, wouldn't he, and he'd lose his temper. I can't
plot against my own body.

MARIA: Your hand doesn't look that lethal—

EL COCO: You don't know what appetites . . . (*The right hand takes hold of Maria by the throat*) Did you see this on my hand? Did you see this Maria Reina Duran?

MARIA: How do you know my name?

EL COCO: I listen. I'm behind every wall.

MARIA: Please don't . . .

EL COCO: Why didn't you run from me? I wanted you to.

MARIA: There's more—

EL COCO: What?

MARIA: On your hands. Worse. I'd rather be dead.

EL COCO: What else?

MARIA: Kill me.

EL COCO: What?

MARIA: Kill me!

EL COCO: Yes. Yes. Yes.

HE STRANGLES HER, SINGLE-HANDED.

EL COCO: (*To his hand*) Now look what you've done. Ah! Cockatoo, Cockatoo! Find me, please. Come and find me red-handed. I'll wait. Just come, kill me justly. Let me go home Cockatoo, stop me before I kill everyone who has ever loved me. Kill me. (*He changes—a wolfish grin*) Or give me the world. I have a hunger, I have an endless thirst. Give me the world. (*Looks down at the body of Maria*) Beautiful. Sweet. Beautiful. (*Caresses the body*) I dreamt last night, Maria. I dreamt all the men and women on earth were one huge beast. Are you listening? It had a billion arms, this beast, and a billion eyes, and it was roaming through the stars like a wild thing, peering behind planets, putting its head into the hearts of suns. Then it turned its head toward me, and its eyes rested on me, and I knew its look. It was searching for love Maria, for another like itself, aching not to be left alone. It's the only thing we have in common—a lack of love. The lice are leaving your hair. I must be going too. Good night.

HE EXITS. AFTER A BEAT, MARIA SITS UP.

MARIA: Cheek! Lice. I don't have lice. He was gentle, killing me.

Not cruel, like the lovers I've had. And the hands, I didn't guess what it meant. Well, what would you think? Bad workmanship, he said. That was the truth, had I known it. Well, that's my murder over. I needn't pretend life any longer. The ghost goes her way, rejoicing.

MARIA DOESN'T LEAVE. PERHAPS SHE HELPS TO SET THE NEXT SCENE. A BOY SOPRANO BEGINS TO SING. THE LIGHTS CHANGE.

Scene Three

AN ALTAR. ENTER CARDINAL ARMITANO. HE KNEELS IN FRONT OF THE ALTAR AND PRAYS.

MARIA: Useless, praying for a miracle.

CARDINAL TURNS. HE HAS A LARGE KNIFE.

CARDINAL: (*With disgust*) Ah. One frightened whore.
MARIA: And one frightened Cardinal. We make quite a pair.
CARDINAL: They stole the Holy Relics.
MARIA: No.
CARDINAL: The phial of the Virgin Mother's milk, and the sacred bones of St. Paul.
MARIA: Three shin bones.
CARDINAL: This is the apocalypse.
MARIA: My very words.
CARDINAL: The four horsemen are riding up from the corners of the world to cut us down. All of us.
MARIA: How will they know the Marxists from the Catholics?
CARDINAL: No one will survive. The time for distinctions is past. Everyone goes to the wall.

MARIA: You too?

CARDINAL: I won't be here.

MARIA: But your flock?

CARDINAL: So much mutton.

MARIA: I thought I heard you praying for a miracle.

CARDINAL: I was praying, if you must know, for a well-fueled Ford sedan. I can't wait much longer. If he doesn't come soon, I'll go without him.

MARIA: Who are you expecting?

CARDINAL: Frankenstein. You won't have heard of him, but he's a great man.

A NOISE

CARDINAL: Joseph? Is that you? Joseph. Come out of the dark, please. Go on whore, fetch him.

MARIA: He's your friend—you fetch him.

CARDINAL: (*Steps forward*) Joseph?

ENTER VERONIQUE, CARRYING A HEAVY BOX.

CARDINAL: Who are you?

VERONIQUE: The doctor's not here.

CARDINAL: Why not?

VERONIQUE: He's wounded.

CARDINAL: Badly?

VERONIQUE: He was shot trying to make his escape. He's dying.

CARDINAL: Animals! How did you get in here? The children at the doors are armed. They had instructions not to let anyone in but Frankenstein.

VERONIQUE: The boys have gone. There's nobody here.

CARDINAL: Oh yes, there's a whore—(*Can no longer see her*) somewhere. What is it smells?

VERONIQUE: Me. I came through the sewers. It's safer.

CARDINAL: Is there rioting?

VERONIQUE: Not now. They have entertainments, to keep the people happy. Fire-eating—

CARDINAL: Ha! When the Perez Junta took power they blindfolded the Democrats, gave them axes, and set them on each other. Now that's what I call entertainment. You know they've shot priests, these gentlemen fire-eaters? Godless bastards. In cold blood. At the alter. Wafer in hand. The body of Christ—

VERONIQUE: Dr. Frankenstein sends his love to you.

CARDINAL: And mine to him. The Holy Mother bless him and keep him.

VERONIQUE: And he sends you this. By way of farewell.

CARDINAL: A gift?

VERONIQUE: A gift.

CARDINAL: He's kind. He was the kindest man I ever knew. Too kind, with all his good works. What is this?

VERONIQUE: A keepsake.

CARDINAL: Is there a key?

VERONIQUE: In the lock.

THE CARDINAL TURNS THE KEY. A SMALL PANEL OPENS IN THE BOX.

CARDINAL: I can barely get my hands inside. Is this some sort of game? I can see Joseph's sense of humor in this. I know what it is. It's the ring, isn't it. It's the Auschwitz ring. I've always coveted it. He knew. Dear Joseph. (*Puts his hands in eagerly, the box makes a grinding noise*) It's empty. Ah! (*Screams*) Oh Christ in Heaven help me—my hands—ah! My hands!

(*Wrestles with the box*) Help me woman—help me, there's something skewering my hands. They're being cut to ribbons. Make it release me. Make it release me. Why has he done this to me? (*Screams and pulls his hands out*) I'm being crucified. (*His hands are transfixed by two blades, straight through the middle of the palms*) Why Joseph? Why, why, why?

VERONIQUE: This isn't his doing.

CARDINAL: Then who?

VERONIQUE: You won't remember me.

CARDINAL: Help me.

VERONIQUE: Veronique Flecker.

CARDINAL: It's excruciating.

VERONIQUE; I was in hell last time we met, naked under his needle, faceless. But I have friends you may remember.

THE CARDINAL COLLAPSES TO THE FLOOR AS TWO EXTRAORDINARY MONSTERS ENTER: FOLLEZOU

AND MATTOS. THEY ARE DRESSED IN A PATHETIC
PARODY OF CIVILIZED CLOTHING. A SUIT, MAYBE A
TIE EVEN, CAN BE GLIMPSED, SHITTY AND BLOODY,
MINGLED WITH GANGRENED BANDAGES AND
RAGS. PHYSICALLY, THEY FORM A CONTRAST.
FOLLEZOU HAS THE FACE OF A CADAVER, WELL—
PUTREFIED. HIS FLESH IS DARK GREEN, GREY AND
BROWN, WITH LIVID SORES WHERE HIS WOUNDS
FESTER. MATTOS RESEMBLES A GROTESQUE FETUS,
HIS CRANIUM UNNATURALLY LARGE, PALE PINK
AND ALMOST BALD. THEIR BODIES REFLECT THIS
CONTRAST. FOLLEZOU SKELETAL, MATTOS PULPY-
FAT. MATTOS CARRIES A BUNDLE OF TOOLS.

VERONIQUE: Senor Edmundo Follezou. Eddie, the Cardinal.

FOLLEZOU: My pleasure.

VERONIQUE: And Salvador Mattos. Excuse me, Salvador doesn't
hear well. (*Louder*) Salvador.

MATTOS: Huh?

VERONIQUE: The Cardinal.

MATTOS: At least he's not fat.

FOLLEZOU: You were present at Mattos' marriage Cardinal, when
good Dr. Frankenstein sewed his top half to his bottom half.
Do you not remember?

CARDINAL: Help me.

MATTOS: He seems distracted.

CARDINAL: Somebody help me.

FOLLEZOU: The boys ran away.

MATTOS: They didn't like the looks of us.

FOLLEZOU: So we're your only hope.

CARDINAL: Hope? You?

FOLLEZOU: Oh yes.

MATTOS: Why not?

CARDINAL: Help me then. Staunch these wounds before I drain away.

MATTOS: No.

CARDINAL: Why not?

FOLLEZOU: You offend us, with that look of horror on your face.

MATTOS: Just because we've been tampered with, are we any less
reasonable, any less sensitive?

FOLLEZOU: Close your eyes, listen to his voice—(*Mattos sings a*

fragment of Ave Maria) Is that such a terrible sound? There's a
sweet natured soul in there. We're just men. I myself was a
philosophy teacher before the purges. And a friend of
Cicero. Remember Cicero?

MATTOS: I was a violinist at the Opera House. I'm going to play again.

CARDINAL: Won't you help me? Sensitive men.

FOLLEZOU: We are helping you.

CARDINAL: I'm dying.

MATTOS: There you are then.

CARDINAL: Veronique, is that your name? Veronique, a little mercy.

VERONIQUE: It was Follezou made the box. Fine handiwork,
don't you think? His limbs don't have the strength to kill
you personally, so he devised a trick.

CARDINAL: Why would anyone want to kill me?

VERONIQUE: You blessed the scalpels.

CARDINAL: A joke.

VERONIQUE: The slab was washed down with holy water.

CARDINAL: He made me do it.

VERONIQUE: You used to watch. Smiling. Why?

FOLLEZOU: Please explain. I want to understand how you could
be so dispassionate. I'm a man you see, who can barely
stand to crush a wood-louse. To do what you did—

MATTOS: Was it morbid fascination?

CARDINAL: I hate you.

FOLLEZOU: Is it that simple?

CARDINAL: I hate every living thing, and I always have.

MATTOS: Women?

CARDINAL: Decay. Flatulence. Grease.

MATTOS: You must know some strange women.

CARDINAL: But Frankenstein, oh dear Joseph, he always loved
humanity.

VERONIQUE: Never.

CARDINAL: Oh yes. He had a passion for its intricacies, its
strength, its elasticity. So he wanted to stretch it, shape it,
remake it by his own rules. To make a law for the flesh, a
physical morality he called it. I just saw a blood-letter, a tor-
mentor. And it pleased me, watching him silence their com-
plaints, sluice out their minds with agonies. I'd put my finger
sometimes, into their hot heads, buried in thought up to the
knuckle, and see their lives go out a little further with each

prod. That pleased me too. He worked out of love, I out of loathing.

MATTOS: Sounds like the perfect marriage.

FOLLEZOU: I understand. Thank you.

CARDINAL: He claimed he was sowing seeds that would one day change humanity. Drawing the sap out of vivisected fetuses and injecting it—

VERONIQUE: I don't want to hear.

MATTOS: I do. It makes me feel better hearing about people who are worse off.

CARDINAL: You for one.

VERONIQUE: I know.

CARDINAL: He tampered with you endlessly. You're just a jug, full of him.

VERONIQUE: No.

CARDINAL: He's changing you from inside.

MATTOS: She has pains.

VERONIQUE: Mattos.

MATTOS: Why not tell him? Her body—

VERONIQUE: You want to see the part of me that's sprouting wings? Or the fur? Or the feathers? You want to know what I crave for these days, to eat, to drink, to sleep with?

MATTOS: I don't think he does.

FOLLEZOU: I think he's had enough. Lucky man.

CARDINAL: Will you let me go now?

FOLLEZOU: More or less.

CARDINAL: Help me before I'm bled white.

MATTOS: That's the idea.

CARDINAL: The idea?

MATTOS: To bleed you. We've no taste for blood. Lots of protein, but it makes me sick. It's the meat I want.

FOLLEZOU: We want.

CARDINAL: No.

VERONIQUE: They intend to eat you.

CARDINAL: No!

FOLLEZOU: I think it's time we took him away. His noise offends our lady.

CARDINAL: No! No! No!

FOLLEZOU: Maybe into the crypt.

CARDINAL: No! No! No!

MATTOS: For what we are about to receive may the Lord make us truly thankful.

FOLLEZOU AND MATTOS DRAG HIM AWAY. MATTOS RETURNS A MOMENT LATER AND SELECTS A LARGE SAW FROM HIS BUNDLE OF TOOLS. HE EXITS. OFF-STAGE THE SCREAMS START AGAIN, AND WE HEAR SCREAMING NOISES. MARIA DRIFTS BACK INTO THE SCENE, AND SITS ON THE ALTAR.

MARIA: I've seen fairer trials.

VERONIQUE: What would a whore know about the law?

MARIA: I'm not a whore. I'm a palm-reader.

VERONIQUE: Oh. Forgive me.

MARIA: What do you have to do to get some respect around here?

VERONIQUE: Respect? You want respect? Poor bitch.

MARIA: He said the horsemen were coming.

VERONIQUE: Did he?

MARIA: I hope they're good looking.

VERONIQUE: Feeling lonely?

MARIA: I get listless without some affection.

VERONIQUE: I know how you feel.

MARIA: What did you mean, asking if he wanted to know what you crave for?

VERONIQUE: To eat?

MARIA: To sleep with.

VERONIQUE: That's my business.

MARIA: Tell me. I'm dead. I won't gossip.

VERONIQUE: He was right. I'm a container, a jug, that's all. He put something in me, not human. It gives me thoughts.

MARIA: Such as?

VERONIQUE: Perhaps we're too cautious, just making love to men. Maybe there's more pleasure in bricks, or trees, or fire.

MARIA: I don't think so.

VERONIQUE: Why not? What's to lose?

MARIA: Fire?

VERONIQUE: Nothing is enough. Nothing satisfies. I'm hungry, never full. Do you understand? I went into the Barrios last night, there were some wild sights. God knows who took me,

I didn't discriminate. Even look at their faces. Boys, old men. One after the other. Filthy. I felt nothing at all. Just empty.

A SCREAM FROM THE CARDINAL.

VERONIQUE: That's the end.

ENTER EL COCO

EL COCO: What's the din?
VERONIQUE: You're too late.
EL COCO: I thought it was you at work. Judge and jury.
MARIA: It was the Cardinal.
EL COCO: Who's she?
MARIA: You just murdered me. Men!
VERONIQUE: Did you kill her?
EL COCO: I don't remember.
MARIA: He blamed his hand, which is of course, attached to his arm, and his shoulder and all the rest of his stinking torso. Still, it's all blood under the bridge now. I'm dead. Dogs have found me. They've each taken something home for the pups.
VERONIQUE: You see her too?
EL COCO: Yes.
MARIA: Of course he sees me. He's deader than I am.
EL COCO: Hush.
MARIA: You can't hurt me now. I can tell the truth.
EL COCO: Not your business.
MARIA: The future was my business. I read it on his palm you see. All he was, all he's going to be. I'd steer clear of him if I were you. He's got secrets.
EL COCO: Is the doctor here? Perez said he came here sometimes, to make confession.
VERONIQUE: No.
EL COCO: And the Cardinal?
VERONIQUE: He knew nothing. He was about to make his escape.
EL COCO: I need him . . .
VERONIQUE: Frankenstein?
EL COCO: . . . before I can put my past in order, before I can become a man of state, I have to pay my respects.
VERONIQUE: What is he to you?

MARIA: Answer her.

EL COCO: She doesn't want to know.

MARIA: You don't want to tell her, you mean.

VERONIQUE: Who is he?

EL COCO: My . . . father.

VERONIQUE: Father?

MARIA: Tell her the whole truth.

EL COCO: There's nothing more to tell.

MARIA: Confess it.

EL COCO: I forget.

MARIA: He's not your father. He's your maker.

EL COCO: I have a right to him.

VERONIQUE: Maker?

MARIA: I'm going to bless the Cardinal, if I can remember the
words. Don't be rough, Veronique. He may go to pieces.

EXIT MARIA.

VERONIQUE: Maker?

EL COCO: I'm his child.

VERONIQUE: Cesar Guerrero, the great liberator, is the offspring
of Dr. Joseph Frankenstein?

EL COCO: After a fashion. Each of these parts has a different
father and mother, but he assembled me.

VERONIQUE: From corpses?

EL COCO: I was born in a charnel-house in Prague, eight years
ago. I remember it as yesterday—the heat, his face, the bodies. You said it yourself—meat, meat he moulded to make me.
An abbatoir and me its fruit, its marvelous boy. I don't know
how he did it, unknitting nature, but he was jubilant. For
weeks after he'd look at me, feel the pulse in my neck, kiss me
like a lost child he'd found. I was a clean slate, with no memory of what this brain had been, but I knew my condition.
Living corruption, a crowd sewn together in one skin. Anar-
chy in every limb, and bones that ached to go to dust. I lived
a year with him. Refused to talk. Refused to give a sign of
compliance. Out of spite I'd kill every living thing I could set
this dice-player's hand on. Except him. Him I couldn't touch
in anger, it hurt me. And he told me my history. Whose limbs
I had, whose heart. And the more I learned, the more I

loathed myself. Then one night the house was raided, and he had to make his escape before they arrested him. I killed the men who tried to manacle me, and went out into the world. Now I had to be human again, or be alone. I watched awhile, from the borders, the etiquette, the gloss of life, learning how to resemble a natural man, and when I thought I could pass for a living soul I went back to Prague and picked up his trail. I followed him for five years, across three continents, faithful as only a son can be who longs to see his father's face.

VERONIQUE: Why do you need him?

EL COCO: Sons are always like their fathers, however deeply the resemblance is buried. I wanted to see him once more, know the miseries I'd inherit, then kill him.

VERONIQUE: He never made another like you, not that I saw.

EL COCO: I'm a first failure, doubtless he has the skills now.

VERONIQUE: You're not the worst. You're his triumph.

EL COCO: Then God help his failures. I've precious little control left over my appetites. I have to finish him off and forget I was a monster, make a new world.

VERONIQUE: Without monsters.

EL COCO: They require me. Magic, miracles, the pursuit of the impossible—it all repulses me. Give me order, give me calm, law, reason.

VERONIQUE: And what will you do with the freaks, lunatics, visionaries?

EL COCO: Purge them, for their own sakes. As Plato wanted to drive out the poets for the order of the state.

VERONIQUE: You read Plato?

EL COCO: Without Plato and heroin I'd be a lunatic.

VERONIQUE: The monster reads Plato!

EL COCO: Don't call me that. *I will be human!* And you will treat me as such.

VERONIQUE: You'll never be human. Look at yourself. You're a walking cemetery, a paradox, a contradiction.

EL COCO: Maria said that. I killed her.

VERONIQUE: And proved her point.

EL COCO: I must have reason.

VERONIQUE: Is it reason to forget yourself?

EL COCO: I can't live with my condition, and my condition is death, so I can't die from it. All I can do is try to forget.

VERONIQUE: Or accept it.

EL COCO: Accept—this? (*Looks at his body*) Filth!

VERONIQUE: Meat. The light is here. It burns behind the eyes. I thought you believed in the soul, Cesar.

EL COCO: Not tonight.

VERONIQUE: Believe again.

EL COCO: I'm frightened.

VERONIQUE: What of?

EL COCO: Of myself. I could murder again, unless I control what's in me.

VERONIQUE: Control, yes. I'll help you control . . . but don't deny it, monster.

EL COCO: Help me then.

VERONIQUE: How?

EL COCO: Let me have my father to myself.

VERONIQUE: Forget him. He's probably dead.

EL COCO: No . . .

VERONIQUE: Gone, Cesar. That's not your hope.

EL COCO: Don't fear me.

VERONIQUE: I don't.

EL COCO: Love me. Open yourself to me, let me curl up inside you. I want your womb awhile. I want to dig so deep in you I have a womb for myself. Hear your heart, share your blood, a little ecstasy of hiding. Unborn—again. He sent me out unfinished, as though you'd dress an abortion in its Sunday clothes and send it to school, still wet, with its head still full of the peace it was snatched out of.

VERONIQUE: (*She cradles him*) No harm will come to you here.

EL COCO: Promise me?

VERONIQUE: Ssh.

EL COCO: I'd like to die now.

ENTER MATTOS, CHEWING, WITH THE CARDINAL'S ARM. THERE ARE BITE MARKS IN THE DEAD FLESH.

MATTOS: He's good.

EL COCO: Who's this?

VERONIQUE: A friend.

MATTOS: Salvador Mattos. You're El Coco, aren't you? I know

you from the posters they're pasting up. I didn't know you were friends.

EL COCO: What are you doing?

MATTOS: You want some?

EL COCO: (*Strikes the arm out of Mattos' hand*) Cannibal.

VERONIQUE: Cesar, no!

MATTOS: Oh, you've got an appetite for it as well. I can see it in your eyes.

EL COCO: Be quiet! (*Attacks Mattos*)

VERONIQUE: If you harm him, I'll tell everyone. I'll write it on the walls six feet high: You are Frankenstein's child!

EL COCO WRESTLES TO CONTROL HIS ANGER, AND DROPS MATTOS.

MATTOS: He's one of us?

VERONIQUE: Yes.

EL COCO: Us?

VERONIQUE: Where's Follezou?

MATTOS: Skipping with the gut I shouldn't wonder. Or playing ball. (*Admiring El Coco*) You're well made.

VERONIQUE: Mattos is one of your brothers, Cesar. He understands.

EL COCO: And you?

VERONIQUE: Ask me another day.

MATTOS: Oh, she's the Queen Bee. She's a hive all to herself.

VERONIQUE: I'm going home.

EL COCO: Meet me tomorrow.

VERONIQUE: No.

EL COCO: The day after.

VERONIQUE: No.

EL COCO: I need you.

VERONIQUE: What sort of romance is this?

EL COCO: Please.

VERONIQUE: Do you waltz?

EL COCO: As it happens . . . yes. My feet are Viennese.

VERONIQUE: Then we'll dance in the dark. (*They kiss*)

VERONIQUE EXITS.

MATTOS: (*Takes a bottle from his bundle*) Fine figure of a woman.

You want some Beaujolais? It's not a particularly good year, but it goes with anything.

EL COCO: I don't eat. It makes me sick.

MATTOS: You're the Bogey-Man, and you don't eat human flesh? Tut-tut! At least a child once in a while. (*El Coco rolls up his sleeve, and prepares to give himself a fix*) Oh, that's your meat, is it?

MATTOS: You know, as we started to cut him up, the Cardinal this is, he looked at me and he said "how can you do this?" I said "with a knife." He said "aren't you human under there?" I said "if my mind was crammed into the shell of a crab, I'd have to walk like a crab, sex like a crab, I'd have the appetite of a crab." I said "we must eat you, it's the monsters' imperative, blood and hunger." He nodded. He seemed satisfied. "Do eat." He died for us.

EL COCO LOOKS AT THE MEAT AND STARTS TO EAT.

MATTOS: Oh, (*Looks up*) look at the moon.

Scene Four

A SQUARE. SOUND OF A CROWD. ENTER COCKATOO WITH MARIA.

COCKATOO: Does he eat human flesh?

MARIA: (*In his ear*) You know he does.

COCKATOO: I don't believe it.

MARIA: Three witnesses have seen him, amongst ghouls, devouring haunches of raw human meat. Biting tongues, chewing off fingernails—

COCKATOO: Suppose somebody finds out?

MARIA: Political suicide.

COCKATOO: We should take steps—

MARIA: Maybe the heroin makes him wild.

COCKATOO: Yes.

MARIA: That's the reason.

COCKATOO: I went to the Cathedral.

MARIA: What did you find?

COCKATOO: A lot of blood. And—(*Unwraps the hand, still trans-fixed by a blade, of the Cardinal*) the hand of Cardinal Armitano. The ring is his.

MARIA: He ate a man of the Church?

COCKATOO: That's what made me believe it. A man of the Church. He'd do that.

MARIA: But he's the President-Elect.

COCKATOO: The President-Elect.

MARIA: Even now he's seeing the Russian Ambassador. This morning he was in conference with the American Ambassador. What if he eats them? How do you explain that at the U.N.?

COCKATOO: Maybe if I spoke to him.

MARIA: Traitor.

COCKATOO: No.

MARIA: He'd accuse you.

COCKATOO: We had a traitor in the People's Militia back in the days before the revolution, when we were still camped in the Sierra. I discovered him, he was giving information to Perez's colonels. We'd lost many men from his betrayal. Cesar had a fire lit, it burned all day and all night, with stones in the middle of it. After twenty-four hours they were blisteringly hot, you couldn't go near them. He had the fire raked out, the ashes, the stones, the cinders all spread on the ground. The air was roasting. Then he took the man, and he danced with him, barefoot, in the fire, 'til the traitor was screaming in his arms. The heat didn't even scorch Cesar. He walked in it, danced in it like he was a swimmer in cool water.

MARIA: And the traitor?

COCKATOO: Cremated.

MARIA: He eats human flesh. That makes him a monster. You can't suffer monsters to live.

COCKATOO: I love him better than myself. He's pure, he's strong and he's wise. But he terrifies me shitless.

MARIA: If he becomes President—

COCKATOO: When he becomes President—

MARIA: If the people find out what he does, if he's discovered with a mouthful of eyeballs—

COCKATOO: Everything we fought for, destroyed. I know.

MARIA: Perez was a tyrant, but at least he ate bread.

COCKATOO: I need help. I can't think straight. I'm not clever enough for this.

MARIA: A doctor maybe.

ENTER LAZARO. HE WEARS A BANDAGE AROUND HIS HEAD, WITH A FEW BLOOD STAINS ON IT. HE CARRIES A DRILL. WE DON'T KNOW TO WHAT PURPOSE.

LAZARO: Did somebody say a doctor?

COCKATOO: No.

MARIA: I did.

LAZARO: I know a Jew, great humanist. Children melt at his touch.

COCKATOO: No doctors.

LAZARO: Why not?

COCKATOO: He hates doctors.

LAZARO: It's sick to hate doctors. He should see a doctor.

COCKATOO: I don't trust Jews. They have funny beliefs.

LAZARO: And you a Marxist.

MARIA: He does good works.

LAZARO: No, the man's mind is made up. He will not help his friend because his friend, being sick, has a fear of doctors.

MARIA: That's stupid.

LAZARO: Let him be. Can't you see the fellow has a death-wish?

COCKATOO: I can't betray him.

LAZARO: Health is an appalling betrayal, you're right. You should let him be caught and tried as a cannibal. It's what any friend would do.

COCKATOO: He has his reasons.

MARIA: For eating a Cardinal?

COCKATOO: He wouldn't forgive me.

MARIA: If you helped him in good faith, any man would forgive you.

LAZARO: And he's a man, isn't he?

LIGHTS CHANGE. BEHIND LAZARO, MARIA AND COCKATOO, A ROSTRUM APPEARS, RANGED WITH

*MICROPHONES. A GREAT CONCENTRATION OF LIGHT,
AND THE NOISE OF A VAST AND EXPECTANT CROWD.*

*EL COCO STEPS ONTO THE ROSTRUM TO BE GREETED
WITH A DEAFENING ROAR. THE STARS AND STRIPES IS
DRAPED OVER HIM, LIKE A TOGA. HE RAISES HIS
ARMS AND ACKNOWLEDGES THEIR LOVE.*

EL COCO: This is the first day of our lives. We are born today, and
we come into the world naked, like children, and full of hope
for the future. They will not daub us with their ashes, brothers
and sisters. We are dressed for life and will be heard. Our face
is a single face with ten thousand eyes. With ten thousand
mouths. And it demands the ears of the world. We have overturned tyranny. Now we must speak quietly, and learn wisdom. I have today spoken with the American Ambassador—

*LIGHTS CHANGE. THE AMERICAN AMBASSADOR IS
ON THE PHONE.*

AMERICAN AMBASSADOR: Henry . . . the man's a god-damn
mystic. He talks asshole metaphors every second word and
drinks, wait for this Henry, he drinks brine. Brine Henry, not
brain, brine. Salt water . . . yes, I know . . . I told him it
addles the brain, brine. He refuses all C.I.A. assistance. Says
he's quite capable of growing his own dope. Yeah, clever
bastard—for a fucking peasant. Asked me what I thought of
Democracy as a religion . . . yeah, you got the picture . . .
mad as a two-legged dog . . . oh, and Henry, he eats fire . . .

LIGHTS CHANGE.

EL COCO: —and I have today thanked the American Ambassador for his concern that our country live in peace and freedom. But I told him if it is the peace of the senile, and the
freedom of the whore—our face spits on it. I have today also
spoken with the Russian Ambassador—

*LIGHTS CHANGE. THE RUSSIAN AMBASSADOR IS
ON THE PHONE.*

RUSSIAN AMBASSADOR: Ah—the man's an intellectual, he's not of the people. Talks like a poet, very elliptical vocabulary. He asks me what I think of Communism as a drug. No . . . I don't know what he means . . . but it's not ideologically sound. Then he tries to poison me with salt-water. Salt, Gregor, salt. Not the treaty, the condiment . . . the man's as mad as a two-legged dog . . . oh, and Gregor, he eats fire . . .

LIGHTS CHANGE.

EL COCO: —and I have today thanked the Russian Ambassador for his concern that our country live in peace and freedom. But if it is the peace of the ignorant, and the freedom of the dead—our face spits on it. A free man knows he is free because his hands can do good or bad, and he is at peace only when he chooses to do good. If you are beside me and with me and in me, if you will be my face I will teach you to walk on fire, teach you to find that part of you which is without humanity, is strong and wise and deadly. And then my friends, we fire-walkers will take the world!

CHEERS. HE RAISES HIS HANDS TO ACKNOWLEDGE THEM. LIGHTS CHANGE. BUT THE CHEERS REMAIN. COCKATOO, LAZARO AND MARIA.

COCKATOO: They think he's a god.

LAZARO: It's a good impersonation.

MARIA: They press babies to him, to be cured of cholera. People are burning themselves to death trying to emulate his fire-walking.

LAZARO: I wondered what that smell was.

COCKATOO: What does he mean, to find the part that isn't human?

LAZARO: Good question.

MARIA: You know what he means.

COCKATOO: I don't.

LAZARO: The part that has a taste for Cardinals.

MARIA: Get a doctor.

LAZARO: Or a gun.

MARIA: Cure him.

LAZARO: Or kill him.

MARIA: He's losing control.

COCKATOO: This doctor, is he honest?

LAZARO: Do I look like a man with dishonest friends? He taught me everything I know about the labyrinth of the brain, the waters under the skull, the pressures that make a man lose his sanity. He's a genius.

COCKATOO: Then take me to him.

LAZARO: You won't regret it.

MARIA: Give me the hand.

COCKATOO: Why?

MARIA: Evidence.

COCKATOO: What will you do with it?

MARIA: Bury it. I'll take it to the cemetery and bury it.

COCKATOO: Thank you. Do I know you from somewhere?

LAZARO: Come on, no time to lose.

COCKATOO: Is he honest, this doctor?

LAZARO: As the day is long.

THEY EXIT.

Scene Five

A CEMETERY. MARIA HAS COME TO BURY THE HAND. EL COCO AND VERONIQUE ENTER. VERONIQUE HAS CHANGED. HER SKIN HAS TAKEN ON A BLUISH CAST.

EL COCO: I'll have a suit made, like the Ambassador's. But of shrouds and winding sheets.

VERONIQUE: Won't they notice when you walk into the United Nations?

EL COCO: Let them wonder. Let them call me El Coco behind my back, and President Guerrero to my face. Maybe I'll have to be a little more politic in the future. Let them grow their cocaine, let them have their silos.

VERONIQUE: Did you really invite the Ambassador to juggle hot coals?

EL COCO: I asked if he was a diplomat; he said he was. I asked him if he could play with fire; he said he could. Then I threw him a coal or two to prove his point. He caught them; then the screaming started. It serves him right for talking metaphor. If I say play with fire, I mean play with fire. I feel very strong.

VERONIQUE: We're strong together.

EL COCO: You know they'll try to assassinate me? The Americans. They do it to all their favorite people. It's a sign of affection.

VERONIQUE: You'll survive. It'll just add mystery to your reputation that they can't kill you.

EL COCO: I don't want mystery. I want them to know what I am, even if they can't bring themselves to think about it. Let them realize in their hearts that the world's stranger than they'd dared imagine.

VERONIQUE: This'll become a haunted state, you realize that? The outside world will begin to believe it's cursed.

EL COCO: Good. Then we'll be left alone to be ourselves.

VERONIQUE: I wish he'd sewn us together, like twins. So they could never part us, not in a thousand years, unless they cut us up into a thousand pieces.

EL COCO: Then they wouldn't know which piece was which. They'd have to bury the mincemeat in one grave. Eyes, fingernails, hair, skin, lips, all together. And even that wouldn't stop us, would it?

VERONIQUE: Probably not.

EL COCO: I'd love you for every drop of blood, for every particle of skin. The order's irrelevant.

VERONIQUE: Even if I turn into a bird?

EL COCO: You accept me: how could I do less? We'll be equal. Flesh disfigured, flesh remade. You can't repulse me, whatever you become. You'll be my unspeakable wife, and I'll be your disgusting husband.

VERONIQUE: My back feels as though it wants to split. And my face gets tight, as though someone's pressing on it from behind.

EL COCO: Are you frightened?

VERONIQUE: No. I'm curious. (*They kiss*) Do you want to make love?

EL COCO: Some of me does. The dice-player's itching to touch you.

VERONIQUE: Let him.

EL COCO: The blind man's not so sure.

VERONIQUE: *(Takes his hand)* He's just nervous. And the rest of you?

EL COCO: The torso consents, the groin is eager—

VERONIQUE: Well then, the vote's for love, yes?

EL COCO: Yes.

> *THEY KISS AGAIN, AND MAKE LOVE. MARIA, HAVING BURIED THE HAND NOW BEGINS TO PREPARE FOR THE SCENE SHE KNOWS WILL FOLLOW. SHE PREPARES A ROPE, KNOTTING A NOOSE IN IT. SHE PUTS ON LEATHER GLOVES.*

MARIA: *(To the audience)* The French call it the petit mort, the little death after sex. Eyes closed, thinking nothing. Released. Lust's a burden; it makes us ridiculous. But the living live for lust, don't they? Absurd. And they lust to live too, which is insanity. Death's good, like the petit mort—a sense of a duty done. We should curse our mothers and bless our executioners.

> *ENTER COCKATOO WITH LAZARO. LAZARO CARRIES A NET.*

MARIA: But I doubt if he will.

COCKATOO: Cesar.

EL COCO: Spying?

> *SILENCE.*

EL COCO: Well?

COCKATOO: Please, Cesar. Come quietly.

EL COCO: What?

COCKATOO: There's no harm meant. Just help.

VERONIQUE: Run, Cesar, run!

> *EL COCO GETS UP, BUT TOO LATE. THE NOOSE GOES OVER HIS NECK.*

COCKATOO: Hold him.

EL COCO: Cockatoo!

COCKATOO KEEPS VERONIQUE AT BAY WITH HIS GUN.

COCKATOO: Don't! I'll shoot!
EL COCO: Why? Why?
COCKATOO: For the revolution.
EL COCO: Traitor! Bastard!
COCKATOO: We have to help you.

THE NET IS OVER HIM. HE IS CAUGHT.

EL COCO: Cockatoo . . . don't do this.
COCKATOO: Nobody's going to hurt you.
EL COCO: Please . . .
COCKATOO: I've found a doctor.
EL COCO: A doctor?
COCKATOO: To help you.
EL COCO: A doctor?

ENTER DR. JOSEPH FRANKENSTEIN. HE IS SEVENTY, BUT WELL BUILT. NEATLY DRESSED, CLOSE CROPPED WHITE BEARD. HAUNTED EYES SUNK IN A BROAD-BROWED HEAD.

FRANKENSTEIN: Yes, a doctor, golem.
EL COCO: No. No. No. No. No. No.
FRANKENSTEIN: It seems so long . . .
EL COCO: Father . . .
FRANKENSTEIN: . . . since I saw your face.
COCKATOO: This is Dr. Kronhaussen.
VERONIQUE: You've given us into his hands.
COCKATOO: He's going to help you.
VERONIQUE: His hands, you imbecile, into his hands. The angel himself. The angel of Auschwitz.
FRANKENSTEIN: Please don't fret yourself. I really have only the best of intentions toward you. To watch you grow, Veronique. To help you accommodate the agonies of change.
COCKATOO: You know the woman?
FRANKENSTEIN: She's sick, Juan Thomas, and needs my help.
EL COCO: Why, Cockatoo?
COCKATOO: You're unwell, please understand, I thought per-

haps . . . you eat human flesh . . . you've been seen . . .
Cesar . . . you'll destroy us! Don't you see? You'll destroy us.

EL COCO: And him?

COCKATOO: He's a doctor. All he wants is for you to be healthy.

EL COCO: Him? Cockatoo, him? Of all the doctors on earth you
chose him?

FRANKENSTEIN: He didn't choose me, golem. I chose him. You
were so merciless to me; never letting me rest for even a
year. I'm exhausted now. Still, I could have forgiven you
pursuing me, even destroying my work at the Palace . . .

COCKATOO: What work?

VERONIQUE: It was his charnel-house, Navarro, in the bowels . . .
Frankenstein. This is Dr. Joseph Frankenstein.

COCKATOO: No. Kronhaussen. Lazaro . . . ? This is Kronhaussen.

*FRANKENSTEIN HAS TAKEN A HYPODERMIC FROM
HIS POCKET. COCKATOO APPROACHES HIM AND
THE DOCTOR PRESSES IT INTO HIS NECK.*

FRANKENSTEIN: Forgive the deception, Juan Thomas.

COCKATOO: What is that?

FRANKENSTEIN: Taquiflaxin.

COCKATOO BUCKLES.

FRANKENSTEIN: It will take you as close to death as you will
care to get. Bring me a report, will you?

COCKATOO: (*Falls over*) Cesar . . . Cesar . . . (*Loses consciousness*)

FRANKENSTEIN: It has taken courage for me to face you, golem.
After all these years. You are almost my ruin . . . and yet
when I look at you, the years, the agonies . . . I want to forgive you.

EL COCO: I was your triumph, is that right?

FRANKENSTEIN: Is that an appeal for life? Wasted, golem. As I said, I
would have forgiven you but—*you never loved me!* You never
loved me! I damned myself for you, and yet you never loved me.

EL COCO: I want to erase you completely.

FRANKENSTEIN: Never. You're just the child, and a decaying
child at that. I am the power, golem. I always was and I
always will be. I made you, and having seen you, I will dis-

patch you (*To Lazaro*) Flay him! Strip his skin from head to foot and bring him to me as a keepsake. The rest, burn.

EL COCO: That's not so bad.

FRANKENSTEIN: Are you a stoic as well as a Platonist? It's a good brain I put in there. He was a doctor you know, like me.

VERONIQUE: Don't do this. He's your creature.

FRANKENSTEIN: Take him to the mausoleum, where you won't be seen. Unman him, unmake him.

MARIA AND LAZARO DRAG HIM AWAY.

FRANKENSTEIN: (*To Veronique*) Well what shall we do tomorrow? Mourn I suppose. (*Sneezes*) Ah! I have a chill . . . the sweat gets cold on me, at my age. You could have helped him you know. But you didn't, did you? Why was that do you suppose? Perhaps because you feared death, and the terror of that thought prevented action. Think about that, Veronique. You feared death, so you couldn't act. Now . . . suppose I could make a world without death, then nothing would be forbidden by fear. We could act and love and never think of darkness.

A SCREAM, OFF-STAGE.

FRANKENSTEIN: The stoic speaks.

VERONIQUE: Murderer.

FRANKENSTEIN: The word means nothing. Its significance is washed away by untold crimes. I will nurture what you're becoming, and make you well. I promise. I have affection for you, Veronique. And you have no secrets from me, because I have seen you inside and out. You are transparent. (*Looking at Coockatoo*) We'll make the parrot king for a while; he can breed with you. That should please him. Cockatoo . . .

COCKATOO: (*Stirs*) Ah!

FRANKENSTEIN: You're not dead, and you won't die as long as you keep hold of this hand. Take it. (*Puts Veronique's hand in Cockatoo's*)

COCKATOO: I can't see.

FRANKENSTEIN: The drug blinds you for a while. You'll see again soon.

COCKATOO: I can't breathe.

FRANKENSTEIN: You'll survive.

COCKATOO: (*Crying*) Help me.

FRANKENSTEIN: You see how fertile I am. How well I make babies. It's easy. You just put men in the dark.

ENTER MARIA AND LAZARO, WITH EL COCO'S TORN AND BLOODY SKIN, WHICH THEY DISPLAY FOR FRANKENSTEIN BY HANGING IT UP. LAZARO PHOTOGRAPHS IT WITH A FLASH CAMERA.

VERONIQUE: Oh Jesus, Jesus, Jesus . . .

FRANKENSTEIN: Take Cockatoo back to the Palace. Escort them Lazaro. This isn't your business.

EXIT COCKATOO, VERONIQUE AND LAZARO.

FRANKENSTEIN: Nor yours.

MARIA: He murdered me.

FRANKENSTEIN: He murdered me too.

MARIA: Are you dead too?

FRANKENSTEIN: Nothing so simple. Have you lit a fire for him?

MARIA: Yes.

FRANKENSTEIN: Well. That's good.

MARIA: Do you want the skin brought back to the Palace?

FRANKENSTEIN: No. Leave it here. Someone will have an appetite for it. The world is very tidy. Good night.

EXIT FRANKENSTEIN.

MARIA: And so to bed.

EXIT MARIA.

END OF ACT ONE.

Act 2:

<u>Scene One</u>

*A YARD BEHIND A MORTUARY. CENTER-STAGE,
ROUGHLY WRAPPED IN STAINED CANVAS AND
BURLAP, IS THE BODY OF EL COCO. ON THE FLOOR A
BUCKET, WITH THE WORDS 'SOILED DRESSINGS' ON
IT, OVERFLOWING WITH BLOODY BANDAGES AND
PUTRID LINT. ENTER MARIA, PARTIALLY DRESSED AS
A NUN. SHE ADDRESSES THE AUDIENCE.*

MARIA: Of course, this isn't the end of the world. The end of the
world was yesterday. You are already dead, you just remember having tickets to the theatre tonight and as your brain
cools it dreams you're here. Soon you'll hear a hammering as
they nail down the lid on you, and the only sound left will
be the whine in your head. Frightened? No? I'll have to try
harder. I know I promised a romance and I swear, there'll be
love in the second act, albeit love in a grave. Well, at least it's
private. It's warm tonight, have you noticed? And mortuaries
get so stuffy. It's putrescence you see, it generates heat. Oh
yes, many a time I've warmed my hands on something rot-
ten. (*Puts her costume on completely*)

*ENTER CAMILO BOZUFFI, A TAILOR. HE IS IMMACU-
LATELY DRESSED IN A VERY LIGHT SUIT, AND HAS A
SMALL, BEAUTIFULLY KEPT MUSTACHE. HE PICKS
HIS WAY THROUGH THE MESS WITH A LOOK OF
DISTASTE ON HIS FACE. HIS SPECTACLES ARE*

SLIGHTLY TINTED, SO WE DON'T SEE HIS MAS-
CARAED EYES UNTIL HE TAKES THEM OFF. HE
STARES A WHILE AT THE WRAPPED BODY.

BOZUFFI: Sister?

MARIA: God be with you.

BOZUFFI: And with you, Sister.

MARIA: Can I help you?

BOZUFFI: I do hope so. I have to see the pathologist, Dr. Fook.

MARIA: Dr. Fook is busy at the moment—

BOZUFFI: It's urgent.

MARIA: There's a new dispatch of cholera victims come in from the city. We've got to have them all sorted out by dawn. Some of them die in the cramps you know; it's the Devil's own job straightening them out. Takes two or three of the sisters to do it sometimes. One sitting on the face, someone else breaking the legs—

BOZUFFI: Could you simply tell Dr. Fook that Senor Bozuffi is here?

MARIA: He won't see you. I'll lay you ten to one he won't see you.

BOZUFFI: I'm not a betting man.

MARIA: No comment.

BOZUFFI: (*As Maria exits*) Bitch.

MARIA: I beg your pardon?

BOZUFFI: You heard me.

MARIA EXITS AND BOZUFFI PUTS DOWN THE
SMALL CASE HE CARRIES AND TAKES OUT A SELEC-
TION OF NUTS AND A NUT-CRACKER. HE CRACKS A
NUT AND EATS IT. THUNDER RUMBLES AROUND.
THE LIGHTS FLICKER AND THREATEN TO FAIL.
BOZUFFI LOOKS AT THEM, AND EATS ANOTHER
NUT. HE GOES ACROSS TO THE BODY AND IS ABOUT
TO UNCOVER THE FACE WHEN DR. FOOK ENTERS.

FOOK: Don't.

BOZUFFI: Ah! You scared me.

FOOK IS WEARING A BLOODIED GREEN APRON
AND BLOODIED GLOVES. A CIGARETTE HANGS

FROM THE CORNER OF HIS MOUTH. HE CARRIES A
HAMMER AND CHISEL, ALSO BLOODIED.

FOOK: Leave it alone.

BOZUFFI: Why?

FOOK: Take it from me, he's not your type. For one thing, he's
over seventeen. And for another, he's got no skin.

BOZUFFI: No skin?

FOOK: That's what I said. Peeled off like a peach, God help him.
He was found in a fire, or what was left of a fire. But he was
dead before the flames hit him.

BOZUFFI: What of?

FOOK: Blood loss, shock. As if there wasn't enough work for a
hard-working pathologist without having to deal with murder victims. We had another hundred and seventy carcasses
in this evening. Falling like flies.

BOZUFFI: I won't keep you long.

FOOK: You've got two minutes, then I must get back or I'll lose
the rhythm.

BOZUFFI: I need your assistance.

FOOK: How?

BOZUFFI: The same as before.

FOOK: Out of the question.

BOZUFFI: Just enough to make a few designs.

FOOK: We're up to our necks.

BOZUFFI: All the easier.

FOOK: Camilo, I can't. I'm sorry.

BOZUFFI: What am I asking for? A few old shirts, a couple of suits,
a shroud or two? My shop was gutted in the riots. I've got no
material to work with. How can I be a tailor with no cloth?

FOOK: It's difficult all around.

BOZUFFI: Don't be so condescending, damn you.

FOOK: I'm overworked, Bozuffi. I haven't slept in three nights. It's
like a crazy-house in there, bodies on the floor, bodies in the
sink. We've requisitioned every ice-cream truck in the city to
keep them in; the rot sets in so quickly in this weather. Two
minutes and they're black with flies, another two and their
eyes pop, maggots everywhere. I'm reduced to a mere func-
tionary. It's difficult just keeping them from sticking
together.

BOZUFFI: I know what you're doing. Digging out gold teeth. Ripping off jewelry.

FOOK: There's very little jewelry.

BOZUFFI: So you admit it.

FOOK: Gold's worth something. I'd be a fool not to take advantage. A man has to live.

BOZUFFI: So do I! So do I!

FOOK: I can't start stripping them, Camilo, looking for the odd silk shirt or a pair of leather knickers. We're racing against time here. You can practically watch them rot. When the generator fails, which it does with monotonous regularity, you can see the phosphorescence off them as they decay. They glow in the dark; you could read by it. I can't help you, Camilo. I'm sorry.

BOZUFFI: Thank you. Thank you, I'll remember this. Thank you.

FOOK: Now don't pout.

BOZUFFI: You'd have helped me once, when you needed me.

FOOK: Well I don't any longer, that part of my life is over. And if I supplied you with cloth, how long before the opticians would want spectacles and the doll makers want glass eyes? I can't keep the economy going single-handed.

BOZUFFI: If it's man-power you want, I'll find you a boy—

FOOK: One of your apprentices? Pretty as a picture and hung like a horse—no thank you. I've got a reputation—

BOZUFFI: You could have a reputation and a half if I opened my mouth.

FOOK: What?

BOZUFFI: It wouldn't take much. I've got letters, your instructions, how you wanted your dresses made.

FOOK: Ssh!

BOZUFFI: Dr. Fook in skirts.

FOOK: Bozie, don't be silly.

BOZUFFI: Help me then. So I won't be silly anymore.

FOOK: Is this blackmail?

BOZUFFI: Yes. But strictly between friends.

FOOK: Damn you. (*Calls*) Sister Maria.

BOZUFFI: I am in your debt.

FOOK: You're unforgivable.

BOZUFFI: Then maybe we should go into business together.

OFF-STAGE, A SCREAM.

BOZUFFI: Who was that?

FOOK: An error, probably.

BOZUFFI: Error? What sort of error?

FOOK: Premature burial.

BOZUFFI: Oh God—

FOOK: We're all overworked here, and frankly at four o'clock in the morning the difference between the dead and the almost dead is academic. So once in a while some poor bugger wakes up in a shroud with all his gold teeth missing and screams blue murder. The shock usually kills them.

BOZUFFI: And him? The peach? What are you going to do with him?

FOOK: He'll go into the lime-pit with the others. We're well past the niceties of funerals, Camilo.

BOZUFFI: Is there no dignity left?

FOOK: This nation is finished. Our glorious leader disappeared after one day in office, probably assassinated. Perez was hung up by his heels and bled like a pig. There's a parrot in the President's chair, some half-wit rebel called Cockatoo. We may as well let the Americans and Russians tear us apart and be done with it.

BOZUFFI: Does it frighten you?

FOOK: Of course it frightens me. I want to live, Camilo. Most people do.

BOZUFFI: What will you do if the Americans invade? Or if there's another coup?

FOOK: I've made plans for my escape. I could be out of here in two minutes flat and nobody would know my face.

BOZUFFI: How?

FOOK: You've got your secrets, I've got mine.

BOZUFFI: He moved!

FOOK: What?

BOZUFFI: There was a movement under the shroud.

FOOK: Don't tell me the rats have got to him.

HE REACHES TO UNCOVER THE BODY, BUT IS INTERRUPTED AS SISTER MARIA ENTERS.

MARIA: Dr. Fook. You wanted me?

FOOK: Who was screaming?

MARIA: Senor Gargas. He woke up—

FOOK: Who examined him?

MARIA: You did.

FOOK: Then I suppose I must make my apologies.

MARIA: No need. His wife wanted him embalmed, you recall.

FOOK: Ah—

MARIA: We were draining him when he woke. It was too late. He just ran away into a bucket. He only lived a moment.

BOZUFFI: Quite a moment.

FOOK: What was his suit like?

MARIA: Very good quality.

FOOK: Silk shirt?

MARIA: I think so.

FOOK: Fetch them for Senor Bozuffi. Bring a few winding sheets too. The Senor gets cold at night.

MARIA: Yes Doctor.

MARIA EXITS

FOOK: And bring me another pack of cigarettes. (*He lights another cigarette*) Don't mind me smoking, Bozie. I know how it disgusts you but it keeps the flies off me.

BOZUFFI: Are there rats here?

FOOK: Of course there are rats.

BOZUFFI: And they eat the bodies?

FOOK: It's just another meal to them. It spreads the disease, of course, as you will be doing, taking dead men's clothes. It lingers in the weave, the breath of cholera. We fumigate, we disinfect, but it hangs on. So make sure you don't wear any of your own fashions, Bozie. We don't want to find you burying yourself in your work.

BOZUFFI: That's in poor taste.

FOOK: You're about to steal clothes from the dead, and you say I'm in bad taste?

BOZUFFI: I don't like doing this.

FOOK: So you insist.

BOZUFFI: I'm forced to these extremes by circumstance. I disgust myself, I hate myself, stealing from the dead.

FOOK: The dead don't care.

BOZUFFI: So you say.

FOOK: They're passive, Bozie. Never a murmur. You can put your fingers down their throats, up their backsides to the elbow, do they complain?

BOZUFFI: No respect, no heart . . .

FOOK: Camilo, there's nothing left in the world to respect. I've seen everything and the thrill's gone out of it. I've looked at atrocities, bodies in states that defy description, and picked my teeth. Whereas you, in the presence of death, you sweat and shake.

THE LIGHTS FLICKER.

FOOK: Because it's still a mystery to you, you're still capable of being intimidated by it. I dare say you linger around car accidents, don't you? Half hoping to see something gruesome, revolted by yourself but unable to walk the other way. Whereas I'm indifferent, because I know the truth. That death's very commonplace, very unsensational. Not worth a second glance. It's just . . . an absence. It's the place where something was, it's the silence after a scream that almost makes you long to hear the scream again, even if it's your own.

BOZUFFI: I dreamt this.

FOOK: What?

HE CROSSES TO THE BODY, AND AN ARM SEIZES HIM AS HE BENDS TO LOOK AT IT. THE BODY SITS UP. THE MATCH GOES OUT. FOOK SCREAMS. BOZUFFI SCREAMS.

BOZUFFI: Lights! Lights!

THE LIGHTS FLICKER ON, NOT CERTAIN OF THEM-SELVES. WE SEE BOZUFFI ON HIS KNEES, PRAYING. HE SPEAKS THE LORD'S PRAYER, IN SPANISH, IN A CONSTANT FLOW OF PANIC. THE CORPSE HAS STOOD UP, AND HAS HOLD OF DR. FOOK. IT IS EL COCO, DRESSED ROUGHLY IN A WRAPPING OF STAINED CLOTH. HE IS SKINNED.

EL COCO: Raise no alarm and I'll let you be.

FOOK: Yes. Yes.

EL COCO: (*Drops Fook*) I mean you no harm. Silence your prayers, tailor. They're not necessary. You won't be going to Heaven just yet.

BOZUFFI: One of your errors?

FOOK: God knows.

EL COCO: God knows nothing about me, Dr. Fook. God doesn't care for me. No angels attend me, nor devils. I am as naked of morality or metaphysics as I am of skin. And I say again, if you mean me no harm, I mean you none. Indeed, I am pleased to meet you.

FOOK: You're dead. You can't be pleased, you can't know or see or feel a thing.

BOZUFFI: I dreamt this conversation, the flickering lights, the thunder—

FOOK: I get déjà vu all the time. One body looks so much like the next.

BOZUFFI: But when I dreamt it, I swear—

FOOK: You look very pale.

BOZUFFI: I swear there were three of us.

THE LIGHTS FLICKER AND FAIL ALTOGETHER.

FOOK: Damn generator.

BOZUFFI: (*In the dark*) There were. There were definitely three of us.

FOOK: They'll come back on in a moment.

BOZUFFI: Fook. I think I'm going to shit myself.

FOOK: They'll come back on in a moment.

BOZUFFI: I hate the dark.

FOOK: I've got a match somewhere—

BOZUFFI: Quickly.

FOOK: Wait. (*Strikes the match*) Better?

BOZUFFI: Yes. (*Sees the shroud move*) Fook!

FOOK: What?

BOZUFFI: The body! Fook! The body!

FOOK: There's nothing there.

EL COCO: Wrong. I live by my will, and I will continue to live until my will is done.

FOOK: Why don't you lie down and let us bury you?

EL COCO: Because I have work to do. Oh, the grave has its

pleasures, but I must postpone them for a while. I want . . . vengeance.

FOOK: On whom?

EL COCO: The men that did this to me. They think I'm dead.

FOOK: It's a reasonable assumption.

EL COCO: But I will come again. With your help.

FOOK: Mine?

EL COCO: The tailor.

BOZUFFI: Mine? What can I do? He's the doctor.

EL COCO: I don't need doctors, I've had an excess of doctors. I need a tailor, to dress me for life.

BOZUFFI: A suit! You want a suit? Why didn't you say so? A suit I can provide.

EL COCO: Good.

BOZUFFI: (Relieved) A suit! He wants a suit!

EL COCO: What do you think of me Doctor? A walking anatomy lesson. Feast your eyes, you'll never have such a specimen again. Why the look? Do I offend you?

FOOK: Your body . . . it's sewn together.

EL COCO: Yes.

FOOK: From many pieces.

EL COCO: Right again.

FOOK: You're not a natural man.

EL COCO: No. I despise natural men.

FOOK: You're constructed somehow, a jigsaw—

EL COCO: A hash, a human stew, yes. And still, without their gloves, these hands have desires of their own. This one, it doesn't trust you, Doctor.

FOOK: Oh?

EL COCO: I think it sees the chisel in your hand. (Grabs Fook's arm and makes him drop the chisel) And it sees too the other face you wear. (Pulls at Fook's apron, which comes off to reveal women's underwear) Senorita.

BOZUFFI: Fook, I thought you'd given that up forever.

FOOK: I had to make my escape somehow.

EL COCO: It suits you. Will you take fingers in your mouth, Fook? Will you lie down and put your legs in the air like the dead have for you?

BOZUFFI: What are you accusing him of?

EL COCO: He knows. I wanted to overcome my natural antipathy to your profession, Doctor. I wanted to forgive your grave-robbing, your rapes, your exploitation of my people.

FOOK: Your people?

EL COCO: The dead. The great, silent majority. The powerless nation. Well that changes from tonight. From tonight the dead will walk, Doctor, they will get up from their pits and you will wish you had never been born. You would murder me—

FOOK: No.

EL COCO: Twice.

FOOK: No.

EL COCO: Come closer, Doctor. See the way my nerves show? The tracery of tendons, the ebb and flow of me. Come and embrace me, Doctor. I'm only yourself. Or am I too common-place, too forgettable, not worth another glance? I am a tri-umph! I am a miracle! And you would put me out like a light.

FOOK: You terrify me.

EL COCO: Then respect me and be polite. I was nothing. I was floating in a darkness so deep there was no bottom to it. Previous to algae, previous to the first cell that winked in the salt-sea. No thought, no self. I waited, not choosing to live or die. Then I heard that scream, that agony from the world, and your voice, Doctor, dispassionate as stone. And I had to come, had to come, just to make peace with myself.

ENTER SISTER MARIA, WITH SUIT.

MARIA: Sir, I could only find—(*Screams*)

EL COCO: Hush. Hush, Sister.

MARIA: Ave Maria Purisima. (*Falls to her knees and prays*)

EL COCO: Why does everyone fall to their knees when they see me? Get up.

FOOK: Do as he says.

EL COCO: I've shocked the good Sister. She's never seen a man quite so naked in her life.

MARIA: I brought the suit.

EL COCO: Take it back.

BOZUFFI: But I have no cloth, you see. I don't like stealing. My shop—burned down—

EL COCO: Return the garments to their owner. They mustn't go naked.

MARIA: Doctor?

FOOK: Don't contradict him. He'll kill you.

EL COCO: Why assume that's the ultimate sanction, Doctor?

MARIA: Don't hurt him.

EL COCO: I won't.

MARIA: I know he's a morbid bastard, but I love him.

EL COCO: Ha! She loves him. The nun loves the mortician who loves his corpses—how could I refuse a request like that? The woman loves you, Doctor, in your skirts and out of them. That's good, because after death, love is the only hope we have. Go about your business.

FOOK: Thank you.

EXIT FOOK AND SISTER MARIA.

BOZUFFI: How can I make a suit without cloth? He was my supplier.

EL COCO: The suits come later, Camilo. First I have to have a skin.

BOZUFFI: A skin.

EL COCO: Several skins in fact, but not mismatched like my others, not a patchwork. I want beauty, Bozuffi, like others have. I want to seem a perfect gentleman.

BOZUFFI: Whatever you say.

EL COCO: And I need heroin too, badly. You can get me that?

BOZUFFI: I suppose so. Do you have money?

EL COCO: There's no pockets in my suit.

BOZUFFI: I have some. Enough for one fix perhaps.

EL COCO: I trust you, Bozuffi.

BOZUFFI: Do you?

EL COCO: Like a brother.

BOZUFFI: I—

EL COCO: You don't want to be my brother.

BOZUFFI: Well, it's not that—

EL COCO: You have forbidden love, don't you, Bozuffi? An unnatural love. One day I shall have a government made up of men like you, who are not quite natural. I will never trust a natural man again. They have too many fears.

BOZUFFI: Do you like boys too?

EL COCO: No. But if you want beauties with slim hips and buttocks like melons, you shall have them, Bozie. Happily. When I am dressed.

BOZUFFI: Do we get the skins from the mortuary? Fook would do the job, the peeling and so on. I can do the sewing.

EL COCO: Fook is a Philistine. He has no eye, no wit, no style. You must remake me, Camilo. You and you alone. I am Adam. I feel too naked. If I had cheeks, I'd blush. We'll work together, choose my new flesh carefully.

BOZUFFI: From living people? But that means—

EL COCO: Murder.

BOZUFFI: No.

EL COCO: Bozie!

BOZUFFI: I draw the line at murder.

EL COCO: Why?

BOZUFFI: It's the first sin. Cain killed his brother—

EL COCO: Because he was Abel.

BOZUFFI: What?

EL COCO: Cain killed his brother because he was Abel . . . to kill his brother. Murder is one part necessity, nine parts opportunity. You'll get the hang of it, Camilo.

BOZUFFI: Do you know the bandit song? "We've made many mothers weep, we've widowed many wives, Many more have we made orphans, for we are childless men ourselves."

EL COCO: Childless and fatherless. All we have is each other, Camilo.

BOZUFFI: There's a club, in the Barrios. We'll find a face for you there.

EL COCO: Something gentle.

BOZUFFI: A wry smile.

THE LIGHTS FLICKER.

BOZUFFI: The generator's on the blink again.

EL COCO: Why don't you flinch? I thought you hated the dark.

BOZUFFI: What could be worse than you? The Bogey-Man's got me. There's nothing left to fear.

THE LIGHTS FLICKER OUT.

Scene Two

THE PRESIDENT'S PALACE. FAR-OFF, WE CAN HEAR GUNS. A WIND PROWLS AROUND, RATTLING AT THE DOORS. ENTER COCKATOO. HE IS DRESSED AS THE PRESIDENT, BUT HIS CAP IS STILL FULL OF FEATHERS. HE LOOKS ILL; HIS EYES ARE RINGED WITH DARKNESS. HE EATS TINNED FRUIT WITH A FORK. HE IS FOLLOWED BY MARIA. SHE SETS UP CANDLES.

COCKATOO: Are all the windows sealed?

MARIA: Yes sir.

COCKATOO: Good. And the doors?

MARIA: Yes.

COCKATOO: Locked and bolted?

MARIA: Every one.

COCKATOO: Nothing can fly in?

MARIA: Fly in sir?

COCKATOO: Cholera. It mustn't find a chink.

MARIA: No.

COCKATOO: It comes as a bird sometimes. A fat black bird. That's its disguise. Sometimes it's a snake, a black snake.

MARIA: *(As to a frightened child)* We're sealed in.

COCKATOO: That's a job well done. The Doctor and I are very pleased. We should keep the flies out too. Even flies carry the pest. If I see a fly in here, I'll make you eat it. Understand? Then we'll see . . .

ENTER VERONIQUE. THE TRANSFORMATION OF HER FACE CONTINUES. A BLOOM OF SCALES ON HER FOREHEAD AND NECK.

VERONIQUE: It's like a furnace in here, Cockatoo.

COCKATOO: It's noon. The sun's high.

VERONIQUE: We should open one window at least.

COCKATOO: No.

VERONIQUE: We'll cook. We'll die of heat exhaustion.

COCKATOO: There's no harm in sweat. It lets out the poisons in the skin.

VERONIQUE: How long do we have to live like this?

COCKATOO: When it's safe, when the plague's over, then we'll take a stroll together, around the city. Visit the sick—

VERONIQUE: If we stay in here, there'll be no city left to visit. You're supposed to be President, Cockatoo.

COCKATOO: *(Dreamily)* President.

VERONIQUE: You should be taking charge. Martial law—

COCKATOO: Law.

VERONIQUE: Answer me, Cockatoo.

COCKATOO: Law.

VERONIQUE: You remember Cesar. He wanted law.

MARIA: Don't speak to him about—

VERONIQUE: Cesar, Cockatoo. Remember?

MARIA: It's forbidden. If the Doctor hears you—

VERONIQUE: El Coco.

MARIA: Jesus.

VERONIQUE: El Coco.

COCKATOO: El Coco.

MARIA: He doesn't remember. Let him be.

COCKATOO: El Coco.

MARIA: I think it's time you took your medication, isn't it?

COCKATOO: There is natural law and unnatural law. The natural law protects all natural acts by natural men, it is repressive. The unnatural law is made . . . is made . . .

VERONIQUE: Go on.

COCKATOO: I forget.

MARIA: Come with me.

VERONIQUE: *(To Maria)* Why do you do this? Why do you serve Frankenstein?

MARIA: Because he's kind. He understands.

VERONIQUE: We'll die in here, you stupid woman. We'll never see the sun again. He's locked us in our graves, all of us.

MARIA: No. It's wise. There's horrors outside, I've seen for myself. Little coups and counter-coups. You hear the shooting? And

the dead just lying in the streets, bloated by the heat, crawl-
ing with flies. You want to be out there?

VERONIQUE: We can't lock it out forever. It'll find its way in, in
one form or another. Disease gets hungry. It'll want us all.

MARIA: The Doctor will protect us.

VERONIQUE: From every fly? From every breath of wind under
the door?

MARIA EXITS WITH COCKATOO.

VERONIQUE: You see how I'm left, Cesar. With idiots, and lunatics.
And the dead. (*She looks at herself in a hand mirror*) I dreamt I
was sitting in this room on a crate, and the crate was full of
men. Hyenas prowled around. I fed them slivers of meat from
between my teeth. Sooner or later I knew I'd let them out of the
crate, those whining prisoners, and let the hyenas and men
fight it out for me. Would I go to the beasts or the men? I didn't
care. I chewed on raw meat and let them sweat, and didn't care.

ENTER DR. FRANKENSTEIN.

FRANKENSTEIN: Do you hear the wind? It wants to get in. But
all the doors are locked, and all the windows are shuttered.
Lazaro bricked some of them up, the big ones. That was
wise, don't you think? You can't be too careful. There's so
much out there that wants our blood, Veronique. The whole
of suppurating humanity would like to get in here and taste
our safety. I hear its voice, don't you? In the wind.

VERONIQUE: What are you doing to Cockatoo?

FRANKENSTEIN: Just keeping him sedated. But he refuses to eat,
and he tries to hurt himself. Sometimes I think his will is too
strong, he surfaces through the drug, remembers his past,
his betrayal of the monster. That hurts him, and he has
wounded himself in atonement for his mistake. I think he'll
kill himself, which is a pity.

VERONIQUE: You don't seem to care.

FRANKENSTEIN: If a man has one head, I can give him two.
Guilt I can do nothing about. The wounds in the mind must
be bred out, generation by generation. People must be
taught not to hate themselves so much. Like you, you hate

yourself, don't you? You think you'll be something venomous, disgusting. Oh, I watch you Veronique, with your mirror and your tears. I watch you naked as you look at the changes in your substance, and the horror with which you greet each new transformation. But you must learn not to fear change, and if not you, your children—

VERONIQUE: I'll have no children.

FRANKENSTEIN: My dear, you must, or all our suffering is for nothing.

VERONIQUE: What kind of husband could you find me?

FRANKENSTEIN: Beast or man, you mean?

VERONIQUE: You were listening.

FRANKENSTEIN: I won't mate you with a hyena. I want you to produce undying human children. Capable of endless regeneration of their bodies. As though the butterfly could return to the chrysalis after its day and be born again the next. Until we are without death, we will be beasts, sweet.

VERONIQUE: Everything dies. Even suns go out.

FRANKENSTEIN: But we predict our deaths, that's the unbearable part. We know it's coming. When we're children we think death's a kind of sleep, curable in a while. Gradually the truth dawns: death is a permanent complaint. We look at our bodies and we see them putrefying around our living minds and we know, finally, that the enemy is our flesh. The body is a prison and must be escaped by metaphysics, or changed by wit and knife and courage. I have changed you, made your womb the birthplace of a deathless thing. Your breasts are its meat. It lacks only a father. I wanted Cockatoo to breed with you, but he has murdered his manhood.

VERONIQUE: What do you mean?

FRANKENSTEIN: In a moment of lucidity, two nights ago. He castrated himself.

VERONIQUE: No, Cockatoo. No.

FRANKENSTEIN: He'd gelded foals; he knew the cut. So . . . it must be us. You and I.

VERONIQUE: You? My husband?

FRANKENSTEIN: I love you, Veronique.

VERONIQUE: You're incapable of love. You saw the heads off living men. You scoop out their eyes while they plead—

FRANKENSTEIN: I do it all of the same, indivisible love. For you, for them, for the future. I want you to prosper.

VERONIQUE: You're insane. You stink of blood.

FRANKENSTEIN: Would you accuse me of insanity if I bred a new orchid, with a sweeter scent? If I live in blood to make new blooms, that is the condition of my study. I don't expect you to love me. Of course not. But you have my heart, Veronique.

VERONIQUE: And if I refuse?

FRANKENSTEIN: You'll be let out into the world. You'll be a monster. Like the pin-head and the two-headed cow. You must have stared at freaks. Well, that's what you are. Nature undone. You drink hot blood, Veronique. In the eyes of the common bourgeois that is in questionable taste. Only I . . . only I will happily satisfy your appetites, love you with all the passion I am capable of.

VERONIQUE: You are the angel of Auschwitz.

FRANKENSTEIN: I am a Jew, Veronique. I was in Auschwitz to die. We have a legend of the golem, the unfinished thing. Adam was God's golem, until he was given a soul. There are stories of Rabbis who made such creatures from dust, and set them to work. In Auschwitz I conceived of such a thing to do work for me, to change the world by force. See how obedient he was, my golem? So I must work another way, through you. Marry me, I put my religion aside. We'll have the Cardinal marry us. Well?

VERONIQUE: Yes. I will marry you.

FRANKENSTEIN: You'll find me an attentive lover. As a young man in Vienna, women were always happy in my bed. So many husbands, you know, have a pitiful understanding of love's anatomy. But I have a skill, with my hands and—you won't regret your decision.

VERONIQUE: Thank you.

FRANKENSTEIN: May I kiss you?

VERONIQUE: No.

FRANKENSTEIN: Once.

VERONIQUE: Later.

FRANKENSTEIN: I will adore you, Veronique. Don't cry, sweet. You're safe with me. Quite, quite safe. Nothing can find us here, nothing can touch us or hurt us. Oh please don't cry, Veronique, please.

VERONIQUE: You killed Cesar.

FRANKENSTEIN: You wanted him.

VERONIQUE: Not wanted. That's past, wanting.

FRANKENSTEIN: It's all right. He was my son, Veronique. He hurt me too. I understand. Hush. Hush. Where is Lazaro? I wonder, is he listening?

VERONIQUE: He always listens.

FRANKENSTEIN: He doesn't understand what we say.

ENTER LAZARO.

LAZARO: Yes. I do.

FRANKENSTEIN: Poor child. You couldn't know.

LAZARO: What can I do? How can I help? Is the lady ill? Does she need her head drilling? It's very good, it releases the pressure on the brain. I drill holes in my skull all the time. Shall I demonstrate?

FRANKENSTEIN: No. Not now.

LAZARO: Just to relieve the pressure.

FRANKENSTEIN: Lazaro. Go and fetch the Cardinal. We're going to be married.

LAZARO: I didn't know you loved me that much.

FRANKENSTEIN: Veronique and I.

LAZARO: Oh, the lady. You're marrying the lady.

FRANKENSTEIN: I am. And I want the Cardinal here, in attendance.

LAZARO: That's a good idea. We should celebrate.

FRANKENSTEIN: Perhaps you can find flowers for the lady? And a dress. Find her a wedding dress, Lazaro.

LAZARO: White? For a virgin. I'll find something for her. I'll find a thousand things.

FRANKENSTEIN: Good. Then go.

LAZARO: It may take me all day and all night, but you'll have a wedding to be proud of, I promise. We all love you, you know, the ghost and Cockatoo and—we all love you.

EXIT LAZARO. FRANKENSTEIN KISSES VERONIQUE.

FRANKENSTEIN: I'll send Maria with your pills, my sweet. God loves you.

EXIT FRANKENSTEIN. VERONIQUE BEGINS TO LAUGH, THE LAUGH GROWS UNTIL SHE IS PRACTI-CALLY HYSTERICAL.

VERONIQUE: God loves you, Veronique. God loves you. So I
have your adoration, do I husband? You know my biology
intimately of course. Off by heart. By heart. Well, I hope you
satisfy me. The female spider, having mated, eats her husband. I will not be less considerate.

ENTER MARIA WITH A PILL, A BOTTLE, AND A GLASS.

VERONIQUE: Ah, Maria. How are you?
MARIA: Cool.
VERONIQUE: You look well.
MARIA: I forget my name sometimes.
VERONIQUE: You know I'm getting married?
MARIA: Congratulations.
VERONIQUE: Who shall I invite? That's the problem. With half
the city dead, and the other half in mourning, who can a
lucky girl like me possibly invite? I tell you what, Maria. You
can do me a favor, as your wedding present to me. Find
yourself a spade and dig up a few wedding guests, will you?
MARIA: Dig them up. You're joking.
VERONIQUE: This is my house, phantasma, and those are my orders.
Bring me rot. Puerile, smiling rot. Attend me with gangrene, and
spoil, and every wormy, fecal thing you can unhouse. Pollute
me. Revolt me. Do your worst. Please. The blushing bride must
find her blushes somewhere. Let mine be sores.
MARIA: Yes, lady.
VERONIQUE: Maybe this world will retch me out Maria, and sick
me into heaven. Look at me. Is the ghost afraid?
MARIA: No.
VERONIQUE: Where's Cockatoo?
MARIA: He had a fit. He half-remembers—
VERONIQUE: I did it to make him remember.
MARIA: Well he has his imitators now, your fire-walker.
VERONIQUE: Oh?
MARIA: He's not forgotten.
VERONIQUE: There are true fire-walkers and false.
MARIA: I know. Real fire-walkers go barefoot.
VERONIQUE: No, Maria. Real fire-walkers make the fire them-
selves. Every pace is a flame.
MARIA: Who told you that?

VERONIQUE: Nobody. I just hope it. Don't you watch sometimes, see the air shimmering, waiting for someone to come,
walking flames, to take you into hell with him.

MARIA: I'm biding my time.

VERONIQUE: But maybe we are alone.

MARIA: I don't think so.

VERONIQUE: Maybe nobody comes. All the true fire-walkers are
maybe dead.

MARIA: There's one, in the Barrios. They call him the Salamander.

VERONIQUE: Salamander.

MARIA: Because he's supposed to live in fire you see. (*Gives
Veronique the pills*)

VERONIQUE: Salamander.

MARIA: He heals the sick too.

VERONIQUE: Bring me Cockatoo.

MARIA: He's had a fit.

VERONIQUE: Bring him here.

MARIA: Yes.

VERONIQUE: Thank you.

*EXIT MARIA. VERONIQUE POURS HERSELF A GLASS
OF BLOOD AND DRINKS IT DOWN.*

VERONIQUE: Blood gets thick in the air, and dark, and meaty.
Let it be him. I like blood that's fresh, but cool. Let it be
him. We must stay cool. Him. Until the fire.

Scene Three

*SOMEWHERE IN THE BARRIO. ENTER MARIA. SHE
ADDRESSES THE AUDIENCE.*

Maria: Seems to me, if you want to know my opinion, that we're
all swimming around in sewerage. That's what the nice people call it. Sewerage. And not wanting to offend you, that's
what I call it too. You know what I mean. So here we are,
barely keeping our mouths from filling up, and there's these
buggers floating past in boats. Oh yes, big white boats.
Americans most of them, and they're floating around like
there was no tomorrow. But I'll tell you something. They
haven't got sails on their nice, white boats, no oars, no rud-
ders. They're going with the current same as the rest of us.
Down the drain, all of us, down some dark and filthy drain,
covered in shit. Sorry, sewerage. That's my opinion.

*THE NOISE OF A CROWD. ENTER BOZUFFI, ELEGANT
AS EVER.*

MARIA: Ah! Bozuffi.
BOZUFFI: You can't come in here; the Salamander will not be
healing anyone today.
MARIA: I don't need healing.
BOZUFFI: Aren't you Sister Maria?
MARIA: I was.
BOZUFFI: Given up virginity, have you?
MARIA: I was hoping for a Papal Bull, but it didn't turn up. What
are the boys like here?
BOZUFFI: I beg your pardon?
MARIA: There's a lot of kids who'll bend over for the price of a
cigarette, eh?
BOZUFFI: I resent that remark.
MARIA: No easy pickings then?
BOZUFFI: I cover the waterfront. If you take my meaning.
MARIA: Happy?
BOZUFFI: Could be worse.
MARIA: Despite all the disease?
BOZUFFI: You can get used to anything.
MARIA: Let me see your hand.
BOZUFFI: What?
MARIA: Short life-line.
BOZUFFI: I have cholera. Caught it off a blue-eyed . . . I'll be
dead in a few days, that's my prognosis.

MARIA: You don't seem to care.

BOZUFFI: Life's a nice place to visit, but I wouldn't want to stay here. It's too arbitrary, too unperfectable. Like a suit you can never quite get to fit.

MARIA: Did you commit murder for the monster?

BOZUFFI: How did you know about that?

MARIA: I've been eavesdropping.

BOZUFFI: I didn't wield the axe personally. But I've got quite used to skinning bodies. He's taught me a lot, Cesar Guerrero. I think I may even learn to juggle hot coals before King Cholera takes me.

MARIA: From behind.

BOZUFFI: From behind? Oh yes. From behind.

MARIA: What's the crowd?

BOZUFFI: They come every day to have him heal them, and see him do his tricks. He's fire-walking today.

MARIA: I saw the coals.

BOZUFFI: He never flinches. Never.

MARIA: Is it a trick?

BOZUFFI: Of course it's a trick. They just need a God, and he's conveniently situated. They call him the Salamander.

MARIA: I know.

BOZUFFI: Because salamanders have this urge to sit in fires apparently. Which is probably why they're a dying species.

ENTER EL COCO. HE IS DRESSED IN LIGHT, SIMPLE CLOTHES. HIS FACE IS STILL COMPLETELY BANDAGED. HE EMBRACES BOZUFFI.

EL COCO: Ah, Camilo. Today, the last piece—

BOZUFFI: The last piece.

EL COCO: And I'm a new man.

BOZUFFI: Perfect in every detail.

EL COCO: Will she recognize me, do you think?

BOZUFFI: Your bones are the same. The face won't have changed that much.

EL COCO: Do you think she's well, Bozuffi?

BOZUFFI: Who knows? She could have flown away by now.

EL COCO: Don't say that.

BOZUFFI: Take off your bandages and sit down. We have to work to finish before your next performance.

EL COCO SITS WITH HIS BACK TO THE AUDIENCE AND TAKES OFF HIS BANDAGES. BOZUFFI OPENS A BOX AND TAKES OUT A PIECE OF CLOTH. HE UNFOLDS IT AND LIFTS A PIECE OF BLOODED SKIN WITH TWEEZERS. IT IS A FACE.

BOZUFFI: Who did we get this from?

EL COCO: The tax-inspector.

BOZUFFI: So we did.

EL COCO: The one with the flawless complexion.

BOZUFFI: He was sweet. I was quite in love, until he opened his mouth. Vicious pimp. I mean, a tax-inspector pimping. Oh mercy, how far have we fallen?

EL COCO: Get on with it.

THE WORK ON EL COCO'S FACE BEGINS WITH BOZUFFI SEWING AROUND THE EDGE OF THE FACE, APPARENTLY SEWING THE SKIN IN PLACE.

BOZUFFI: I was never beautiful, which I always regretted. Being beautiful makes everything so much easier, doesn't it? I've always had to fight for what I had. And I've relied on the kindness of strangers. This is going to be a fine face when it's finished. The skin tone perfectly matches your eyes. Of course you won't be able to grow a beard for a while, but you're manly enough without a lot of hair. Who wants hair anyway? Not me. Give me a smooth body, slim and lithe and smooth.

EL COCO: Sounds like a snake would suit you fine.

BOZUFFI: Keep still and shut up. You know I can't bear snakes. Especially the little black ones that swim. Those are the worst. Keep still. How can I sew your face back on if you won't keep still? It's almost done—

OUTSIDE THE CROWD ROARS.

EL COCO: What's that?

BOZUFFI: Stay still . . . a few moments more. *(To Maria)* Go and look for him, sweetheart—

EL COCO: Who's she?

BOZUFFI: Some ghost.

MARIA EXITS

BOZUFFI: You will bury me properly, won't you my darling?

EL COCO: Of course.

BOZUFFI: I don't want to be flung in a lime-pit. I don't want Fook to get his thieving hands on me.

EL COCO: He won't.

BOZUFFI: Promise.

EL COCO: Cross my heart and hope to die.

BOZUFFI: The wit of the man.

MARIA: There's somebody trying to walk on the coals—

EL COCO: (*Gets up*) What?

HE TURNS ROUND. THE JOB IS ALMOST COMPLETE. THE NEW SKIN IS IN PLACE; THE THREAD AND NEEDLE HANG FROM THE CORNER OF HIS JAW.

MARIA: A moment more—

EL COCO: On the coals—no!

OFF STAGE, A SCREAM.

BOZUFFI: Dios mio!

EL COCO: Stop him—

BOZUFFI: (*Gets hold of El Coco*) You can't go out like that! Let me—(*Gives up*) finish it yourself.

EXIT MARIA AND BOZUFFI. EL COCO SITS BACK IN THE SEAT AND STARTS TO SEW UP THE REST OF HIS FACE, BUT HE IS TOO CLUMSY.

EL COCO: Ah! Damn it!

ENTER MARIA AND BOZUFFI CARRYING A MOANING MAN WHOSE FEET ARE BURNED BLACK. THEY SMOKE. HIS TROUSERS ARE CHARRED. HIS SHINS ARE PEELING AND BLISTERED. HIS HEAD IS TURNED AWAY FROM US. HE WEARS THE REMNANTS OF A STRAIT-JACKET ON HIS UPPER BODY. IT IS COCKATOO.

EL COCO: Cockatoo!

BOZUFFI: You know him.

EL COCO: Oh Cockatoo. (*Kneels beside him*) What can we do for his feet?

BOZUFFI: Without medication, very little.

MARIA: Shall I find a doctor?

COCKATOO: No doctors.

BOZUFFI: But it'll fester.

EL COCO: He wants no doctors.

COCKATOO: Enough of the doctors.

EL COCO: What brought you here?

COCKATOO: She sent me.

EL COCO: Veronique?

COCKATOO: I forget her name.

EL COCO: Veronique, Cockatoo. Tell me it was Veronique.

COCKATOO: I saw you.

EL COCO: Did you?

COCKATOO: Yes Cesar, I saw you. I saw you in the flames, walking in the fire, like the old days. In the, in the—

EL COCO: Sierra.

COCKATOO: In the Sierra. We lived, didn't we?

EL COCO: We did, Cockatoo.

COCKATOO: I wasn't dreaming it. We lived. There was rain, birds—

EL COCO: Yes.

COCKATOO: I forgot for a while . . . then when I remembered, I thought I'd dreamt it. Cesar . . .

EL COCO: What is it, my friend?

COCKATOO: I did you harm. I don't remember what, but I pained you somehow. It hurts me to think of it . . . my eyes ache. But I harmed you.

EL COCO: Not knowingly.

COCKATOO: I was envious, you know. I wanted to harm you until . . . forgive me.

EL COCO: There's nothing to forgive.

COCKATOO: Don't deny me contrition, my brother. Don't take that away from me. Forgive me, please. Let me have sinned against you and then forgive me.

EL COCO: I forgive you.

COCKATOO: I saw you in the fire. I wanted to walk with you.

EL COCO: I wasn't walking on the coals.

COCKATOO: You had your back to me . . . walking. Like you used to, a slow walk, steady like a soldier, and I thought I could do it. I came after you; it didn't hurt that much. There was a smell. I was burning but I didn't notice. I ran to you, and you turned and looked at me. And it wasn't you at all, it was me. It was my mirage, in the heat. Me. I was alone Cesar, alone in the fire, and you weren't there to save me. Then I screamed.

EL COCO: It's over now.

COCKATOO: No. There's more fires yet.

EL COCO: Where?

COCKATOO: At the Palace. You must go to the Palace. Veronique—

EL COCO: What about Veronique?

COCKATOO: Veronique. *(He seems to die)*

EL COCO: Cockatoo, answer me. What about Veronique? You will not die yet. I forbid you to die. Find another breath. *(Blows breath into Cockatoo's mouth)* What about Veronique?

COCKATOO: *(Coughs and flings his head back, eyes showing white, in some fugue state, neither alive nor dead)* Marriage.

EL COCO: To whom?

COCKATOO: Frankenstein.

EL COCO: When?

COCKATOO: Tonight.

EL COCO: At the Palace?

COCKATOO: Yes.

EL COCO: Thank you.

COCKATOO: May I die now?

EL COCO: Is that all you have to tell me?

COCKATOO: Yes.

EL COCO: Die then, Cockatoo.

COCKATOO: If you come to hell, Cesar . . .

EL COCO: What?

COCKATOO: If you come to hell . . . after a while . . . you must teach me to walk on fire. Please. *(He dies)*

BOZUFFI: A wedding.

EL COCO: A wedding. *(To Maria)* Did you see this on my palms?

MARIA: Of course.

EL COCO: No wonder you wanted to die.

BOZUFFI: Will he—

EL COCO: Bozuffi, what's wrong?

BOZUFFI: I was just thinking out loud.

EL COCO: Tell me.

BOZUFFI: Will he go to hell?

EL COCO: Camilo, he just left it.

BOZUFFI: I wondered. The way you do, once in a while. What it's for.

EL COCO: Wash my face.

BOZUFFI: Oh yes.

EL COCO: And then I must find a suit of clothes. For the wedding.

BOZUFFI: We could go to the hospice. See if Fook has something for us.

MARIA: Fook died three days ago.

BOZUFFI: Oh?

MARIA: One of the errors lost patience and strangled him.

BOZUFFI: Poor Fook. Still, we'll find you a suit somewhere. (*Cuts the cotton*) There.

EL COCO: (*Turns round; the face is finished*) Thank you. (*Embraces Bozuffi*) See me Cockatoo? See me? Aren't I a prodigy? A nightmare never had a smile as sweet as mine.

LIGHTS DOWN.

Scene Four

THE PRESIDENTIAL PALACE. ENTER MARIA. A MUR-MURING IS HEARD OF DEAD VOICES, AND THE SOFT SCRATCHING OF NAILS ON COFFIN LIDS. MARIA DRESSES HERSELF FOR THE WEDDING, PER-HAPS ADORNING HERSELF WITH FLOWERS.

MARIA: It is the last long night of the world. We hear voices, we see signs. Things on the wall, noises in the vaults. When we think we are alone, we find strangers hiding in the corners of the room. When we are amongst friends we find them suddenly insubstantial, fading, leaving us alone. Suddenly nothing is what it seems. Especially the first fact—flesh. Somebody sent me a rose. I don't know who. A fresh rose. Where would you find a fresh rose on a night like this?

ENTER DR. FRANKENSTEIN.

FRANKENSTEIN: You.
MARIA: Sir?
FRANKENSTEIN: The voices.
MARIA: What about them?
FRANKENSTEIN: Do you hear them?
MARIA: Certainly.
FRANKENSTEIN: What are they?
MARIA: Guests, I imagine.
FRANKENSTEIN: There's noises at the windows, cuticles on wood, eh? Scratching away.
MARIA: Apparently somebody wants to get in.
FRANKENSTEIN: Well don't you let them.
MARIA: Heaven forbid.

MARIA BEGINS TO DECORATE THE STAGE WITH SKELETONS AND MUMMIFIED BODIES SHE HAS GATHERED FOR THE WEDDING. SOME SHE MIGHT UNVEIL, ALREADY IN POSITION. OTHERS SHE MIGHT BRING OUT OF THE CRATES, COVERED IN DIRT, AND ARRANGE. ROWS OF MUMMIFIED HEADS, THEIR DRIED FACES CAUGHT IN SHRIEKS AND HOWLS, THEIR LEATHER TONGUES CURLED AND COILED. THE STAGE SEEMS TO FILL WITH THE DEAD.

FRANKENSTEIN: I went up to the roof.
MARIA: Did you?
FRANKENSTEIN: It's too dark to see much. Just the plague pits burning. They must have run out of lime.
MARIA: Yes.
FRANKENSTEIN: I could see no crowd. And yet the voices *(Turns; sees the cadavers)*—my God woman, what are these?
MARIA: Your bride-to-be, she asked for guests.
FRANKENSTEIN: Guests?

MARIA: She asked me to exhume some friends.

FRANKENSTEIN: Ha! Is this what I can hear in my head? (*Picks up a dried, howling head*) Is it you, choirmaster? Are you leading this music? You've got a tongue in there—I can see it. A little leather tongue. Well, damn you, I can silence you. (*Tears out the tongue*) I insist you be quiet. I insist! (*Puts his hand deep into the head's mouth and pulls out worms*) Maggots where you should have thought. No wonder he doesn't listen. Never mind, choirmaster, I understand your confusion. Unable to be quiet, obliged to go on crying. It's my condition absolutely. Where is the Cardinal?

MARIA: (*Offers a head*) Is this him?

FRANKENSTEIN: No.

MARIA: This one?

FRANKENSTEIN: He's still alive.

MARIA: Oh. He's one of those. I don't know where he is.

FRANKENSTEIN: As soon as he arrives, I want him to bless this room. Bless the whole Palace. Drive out these voices with the Blood of the Lamb.

MARIA: He's bringing meat? Where'd he get that?

FRANKENSTEIN: Christ is the Lamb.

MARIA: Pity. I fancied a little meat.

FRANKENSTEIN: I don't mind taking the Church to bed with me. A lot of men, more Godless than me, do it at the end. Just to be sure. To play safe. God forgives them everything, doesn't he, like the perfect father. He rocks the contrite to sleep with equal love whether the sin was murder or bedwetting. I will be forgiven. What have I done but served life? (*Closes his eyes*) I think I see him coming.

MARIA: The Lamb?

FRANKENSTEIN: The Cardinal.

MARIA: The windows are closed. How can you see him coming?

FRANKENSTEIN: In my mind's eye. I close my lids and he's there.

MARIA: What does he look like?

FRANKENSTEIN: I can't see his face. He's dressed in black. Coming to bless the union.

MARIA: Hallelujah.

THE MURMURING BEGINS TO FADE.

FRANKENSTEIN: I think maybe tomorrow the Americans will come.
MARIA: Is that good?
FRANKENSTEIN: Oh yes. We'll have law, and Coca-Cola.
MARIA: Not necessarily in that order.
FRANKENSTEIN: And I shall win the Nobel Peace Prize.
MARIA: It's been known.
FRANKENSTEIN: Move to New York. Take up cosmetic surgery.

ENTER LAZARO, HIS HEAD FAR BLOODIER THAN BEFORE. HE CARRIES A CROSS.

LAZARO: Oh. Everything's so beautiful. Brings tears to the eyes.
MARIA: Thank you.
LAZARO: Isn't she clever?
FRANKENSTEIN: Any sign of the Cardinal?
LAZARO: Isn't she clever?
FRANKENSTEIN: Lazaro.
LAZARO: I drilled a big hole in my head. It was aching so much. The Cardinal has a strange head, hasn't he?
FRANKENSTEIN: Not that I remember.
LAZARO: I saw him coming, from the roof.
FRANKENSTEIN: Oh—
LAZARO: I think it was him.
FRANKENSTEIN: I'd better get dressed.
LAZARO: Wear your apron. It's your color—red and white.
FRANKENSTEIN: Come for me as soon as he arrives.

EXIT FRANKENSTEIN.

LAZARO: Do you think we're all going to die? I do. What does it matter? What's the worst they could do to me? Graft my head onto a cow? So what? I like being milked.

HE OPENS A BABY'S COFFIN WITH A SCREWDRIVER, UNSCREWING IT CAREFULLY.

MARIA: You're as bad as he is.
LAZARO: Worse, I daresay. I sucked out part of my brain last night, trying to relieve the pressure. I put a little hose into one of the holes, and sucked. First I got a mouthful of brain-

pan water. That made me feel better. So I got a little overzealous you know, as you do, and I sucked again and got a mouthful of offal. Not bad actually. Better with onions. (*Has the lid off the coffin*) Where did you get the baby?

MARIA: One of the mausoleums.

LAZARO: Quite a child. (*Takes the baby out: its hair is very long and white, its dress is lace, its teeth are those of a beast*) All these treasures buried underground. People don't realize, do they, what they're walking on. (*Puts the child on the altar, having molested it*) The problem is, I run out of outrages.

ENTER VERONIQUE, IN HER WEDDING GOWN. THE TRANSFORMATION GOES ON. HER HAIR IS COPPER, HER SKIN SPECKLED LIKE A SNAKE'S. HER DRESS IS A FANTASTIQUE: A POTPOURRI OF LACES, SHROUDS, RIBBONS AND ROPES. EXQUISITE, SEXUAL. HER SKIN GLINTS THROUGH THE LACE. SHE HAS NO VEIL HOWEVER.

LAZARO: Our lady of the shrouds.

VERONIQUE: Oh Maria, you've done well.

MARIA: Thank you.

VERONIQUE: We need incense.

LAZARO: I have it.

VERONIQUE: Light the censers then.

LAZARO: Yes. Yes.

VERONIQUE: Where's the bridegroom?

MARIA: Getting ready for the ceremony.

LAZARO: I think he's too old for you. When you're coupling he won't know if he's coming or going.

MARIA: (*Laughs*) He's right. You'll have to take lovers.

VERONIQUE: I suppose I will.

MARIA: Younger men. With sweat to spare. I've got a rose you know. You look parched.

LAZARO: You need a wet man, oozing out of every pore.

MARIA: Fountains.

LAZARO: Me, I could be your lover. I'm good with virgins, especially docile virgins who died early.

VERONIQUE: The dress is exquisite.

LAZARO: Thank you.

VERONIQUE: But I have no veil.

LAZARO: No veil! Ah! I could kick myself. In fact I will! (*Kicks himself around the stage, much to Veronique and Maria's amusement; he is basking in their attention*) I'm an idiot! I'm a brainless cretin! No veil! Ah! No veil! (*Goes into the baby's coffin, throwing out dead flowers, and hauls out a length of lacy shroud*) What about this? Hand-sewn.

VERONIQUE: Let me see. Yes, that's beautiful.

LAZARO: It smells of children.

VERONIQUE: Why not? So do I.

LAZARO AND MARIA FUSS AROUND THE BRIDE, PUTTING THE VEIL ON HER HEAD, ARRANGING HER DRESS AND TRAIN.

LAZARO: (*Giving her flowers; fantastic blossoms made of human tissue with eyeballs at their centers*) There! There! Are those gross enough for you?

VERONIQUE: Perfect.

LAZARO: Let me take a photograph.

VERONIQUE: Maria.

MARIA: Lady?

VERONIQUE: Did Cockatoo come home?

MARIA: No.

VERONIQUE: No message?

MARIA: Nothing. He was ill. He shouldn't have been let loose.

VERONIQUE: Was it a trick then? Your talk of the Salamander?

MARIA: I heard nothing more.

VERONIQUE: Did you say it to hurt me? Is that it? Because I'm getting a husband and you're going to fret on with an ache between your legs? Jealousy was it?

LAZARO: Ladies. Ladies. Let me shoot the blushing bride. (*Photographs Veronique*) Beautiful. Beautiful. One more.

A BANGING ON THE DOOR.

LAZARO: The Cardinal.

VERONIQUE: He's here.

MARIA: At last.

LAZARO: I'll fetch him.

VERONIQUE: Do that.

LAZARO: Don't forget me, lady. Brides have wishes granted. Pray I understand soon.

VERONIQUE: Understand what?

LAZARO: What the hell it's all about, eh?

EXIT LAZARO.

VERONIQUE: What's it like outside?

MARIA: Warm, I believe. Stars.

VERONIQUE: I didn't mean—

MARIA: I know.

VERONIQUE: I'm sad, that's all. For you and for me.

MARIA: Don't be sad for me. I've got a lover.

VERONIQUE: Where?

MARIA: He's coming. He isn't here yet, but he's very close. Perfectly faithful, utterly diverting.

VERONIQUE: What are his intentions toward you?

MARIA: Entirely honorable. He wants to lie me down and make an honest woman of me.

VERONIQUE: That's good. I'm pleased. *(They kiss)*

MARIA: I'll fetch the groom.

VERONIQUE: Maria. What's his name?

MARIA: Honorable men don't have names, do they?

MARIA EXITS.

VERONIQUE: Wherever you are, Cesar, whatever wind took your ash, I love you. He takes nothing of any worth from me. He steals nothing, because it was all given to you. My hands are empty.

ENTER THE CARDINAL, HOODED, CARRYING A BOX. LAZARO FOLLOWS. VERONIQUE KISSES THE CARDINAL'S RING.

LAZARO: He came! He came!

VERONIQUE: Of course he came.

LAZARO: Can I sing *Ave Maria*? Shall I take your cloak? No? What's in the box? Is it holy water? Is it? He's very quiet, isn't he, for a Catholic?

ENTER DR. FRANKENSTEIN.

FRANKENSTEIN: Good evening. You came.

LAZARO: Of course he came.

FRANKENSTEIN: I was afraid something had happened to you. We hear such terrible reports.

LAZARO: Bang! Bang! Bang! Bang! All night.

FRANKENSTEIN: Shall we begin?

THE CARDINAL NODS.

FRANKENSTEIN: Good. Good.

THE CARDINAL CROSSES HIMSELF IN FRONT OF THE ALTAR AND PRAYS. MARIA BRINGS THE VEIL DOWN OVER VERONIQUE'S FACE.

LAZARO: *(To Frankenstein)* Good luck, sir.

FRANKENSTEIN: Thank you, Lazaro.

LAZARO: Here's the ring. The Auschwitz ring. Don't forget your line: I do.

FRANKENSTEIN: I won't.

LAZARO: No—I do. I do.

FRANKENSTEIN GOES TO THE ALTAR AND KNEELS DOWN. VERONIQUE JOINS HIM. CARDINAL HAS TURNED AND BLESSES THEM. DOWNSTAGE, LAZARO APPROACHES THE BOX.

LAZARO: I could never resist boxes. It's a weakness of mine. Especially closed boxes. *(Tries the lid)* Locked. There's always something interesting in locked boxes, isn't there? There is. There is.

MARIA: I wouldn't if I were you.

LAZARO: Well, you're not me. I'm me. I think. I wonder what's in it. What do Cardinals keep in boxes? Besides their balls. *(Forces the lid—the box is lined with scalpels, set into the sides and the lid, glinting, pointing inwards)* Oh, how pretty. Look at all those lovely knives. Dozens of them. Pristine. *(Touches one)* Ow! Savage little things. What would he want this for?

MARIA: Put the lid down.

LAZARO: (*Hypnotized*) Beautiful. Look at the way they wink and glitter. Like teeth. There's something written on the bottom of the box, see?

MARIA: Don't look.

LAZARO: It's very small writing. (*Peers into the box*) Tiny, Tiny words. (*Leans further in*) I can hardly read it. (*His head is in the box*) "Smile . . . and say . . . goodnight." (*Lid slams down and locks—Lazaro screams as his head is encased in a sheath of scalpels, his limbs thrash—the wedding is disrupted*) Ah! Help me! Help me!

FRANKENSTEIN: (*Gets up*) Lazaro!

MARIA: He looked inside.

FRANKENSTEIN: Lazaro!

LAZARO'S VOICE IS ONE SOLID SHRIEK NOW. FRANKENSTEIN WRESTLES WITH HIM, TAKING HOLD OF HIS THRASHING HEAD. HE UNBOLTS THE BOTTOM OF THE BOX. THE BOTTOM IS ON A HINGE, AND IT FALLS OPEN. THE BOTTOM TOO IS LINED WITH SCALPELS, AND LAZARO'S HEAD HAS BEEN PUNCTURED IN A DOZEN PLACES. HIS FACE HAS CUTS ALL OVER IT; SCALPELS HAVE PUT OUT HIS EYES. BLADES SET IN THE SIDE OF THE BOX HAVE IMPALED HIS HEAD. THE SCREAM DIES. LAZARO COLLAPSES IN FRANKENSTEIN'S ARMS, THE BOX STILL ON HIS HEAD, LIKE AN ABSURD PIETA.

FRANKENSTEIN: Who did this?

MARIA: Not me.

CARDINAL: I did.

FRANKENSTEIN: Armitano, why?

CARDINAL: I'm not Armitano. (*Pulls off his hood*)

FRANKENSTEIN: Follezou.

VERONIQUE: Eddie!

FOLLEZOU: My lady.

FRANKENSTEIN: Where's the Cardinal?

FOLLEZOU: Dead and defecated. Weeks ago.

FRANKENSTEIN: This little box is your doing?

FOLLEZOU: It was meant for you. A wedding present.

FRANKENSTEIN: Not very loving.

FOLLEZOU: Kind, by comparison with your gifts to me.

FRANKENSTEIN: You've spoiled my wedding day.

FOLLEZOU: My pleasure.

FRANKENSTEIN: (*His expression changes*) But it was a fine joke.

FOLLEZOU: Joke?

FRANKENSTEIN: I enjoyed it immensely.

FOLLEZOU: It wasn't meant as an entertainment.

FRANKENSTEIN: I thank you for it. What can I give you in return?

FOLLEZOU: (*Confused, approaches Frankenstein*) I wanted you to die.

FRANKENSTEIN: Those hands of yours are weak, aren't they? The muscles have withered; your grip is less than a child's. So what hope is there for you now? Those rickety legs weren't made for running, and your good eye is almost blind.

VERONIQUE: Don't hurt him.

FRANKENSTEIN: He is a forfeit. Simply that. The joke misfired. It would be bad form to avoid the consequence. He's a gentleman, he understands.

VERONIQUE: If I begged.

FRANKENSTEIN: What for?

VERONIQUE: His life.

FRANKENSTEIN: It's not in my hands.

FOLLEZOU TAKES OUT A SMALL BOTTLE AND SWALLOWS ITS CONTENTS.

VERONIQUE: No, Eddie.

FOLLEZOU: Lady, I failed. He won't have me again. Don't let him touch me, please. The dead should lie down—(*He collapses, dead*)

FRANKENSTEIN: I wouldn't tamper with you, Follezou. I've prettier things to play with. (*Steps on his face*) Your face offends me.

VERONIQUE: Let him alone.

FRANKENSTEIN: Imperfect wretch.

VERONIQUE: Are you such a miracle?

FRANKENSTEIN: I don't like this change of tone, Veronique. This isn't the behavior of an attentive bride. Maybe I shouldn't do the decent thing—maybe I should lash you to the wall and take you anyway.

VERONIQUE: Don't touch me.

FRANKENSTEIN: Resist me then. I'll let you be. You can burn a while, without my skill to help you through your agonies. Love has many faces, a smile is just one. A bloody sheet is no less lovely. A bare back, a lost life . . . all signs of love. Love is a wound, and a shaft that makes a wound. An emptiness suddenly filled to brimming. (*He starts to strip her*). You don't need your virgin's veil. You can go naked, so I can see the tail you've sprouted. From now on, always naked, Veronique. Naked. Naked. My object, utterly.

VERONIQUE: No.

FRANKENSTEIN: My freak, my jug, my womb.

VERONIQUE: Never. I'll die. I'll die.

ENTER EL COCO, DRESSED TO KILL.

EL COCO: No need.

FRANKENSTEIN: You're not here.

EL COCO: Don't press your suit. It's impolite. I come to your wedding, Father.

FRANKENSTEIN: And you may stay to watch the rape, phantasma, if you wish. You're only in my head. Lust will wash you out. (*Takes hold of Veronique and kisses her*) Don't stare, my love. There's no one there.

VERONIQUE: I see him.

FRANKENSTEIN: You share the delusion, that's all.

VERONIQUE: I see him! Cesar! Cesar! (*Breaks away and they embrace, kissing*) The scars have gone.

EL COCO: I found a better surgeon.

VERONIQUE: Darling—

EL COCO: How is my abominable wife?

VERONIQUE: Well. And my disgusting husband?

EL COCO: Blooming.

FRANKENSTEIN: You are in my head.

EL COCO: Am I?

FRANKENSTEIN: Maybe sons are always in their fathers' heads.

Figments of their manhood, not to be believed. Then the world is full of sons who are dreamt by their fathers, who are in their turn only dreamt.

EL COCO: Then we're all ghosts and equal under the law, and my hands can take you apart at the seams.

FRANKENSTEIN: You're dead. I have your skin.

EL COCO: I grew a new skin. We lizards can.

FRANKENSTEIN: Your body was burned.

EL COCO: The salamander learned to live in fire. Could he die in fire? No. I've set the vaults alight. Do you smell them? The flames are licking their way up the stairs. We must do our familial duties, father, and be finished before the fire brings the house down. (*Approaches his father*)

FRANKENSTEIN: Don't touch me.

EL COCO: Afraid at last. At last, afraid.

FRANKENSTEIN: For you. Not for me. For you.

EL COCO: I'll kill you quickly. I've learned all I need to learn. I understand your nature, father. The selfless pursuit of life against all reason. I won't repeat your error.

FRANKENSTEIN: Don't touch me, son. It's not wise, believe me.

EL COCO: You can't frighten me. You've taken my life, I'm still here. Look at me. Couldn't I pass for a man? Look! And so, appearing to be a man, I claim the right of every natural son: to murder his father.

FRANKENSTEIN: Lay your hands on me, you'll see how natural you are. Monster.

EL COCO: (*Takes hold of his father*) Well?

FRANKENSTEIN: Your hands ache. Your palms feel as though they're spiked. Blood begins.

EL COCO: (*Lets his father go*) Ah!

FRANKENSTEIN: Yes?

EL COCO: What's this wound?

FRANKENSTEIN: Stigmata perhaps.

EL COCO: What have you done?

FRANKENSTEIN: Too many of my predecessors died at the hands of their creations. I don't intend to suffer the same fate. You are incapable of harming me. Your flesh opens like a flower if it's laid on me in anger. That is the first law I taught you, son. It's built into your fabric, at your core. To touch me in anger is to bleed. The perfect psychosomia for an erring child.

EL COCO: No, damn you! *(Takes hold of Frankenstein again)* You won't defeat me.

FRANKENSTEIN: Your hands sprout agonies. Your eyes wither in their sockets because they look at me with hatred. You cannot bear to hold me.

EL COCO: I will! I will! I've risen twice—once under your hand, against my will—now again. I choose to live, to root you out. You won't . . . won't . . . *(He has to let go—the agony is unendurable)*

FRANKENSTEIN: You are my beauty, my body, perfected. All I was, drained off into you. When you went, my health went with you—leaving a moral morbidity I smell in my sleep. The acts I committed for the love of you. Acts I can never forget. I crawled into the bellies of the dead to fish out a little life.

EL COCO: I didn't ask to be born. *(Collapses)*

FRANKENSTEIN: I have an appetite for it now. I have an unrelenting lust for death. To see its procedures, its wit, that certain smile. What shall we do? Look at me, child. What shall we do? *(Kicks the body)* Dead? No, damn you. *(Kicks again)* No! No! Never! Never! *(He kicks and prods and dances on the body, an obscene exhibition of hatred)* Suicide! Suicide! The room is full of suicides. You wanted to kill me and you killed yourself. Imbecile.

VERONIQUE: No.

FRANKENSTEIN: I laid no hand on him. *(Going to El Coco)*

VERONIQUE: Cesar . . .

FRANKENSTEIN: That wasn't his name. He had no name. I never called him anything.

VERONIQUE: He was an angel.

FRANKENSTEIN: I was kind, after my fashion. I warned him, didn't I?

VERONIQUE: Yes.

FRANKENSTEIN: A considerate father.

VERONIQUE: Yes. Too kind.

FRANKENSTEIN: I spoilt him.

VERONIQUE: The fault wasn't yours.

FRANKENSTEIN: I'm not a cold man, Veronique.

VERONIQUE: No.

FRANKENSTEIN: I have a heart.

VERONIQUE: Yes.

FRANKENSTEIN: Capable of feeling.

VERONIQUE: Is it?

FRANKENSTEIN: Yes. Yes.

VERONIQUE: Show me.

FRANKENSTEIN: I love you.

VERONIQUE: Show me your heart. *(Lays her hand on his chest)* Show me your heart, dearest.

FRANKENSTEIN: That hurts me.

VERONIQUE: Then fight.

FRANKENSTEIN: Ah! Your hands—what are you doing?

SHE HAS TORN AT HIS SHIRT AND IS NOW CLAW-ING AT HIS FLESH.

FRANKENSTEIN: *(Screams)* Veronique!

VERONIQUE: Show me. Show me. Prove yourself a lover, Joseph.

FRANKENSTEIN: Ah!

VERONIQUE: There's strength in me. Feel it? Feel it? *(Has her hands in his chest)* Physician, heal thyself.

HE SHRIEKS AND COLLAPSES AS SHE DRAGS HIS HEART OUT.

VERONIQUE: You do have a heart, Joseph. I see it. *(To Maria)* Don't look away. It's only meat. What could be simpler? *(Flings it down)* Take these things away.

MARIA GOES TO EL COCO.

VERONIQUE: Not him. Not him.

MARIA BEGINS TO HAUL THE BODIES OFF, AS VERONIQUE LOOKS AT EL COCO.

VERONIQUE: *(Crying)* You have a choice. I know you hear me. Choose to go, it's not so far. There's silence, earth. I wouldn't blame you, sweet. Or stay. I'm here. I won't say I need you. That's not fair to you. And yet . . . I . . . I am . . . in love with you. *(Touches him)*

EL COCO: *(Snatches her hand)* Never leave me. *(Sits up, they kiss)*

VERONIQUE: Never.

ENTER MARIA.

MARIA: The fire is on the stairs.

> *THE NOISE OF THE FIRE HAS GROWN. FROM BENEATH THEM, A RED GLOW AND SMOKE.*

VERONIQUE: We must go.
EL COCO: No need.
VERONIQUE: We'll burn.
EL COCO: We can walk on fire.
VERONIQUE: I don't know the trick of it.
EL COCO: I'll teach you.

> *FROM UNDER THE ROAR OF THE FIRE, A WALTZ, WITH STRINGS AND PIANO. AS THEY BEGIN TO DANCE, THE NOISE INCREASES, AND THE WHIRLING DANCE GATHERS MOMENTUM FROM THE DEAFENING ROAR AND MUSIC. THE WALTZ REACHES A SPECTACULAR CONCLUSION AS THEY DANCE, LOCKED IN EACH OTHER'S ARMS. SUDDEN DARKNESS. NO LIGHT. NO SOUND.*

> *THEN SLOWLY, A LIGHT COMES UP ON MARIA REINA DURAN.*

MARIA: If the world fails, so what? If sin disappoints, never mind. He will come, and at his arrival the trap is sprung.

> *ENTER DEATH, IN SOFT CLOTHES. GENTLE.*

MARIA: He is honorable, dutiful, kind. Good night, flesh. I'm in love. No time for tears—

> *DEATH HAS EMBRACED HER, AND SHE HAS MELTED INTO HIS ARMS. THE LIGHTS FADE, SLOWLY.*

> *THE PLAY ENDS.*

THE HISTORY OF
THE DEVIL

OR

SCENES FROM
A PRETENDED LIFE

Production Notes

The Devil is an actor: a man of masks, never the same tempter twice. It's appropriate then that a play exploring his life and times should be an actor's piece, using word-pictures in place of elaborate sets, in the stream of which a large number of characters are carried, some of them healthy swimmers, many swept away by the protean evil that is the play's true constant.

In choosing this style, I was to some extent making a virtue of a necessity—the company for which the play was written had no money for sets or costumes—but the consequence of the choice was liberation. The play is full of extravagant scenes that I would never have dared make a part of the tale if we'd been attempting a realistic staging. A sky-ride on the Devil's back, the destruction of a Greek city, a descent from heaven—these are hopelessly expensive effects for a playwright to put into a text unless they're to be evoked with some stylized physical business and a few lines from a commentating actor. The audience then has the pleasure of co-creating the illusion with the performers; enriching the experience for both sides of the equation.

The space in which these low-budget miracles are achieved must be as malleable as possible: as stark, in fact, as the region around Lake Turkana where the Devil's trial is ostensibly taking place. For anyone interested in producing the play and who wants a glimpse of this landscape, may I suggest *Eyelids of Morning: the Mingled Destinies of Crocodiles and Men,* by Alistair Graham and Peter Beard, a book I had at my elbow when writing the play? It is filled with photographs of Lake Turkana and its inhabitants. The landscape is, as Satan points out in the play, a pretty "Godless" place. Black sand underfoot, a blank, unforgiving sky: brilliant light falling on an unlovely barrenness. Though a designer might want to render all this schematically rather than realistically, the photographs in this book are a wonderful starting place.

As to how this space turns into a cornfield outside Chartres, or a prison-cell, or a forest, that's completely open to the designer's and director's invention. I only advise this: keep it simple, keep it witty, keep it quick. Part of the pleasure of the play lies in the speed with which it changes locations and atmospheres. One moment the stage is buzzing with all the furor of a boxing match. The next it's midnight, and terrible deeds have been done to the victor. All in the twinkling of a Devil's eye.

This ever-shifting theatrical reality approximates thought pro-cesses far better than so-called cinematic techniques (short scenes with black-outs between) ever could. The arena of the play thus becomes analogous to the mind: a space where thoughts can free-associate, folding one into the other. When a particular place and time is being evoked, lighting and sound should do all they can to intensely evoke the spot, like a crystalline memory. But at any moment, an actor may enter and carry the action away to some-where new.

The same rules of particularity apply to the performance style. The more distinct the nuances are—for however brief a time a character is on stage—the better. The trick is to avoid tricks. To give the audience a specific, not generic, choice. That is always a performer's ambition, of course, but in a piece like *Devil* the temptation to sink into caricature is stronger because many of the characters—a demon, a witch, a soldier lost in a forest—are pri-mal, almost fairy-tale figures, and can be readily played in broad strokes. This is a mistake. If I've learned anything from two decades of *fantastique* writing it's that the more extraordinary the subject matter the more specific the details need to be. This is not a dream-play; not a medieval mystery play, parading semi-sym-bolic figures for a moral purpose. It's a history.

Finally, of course, if this story's worth telling it's because it's about being human. The Devil's tale is the tale of our own confu-sion, ego and inability to live without hope for Heaven. His wings removed, Satan is dropped into the world wounded, and though he conceals his frailty well enough, putting on a fine show of dis-passion, he's never far from throwing back his head and raging like an abused child. If the play persuades its audience to look at what this mirage of external evil is—in short, an excuse; a brush-ing off—then it has done something of what I intended.

The rest of my intentions are buried in the story itself. They are part of every exchange, sour or sweet; part of who these people are, whether victims or victors. How those intentions emerge is a function of the performance, design and directorial choice, over which I, sitting here, have no control. When I first wrote this play that powerlessness would have made me crazy. Now it pleases me. Unlike a book, which goes from my desk to my readers with only an editor and a type-setter between, or a movie, which is set in celluloid at its premiere and will not change significantly thereafter, *The History of the Devil* is protean and subject to the influence of many minds. The Devil, exiled shape-changer that he is, has found his home.

Clive Barker—Los Angeles, 1995

The Cast:

JACK EASTER
DANIEL MENDOZA
MRS. MENDOZA
DUKE OF YORK
MARY ANN CLARKE
LILITH
GEORG KEIPENHAUER
ACTORS

Act 1

The First Day

A BRIGHTLY LIT LONDON STREET. AN ACTOR ENTERS AND ADDRESSES THE AUDIENCE WITH THE CONFIDENCE OF ONE WHO KNOWS THERE'S A GOOD STORY IN THE WIND.

ACTOR: History always begins with a cry: of anger perhaps, of jubilation, of panic—

A WOMAN SCREAMS OFFSTAGE.

ACTOR: Like that.

ENTER A WOMAN IN HYSTERICS. TEARS OF TERROR POUR DOWN HER CHEEKS.

WOMAN: Get off the street!
ACTOR: Why?
WOMAN: Smell that? Burning hair. The ground's opening up.
ACTOR: I'm working.
WOMAN: I wouldn't stay here if I were you. There's a hole in the road, and something came up out of it, howling like a dog under a car.

SHE LOOKS AS THOUGH SHE'S ABOUT TO LOSE CONTROL OF HER BLADDER, AND EXITS.

ACTOR: *(Turning back to the audience, casually)* A shout, yes. And finally, silence. But in between? *(Expansively)* The great panorama: the triumphs, the casual atrocities. Love, death. The spectacle of the world cut open. And of course the next corner, children playing; the front door. Home.

HE STEPS ASIDE AS THE LIGHTS CHANGE, EVOKING A DOMESTIC INTERIOR. ENTER NANCY KYLE, A NORMAL WIFE ABOUT HER NORMAL MORNING BUSINESS.

NANCY KYLE: Did you hear that?
SAM KYLE: *(Off)* Nancy?

A BANGING ON THE DOOR.

ACTOR: *(To the audience)* February: to the London house of Samuel Kyle, lawyer, comes something smelling faintly of the Abyss.

THE ACTOR EXITS.

NANCY KYLE: Leal's here. I'll give him a cup of coffee.
SAM KYLE *(Off)*: Nancy?
NANCY KYLE: He's ten minutes early.

EXIT NANCY. ENTER SAM. HE IS HALFWAY THROUGH SHAVING. A HANDSOME FELLOW, IN A LAWYERLY SORT OF WAY.

SAM KYLE: *(Confounded)* There's mud coming through the taps—
NANCY KYLE: *(Off)* Did you hear the shouting?

THE BEATING AT THE DOOR IS LOUDER NOW.

NANCY KYLE: *(Off)* I'm coming, I'm coming.

SAM KYLE: I can't shave with mud.

*SAM EXITS. THE STAGE IS EMPTY FOR A MOMENT.
DO THE LIGHTS FLICKER?*

NANCY KYLE: (*Off*) Come on in.
SAM KYLE: (*Off*) Give him a cup of coffee, will you, sweet?
NANCY KYLE: (*Off*) Wait, you're not Leal—
SAM KYLE: (*Off*) Make me a cup, too.

ENTER NANCY.

NANCY KYLE: (*Alarmed*) Sam? Are you there? Sam!

*ENTER THE DEMON VERRIER. HIS MANNER
THROUGHOUT IS HIGHLY CIVILIZED, BUT HIS
BOOTS SMOKE AND HIS SPECTACLES ARE CON-
STANTLY STEAMED UP. HE SHOULD BE PLAYED BY
A WOMAN, WITHOUT A TRACE OF CAMP.*

NANCY KYLE: Get out.
VERRIER: (*All reason*) But you just invited me in.
NANCY KYLE: That's because I thought you were Leal.
VERRIER: Ah, the chauffeur? Well . . . I'm his replacement.
NANCY KYLE: Oh, I didn't realize—
VERRIER: For today, only. Verrier.
NANCY KYLE: My husband's still shaving. Do you want a cup of
    coffee?
VERRIER: Thank you, I'd like that. I take it black and very sweet.
NANCY KYLE: I'll fetch Sam.
VERRIER: Tell him to dress for Africa.
NANCY KYLE: (*A double-take*) I beg your pardon?
VERRIER: By all means beg it.
NANCY KYLE: *Africa?* You are from the courts?
VERRIER: Not from any court you've ever heard of, no.
NANCY KYLE: (*Suddenly chilly*) If you want to see my husband on
    business, then make an appointment.
VERRIER: No time, I'm afraid.
NANCY KYLE: By all means, be afraid. Please leave.
VERRIER: With your husband: not before.

ENTER SAM. HE'S GIVEN UP ON THE SHAVING. HE'S PUTTING ON HIS SHIRT.

SAM KYLE: (Irritated) Now there's a noise in the pipes. It sounds like—voices. (Sees Verrier) Where's Leal?

VERRIER: Indisposed. My name is Verrier. At your service.

NANCY KYLE: He's not from the Bailey, Sam.

VERRIER: Please get dressed. Boots are appropriate—

NANCY KYLE: He wants you to go to Africa.

SAM KYLE: He wants what?

NANCY KYLE: I'll call the police.

VERRIER: No need for an escort. We're flying.

SAM KYLE: Better an ambulance, Nancy.

VERRIER: Speed's essential.

SAM KYLE: Thanks for the invitation, but I can't manage Africa this morning.

VERRIER: I'm prepared for incredulity. I'm authorized to bind you.

HE REACHES INTO HIS THROAT AND PULLS OUT A KNOTTED ROPE.

SAM KYLE: Good God.

VERRIER: And I shall bind you if you resist me.

NANCY KYLE: There's no need.

SAM KYLE: (*Incredulous*) No need? What are you—?

NANCY KYLE: I think he means it, Sam.

SAM KYLE: Call the police, Nancy. *Call the police! (She doesn't move)* I'll call them if you won't.

EXIT SAM.

VERRIER: Wise, not to resist.

NANCY KYLE: The rope—

VERRIER: You recognize it?

NANCY KYLE: Something like it—in dreams. Are you what I think you are?

VERRIER: Less than an angel, more than a man.

NANCY KYLE: (*Fatalistic*) Be kind. He's used to being treated well. I pamper him.

EXIT VERRIER, IN PURSUIT OF SAM. ENTER ACTOR.

ACTOR: (*To Nancy*) You're accepting this very calmly.

NANCY KYLE: Trivia annoys me. Dirty underwear left on the floor. This is merely . . . cataclysmic.

ACTOR: He could be going to a hideous death.

NANCY KYLE: My sister fell under a train. He could do worse?

ENTER SAM AND VERRIER. VERRIER CARRIES A SMALL CASE. THE ACTOR EXITS.

SAM KYLE: He just packed a case without laying a hand: *what is he?*

NANCY KYLE: You'd better go with him.

SAM KYLE: Nancy—

VERRIER: (*Respectfully*) No harm is going to come to you. You've been chosen from every appeal lawyer in the world as my master's Advocate. We're going to what is being touted in certain circles as the greatest trial in history.

SAM KYLE: Back up a moment. Your master?

VERRIER: Your wife knows.

NANCY KYLE: The Devil, Sam.

SAM KYLE: Who?

NANCY KYLE: You listen to me, Verrier. You bring him back intact, healthy and happy, or he doesn't step out of this house.

VERRIER: You couldn't stop me.

NANCY KYLE: I could make you very late.

SAM KYLE: Wait. We've got a dinner party tonight.

VERRIER: Cater for four. If he can't be back, I'll raise a friend to make up the quartet. Time to go.

NANCY KYLE: (*Very close to tears*) Kiss.

SAM KYLE: I don't understand this.

NANCY KYLE: I'm *very* proud of you.

THEY KISS, LIGHTLY AT FIRST. THEN SHE PRESSES HER MOUTH HARD AGAINST HIS. A SOUL-KISS. SHE EXITS.

SAM KYLE: (*Amazed*) I'm only going along with this for two reasons. One: it isn't happening. Two: I'm terrified.

VERRIER TAKES HOLD OF SAM'S NECK.

VERRIER: Excuse fingers. Undignified, but the best way to travel.

ENTER ACTOR. THE LIGHTS CHANGE. THE SOUND OF WIND.

VERRIER: Count to three.
SAM KYLE: One.

A BLAZE OF SKY AND MOTION.

ACTOR: (*To the audience*) Up they leap. Three miles in a single bound.
SAM KYLE: Two.
ACTOR: The stratosphere is bright with ice and music.
SAM KYLE: Three.
ACTOR: And the fall's like lightning. Africa's below, and Lake Turkana, jade with stagnation, stinking in the sun.

EXIT ACTOR, AS A BRILLIANT LIGHT BURNS ON THE SCENE. THE WHINE OF HEAT AND INSECTS. A PRIMITIVE COURT HAS BEEN SET UP IN THIS WRETCHED, DUSTY WILDERNESS. CHAIRS, TABLES, UMBRELLAS TO KEEP THE HEAT FROM COOKING THE CONTESTANTS' BRAINS. UNDERFOOT, BLACK SAND.

SAM KYLE: Where are we?
VERRIER: Kenya. Sixty miles east of where Eden stood.
SAM KYLE: It stinks.
VERRIER: So did Eden. Please follow: we must find our tents.
SAM KYLE: There's going to be a trial here?
VERRIER: It's his right.
SAM KYLE: But the heat—
VERRIER: It suits him.
SAM KYLE: No, you're not listening to me. I can't work in this heat. I get sunstroke in England, for God's sake.
VERRIER: So much done for God's sake. Mr. Kyle, you are The Devil's Advocate whether you like it or not. Work, and maybe you'll eat with your wife tonight.

SAM KYLE: (*Slapping himself*) I've been bitten.

VERRIER: You shouldn't be so warm blooded. Follow, and take care. There are crocodile eggs buried in the sand.

SAM KYLE: Oh my Lord. Where are the mothers?

VERRIER: In the lake, wallowing. The meat's good, I hear. (*Smirks*) It tastes like . . . dragon.

EXIT VERRIER AND SAM. ENTER JANE BECK AND CATHARINE LAMB, WHO ARE SCARCELY BETTER DRESSED FOR THIS ORDEAL THAN SAM. JANE IS THE YOUNGER OF THE TWO. PRETTY, IN SPITE OF HER BEST EFFORTS. SHE'S THIRTY-THREE. CATHARINE IS A POWERFUL WOMAN, AMBITIOUS AND ANGRY. KATE CARRIES BOOKS AND FILES.

ACTOR: (*To the audience*) Catharine Lamb and Jane Beck, lawyers for the Prosecution.

EXIT ACTOR

JANE BECK: Is all Africa this empty, Kate?

CATHARINE LAMB: The Turkana live here on the shore. Apparently.

JANE BECK: I see nothing. And more nothing.

CATHARINE LAMB: You'll know them when you see them. They go stark naked. The men consider themselves properly dressed as long as their foreskins are not peeled back.

JANE BECK: Are we in any danger?

CATHARINE LAMB: Not unless we try and convert them.

JANE BECK: Not from them, from the defendant.

CATHARINE LAMB: How would I know? We're prosecuting The Devil, Jane, there's no precedent that I know of.

JANE BECK: We could be murdered.

CATHARINE LAMB: It's a possibility. But who could resist the chance to grind his face into the ground?

JANE BECK: You're so confident.

CATHARINE LAMB: You have some objection to that? Why? Because I'm here out of ambition? Because I'm not playing the lawyer, impartial to my toes?

JANE BECK: If I wanted impartiality I wouldn't come to you for it. But I'm here, aren't I?

CATHARINE LAMB: (*Gently, indulgently*) Yes.

JANE BECK: Besides, I've researched him. His life. His times. And you know what I think? When it comes down to it, he's an unexotic thug like all the others you've put behind bars. Five thousand years old, but a thug.

CATHARINE LAMB: I hope you're right. And won't they point us out when this is over, won't everyone see us and say: they prosecuted The Devil himself.

JANE BECK: (*A joke*) As long as we can hear them, six feet under.

CATHARINE LAMB: This is a court of law, Jane.

JANE BECK: Oh is it? You surprise me.

CATHARINE LAMB: Maybe a little primitive.

JANE BECK: A little? The only entertainment we have between sessions is watching the locals play with their foreskins.

CATHARINE LAMB: What's your point?

JANE BECK: He chose this place, Kate. He wanted to be tried here, in this filth: in this air. Why? Bit of a puzzle, isn't it? What happens to a thing that's lived five thousand years: What's beyond the wisdom of Methuselah? Decadence: a slow descent back into the mud. I think the law looks a little insubstantial out here: I think it looks like . . . words.

CATHARINE LAMB: Do you want to go home?

JANE BECK: Does that matter right now?

CATHARINE LAMB: I don't want—

JANE BECK: You to go. Please say it.

CATHARINE LAMB: I don't want you to go.

JANE BECK: I won't. Besides—

CATHARINE LAMB: Besides?

JANE BECK: Ridiculous, but I have the strangest feeling I'll never be home again. That I'm in some departure lounge with a one way ticket.

ENTER THE DEMON BELIAL DISGUISED AS A LAWYER. HE SWEATS PROFUSELY. MOPS HIS BROW. MOPS HIS LIPS, WHICH ARE SPITTLE-SPATTERED.

BELIAL: (*Gushing*) Kate? Kate Lamb?

CATHARINE LAMB: Yes.

BELIAL: Henessey. George Henessey. Law School. You remember me.

CATHARINE LAMB: (*A lie*) Of course.
BELIAL: Amazing to see you. Clerking, are you?
CATHARINE LAMB: Prosecuting, actually.
JANE BECK: Kate—
CATHARINE LAMB: George Henessey—Jane Beck, my colleague—
BELIAL: Oh. Delighted.

*THEY SHAKE HANDS. JANE FINDS BELIAL'S CLAMMY
TOUCH UNPLEASANT.*

CATHARINE LAMB: We were at law school together.
BELIAL: Happier days.
CATHARINE LAMB: What are *you* doing here?
BELIAL: Prurient interest: never seen a massacre firsthand before.
    I'm sorry you're prosecuting. You can't win, of course.
CATHARINE LAMB: Not a hope in hell?
BELIAL: He's unpredictable.
JANE BECK: Are you trying to scare us off?
BELIAL: Even if you had evidence worth a damn—which you don't.
JANE BECK: We've got enough to sink him.
CATHARINE LAMB: Jane—
JANE BECK: Witnesses, testimonies—
BELIAL: (*Quick-silver*) What's it worth?
CATHARINE LAMB: What's it worth?
BELIAL: Name your price. A straight deal. I take no percentage.
JANE BECK: A bribe, in broad daylight?
CATHARINE LAMB: And the alternative?
BELIAL: Oh. Oh. Agony beyond imagining. The first day.
CATHARINE LAMB: You're not George Henessey.
BELIAL: (*To Jane*) She's fast. (*To Kate*) His Sable Majesty is not
    concerned with equity. He wants the appeal passed.
CATHARINE LAMB: Who are you?
BELIAL: Belial.
JANE BECK: A demon of the first order.
BELIAL: (*Reaches for Jane's briefcase*) Give me the case.
CATHARINE LAMB: Don't.
BELIAL: I implore you.
CATHARINE LAMB: Ignore him.
BELIAL: Think of your most intimate pain, times a thousand. You'll
    feel that in the first joint of your thumb. Give me the case.

JANE BECK: Don't touch me.

BELIAL SNATCHES THE CASE. JANE SHRIEKS.

BELIAL: Thank you. (*He opens the case*) It's empty.
JANE BECK: Well played, I thought.
BELIAL: Where is the evidence?
CATHARINE LAMB: I knew: tell him I knew, will you? And tell him the evidence is here: (*Points to her head*) where no fifth-level, slit-nosed piece of demon shite like you is going to touch it.
BELIAL: You cunty little Christians. How I hate you.
CATHARINE LAMB: Oh, please, Belial, understand me. The Lord's not my shepherd.

EXIT CATHARINE LAMB.

BELIAL: (*To Jane*) No Lord to go by? Oh. Oh. He'll open her up. You don't know . . . what he will do.
JANE BECK: (*Lightly*) Did somebody fart?

EXIT JANE BECK.

BELIAL: (*To the audience*) Consider the lilies of the field. (*He looks around*) None. Consider the birds of the air. (*He looks up*) Gone. Consider me: I sow not, neither do I reap, so why am I in agony?

AS BELIAL EXITS, ENTER JUDGE FELIX POPPER, FOL-LOWED BY MILO MILO, A CLERK OF COURT, ACCOMPANIED BY AN ACTOR. POPPER IS A WIRY, DYSPEPTIC OCTOGENERIAN. MILO MILO IS A BIRD OF A FELLOW.

ACTOR: Judge Felix Popper, and Clerk of Court, Milo Milo.
POPPER: (*To Actor*) Will you join me in a peppermint?
ACTOR: Thanks.

EXIT ACTOR. ENTER CATHARINE LAMB.

CATHARINE LAMB: Popper, I want to make a complaint.

POPPER: Oh Christ, already?

CATHARINE LAMB: I've been harassed.

POPPER: I know, I've had the same. Just ignore it.

CATHARINE LAMB: I don't ignore things. It's not in my nature.

POPPER: Why am I surprised?

CATHARINE LAMB: They should be reprimanded.

POPPER: Listen Ms. Lamb. I'm the only man they could find to take this responsibility. That makes me a fool, but I'm a tough fool. I'm treating this like a normal court of law. No harassment of witnesses, or counsels, no bad logic, no tuppenny-colored theatrics. And I'll be just as tough with you as with them. The law's the law.

CATHARINE LAMB: And justice is justice.

POPPER: Then we agree.

CATHARINE LAMB: Do we?

EXIT CATHARINE LAMB.

POPPER: I've always said, the better the person, the worse the lawyer. (*To Milo*) Go fetch my hat, will you Milo?

MILO MILO: Yes, sir.

POPPER: Why are you walking like that?

MILO MILO: The crocodiles, m'lord.

POPPER: Jesus, Milo, there isn't a crocodile in creation that'd eat you. Get your arse *moving*.

EXIT MILO MILO AND JUDGE POPPER.

ENTER BELIAL AND VERRIER, SWEATING AND STEAMING, JITTERY WITH ANTICIPATION. A SUBTLE AGITATION HAS BEGUN IN THE AIR, SLOWLY MOUNTING AS THEIR DIALOGUE PROCEEDS. VOICES THAT SOB AND SING.

BELIAL: I feel him near. Handle him gently.

VERRIER: The hands of a Jew, the lips of an Englishman.

BELIAL: Oh. In Heaven soon. Oh. In Heaven.

VERRIER: In Heaven, Belial.

BELIAL: He's coming fast now.

VERRIER: Hush.
BELIAL: Perfect life.
VERRIER: Perfect love.
BELIAL: Here! Here! He's here!

*VERRIER EXITS. ENTER JUDGE POPPER, ALARMED.
THE SOUND IS BECOMING DELIRIOUS.*

POPPER: Milo! Milo!

ENTER CATHARINE LAMB.

CATHARINE LAMB: What's that noise?
POPPER: There's a cloud over the lake. Look.
CATHARINE LAMB: I see it.

ENTER JANE BECK.

JANE BECK: It's getting very dark.
POPPER: Where the fuck's Milo?
JANE BECK: Is it going to rain?
CATHARINE LAMB: I don't think so.
POPPER: My God, what is it?
CATHARINE LAMB: God it's not.

ENTER MILO MILO.

MILO MILO: Sir, have you seen?
POPPER: We've seen it.
JANE BECK: The cloud.
CATHARINE LAMB: Yes.
JANE BECK: It's *birds!*

*THE DIN OF VOICES HAS BECOME THE CLAMOR OF
COUNTLESS BIRDS.*

MILO MILO: What do we do?
CATHARINE LAMB: It's blotting out the sun.
JANE BECK: Pazuzu.
POPPER: Uh?

JANE BECK: It's one of his names.

POPPER: The defendant?

CATHARINE LAMB: Call him by his proper name. Call him
    Satan: The enemy.

POPPER: Perhaps it's a natural phenomenon.

CATHARINE LAMB: Ten thousand birds and a boiling lake?

MILO MILO: (*Fleeing*) Look! They're congealing in the air.

POPPER: Come here, Milo, it's not going to bite.

MILO MILO: I never believed until now.

POPPER: Hush, will you?

MILO MILO: I thought it was a joke—

CATHARINE LAMB: It's landing on the water—shaped like a man—

MILO MILO: Better not to look: you can go blind.

CATHARINE LAMB: Walking on water.

ENTER VERRIER.

JANE BECK: Darkness at noon. Quite an entrance.

VERRIER: Prepare yourselves.

CATHARINE LAMB: Immaculate stagecraft, don't you think, Popper?

VERRIER: The Prince of the World is here.

POPPER: I've said before, I won't tolerate—

*ENTER THE DEVIL, SMILING. HE IS A STAR IN HIS
OWN ROTTED FIRMAMENT. AS GLAMOROUS—AND
AS ARTIFICIAL—AS ANY HOLLYWOOD ICON. A
COAT OVER HIS SHOULDER, PERHAPS. SUN-
GLASSES, PERHAPS. PERHAPS NOTHING.*

THE DEVIL: (*Picking up Popper's litany*)—the harassment of wit-
    nesses, or counsels. Bad logic. Tuppenny-colored theatrics.
    (*He bows*) Sir, I salute you.

POPPER: You're late.

THE DEVIL: I come before you a supplicant already tried by his-
    tory: treat me as the pickpocket I am. It's my only crime.
    That and being in need of a new timepiece.

POPPER: Milo, assemble the court.

THE DEVIL: Why? Are they in pieces?

MILO MILO LAUGHS.

THE DEVIL: (*Touches Milo's face*) You see, Milo, nothing to be afraid of. Nothing in the world.

MILO MILO RETREATS, DAZZLED, AND EXITS.

POPPER: Will you take your place in court?

POPPER TURNS HIS BACK ON THE DEVIL.

THE DEVIL: Would that be at your feet? I beg a moment to consult with my Advocate. (*To Verrier*) Fetch him.

EXIT VERRIER.

POPPER: You have five minutes.

EXIT POPPER.

THE DEVIL: Will the ladies be attending?
CATHARINE LAMB: The *women* will be prosecuting. But you know that, you—
THE DEVIL: For brevity's sake, call me sir.

ENTER AN ACTOR, NERVOUS.

ACTOR: (*A whisper*) What's he like?
CATHARINE LAMB: I expected more.
JANE BECK: He smells faintly—perfume—
ACTOR: He seems civil.
CATHARINE LAMB: Wars can be civil.

EXIT CATHARINE LAMB. JANE STARES AT THE DEVIL'S BACK. THE ACTOR WATCHES FROM A DISCREET DISTANCE. HE HAS AN AUTOGRAPH BOOK.

THE DEVIL: No, Jane, I never had horns on my head.
JANE BECK: Can you read my mind?
THE DEVIL: Only the first few coils: after that you get a little too *profound* for me.
JANE BECK: Good.

THE DEVIL: But I'll persevere.

JANE BECK: Don't: you'll be disappointed.

THE DEVIL: I think you're the disappointed one.

JANE BECK: Why?

THE DEVIL: No Leviathan. I'm really so remarkably . . . unremarkable.

JANE BECK: I predicted that.

THE DEVIL: But you hoped you'd be wrong. In your heart. You
prayed I'd be wonderful.

JANE BECK: (*Eyes closed*) Leviathan: huge ship or sea-monster.
Person of formidable power, ability or wealth.

THE DEVIL: Do you eat dictionaries?

JANE BECK: Or, as in Hobbes, autocratic monarch or state.

THE DEVIL: Ah, I am by instinct an autocrat. Was that a faux-
pas? Should I have admitted to a lawyer that I consider
myself a law unto myself?

JANE BECK: Will you accept this court as binding?

THE DEVIL: Of course.

JANE BECK: Why?

THE DEVIL: So that I may be returned into Heaven, where I belong.

JANE BECK: Then you're right, you're no Leviathan. A real monster would overthrow Heaven before accepting any law.

THE DEVIL: Well, I tried storming the gates, you know: it came
to grief. It all came to grief.

*THEY STARE AT EACH OTHER FOR A LONG
MOMENT. ENTER CATHARINE.*

CATHARINE LAMB: Jane?

JANE BECK: Yes . . .

THE LOOK IS BROKEN. EXIT JANE AND CATHARINE.

THE DEVIL: You—

ACTOR: Sir?

THE DEVIL: (*Signing the autograph book*) Would you care to kneel
and kiss my behind?

ACTOR: No, I wouldn't.

EXIT ACTOR.

THE DEVIL: First refusal.

ENTER VERRIER, WITH SAMUEL KYLE. SAM IS PALE, SWEATY AND SHAKING.

VERRIER: You were late. With respect, that's not wise.

THE DEVIL: I made up for it.

VERRIER: They're not so impressionable as they were. They see stuff like that all the time.

THE DEVIL: Am I competing with Hollywood? God help me.

VERRIER: I want to go home like you. I'm riding on your back, Lucifer.

THE DEVIL: Only you dare say that: and only you I allow to dare.

SAMUEL STARTS COUGHING.

THE DEVIL: (*Brightly*) Cough it up, it could be a gold watch.

VERRIER: This is your Advocate.

THE DEVIL: (*Studying Sam*) He favors his father.

SAM KYLE: (*Refusing to look at The Devil*) I'm not well.

VERRIER: He constantly vomits. He insists that this is unnatural.

SAM KYLE: Look, I'm no use to you like this. There must be other appeal lawyers.

THE DEVIL: None with your heritage, Samuel. My trust is in you, as a finger. So.

HE PUTS A FINGER IN SAM'S MOUTH. VERRIER LAUGHS.

SAM KYLE: My bowels—

THE DEVIL: (*Quietly, soothingly*) Yes.

SAM KYLE: This stinking place.

THE DEVIL: God-forsaken is in the phrase. Have you seen the lake? Dirty floats and coils of flesh; human, crocodile, indistinguishable.

SAM KYLE: I want a cool palm.

ENTER TWO FEMALE DEMONS, PROCELL AND SON-NEILLON.

THE DEVIL: Close your eyes—forget Africa. You're a tiny child again.

THE DEMONS PICK HIM UP.

THE DEVIL: You're being rocked in your mother's arms. She's pressed
 so close to you, you can feel her heartbeat. There's a dribble of
 thick milk on your lip. There, there. Doesn't that feel better?
SAM KYLE: Yes.
THE DEVIL: Rock-a-bye-baby.
SAM KYLE: Yes.
THE DEVIL: Do you feel stronger?
SAM KYLE: I'm . . . beginning to.
THE DEVIL: Ready to give yourself to your mother: do what she asks?
SAM KYLE: Yes.

*THE ROCKING STOPS. THE DEMONS PLACE
SAMUEL IN FRONT OF THE DEVIL.*

THE DEVIL: Open your eyes. There's a little miracle. Better?
SAM KYLE: (*Surprised*) Yes.
THE DEVIL: Sir.
SAM KYLE: Sir.
THE DEVIL: Trust me. Serve me and you serve your history.
SAM KYLE: What do you mean?
THE DEVIL: Hold the feeling you have now. It's innocence. And
 it's very precious.

*THE DEVIL AND SAM STARE AT ONE ANOTHER. A
LONG, MYSTERIOUS BEAT.*

THE DEVIL: (*Briskly*) Gentleman, shall we go to court?

*EXIT THE DEVIL, VERRIER AND DEMONS. SAM
LINGERS A MOMENT, PUZZLED. THEN HE FOLLOWS.*

THE LIGHTS DIM.

END OF ACT ONE.

Act 2

ENTER AN ACTOR.

ACTOR: (*To the audience*) In law, there are no certainties. Suppose we tried our loved ones? Made a list of offenses against us. How long before we'd amassed enough resentment to hang them by? Now, we put the Enemy on trial. How long before we find enough reasons to love the Prince of the World?

THE DEVIL ENTERS.

THE DEVIL: (*To the Actor*) Are you sure you won't kiss me?
ACTOR: I told you already.
THE DEVIL: You'll change your mind.

EXIT ACTOR. ENTER POPPER, KYLE, CATHARINE LAMB, JANE BECK AND MILO MILO. THROUGHOUT THE PROCEEDINGS THAT FOLLOW, WE SHOULD NEVER FORGET JUST HOW UNCOMFORTABLE THEY ARE IN THIS OVERHEATED, INSECT RIDDEN PLACE. THEY FAN THEMSELVES, SLAP MOSQUITOES, SLATHER THEMSELVES IN SUNBLOCK AND INSECT-REPELLANT. THEY PANT. THEY SWEAT. THEY DRINK WATER, THEN PANT AND SWEAT SOME MORE.

POPPER: (*To the audience*) We're here gathered to try The Devil. Why? Because for reasons the Counsels will undoubtedly make clear, he was thrown from Heaven—
SAM KYLE: Not proved.
POPPER: Allegedly thrown by God Almighty some several thousand years ago. Now, he's up for parole, and by the terms of his exile, his appeal for a return to the City of

God is to be judged by us, the humanity whose world he's shared. If it's found that his ministry tended more to evil than to good, he'll be condemned to earth indefinitely. If, however, his Advocate can prove his time on earth hasn't adversely affected mankind, he must be judged innocent and returned to Heaven. Whatever the jury—whose pure and invisible souls are watching us even now, twelve just ghosts and true—whatever they decide, to that judgment the defendant is bound. Is this sworn?

THE DEVIL: I set my life on it.

POPPER: So you forfeit your very existence if you disobey the court's ruling, whichever way it goes.

THE DEVIL: I understand.

POPPER: One thing I insist of Counsels: in a case like this we may have to juggle abstracts, but please keep a low profile on the metaphysics. A little theology goes a long way at the best of times. And in this heat...

CATHARINE LAMB: His Lordship recognizes however that this *is* fundamentally an ethical question.

POPPER: His Lordship recognizes that if he has the pants bored off him, he'll rapidly lose patience.

THE DEVIL: (*Beaming*) He's a good man. Straight forward.

POPPER: Opening statements. Ms. Lamb for the prosecution.

CATHARINE LAMB: The Prosecution will seek to prove that the defendant is the Prince of all sickness, the enemy of truth, the inventor of depravity, error and anguish—

POPPER: Thank you.

CATHARINE LAMB: I haven't finished.

POPPER: Advocate: you've got thirty seconds—

SAM STANDS, BUT THE DEVIL RISES AND PUSHES HIM BACK ON TO HIS CHAIR.

THE DEVIL: Allow me. (*To the audience*) I sniff you, invisibles. I sense your sweet souls. Let me tell you . . . I'm not your enemy. I'm not harm or depravity. I'm no more unnatural than a fish, nor as mysterious. My loins aren't iron, my teeth are thirty two, my blood's temperate. I'm not Old Nick, not the Bogeyman, not the Lord of the Abyss—

POPPER: What are you then?

THE DEVIL: Innocent. But you may call me Lucifer. I'm finished. Judge me, and I'll go.

CATHARINE LAMB: (*Incredulous*) What?

THE DEVIL: Make your decision, please.

POPPER: Mr. Kyle, please ask your client to sit down.

THE DEVIL: I've told you what I am—

JANE BECK: He thinks it's over.

THE DEVIL: Judge me, and let me go to my Father.

POPPER: That was just the opening statements.

THE DEVIL: I've done my time—I demand to be judged!

POPPER: Silence! Mr. Kyle—

THE DEVIL: (*Suddenly emotional*) I'm innocent!

SAM KYLE: Please sit down!

THE DEVIL: Tired, angry and innocent.

POPPER: Then you've nothing to fear. Sit down. Prosecution, your first witness.

SAM KYLE: (*To The Devil*) You have to obey the rules.

RELUCTANTLY, THE DEVIL SITS.

THE DEVIL: The judge: what's his name?

SAM KYLE: Felix Popper.

THE DEVIL: (*Dangerously*) Felix Popper. Who'll be the judge of the judges, eh?

CATHARINE LAMB: I call the Archangel Michael.

THE DEVIL: (*Outraged*) What?

SAM KYLE: Objection: this court is concerned only to judge my client's behavior on earth.

POPPER: Lamb? He has a point.

CATHARINE LAMB: M'lord, we must first establish why the defendant was thrown out of the City of God. His fundamental sin.

POPPER: That seems reasonable to me. Let's see what the angel's got to say for himself. Milo? Fetch the witness, will you?

ENTER MILO MILO.

MILO MILO: He's not here, sir.

POPPER: Did you send out a summons?

MILO MILO: Of course, sir. Macready carried it.

POPPER: Well then find Macready. (*Already exasperated*) Jesus.

EXIT MILO MILO.

POPPER: Sorry, Lamb. It looks as though you've got no witness.
SAM KYLE: Round one to us, I think.
POPPER: This isn't wrestling, Mr. Kyle.
THE DEVIL: (*Smirking*) Is this the law? It could be entertaining.
POPPER: Have you another witness, Lamb?
CATHARINE LAMB: No more angels, I'm afraid. M'lord. I'd like to call Ulla Shim.
POPPER: Ulla Shim!
MILO MILO: She's here, sir.

A SIGHING, OUT OF THE EARTH, AS IT GIVES UP THE DEAD. A MOMENT LATER ULLA SHIM ENTERS, WIZENED, AND IN RAGS. A PITIFUL, DIMINUTIVE FIGURE.

POPPER: Is she sworn in?
MILO MILO: Oh, yes m'lord. We swore them in at their resurrections.
THE DEVIL: Sworn to truth, eh? That's a nice touch.
ULLA: May I sit down? I'm very tired.
POPPER: Have you come a long way?
CATHARINE LAMB: The witness is dead, m'lord.
POPPER: What?
CATHARINE LAMB: We are permitted to call the dead?
POPPER: It's allowed: I just didn't think anybody'd do it. A chair, somebody. Or would you prefer to lie down?
SAM KYLE: You didn't tell me there'd be dead witnesses.
THE DEVIL: Dead or alive: it's a matter of degree.
POPPER: Silence, please—
CATHARINE LAMB: Ulla Shim: I want to take you back to your home in what is now Soviet Russia. Can you remember that far back?
ULLA: Oh yes. I've lain in my rot remembering.

THE SCENE CHANGES. THE COURT, WITH THE EXCEPTION OF CATHARINE LAMB, FADES FROM VIEW. SUDDENLY, WE'RE IN A BITTERLY COLD WASTELAND. AN ACTOR ENTERS.

CATHARINE LAMB: The year is—
ACTOR: 1212 B.C.
CATHARINE LAMB: And the month?
ACTOR: November. Early snows. Bitter winds, even in the forest.

> *EXIT CATHARINE LAMB. ULLA SHIM GETS UP FROM HER CHAIR. ENTER PIA SHIM: TOO YOUNG TO HAVE BEEN BROKEN, LIKE HER MOTHER.*

ACTOR: Ulla Shim and her retarded daughter, Pia, are digging for roots in the hard ground, when suddenly all the birds stop singing—
PIA: Mama—
ACTOR: And the snows turn bloody.
PIA: Ah!

> *PIA TRIES TO WIPE THE SNOW OFF HER.*

ACTOR: (*Looking up*) Will you look at that?
ULLA: (*Averting her eyes*) No.
ACTOR: The sky's turned yellow—
ULLA: (*Shouting*) Keep your head down, girl!
ACTOR: Then a thunder. She looked up.

> *PIA LOOKS UP. LETS OUT A CRY.*

ULLA: (*Hits her*) Hush, bitch!
ACTOR: The sky had opened, like a wound.
ULLA: People are falling out of the sky. It isn't possible. One, two, three. One, two, three. One, two—
ACTOR: Not people, angels.
ULLA: Now I hear their voices, louder as they drop. Most are falling to the northeast, but one or two—
ACTOR: There!
ULLA: Almost straight down.
ACTOR: It hits the upper branches.

> *THE DEVIL HOWLS OFFSTAGE. A HEART-CRACKING SOUND.*

ACTOR: The branches flays it as it falls.

*THE DEVIL ROLLS ON STAGE, NAKED AND WING-
LESS. BORN INTO THE WORLD RAW AND CRAZED.*

ACTOR: And it falls ten meters from her.
ULLA: Fire. Wrapped up in a cloth.
ACTOR: Face covered.
ULLA: Blood seeping out.
ACTOR: Lucifer.
ULLA: Of all the angels.
ACTOR: The rebel of rebels.
ULLA: Not that I knew. Pia—
PIA: Mama?
ULLA: Come here.

PIA DOESN'T MOVE.

ULLA: *Bitch!* Come here—
ACTOR: (*To Ulla*) Don't touch it.
ULLA: I won't, she will.
ACTOR: It may be alive.
ULLA: (*Certain*) You fall off a tree, you break your back. You fall
    off Heaven, you're dead.

*ULLA SHIM PICKS UP PIA AND PUSHES HER
TOWARD THE BODY.*

ULLA: Let's see his face.
ACTOR: Why?
ULLA: If he's white, we'll bury him. If he's any other color: the
    pigs are hungry. The face, bitch.

*PIA TENTATIVELY APPROACHES AND TOUCHES THE
BODY. AS SHE DOES SO, THE DEVIL SPEAKS.*

THE DEVIL: Am I forgiven?
ULLA: (*To the Actor*) Did you speak?
ACTOR: No.
THE DEVIL: (*Panicked, crazed*) No, don't! I meant nothing by it!

High spirits! That's all! You're hurting me! My wings. Aah! Aah! My wings, what are you doing to my wings?

ULLA: He thinks he's a bird. Uncover his face, Pia.

PIA UNCOVERS THE WOUNDED, CRIMSON FACE.

THE DEVIL: Father!

ULLA: He's not white.

THE DEVIL: (*Sees the women*) Who are you?

HE SEIZES HOLD OF PIA.

PIA: (*In terror*) Mama!

ULLA: Run! (*To the actor*) And you! Run!

ACTOR: I feel like a coward. (*Pia screams again*) Shit!

EXIT ACTOR AND ULLA.

THE DEVIL: (*Still holding Pia*) Who is this?

PIA: Mama!

THE DEVIL: Am I vertical and you horizontal, or the other way about?

PIA: Mama!

THE DEVIL: You're upright, I'm on my back. Ah! My back! Help me stand.

PIA PULLS HIM UP. IT TAKES A GREAT DEAL OF EFFORT.

THE DEVIL: (*Looks at himself*) What's this out of me? Am I painted?

PIA: Blood.

THE DEVIL: I'm incomplete, somehow. This hot red water out of these holes in this flesh I don't even have a name for: Who am I?

PIA: Blood.

THE DEVIL: Blood, yes, that's what they call it; I've seen it before, but never on me. What's my name?

PIA: Shit-face.

THE DEVIL: Why are you grinning?

PIA: You are me.

THE DEVIL: Uh?

PIA: Loose head.

THE DEVIL: Possibly. Come closer. Let me see in your eye: my reflection. Ah! What sort of face is that?

PIA STARTS TO COPY HIM IN HER IMBECILIC FASH-ION. THE ACTOR CREEPS BACK ON, STILL FEARFUL, BUT CURIOUS. ULLA FOLLOWS.

PIA: That?

THE DEVIL: What sort of face?

PIA: What sort of face?

THE DEVIL: I asked you.

PIA: I asked you.

THE DEVIL: (*Disgusted*) Ah!

PIA: Ah!

THE DEVIL: (*Furious*) Don't copy me.

PIA: Ah!

THE DEVIL: I said—

PIA: Ah!

ACTOR: Was he mad?

ULLA: I thought so.

ACTOR: But you let him stay?

ULLA: A madman's better than no man at all. He could work.

ACTOR: And did he?

ULLA: Oh yes. He could light fires touching his fingers together. But he was a child, he knew nothing. She was the one taught him—

ACTOR: Taught him?

ULLA: Knots. She could tie such knots—

PIA AND THE DEVIL ARE SITTING TOGETHER, TYING KNOTS IN A PIECE OF ROPE.

PIA: So. So. Now you.

THE DEVIL: Like this?

PIA: No.

THE DEVIL: Like this?

PIA: Yes, and pull. Pull—

THE DEVIL: This is a good knot.

ULLA: (*Snatches the rope*) Useless! Knots for nothing: knots, knots, knots—

*ULLA RECEDES. PIA COMES FORWARD WHILE THE
DEVIL TIES ANOTHER KNOT.*

ACTOR: Pia?
PIA: Uh?
ACTOR: Do you like him?
PIA: Yes.
ACTOR: And he lives out the winter with you, yes?
PIA: Yes.
ACTOR: And what do you teach him?
PIA: Knots.
ACTOR: And what does he teach you?
PIA: Knots.
ACTOR: No, what does *he* teach *you?*
PIA: Words.
ACTOR: Yes, words.

THE DEVIL AND PIA.

THE DEVIL: (*Patiently*) Don't say Mama—
PIA: Mama—
THE DEVIL: Say mother.
PIA: Mother.
THE DEVIL: Mother.

PAUSE.

THE DEVIL: Mother and Father.
PIA: Fafa.
THE DEVIL: Again. Father.
PIA: Father.
THE DEVIL: Your *father.*
PIA: Your father—
THE DEVIL: Say father—
PIA: Father. Father. Father.

*NOW, A TERRIBLE GRIEF PASSES ACROSS THE
DEVIL'S FACE, AS HE STARTS TO REMEMBER.*

THE DEVIL: Who art—

PIA: Father—

THE DEVIL: Who art—

PIA: Father—Father—

THE DEVIL: Hush! Father who art—who art—I know some words in my head—

PIA: Father.

THE DEVIL: Hush, will you? It's on the tip of my brain. Our father who art—don't cry.

PIA: Don't cry.

THE DEVIL: Say after me—

PIA: After me—

THE DEVIL: Our father who art—

PIA: Our father who art—

THE DEVIL: In Heaven!

PIA: In Heaven!

THE DEVIL: Hallowed be thy name—

PIA: Hallowed be thy name—

THE DEVIL: Thy kingdom come—thy will be done, on earth—

PIA: Thy kingdom come—thy will be done, on earth—

THE DEVIL: On earth—ah!

PIA: Ah!

THE DEVIL: Damn words—I spit them out—on earth—

PIA: As it is in Heaven. Give us this day our daily bread, and forgive us our trespasses as we forgive those who trespass against us—

THE DEVIL: Yes! Yes! How did you know?

PIA: In sleep—

THE DEVIL: I say it?

PIA: Yes.

THE DEVIL: For thine is the Kingdom, the Power and the Glory, for ever and ever—

PIA: For thine is the Kingdom, the Power and the Glory, for ever and ever—

THE DEVIL: But what does it mean?

PIA: Amen.

THE DEVIL: What does it mean?

PIA: Amen. Amen. Amen.

THE DEVIL: And why does my tongue ache when I make the words?

PIA: Never mind.

THE DEVIL: I almost remember.

PIA: Forget the words. I'll teach you a knot. Look—
THE DEVIL: (*Frustration erupting*) I don't want knots!

A SILENT MOMENT. PIA IS FRIGHTENED, AND AROUSED.

PIA: Do you see the animals?
THE DEVIL: Huh?
PIA: They do violence to each other all the time: one on top of the other.
THE DEVIL: I've seen. It's senseless, like everything in this world. I know nothing: I understand nothing. My head is one big knot—
PIA: I could untie it—
THE DEVIL: Don't touch me—my skin—
PIA: We should do as the animals do.
THE DEVIL: Why?
PIA: It's the season.
THE DEVIL: You smell strange.
PIA: I bleed.
THE DEVIL: Then wash your wound, like mine. It'll close up.
PIA: No.
THE DEVIL: Shall I? I don't mind.

NOW HE TOUCHES HER.

PIA: (*A pained sigh*) Aah!
THE DEVIL: Hot.
PIA: Here—

SHE WRAPS THE ROPE AROUND HER NECK, AND EMBRACES HIM. THEY PRESS CLOSE TO ONE ANOTHER.

THE DEVIL: I feel—
PIA: I don't mind—
THE DEVIL: I feel as though I'm climbing.
PIA: Come into me—
THE DEVIL: Yes . . . Yes . . .
PIA: No harm.
THE DEVIL: . . . I'm climbing the air . . .

PIA: Soft, soft . . .

THE DEVIL: . . . there's a light in my head . . .

PIA: Soft, soft . . .

THE DEVIL: What's that voice? I can hear a voice—

HE HAS TAKEN HOLD OF THE ROPE AROUND PIA'S NECK, LIGHTLY. HIS HEAD IS THROWN BACK. HE'S IN AN ECSTASY OF REMEMBRANCE.

THE DEVIL: I hear: yes I hear. Louder. I'm climbing toward it. Up, up—yes—yes—I hear you. Who calls me? Who calls me—Lucifer. Lucifer! Who calls me *Lucifer?*

HE OPENS HIS EYES. IN HIS EXCITEMENT HE'S UNWITTINGLY STRANGLING PIA.

THE DEVIL: Ah! Where's the light? What is this flesh? This smell of blood, this heavy being? Take it off me, God! Take it away. I want to be light. Please God! God! Lucifer begs you!

PIA IS DEAD IN HIS ARMS, CHOKED BY THE ROPE. HE LETS HER BODY DROP FROM HIS ARMS, ASTONISHED BY WHAT HE IS REMEMBERING.

THE DEVIL: Lucifer! I'm called Lucifer! My angels. Verrier. Belial. Beelzebub. I remember who I am, what I am. Lucifer.

ULLA APPEARS OUT OF THE DARKNESS.

ULLA: That's how I found him. The girl was dead.

THE DEVIL: (*Flatly*) I meant no harm.

ULLA: There were tears on his face. Human tears.

THE DEVIL: (*To the audience*) One loves songs, and forgets them. An age later, you hear the melody, half a line, and the whole song comes back, as though never forgotten. It was though I was in Heaven yesterday, sitting on His hand.

ENTER CATHARINE LAMB AS THE ACTOR REMOVES PIA'S BODY.

CATHARINE LAMB: Did he attack you?

ULLA: No.

CATHARINE LAMB: Touch you at all?

ULLA: I doubt if he even saw me. He just got up and left.

CATHARINE LAMB: And the girl?

ULLA: I fed her to the pigs. I know a mother shouldn't say this about her own flesh, but I was glad she was gone. It was quick, I'm sure. There's nothing in life for those with all their brains: what chance had she got? Can I go?

THE COURT REAPPEARS. VERRIER AND BELIAL ATTEND UPON THE DEVIL, MOPPING HIS SWEATED FACE AND ADJUSTING HIS CLOTHING.

POPPER: Cross examination?

SAM KYLE: No.

POPPER: (*To Ulla*) You may go.

ULLA: I hate the heat.

SHE CROSSES TO THE DEVIL. STARES AT HIM.

ULLA: I wonder sometimes, in my grave, what you were like with wings.

THEY STARE ON. THEN ULLA EXITS.

SAM KYLE: May I ask the Prosecution what that nonsense proved?

CATHARINE LAMB: That your client's first activities on earth were murder and rape.

SAM KYLE: Nonsense. The intercourse was instigated by the girl and her death was entirely accidental.

CATHARINE LAMB: *Please.*

POPPER: Thank you, counsels.

THE DEVIL: (*To the audience*) A little while after, I was in Turkey. In a tiny stinking street a voice said: Lucifer. It was Kawka-bel, an angel I'd skipped the sky with. He had been a rain-bow. Now he was again. All colors: bruised, gangrened, puss-sodden and bloody. This who had been of the order of dominations. He died in my arms.

CATHARINE LAMB: One demon more or less—

THE DEVIL: (*Pained*) That's cruel.

POPPER: They didn't all die, then? Your fellow angels?

THE DEVIL: Oh no. As I went through the world I sought them out, one by one. Verrier was running a boy's brothel in Rome. Araziel was Solomon's mistress.

CATHARINE LAMB: You still had rebellion in common.

THE DEVIL: No. The only thing we shared was wounds. Being angels, they'd survived the most terrible mutilations. They were remade: You'd call them monsters. Lump scars, livid flaps of meat on them, half healed and pulsing. New mouths in their backs, toothed with scabs, leaking bile. But I loved them.

POPPER: We're touched. Is that all?

THE DEVIL: It is.

POPPER: Advocate. The floor's yours. Do you wish to call a witness?

SAM KYLE: I do, m'lord.

JANE BECK: (*To Lamb*) We have to stop that sort of speechifying. It plays on the jury's sympathies.

CATHARINE LAMB: Easier said than done.

SAM KYLE: The Prosecution's claimed my clients first works in the world came out of malice. Quite the reverse. They came from innocence—

CATHARINE LAMB: Murder, from innocence?

SAM KYLE: —of the world, of the human condition. In evidence of this: in 88 B.C., my client, now a much travelled man—

CATHARINE LAMB: Objection, the client is not a man.

SAM KYLE: M'lord, if the Prosecution wishes to win this case by challenging common vocabulary, we'll be here forever.

POPPER: He's not a man, Kyle; objection sustained.

SAM KYLE: (*To Lamb*) What suits you then? Creature? Entity? A much travelled entity—was in North West India, the Kabul Valley. There was there a Greek settlement left by Alexander, a little Athens called Bucephalus. The great man had named it after his horse.

POPPER: Why the hell did he take himself off there?

THE DEVIL: I was a student of the world, sir, and something of a sybarite. I wanted to taste every pleasure. I'd been a while in Athens, and I'd heard of these towns on the very edge of the civilized world.

POPPER: What were you in Athens, may I ask?

THE DEVIL: I'm ashamed to tell you. A critic.

SAM KYLE: The defense calls Yapshi Kanishka.

THE DEVIL: Ah, my little Yapshi.

ENTER YAPSHI KANISHKA, A TWELVE YEAR OLD BOY, BRIGHT-EYED, PRETTY AND—LIKE MOST PRE-PUBESCENT BOYS—A LITTLE LETHAL.

SAM KYLE: You are Yapshi Kanishka?

YAPSHI: (*Dry-mouthed*) I am.

SAM KYLE: There's no need to be nervous.

YAPSHI: I meant no harm.

SAM KYLE: You're not accused of anything. You're just a witness. Please, tell the Court what happened the day the barbarians came—

YAPSHI: (*To Popper*) Do I have to?

POPPER: Yes, child. You do.

THE SCENE CHANGES. WE ARE IN A GARDEN, FILLED WITH FLOWERS AND BIRD SONG. ENTER CALLIMACHUS—THE GREEK MASTER OF THIS WELL-KEPT HOUSE—WITH A BUNDLE AND A STICK.

YAPSHI: (*To the audience*) I was in the garden.

CALLIMACHUS: You depraved filth! Can't you behave like a decent Greek? My wife could have found your disgusting little god.

YAPSHI: (*Shaking his head; eyes downcast*) I don't understand.

CALLIMACHUS: I don't understand: a great shaking of the head.

HE UNCOVERS THE ITHYPHALLIC STATUE IN THE BUNDLE. IT'S DICK HAS BEEN BROKEN OFF.

CALLIMACHUS: Whichever of your over endowed divinities this obscene statue represents, if ever I see its like in my house again I shall, before removing you into the street, remove the skin off your back.

YAPSHI: Yes, sir.

CALLIMACHUS: I've already destroyed its offending part. Smash the unholy thing to pieces—

CALLIMACHUS GIVES YAPSHI THE BUNDLE AND
EXITS. ENTER LYSIAS: (THE DEVIL) AND CALLI-
MACHUS' BORED, OVERHEATED WIFE, POLYXENE.

POLYXENE: (*To Yapshi*) What have you got there?
YAPSHI: Lady?
POLYXENE: In the bundle?
YAPSHI: A dead god, lady.
POLYXENE: Surely you mean dog. (*To Lysias*) He means dog.
    Take it away, Yapshi.
YAPSHI: (*Bowing*) Lady.

    EXIT YAPSHI.

LYSIAS: He has fine eyes.
POLYXENE: Really?
LYSIAS: Very fetching.
POLYXENE: Do you want him?
LYSIAS: Later, maybe. The garden really is beautiful.
POLYXENE: No it isn't. It's parched.
LYSIAS: But such roses.
POLYXENE: I had them brought from Athens. The native blooms
    are dull. Everything in India smells except the flowers.
LYSIAS: (*Laughs*) I like it here.
POLYXENE: In Meander's time, maybe it was a brave place to be.
    The edge of the world. But now? It's stale.
LYSIAS: I heard there were nomads in the mountains. Dangerous
    men—
POLYXENE: I want to go back to Athens, before I lose my mind.
    That's why you're such a friend, Lysias, you remind me of
    the life there.
LYSIAS: Is it so wonderful? The theatre, the races, the dinners—
POLYXENE: And the mysteries. Don't forget those. Oh, for a little
    civilised paganism. The Villa you told me about where they
    have the ceremonies—
LYSIAS: Yes?
POLYXENE: Tell me again.
LYSIAS: It was just a rumour.
POLYXENE: At the crescent moon, you said—
LYSIAS: Did I?

POLYXENE: (*Insistent*) *Tell me.*

LYSIAS: What is there to tell? Acolytes, initiates with their flesh oiled, lambs under foot, priests, chosen for their prowess as lovers, men dressed as children, blindfolded, rose petals everywhere, so thick they can be lain on, and the thorn stems kept to prick the exhausted into life. They all pray Dionysos will come—

POLYXENE: And will he?

LYSIAS: He's effeminate, they say, and a little overweight.

POLYXENE: No.

LYSIAS: His divinities are with him.

POLYXENE: Nubians?

LYSIAS: Half goat.

POLYXENE: (*Delighted*) Monsters.

LYSIAS: Forbidden flesh.

POLYXENE: And the women give themselves to them?

LYSIAS: And to the god himself. Women die with him pressing upon them.

POLYXENE: How do their husbands explain that: finding their dead wives with smiles on their faces?

LYSIAS: They bury them with due honors, and wither up inside.

POLYXENE: Lysias, I can't bear it here any longer.

LYSIAS: I brought you the statue.

POLYXENE: Yes, I pray to it, I smear it with honey, but he doesn't come. Dionysos is too busy in Athens.

LYSIAS: He might send a representative.

POLYXENE: Who?

LYSIAS: Dark meat. Forbidden flesh.

POLYXENE: Yapshi?

LYSIAS: Why not?

POLYXENE: These people aren't lovers.

LYSIAS: How do you know?

POLYXENE: He's too young.

LYSIAS: Then perhaps you're better off here, Polyxene, where the god himself won't come and find you, because he never forgives those who refuse him.

POLYXENE: I'm not refusing. But a boy?

LYSIAS: Perhaps you should ask the god himself. Go. Ask your little statue.

POLYXENE: I will.

EXIT POLYXENE. ENTER ACTOR.

ACTOR: Why are you here?
LYSIAS: I like the heat.
ACTOR: There are hotter places.
LYSIAS: I like the flowers.
ACTOR: There are prettier flowers.
LYSIAS: I like the air of impending destruction.
ACTOR: Ah.

ENTER YAPSHI.

LYSIAS: Do you want your mistress?
YAPSHI: No sir, I have a message for Callimachus. It's important.
LYSIAS: Look for him in the house.

EXIT YAPSHI.

LYSIAS: (*To the audience*) Athens is a flat bread. I nibble at the
    edges. It chokes me, it constipates me: but I'm hungry for it.

ENTER POLYXENE.

POLYXENE: (*Panicked*) Lysias. The statue's gone. Callimachus
    must have found it. I'm a disgraced woman. You see how
    Dionysos loves us? The shame, Lysias, the shame.
LYSIAS: He knows the shame, Polyxene, and he knows the irony
    of using shame to bring down conscience altogether.

ENTER YAPSHI.

LYSIAS: Poor Polyxene—
YAPSHI: Can I help, lady?
POLYXENE: No.
LYSIAS: Your mistress has mislaid something, Yapshi, my dear.
POLYXENE: I haven't lost anything.
LYSIAS: A little idol she doted on. Perhaps you know where it is?
    Speak up, Yapshi.

YAPSHI SHAKES HIS HEAD. LYSIAS HITS HIM.

LYSIAS: The statue, now.

YAPSHI: (*Falls to his knees*) Forgive me, lady.

LYSIAS: There, like a little lap dog.

POLYXENE: Get up.

YAPSHI: (*Clasping Polyxene's legs*) Forgive me.

POLYXENE: Don't cling.

YAPSHI: Forgive me; the master told me to destroy it.

POLYXENE: (*To Lysias*) You hear? He found it! Ruined!

YAPSHI: But the statue smiled at me. It meant no harm—

LYSIAS: No harm.

POLYXENE: You kept it?

YAPSHI: I buried it.

LYSIAS: Time for a little digging, perhaps?

POLYXENE: Callimachus is in the house.

LYSIAS: How many omens do you want? Do you want him dressed as a goat? Look—adoration—I'll take care of Callimachus. Take the boy; teach him . . . Greek.

EXIT POLYXENE AND YAPSHI.

LYSIAS: (*Calling after them*) Dig deep. (*After a beat; to himself*) I need a drink.

ENTER CALLIMACHUS, WITH A LETTER.

CALLIMACHUS: Lysias.

LYSIAS: Callie, so very good to see you.

CALLIMACHUS: I've just had word from the outpost at Attock. There are Saka gathering to the north-east.

LYSIAS: How many?

CALLIMACHUS: Can you ever count these hordes?

LYSIAS: Barbarians.

CALLIMACHUS: I was in the Peshawar, after the attacks last year—

LYSIAS: I couldn't go: I had a previous engagement.

CALLIMACHUS: Babies stuck like kebabs, alternating with the heads of their parents.

LYSIAS: (*Offended*) Please.

CALLIMACHUS: But we're prepared this time.

LYSIAS: Polyxene must get to a place of safety.

CALLIMACHUS: No time for her.

LYSIAS: She ought to be told.
CALLIMACHUS: Where is she?
LYSIAS: Amongst the roses, I think. Go quietly. She may be praying.

EXIT CALLIMACHUS.

LYSIAS: (*To the audience*) The Saka are wonderful horsemen, austere and terrible fighters. Their weapon is the long spear. Through the body it passes, and out the other side. Like faith, or a good dinner.

CALLIMACHUS CRIES OUT OFFSTAGE, THEN ENTERS, SHAKING.

CALLIMACHUS: Oh Gods—
LYSIAS: Callie?
CALLIMACHUS: She's with the slave. Don't look. Where's my short sword?
LYSIAS: Are the barbarians here already?
CALLIMACHUS: Here all the time. In the bower, in the heart of my sweet garden, in the lap of my own wife!
LYSIAS: You can't mean it?
CALLIMACHUS: She raised her head; her hair was unknotted, her face was puffed up with lust, eyes like slits. She didn't see me. He did. He looked over his shoulder at me: him with his shining back, he saw me, and he digs deeper, 'til her toes curl.
LYSIAS: Go inside, take a drink—
CALLIMACHUS: The walls have to be manned.
LYSIAS: Do they?
CALLIMACHUS: Of course.
LYSIAS: Will Athens want this gutter preserved?

ENTER POLYXENE, PERSPIRING.

POLYXENE: (*Flustered at the sight of her husband*) Oh, Callie, sweetheart; well, well. Talking men's talk, are we? I won't kiss you, dearest, I seem to have broken out into a perspiration. And I fell over. My thighs are wet.

EXIT POLYXENE.

CALLIMACHUS: Fetch me my sword, Lysias.

LYSIAS: Killing her's no good.

CALLIMACHUS: Not for her, for me. I want to kill myself.

LYSIAS: Wait, my friend. Think a moment. When the hordes come, they'll transfix her, thread her on a spear. She'll ask for forgiveness. You should be there, to give it. Yapshi!

ENTER YAPSHI.

YAPSHI: Sir?

LYSIAS: Go to your master. He wants you.

YAPSHI: Him too?

LYSIAS: No boy—he wants you to open the gate. (*To Callimachus*) Don't you?

CALLIMACHUS: (*An agony of indecision*) Gods.

LYSIAS: Athens will salute you. Give your word.

CALLIMACHUS: Yes.

LYSIAS: You heard him. The North Gate: tell the soldiers to open it, just a little. Callimachus, give him authorization.

CALLIMACHUS REMOVES HIS RING OF OFFICE, AND GIVES IT IT YAPSHI.

LYSIAS: Here boy, wait. There's a hair, at the corner of your mouth. (*Removes it*) That's better.

CALLIMACHUS: *Get out!*

EXIT YAPSHI. CALLIMACHUS STARTS TO CRY.

THE SCENE CHANGES. THE SOUND OF MASSACRE, AND LIGHTS FROM A TERRIBLE CONFLAGRATION. LYSIAS WATCHES THE ATROCITIES FROM A HIGH WINDOW, JOINED BY AN ACTOR.

ACTOR: They're getting closer, street by street.

LYSIAS: Bring poor Callimachus, will you? His eyes may need opening.

ACTOR: (*Fetches Callimachus*) Come and look at the barbarians.

LYSIAS: Really, it's better than Rome.

ACTOR: And so much cheaper.

LYSIAS: Look at that. Three babies on one spear. Four! Four! (*To Callimachus*) Are you looking?

CALLIMACHUS: No.

LYSIAS: Oh, come, come—

ACTOR: They've got into the baths!

CALLIMACHUS: (*Becoming interested*) So they have.

ACTOR: Here come the bathers!

LYSIAS: Shocking.

CALLIMACHUS: Isn't that Melissa?

ACTOR: It is.

CALLIMACHUS: She should pick up her bowels.

LYSIAS: There's Zeno, the old pederast.

CALLIMACHUS: Straight through the chest.

LYSIAS: Nice shot!

CALLIMACHUS: Clean as a whistle.

LYSIAS: Enjoying it?

CALLIMACHUS: I . . . suppose I am. I never knew it would feel so good, watching it all disappear.

ACTOR: They'll be here soon. If you're going to try and escape—

CALLIMACHUS: Let them come. She's here, I'm here.

ACTOR: Oh look, there's that athlete, Timotheus.

CALLIMACHUS: Where?

ACTOR: By the fountain—

CALLIMACHUS: I see.

ACTOR: He's running! (*He shouts*) Go, boy, go!

CALLIMACHUS: They see him.

LYSIAS: Run, boy!

CALLIMACHUS: They're overtaking—

LYSIAS: Run!

CALLIMACHUS: No chance. Almost got him.

LYSIAS: Watch; this is their specialty. Look. Two scoops.

ACTOR: (*Looks away*) Oh, that's too much; to do that.

CALLIMACHUS: (*Retreating from the window*) He didn't even cry out.

EXIT ACTOR AND CALLIMACHUS.

LYSIAS: Who's to hear?

THE SCENE DARKENS. THE NOISE OF FIGHTING DIMS SOMEWHAT. THE CRIES OF THE WOUNDED

BECOME DESPAIRING SOBS. ENTER POLYXENE. LYSIAS IS PLAYING MUSIC: PAN-PIPES, PERHAPS? OR A VIOLIN.

POLYXENE: Where's Callimachus?

LYSIAS: Oh. He was here.

POLYXENE: How can you sit there, with them at the gate? Don't you know what they'll do to us?

ENTER CALLIMACHUS. HE HAS HIS SHORT SWORD.

CALLIMACHUS: They won't find us alive, Polyxene. We can die well.

POLYXENE: No . . .

CALLIMACHUS: We have no choice—

LYSIAS: He's right—

POLYXENE: Can't we give them something? Beads, or—

LYSIAS: They can take all they want.

POLYXENE: (*A stinging fury*) You did this!

LYSIAS: You said you wanted a little paganism. Go welcome it.

POLYXENE: What kind of filth are you? He's the one, Callimachus, he caused all this—

CALLIMACHUS: Why?

LYSIAS: Curiosity.

CALLIMACHUS STABS THE DEVIL IN THE BACK.

CALLIMACHUS: Bastard!

POLYXENE SHRIEKS. THE DEVIL DROPS HIS INSTRUMENT. HIS EYES GLASS OVER. WE THINK HE IS ABOUT TO PERISH. THEN . . . HE SMILES.

POLYXENE: He doesn't die.

LYSIAS: Of course not.

POLYXENE: This is insanity.

CALLIMACHUS: I've lived a life of reason: how can it end like this?

LYSIAS: Questions, questions.

CALLIMACHUS STABS HIMSELF.

CALLIMACHUS: Ah! Gods . . . it hurts!
POLYXENE: Callie!
CALLIMACHUS: Get out of my sight!

SHE EXITS.

LYSIAS: You've driven her into their hands—
CALLIMACHUS: I won't see them; they'll have no satisfaction from me.

A SCREAM.

CALLIMACHUS: Was that my ears whistling?
LYSIAS: No, it was Polyxene, I think.
CALLIMACHUS: Good.
LYSIAS: I hear them in the dining-room.
CALLIMACHUS: Why don't I die?
LYSIAS: Be quick—they're almost here.
CALLIMACHUS: Help me.
LYSIAS: What?
CALLIMACHUS: Finish me off; I haven't the strength.
LYSIAS: No. I couldn't.
CALLIMACHUS: Please—
LYSIAS: It's unethical.
CALLIMACHUS: You brought this about.
LYSIAS: I may have tapped a column—but the house was unstable.
CALLIMACHUS: Kill me. Damn you. Kill me.
LYSIAS: You're seeping away.
CALLIMACHUS: Not quickly enough.

ENTER YAPSHI, RUNNING.

YAPSHI: Sir! Sir! They've killed the mistress. She's on the table; will they eat her?
LYSIAS: No.
YAPSHI: She looks so silly, without a face.
CALLIMACHUS: Ah—
YAPSHI: Is he dying?

LYSIAS: Slowly.

YAPSHI: Why does he look so peaceful?

LYSIAS: It doesn't hurt after a while; it's warm, isn't it, Callie?

CALLIMACHUS: Yes.

LYSIAS: Like floating in the sea.

CALLIMACHUS: Yes.

LYSIAS: What do you see?

CALLIMACHUS: Nothing.

LYSIAS: No stairs? No mountain tops?

CALLIMACHUS: Gray . . . darker . . . almost black . . .

YAPSHI TWISTS THE SWORD. CALLIMACHUS SCREAMS IN PAIN.

CALLIMACHUS: Aah!

YAPSHI: Does he see me?

LYSIAS: No! . . .

YAPSHI PUTS HIS FOOT ON CALLIMACHUS' FACE.

YAPSHI: Does he feel me?

LYSIAS: Not any longer.

YAPSHI: Dead?

LYSIAS: Dead.

YAPSHI: Are you Siva? Are you a demon?

LYSIAS: Of course.

YAPSHI: Why no faces to frighten them with?

LYSIAS: Why would I want monsters, when I have you? One day, Yapshi, though you won't be alive to see it, Athens will be like this, eaten up.

YAPSHI: Eaten up.

LYSIAS: Now, we must prepare for an audience with the barbarians. And afterwards, if you're very good, you can dance on the bodies . . .

ENTER SAM KYLE. THE LIGHTS START TO CHANGE. SLOWLY, THE COURT REAPPEARS.

SAM KYLE: (*Uncomfortable*) Is that the story?

YAPSHI: It is.

SAM KYLE: Thank you.

POPPER: You're excused.

YAPSHI KISSES THE DEVIL'S PALM.

YAPSHI: Goodbye.

THE DEVIL: Still sweet, after all these years.

CATHARINE LAMB: It's appalling. How is this evidence for the defense?

SAM KYLE: It demonstrates my client's . . . impartiality. At no time was he responsible for an act of violence. He has always been a spectator.

CATHARINE LAMB: He manipulated the situation—

THE DEVIL: As an experiment merely—

CATHARINE LAMB: Are we guinea pigs then?

THE DEVIL: If you were given power over a species, wouldn't you want to examine their passions? It was my sentimental education.

CATHARINE LAMB: So you deny this is evidence of malice against humanity?

THE DEVIL: Culture is evidence of malice. The true will of the masses is as one will: each wishes, with his whole heart, to tread on the rest. Callimachus had his moment of perception: Polyxene had a little love, Yapshi went on to become a father, hated as a tyrant by all his children. I gave them all a chance to be themselves.

CATHARINE LAMB: You're so certain of yourself, aren't you?

THE DEVIL: I have no self to be certain of. Understand that, and you understand me. But you wouldn't dare do that, would you?

POPPER: Who's next?

THE DEVIL TURNS HIS BACK ON LAMB.

SAM KYLE: (*A whispered aside*) Will you listen to little advice?

THE DEVIL: Speak.

SAM KYLE: Don't risk damaging your case with these philosophical bon mots. You're playing into their hands.

THE DEVIL: We're winning, aren't we?

SAM KYLE: I would say not.

POPPER: Ms. Lamb. Next witness?

CATHARINE LAMB: I call Jesus Christ.

SAM KYLE: (*To The Devil*) What are you laughing at?

THE DEVIL: Our case is as good as won.

ENTER MILO MILO.

MILO MILO: I'm afraid the witness is not available, m'lord.

POPPER: Where is he?

MILO MILO: I don't know. The warrant was sent. He simply didn't turn up.

POPPER: Well, let's talk with the warrant carrier.

MILO MILO: Chomsky's dead, sir. He slit his own throat in a bath house. In Istanbul.

POPPER: I'm sorry Ms. Lamb, no witness.

THE DEVIL: Would the prosecution be content with this?

THE DEVIL HOLDS UP A FILTHY, PATCHED-UP BOOK.

CATHARINE LAMB: What is that?

THE DEVIL: The diary of Jesus Christ.

POPPER: Diary?

THE DEVIL: In his own hand: given to me at Golgotha, by his far from virginal mother. There is in it a passage relating to me—

POPPER: Prosecution? What are your views on this?

CATHARINE LAMB: It could be a forgery.

THE DEVIL: M'lord, it would not be wise for a creature in my condition, knowing I'm overlooked by Heaven, to present to the Court a forgery. If this book is not the true word of God's son, may I be struck down now. (*He waits, watching the sky*) See?

POPPER: Well?

CATHARINE LAMB: By all means, let's have the evidence. It was the episode in the desert I was interested in.

THE DEVIL: (*Smiling*) It's here. It's all here.

POPPER: Milo. Do you want to read it to the court?

MILO MILO: (*Taking the book*) Where from?

THE DEVIL: Below the wine stain.

MILO MILO: (*Reads*) It was hot. My hair went yellow. I met a lion. I met another lion. I saw two baboons having a fuck. When I was in the desert four weeks, I was hungry. I was being chased. I ran away, but they chased me. I was thirsty. I met a man—

THE SCENE CHANGES. THE COURT DISAPPEARS. WE'RE IN A BLAZING DESERT. ENTER THE DEVIL, CLOSELY PURSUED BY JESUS CHRIST, WHO CARRIES TWO SHARPENED STICKS.

CHRIST: Don't move.

THE DEVIL: (*Raising his arms in surrender*) I'm past moving. Impale me.

CHRIST: No tricks.

THE DEVIL: Me, tricks?

CHRIST: And if you see the little blue wheels, tell me. Empty your pockets.

THE DEVIL: Nothing.

CHRIST: You must have some food.

THE DEVIL: You're right, I must have some food.

CHRIST: I'll take pork.

THE DEVIL: I'll take it first.

CHRIST: What sort of world is this?

THE DEVIL: As empty one, inside and out. What's your name?

CHRIST: Jesus Christ. The Nazarene.

THE DEVIL: I heard of you, down south.

CHRIST: I'm famous; that's why the blue wheels are after me.

THE DEVIL: My friend, you are suffering from hallucinations.

CHRIST: You think I don't know that? Before you fade away, scratch my back.

THE DEVIL: Anything for a fellow Messiah. (*He obliges*)

CHRIST: Higher: left: left: there. You say you're a Messiah, too?

THE DEVIL: Yes.

CHRIST: That's why I'm here: to purify myself. If I could only stop itching.

THE DEVIL: Ticks.

CHRIST: Nits, ticks, fleas. But you have to go amongst the multitudes.

THE DEVIL: Do you want to put those sticks down?

CHRIST: Any good at hunting? I've seen lizards. Do you think lizard's kosher?

THE DEVIL: Everything's kosher in desperation. Moses ate his mother. Mama from heaven.

CHRIST: (*Outraged*) I wouldn't eat my mother.

THE DEVIL: (*Pained by his lack of humor*) No, I didn't mean—

CHRIST: That's not very kind.

THE DEVIL: No, it isn't.

CHRIST: I think I ought to tell you, you may as well as go home. I'm the Messiah.

THE DEVIL: I think not.

CHRIST: They love me.

THE DEVIL: Cautionary tales. Coins, rainbows: it's not sufficient to win the world, Jesus.

CHRIST: (*Like a child*) Well, we'll fight it out, then.

THE DEVIL: No.

CHRIST: Come on: fight me.

THE DEVIL: I don't want to fight.

CHRIST: Fight! Fight!

THE DEVIL DOESN'T MOVE, SO CHRIST ATTACKS HIM. THE DEVIL QUICKLY WRESTLES HIM TO THE FLOOR.

CHRIST: I won't give up. I won't, you hear me? I won't!

THE DEVIL: What would it take to dissuade you?

CHRIST: I'm the Messiah.

THE DEVIL: I could give you a great deal.

CHRIST: Like what?

THE DEVIL: I've got contacts. Solomon's wife is the family. People in power all across the known world. I could give you cities.

CHRIST: Rome?

THE DEVIL: It might be arranged. But you'd have to give up your pretensions to Messiahdom.

CHRIST: I couldn't do that.

THE DEVIL: What a pity. (*He takes out rope*)

CHRIST: What's that for? (*Realizes*) You can't kill me.

THE DEVIL: Who's to see?

CHRIST: My father. Didn't I tell you? My father in Heaven. I'm the Son of God.

THE DEVIL: What?

CHRIST: So I wouldn't try to hurt me: unless—you wanted to do it in public.

THE DEVIL: Strangle you?

CHRIST: No, no. But the time's coming when I have to make an exit.

THE DEVIL: Why?

CHRIST: I'm running out of stories. And I'm tired. So I'll have to die. You could arrange it.

THE DEVIL: No.

CHRIST: A terrible death.

THE DEVIL: I'm not an executioner.

CHRIST: The worst death imaginable.

THE DEVIL: Torn apart by dogs.

CHRIST: Too messy: I don't want to be resurrected in pieces. I must be marked but . . . intact.

THE DEVIL: Run over by a horse?

CHRIST: It could be comic. No, I want something spectacular. On a hill. A good view. A sunset. Clouds.

THE DEVIL: Crucifixion.

CHRIST: Everyone gets that. They do it to sodomites these days. Half of Israel should be up there. Isn't there something they do in the East with hooks through the skin? Swing you round a pole on hooks? Takes days. And so unusual.

THE DEVIL: I don't know of it.

CHRIST: Damn.

THE DEVIL: You'll have to compromise.

CHRIST: What? Crucifixion?

THE DEVIL: Unless we think of something better.

CHRIST: (*Grabs The Devil*) Will you promise me? Promise you'll arrange it.

THE DEVIL: Yes, I promise.

CHRIST: (*With relish*) I want to be publicly flogged. I must be bloodied, humiliated, reduced to a wounded, whimpering animal. Something on the head—

THE DEVIL: Roses—

CHRIST: —or some such. I'll be naked, hung up there like a slab of meat, then the clouds'll boil, lions roar, perhaps an earthquake, and I'll die. And they'll all know what they did, killing me—you promise you'll do it?

THE DEVIL: I told you, yes. Sure as God made little apples.

CHRIST: Good man. Now get thee behind me.
THE DEVIL: Why?
CHRIST: You're in my way.

> *EXIT JESUS, AT A RUN, LEAVING THE DEVIL BEMUSED
> AND EXHAUSTED. THE COURT REAPPEARS.*

THE DEVIL: (*To the audience*) I kept my word. There was a demon
called Carreau posing as a Roman governor. He had the man
crucified. I was there. He saw me in the crowd: instructed
his mother to give me the diary. Even thanked me. He was
quite changed: sick looking, thinking better of it. But he got
his roses.
POPPER: This makes him sound like an imbecile.
THE DEVIL: Oh no, I was the dupe. Here was me, thinking I was
getting rid of a competitor, and in fact I was stage managing
his apotheosis. I tell you, when I saw them fall down on
their knees at Golgotha, I wept. I was tricked, tricked!—and
you called me the Father of Lies. You put me on trial while
he goes free. He gets a cult to himself, but my synagogue is
blasphemy. When I think . . .

> *A DIN OF SUPPORT HAS RISEN FROM THE DEMONS
> IN THE EARTH.*

POPPER: Order in the court! Please! Please! (*To The Devil*) Will
you hush your faction?
THE DEVIL: (*He puts his fingers to his lips. The din quietens.*) The
earth was given to me: remember that. I was to be Prince of
the World. But now, it was Christian. Though I was an exile,
they found me everywhere. Here's The Devil, they said, pos-
sessing pigs and small boys. Ha! Here's The Devil, they said,
in everything diseased and putrescent. The world rose
against me. Everywhere: slandered, my works twisted, my
ambitions destroyed and my face dragged in fear and
loathing.
SAM KYLE: Could we have a recess?
POPPER: No!
THE DEVIL: That's right: no sympathy for The Devil.
POPPER: Sit down!

THE DEVIL: Do you know how difficult it is not to believe what people say about you? Not to become your own publicity? Be thankful, Felix Popper, I'm not The Devil you think I am, because if I were, if I once believed the image of myself, I'd devour you.

POPPER: Order! Order!

THE DEVIL: Judgment! Judgment!

POPPER: Sit down!

FROM THE EARTH, THE DEMONS CHANT: "JUDGMENT! JUDGMENT!"

POPPER: Order! Order! Silence your faction or I'll throw them out of court!

THE DEVIL: They've been thrown out of finer places. (*A beat*) Silence!

THE DEMONS ARE QUIETENED.

SAM KYLE: (*Unnerved; shaking, in fact*) M'lord, the defense moves that as my client is henceforth removed from the public sphere, we should proceed directly to contemporary evidence.

CATHARINE LAMB: Out of the question.

SAM KYLE: These little anecdotes waste the court's time.

POPPER: Mr. Kyle has a point, Ms. Lamb.

CATHARINE LAMB: With respect, the court commits a familiar error: presupposing that one evil is every evil. This monster—

SAM KYLE: Objection!

CATHARINE LAMB: (*Pressing on*) —may *claim* he was exiled from the world, but I beg the court to remember the name of his refuge: Hell.

POPPER: Point made. Continue.

CATHARINE LAMB: I'd like to ask the defendant why he created Hell.

THE DEVIL: I had no home.

CATHARINE LAMB: So you found a cave, did you? Like a hermit?

THE DEVIL: I had a little more ambition than that. We dug out Hell ourselves, handful by handful.

CATHARINE LAMB: Who exactly worked on this project?

THE DEVIL: Friends.

CATHARINE LAMB: Human?

THE DEVIL: Some.

CATHARINE LAMB: The damned?

SAM KYLE: Objection.

POPPER: Sustained. Inflammatory, Ms. Lamb.

CATHARINE LAMB: These humans: on whose authority did you take them?

THE DEVIL: Their own.

CATHARINE LAMB: And what did they build?

THE DEVIL: A world.

CATHARINE LAMB: A parody of earth?

THE DEVIL: More beautiful, I thought.

CATHARINE LAMB: Stone.

THE DEVIL: More fantastic.

CATHARINE LAMB: Nine circles?

THE DEVIL: We're still building. Soon, a hundred.

CATHARINE LAMB: A refuge?

THE DEVIL: A family residence.

CATHARINE LAMB: Quite the bourgeois.

THE DEVIL: My point exactly. I'm no different from any of you.

CATHARINE LAMB: Not every home is hell.

THE DEVIL: Is it not? I wonder what made you, Ms. Lamb.

CATHARINE LAMB: Not every house is a palace.

THE DEVIL: I have no palace.

CATHARINE LAMB: You had one.

THE DEVIL: I may have done. Once.

CATHARINE LAMB: Designed. I believe, by one of the master architects of Chartres Cathedral. Cast your mind back.

THE DEVIL: (*Stone-faced*) Nothing.

CATHARINE LAMB: Let me refresh your memory.

THE COURT BEGINS TO FADE FROM SIGHT.

CATHARINE LAMB: In 1194, the church of Chartres, which housed the tunic the Virgin had worn at the Annunciation was burned down. The only object untouched by fire was the tunic itself. It was taken as a sign that on this site God intended a great monument to be built.

THE DEVIL: At inconceivable expense, I may add.

CATHARINE LAMB: One of the Architects of the Cathedral was—

THE DEVIL: (*Fatalistically*) Nicholas Vidal, of Toulouse.
CATHARINE LAMB: I call Nicholas Vidal.
THE DEVIL: So did I. But he didn't answer.

> *THE DEVIL EXITS. ENTER NICHOLAS VIDAL: A MAN
> OF HEROIC STATURE AND APPETITE.*

CATHARINE LAMB: Please give your evidence, Monsieur Vidal.
NICHOLAS: I am Nicholas Vidal. I was thirty-five, and the master
architect of the East Face of Chartres. I knew two sisters,
Alette and Madeleine.

> *ENTER ALETTE AND MADELEINE. THE SCENE
> BRIGHTENS ABOUT THEM. A FIELD OF SUMMER
> GRASS AND WILDFLOWERS.*

NICHOLAS: It was a good summer. Hot. Gold grain, blue sky.

> *A POST-COITAL SCENE. NICHOLAS LIES DOWN. THE
> SISTERS LAZE BESIDE HIM. ALL IS BLISS.*

ALETTE: Is it Saturday?
MADELEINE: Sunday.
ALETTE: Are you sure?
MADELEINE: Yes.
ALETTE: Why? I just thought; if it's the Sabbath, we shouldn't sin.
Not three times.
MADELEINE: If you've sinned twice, you're damned anyway.
ALETTE: He's probably exhausted.
MADELEINE: Nicholas?

> *ENTER THE DEVIL, AS A NOBLEMAN.*

MADELEINE: Nicholas?
THE DEVIL: Excuse me . . . ladies . . . I'm looking for Nicholas Vidal.
ALETTE: Oh.
THE DEVIL: Is he here?
ALETTE: Who wants him?
THE DEVIL: My name's Masterna. I've come up from the South,
to find him.

MADELEINE: Are you a bum fancier?
ALETTE: (*Giggling*) Madeleine.
MADELEINE: He doesn't go with men. Even the Bishop.
THE DEVIL: He'll go with me.
MADELEINE: You try it; he'll bust your head.
THE DEVIL: I don't want his body.
ALETTE: Well that's good, because there's not enough to go around.
THE DEVIL: I'm a Lord. I have lands in Spain.
ALETTE: You don't look Spanish.
MADELEINE: He doesn't smell Spanish.
THE DEVIL: (*Chilly*) Please wake the architect.
ALETTE: He's tired. He's been working.

NICHOLAS WAKES, AS FROM A NIGHTMARE.

NICHOLAS: Ah!
MADELEINE: Nick?
NICHOLAS: (*Shaken*) Something fell on me.
ALETTE: There's somebody to see you.
NICHOLAS: I felt a weight on my chest.
ALETTE: A Lord, Nick.
NICHOLAS: Jesus, what do I look like?
THE DEVIL: Your appearance is no concern of mine. You're the architect of the East Face—Nicholas Vidal?
NICHOLAS: I am.
THE DEVIL: I never flatter. Your work is exquisite. I want you to work for me.
NICHOLAS: The cathedral isn't half finished.
THE DEVIL: I have influence in the Church: we can come to terms.
NICHOLAS: No. It's not possible.
THE DEVIL: Reconsider, please. Here, you share the design: I offer you a project to yourself. And here, you're forbidden to mark your work. History will never know your name. Build for me, and you'll be remembered.
NICHOLAS: (*Somewhat persuaded*) I can't make up my mind here and now. Come to my house tonight.
THE DEVIL: Not tonight, it's Sunday.
NICHOLAS: Come tomorrow. The house—

THE DEVIL: I know the house. I'll be there. May I say, a little
    advice for the masons; the hitching knot they use is danger-
    ous. Here, this does the job twice as well. (*He tosses the knot
    to Vidal*)
NICHOLAS: (*Impressed*) Thank you.

*THE DEVIL EXITS. THE BIRDS, WHICH HAVE BEEN
SILENT DURING HIS APPEARANCE, START TO SING
AGAIN.*

ALETTE: Don't listen to him.
NICHOLAS: It's a good knot.
MADELEINE: He smells curious.
NICHOLAS: (*Pulling on the rope*) Look at that. He knows his business.
ALETTE: So do I: that man is sick.
MADELEINE: He's probably deformed.
ALETTE: He *does* walk funny.
MADELEINE: And Spanish. I hate the Spanish.
ALETTE: Nicholas?
NICHOLAS: I've got nothing to lose from hearing his bargain.
MADELEINE: All right. Then we'll come, too.
NICHOLAS: No.
MADELEINE: Why not?
NICHOLAS: It's not your business.
ALETTE: We'll be quiet as mice.
NICHOLAS: (*Dreamily*) He said I can sign the work.

EXIT NICHOLAS.

MADELEINE: A bum fancier.
ALETTE: No.
MADELEINE: The way he looked at Nick. And the perfume.
ALETTE: Masterna. Masterna, I've heard of the place.
MADELEINE: We should watch him. Follow him.
ALETTE: You follow him.
MADELEINE: For Nicholas.

ENTER AN ACTOR.

ACTOR: From the south, a bank of cloud had risen.

ALETTE: I'm cold.

ACTOR: In the grain, the mice miscarried, birds fluttered on lead wings, moths choked—

MADELEINE: Quickly, it's going to rain.

EXIT ALETTE AND MADELEINE AS THE DOWNPOUR BEGINS. ENTER NICHOLAS.

NICHOLAS: I was flattered.

ACTOR: Fool.

NICHOLAS: It seemed a good bargain. That night I slept without the sisters. And I dreamt: oh, how I dreamt.

THE ACTOR TAKES HOLD OF NICHOLAS.

NICHOLAS: Dreamt I was locked in the earth with the Lord Masterna.

THE LIGHTS CHANGE. A NIGHTMARE. ENTER THE DEVIL AND TWO DEMONS, PROCELL AND SON-NEILLON.

THE DEVIL: Do you like riddles, Nicholas?

THE ACTOR HAS GAGGED NICHOLAS WITH KNOT-TED ROPE.

THE DEVIL: Here's one. What knot is that when tied makes a man a comedian, a lover and a dancer? Speak up. You don't know? Show him. A noose, Nicholas.

PROCELL "HANGS" SONNEILLON.

THE DEVIL: Up he goes: up, up, up. See how his feet dance? See how his loins swell? See the faces he pulls? Dancer, lover, comedian. Now, suppose we try the same trick on you?

NICHOLAS STRUGGLES.

THE DEVIL: Or would you prefer to obey me? In everything.

Waking or sleeping.

*NICHOLAS FALLS TO HIS KNEES. THE DEVIL PRE-
SENTS HIS BEHIND. NICHOLAS REFUSES TO KISS IT.
EXIT THE DEVIL, THE DEMONS, AND THE ACTOR.*

NICHOLAS: Five times I dreamt that dream. By morning, I was a
terrified man. I locked myself in my house, and prayed that
he wouldn't come. But he came.

A BEATING ON THE DOOR.

NICHOLAS: Was the last supper like this?
THE DEVIL: (*Off*) Nicholas Vidal!
NICHOLAS: I hid.
THE DEVIL: (*Off*) Nicholas! Nicholas!

THE SOUND OF WIND.

THE DEVIL: (*Off*) Let me in, boy!

*THE WIND RISES. A CRASH. THE WIND IS VERY
LOUD. NICHOLAS IS PRAYING.*

NICHOLAS: Our Lady, Mother of Mothers, perfect in splendor—

*ENTER THE DEVIL. HE RAISES HIS HAND. THE
WIND DIES DOWN.*

THE DEVIL: Hush. Better. Kiss.
NICHOLAS: No.
THE DEVIL: Please.

THE DEVIL KISSES NICHOLAS ON BOTH CHEEKS.

THE DEVIL: You look exhausted.
NICHOLAS: I slept badly.
THE DEVIL: In my country, there's no exhaustion. You'll feel
nothing but the simple urge to make beauty for me.
NICHOLAS: I can't come with you.

THE DEVIL: Why not?

NICHOLAS: I have commitments.

THE DEVIL: The Bishop has released you, as of tonight.

NICHOLAS: I love France.

THE DEVIL: As France is to England, so my country is to France. Warmer, sweeter, altogether more alive. I have here a little contract—would you care to glance over it? Then we would perhaps come to an agreement.

NICHOLAS: This language.

THE DEVIL: French.

NICHOLAS: No French I know.

THE DEVIL: For our protection, it's written backwards. Shall I read it for you? 'I, the undersigned, Nicholas Vidal of Toulouse—'

ALETTE: (*Off*) Nicholas?

MADELEINE: (*Off*) Nicky! Nicky!

THE DEVIL: Jesu! Why have I never learned to close doors after me?

ENTER ALETTE AND MADELEINE. THEY CARRY A BOTTLE OF WINE AND A PIE.

ALETTE: Pleased to see us?

MADELEINE: Of course he is.

ALETTE: Mr. Masterna, what a surprise.

THE DEVIL: We have business at the moment, Nicholas and I.

ALETTE: But we've cooked.

NICHOLAS: Later.

MADELEINE: (*Proffering the pie*) Smell that. Yummy!

ALETTE: After all, we ought to celebrate.

NICHOLAS: There's nothing to celebrate.

MADELEINE: Aren't you going to go with the Lord?

ALETTE: To build him a palace?

MADELEINE: To become famous?

THE DEVIL: I think he is. Are you a dancer, Nick?

ALETTE: No, he can't dance.

MADELEINE: Two left feet.

THE DEVIL: Well, we'll have to teach you.

NICHOLAS: I don't need teaching.

THE DEVIL: What about comedy? Can you pull faces?

ALETTE: Only in bed—

NICHOLAS: Shut up, will you?

THE DEVIL: Can you, Nick?

NICHOLAS: (*Pulls a face*) There.

THE DEVIL: You can do better than that. I have friends who could teach you to pull faces.

NICHOLAS: I'm sure you do.

THE DEVIL: If you don't sign.

NICHOLAS: And make me a lover, too? Swell my loins? How do you get into my dreams?

THE DEVIL: I can't think what you mean.

NICHOLAS: All night, you've been in my head. (*Crazed*) Get out!

THE DEVIL: No.

NICHOLAS: (*Desperate*) Please.

THE DEVIL: Ladies—would you leave us alone awhile? I have a new knot for Nicholas.

ALETTE: (*Ignoring him*) Pie, anyone?

MADELEINE: For me!

ALETTE: And for the Lord. Pie for the Lord.

THE DEVIL: Not at the moment. Get out.

NICHOLAS: Do as he says: he'll kill you.

ALETTE: Just a taste, before we go.

THE DEVIL: In my country, we eat after business.

MADELEINE: Well, this is not your country, so eat.

ALETTE: Then we'll go.

THE DEVIL: Very well. (*He eats*) It's good pie. (*His expression changes*) Ah!

ALETTE: Oh dear.

THE DEVIL: (*Clutching his throat*) *Aah! Aah!*

NICHOLAS: What have you done?

THE DEVIL: *Aah! Aah!*

THE DEVIL IS CHOKING. HE FALLS TO THE FLOOR, WRITHING.

ALETTE: It must be the pie.

MADELEINE: But they were good fruits.

ALETTE: Could it have been the crucifix we cooked into it?

MADELEINE: Surely not.

ALETTE: Maybe it was the holy water. Oh. I feel so guilty. We ought to help him.

THE DEVIL: These women! They've poisoned me! (*Rising*) I'll kill you.

MADELEINE: You want to kill us? We'll die happily. We don't want confession—

ALETTE: We want to come to Hell with you.

MADELEINE: Please, please.

ALETTE: We'll cook for you.

MADELEINE: Make love every day—

ALETTE: —every night.

THE DEVIL: No more. Let me out! You hear me, Nicholas. I'll have you one day, in Hell beside me, and you'll build Elysium before you go to rest.

MADELEINE: Get out! (*Kicks him*)

THE DEVIL: Ah!

ALETTE: And don't come back! (*Kicks him*)

EXIT THE DEVIL. ALETTE, MADELEINE, AND NICHOLAS PUT THEIR ARMS AROUND EACH OTHER, LAUGHING. SLOWLY, ALETTE AND MADELEINE RETREAT FROM HIM, UNTIL THE DARKNESS SWALLOWS THEM.

NICHOLAS: One week later, one of the new knots slipped, and a block of stone fell on my chest. I didn't die outright—there was time, in the dark, to hear his breathing.

ENTER THE DEVIL, PULLING A CRUCIFIX FROM HIS THROAT.

NICHOLAS: So I went into the abyss with him.

THE DEVIL: Such an embarrassment, to so believe in my own evil I choked on the image of good. I was furious with myself. (*He gives the crucifix to Nicholas*) How long will it take to build my palace?

NICHOLAS: Fifty years, perhaps: but I must work unwatched.

THE DEVIL: I was a fool to let you do that.

NICHOLAS: You trusted me.

THE DEVIL: More than that. I wanted the beauty I'd seen at Chartres. A taste of heavenly perfection. I never thought—

NICHOLAS: The day came—the palace was finished. The fires were stoked to light it by—and there was such laughter in Hell—

THE DEVIL: (*Staring up at building*) What have you done?

NICHOLAS: In every circle the word went round that The Devil's palace had been built in the shape of one huge—

THE DEVIL: —*turd!*

NICHOLAS: A palace for the Lord of Shite.

THE DEVIL: I couldn't kill him: he was already dead. And I didn't want him in Hell—reminding me.

NICHOLAS: So I came up out of the abyss. The earth was fifty years older. The summers were not as warm as I remembered. My friends were all dead. After a year, I found Alette and Madeleine, buried in unhallowed graves. So, I dug a hole in the earth between them, and buried myself, with my house on my nose. It was damp, and the worms were not kind, but I stretched my fingers out to the bones of theirs, and, after a long while, I fell asleep. That's it.

THE COURT REAPPEARS.

NICHOLAS: All I ever wanted was the love of my peers. But I'm happy now. In my dreams, there's sun and the sisters beside me. The Devil's a comedy. God is a greater one: all entertainments for us to enjoy and forget.

POPPER: Thank you, you're dismissed.

DANTE: (*Off*) Questo e sacrileggio. Come osa dire cosi? Come osa profanare il nome di dio cosi in publico?

POPPER: Who in God's name is that?

THE DEVIL: Dante, I believe, m'lord. The poet.

POPPER: I know who he is. Your witness, Ms. Lamb?

CATHARINE LAMB: Yes, m'lord.

POPPER: Well, muzzle him!

TOO LATE. A HYSTERICAL DANTE NOW ENTERS, ATTACKING NICHOLAS. THE DEVIL APPLAUDS.

DANTE: Dio e con noi, il suo ci arconda lui e nelle suelle sopra—

POPPER: What's he saying?

JANE BECK: Something about God being in the stars—

DANTE: —la nostra testa e nell'ani che respiriamo—

JANE BECK: (*Translating*) —and in the air we breathe.

CATHARINE LAMB: Calm down! Calm down!

CATHARINE LAMB DRAGS DANTE OFF NICHOLAS.

POPPER: He's hysterical.

DANTE: Si c'e un inferno non c'e anche un paradiso?

JANE BECK: (*Translating*) If there's Hell, there's also Heaven.

POPPER: Is that in question? Lamb, will you stop him shouting? Mr. Vidal, you are excused.

NICHOLAS: Thank you.

DANTE: Lei e un eretico! Lei soffina!

JANE BECK: He calls you a heretic.

NICHOLAS: And proud of it.

EXIT NICHOLAS.

POPPER: (*To Dante*) Now stop shouting, or I'll have you expelled. (*To Jane*) Tell him!

JANE BECK: Espulso!

DANTE: Espulso! Sono Espulso!

JANE BECK: (*Translating*) He says he's already expelled.

POPPER: Tell him to speak English.

JANE BECK: Inglese.

DANTE: (*Contemptuously*) Inglese! Ah!

CATHARINE LAMB: Please: could you tell the court about your visit to Hell?

DANTE: Un inferno?

CATHARINE LAMB: Inferno, yes.

DANTE: Lasciate ogni speranza, voi ch'entrate.

JANE BECK: Abandon every hope—

DANTE: —ye who enter. Ice: fire. The sodomites under rains of fire.

THE DEVIL: He doesn't approve of sodomy.

DANTE: Lust in the seat of filth. (*Points to The Devil*) Look, he smiles. Sornii, si. Smiles! You have taken my redemption from me.

POPPER: What's he talking about?

DANTE: I want to go into the Light of God.

THE DEVIL: I'm not stopping you.

JANE BECK: Aren't you in Heaven?

DANTE: I am not in Heaven! I wait, I wait! Never the call comes. I have always served the natural law. Thou shalt not: not in the bowel! Not in the mouth! I'm a good man. Why am I out of Heaven? You take from me everlasting life. Mai! Mai! Never. Never in the Holy City, never in the light of God! Ah!

DANTE GOES MAD. HE THROWS OVER ALL THE CHAIRS IN THE COURT. HE TAKES OUT A KNIFE.

DANTE: So I cut you. You live as I live: let the world see the bowels of your pain.

HE ATTACKS THE DEVIL, BUT IS DRAGGED OFF BY MILO MILO AND AN ACTOR.

DANTE: (*Crying*) You take from me the only thing I've ever wanted: paradiso. Paradise. Where is justice? Where is Beatrice? Where is love?

POPPER: (*To Milo Milo*) Confiscate that knife! And remove the witness.

DANTE: (*To The Devil; a last, pitiful request*) Perdona mi. Per favore. If heaven will not take me—give me a home.

DANTE IS DRAGGED AWAY.

THE DEVIL: Look what it does to you: going in pursuit of perfection.

CATHARINE LAMB: (*To The Devil*) Have you kept him out of Heaven?

THE DEVIL: With what authority?

POPPER: Mad bloody poet.

CATHARINE LAMB: He was a good man. A visionary.

THE DEVIL: He was a moralist.

CATHARINE LAMB: Is that so bad?

THE DEVIL: Is there a moral sky over me? No. Does this dirt suffer morality? No. In all the natural world there's no moral thing. You ask why you are unhappy. Why, why? Morality. You go against nature. So you will wither, like him: be known as the species that died of conscience.

SAM KYLE: May I suggest the court adjourn?

POPPER: It is getting dark.

THE DEVIL: I don't mind debating through the night—

POPPER: The court will be in recess until tomorrow morning.

THE DEVIL: —I've always found the dark most conducive to thought.

THE COURT BREAKS UP. EXIT JANE BECK, SAM KYLE AND POPPER AND ANY STRAY ACTOR. LAMB AND THE DEVIL ARE ALONE.

CATHARINE LAMB: You obviously watch over us. Tell me, what have you learned all these years?

THE DEVIL: (*He ponders a moment. Then*) I think you have certain inalienable rights which any civilized society must preserve. One, the right to delude yourselves. Two, the right to lose your sanity if and when these delusions fall apart. And three, most significantly, the right to defecate in private.

CATHARINE LAMB: Do you take nothing seriously?

THE DEVIL: Oh, Ms. Lamb, what a question. Of course. Knots, for instance, I take very seriously. Thank God, we're all tied up in knots, bound up in a bundle, or we'd stray: wander off into the dark and lose ourselves completely.

HE SMILES AT HER. AND LEAVES. THE LIGHTS GO DOWN ON A LOST LAMB.

END OF ACT TWO.

Act 3

The Second Day

*IT'S THE LAKESIDE. MIDNIGHT. A FIREWORK DIS-
PLAY IS UNDERWAY, GARISHLY LIGHTING THE
SCENE. ENTER POPPER, LAMB, VERRIER, AND TWO
ACTORS.*

POPPER: What's going on?

VERRIER: A firework display.

CATHARINE LAMB: Courtesy of Hell?

VERRIER: You don't approve?

1ST ACTOR: Oh! Beautiful!

VERRIER: Ms. Lamb is suspicious. There's no ulterior motive.

POPPER: What a surprise. Peppermint anyone?

2ND ACTOR: Look at that.

POPPER: So long since I last saw—

1ST ACTOR: I was about so high.

VERRIER: He thought you'd appreciate a little spectacle.

CATHARINE LAMB: Do you do any thinking of your own?

2ND ACTOR: Ooo—that's exquisite.

1ST ACTOR: And there!

VERRIER: There's some more along the beach.

POPPER: Silver rain?

2ND ACTOR: And rockets?

VERRIER: (*A glance at Lamb*) And Catharine Wheels.

2ND ACTOR: Shall we?

POPPER: The crocodiles come out at night.

1ST ACTOR: We can see by the light of the fireworks.

POPPER: We should still tread carefully.

EXIT 1ST ACTOR, 2ND ACTOR AND POPPER.

VERRIER: He's my master; he always has been: he always will be.
CATHARINE LAMB: You'd never desert him?
VERRIER: Not for the world. Literally.
CATHARINE LAMB: And if he wins?
VERRIER: We'll go to Heaven, all of us. He's promised.
CATHARINE LAMB: Signed in blood?
VERRIER: You're so naive. Do you think a creature lives so long, and is so crude? Age makes us more ourselves, and he was always subtle. Now he's hair-thin: his thoughts are drops on that hair; his malice—and he has malice—swims in the drop hanging on the hair. (*Contemptuously*) Signed in blood!

EXIT VERRIER. ENTER ACTOR.

ACTOR: I thought it was going well, considering.
CATHARINE LAMB: Considering he's cleverer than us by ten thousand years, the greatest liar in history and as smooth as cream.
ACTOR: You might lose?
CATHARINE LAMB: I'm considering the possibility.

ENTER JANE BECK.

JANE BECK: Excuse me.
CATHARINE LAMB: You're not interrupting anything.
JANE BECK: Macready's come back.
ACTOR: Who's Macready?
JANE BECK: The man who carried the first warrant to Heaven—
CATHARINE LAMB: —and then disappeared. Where is he?
JANE BECK: I found him wandering on the beach. He's barely coherent.
ACTOR: Drunk?
JANE BECK: Exhausted. He says he can't sleep.
CATHARINE LAMB: Fetch him.

EXIT JANE BECK.

ACTOR: I think the display's almost over.

CATHARINE LAMB: (*Sour*) Maybe they could put a match to something combustible—like you.

ACTOR: (*Returning the jab*) When you lose, are you going to retire?

CATHARINE LAMB: No comment.

ACTOR: Bitch.

EXIT ACTOR.

CATHARINE LAMB: What am I doing here?

ENTER MACREADY, WITH JANE BECK. HE IS IN TAT-TERS, PHYSICALLY AND MENTALLY.

JANE BECK: This is Macready.

CATHARINE LAMB: He looks sick.

MACREADY: (*Almost to himself*) I haven't slept for months . . .

CATHARINE LAMB: Can you hear me?

MACREADY: Months.

CATHARINE LAMB: You cost us dearly.

MACREADY: (*Coming a little to his senses*) I did my job.

CATHARINE LAMB: Then where was the witness?

MACREADY: Nowhere to sleep.

CATHARINE LAMB: Buck up, man. Why didn't you deliver the warrant?

MACREADY: I went there.

CATHARINE LAMB: The witness did not arrive.

MACREADY: I can't sleep, you see, not now. Every night: I counted sheep, going through the gate. One, two, count the sheep; three, four, going to the shepherd. No shepherd. No more sheep. So I won't sleep. Not ever.

HE WANDERS OFF.

JANE BECK: (*Calling after him*) Macready.

CATHARINE LAMB: Let him go.

JANE BECK: No more sheep?

CATHARINE LAMB: The man's delirious. We'll interview him again tomorrow.

JANE BECK: There's something going on. Some kind of conspiracy.
CATHARINE LAMB: Only one? (*A beat*) Are you coming?
JANE BECK: In a while.

EXIT CATHARINE LAMB. ENTER POPPER, BEING CAR-
RIED BY AN ACTOR. ANOTHER ACTOR FOLLOWS.

POPPER: We don't need a torch, he says. We can see the
    crocodiles by the light of the fireworks, he says. But what do
    we do when the fireworks go out? Total darkness.
1ST ACTOR: Where's Verrier?
POPPER: He flew off.
2ND ACTOR: Did you see those mothers in the mud? Fifteen,
    twenty feet long.
1ST ACTOR: What sort of noise do they make?
2ND ACTOR: They roar, don't they?
1ST ACTOR: I haven't heard them.
POPPER: Go ask one to show you his tonsils.
2ND ACTOR: No thank you.
POPPER: I'm going to bed. Good night.
1ST & 2ND ACTORS: Good night.

EXIT POPPER.

1ST ACTOR: You know what he said to me?
2ND ACTOR: Popper?
1ST ACTOR: No, the big Dee.

ENTER THE DEVIL, UNSEEN.

THE DEVIL: Would you care to kiss my ass?
1ST ACTOR: How did you know?
2ND ACTOR: Know what?
1ST ACTOR: What he said to me. Would you care to kiss my ass?
2ND ACTOR: Are you offering?
1ST ACTOR: Me?
2ND ACTOR: Yes.
1ST ACTOR: Why not?
2ND ACTOR: Your tent or mine?

EXIT 1ST AND 2ND ACTORS. THE DEVIL WANDERS
TO CENTER STAGE, CARRYING A CROCODILE EGG.

THE DEVIL: I've seen men and women in the throes of bubonic
plague, lying beside each other on diseased blankets under a
dirty lamp, suddenly overcome with passion for each other's
bodies, sores notwithstanding. I've seen them grind their last
moments away, grunting out their lives, then collapsing on
to each other, dead. When that's the way most of you touch
Heaven, if at all, how can you believe that I, who didn't
make you, am more malicious than the God who did?

ENTER JANE BECK. DURING THE OBLIQUE
EXCHANGE THAT FOLLOWS, THE TWO FIGURES
MOVE IN AND OUT OF MURKY PATCHES OF LIGHT.
OFTEN THEY ARE BARELY VISIBLE.

THE DEVIL: You should go in: it's getting bitter. Did you enjoy
the fireworks?

JANE BECK: Very pretty.

THE DEVIL: I noticed you today, looking at me.

JANE BECK: Returning your look.

THE DEVIL: Ah.

JANE BECK: You have a certain glamour. Evil does.

THE DEVIL: I don't feel evil.

JANE BECK: I don't feel like a woman, never having been a man.

THE DEVIL: I was an angel: I remember goodness. But here,
everything explodes.

JANE BECK: Explodes?

THE DEVIL: Swells up, becomes over-ripe, bursts. Bang.

JANE BECK: I'm quite stable.

THE DEVIL: No, that bag of meat you occupy is getting tight and
tender, getting too thin to hold your life.

JANE BECK: What do you suggest?

THE DEVIL: Burn it up. Heat is health.

JANE BECK: It just makes me sweat.

THE DEVIL: Passion's nothing to be ashamed of.

JANE BECK: (*Confounded*) Passion?

THE DEVIL: When we exchange looks.

JANE BECK: What are you telling me?

THE DEVIL: Have I been indelicate?

JANE BECK: (*She thinks she understands*) How could I be so slow? Growing tender—

THE DEVIL: It was unlooked for—

JANE BECK: I don't have any words.

THE DEVIL: Say nothing at all.

JANE BECK: I feel, I know it's absurd, honored—

THE DEVIL: Surely you've been in love.

JANE BECK: *I've* been in love?

THE DEVIL: Yes.

JANE BECK: Wait: you *are* telling me you're in love with me?

THE DEVIL: No, I thought you—

JANE BECK: Me?

THE DEVIL: Why would I?

JANE BECK: Well, why would I?

THE DEVIL: There seems to be a misunderstanding.

JANE BECK: Bang.

THE DEVIL: Will you smoke some hash?

JANE BECK: No thank you.

THE DEVIL: Already high enough?

THEY EXIT IN SEPARATE DIRECTIONS, AS POPPER AND MILO MILO ENTER.

POPPER: I can't sleep.

MILO MILO: Macready's dead.

POPPER: Who?

MILO MILO: The warrant carrier, Macready. He just hanged himself.

POPPER: Where?

MILO MILO: There's one tree in ten miles, and he found it. The Turkana found him. Brought him in. Wanted a reward.

POPPER: What did you give them?

MILO MILO: The rest of your peppermints and six jars of coffee. He left a note for Lamb.

POPPER: (*Takes the note*) What does it say?

MILO MILO: It makes no sense.

POPPER: (*Reading*) Do you have any pills?

MILO MILO: No.

POPPER: Looks like a sleepless night.

EXIT POPPER WITH NOTE. ENTER VERRIER AND THE DEVIL.

VERRIER: (*Sizing up Milo Milo*) This one?
THE DEVIL: Any one.
VERRIER: Milo?
MILO MILO: Who?
VERRIER: Milo Milo, isn't it?
MILO MILO: Oh. Yes. My parents . . . weren't very imaginative.
VERRIER: We were just saying: you look a little—
THE DEVIL: Soulful. Thinking of home?
MILO MILO: Not really, no. My wife's pretty unimaginative too.
VERRIER: Oh, surely you must wish you were wrapped up in bed with her.
MILO MILO: Not particularly.
VERRIER: What a waste.
MILO MILO: I beg your pardon?
VERRIER: A friend of mine was saying: how much she'd like to meet you.
MILO MILO: Me?
VERRIER: Mind you, you can be a bit of a handful.
MILO MILO: Is she . . . uh . . . natural?
THE DEVIL: As rain from Heaven.
MILO MILO: Where is she?
VERRIER: Last time I saw her, I think she was down by the lake.
THE DEVIL: I think she was.
VERRIER: If you're interested—
MILO MILO: (*After a beat*) Why not?
THE DEVIL: Why not?
MILO MILO: Down by the lake you said?
VERRIER: That way: just keep on walking.

EXIT MILO MILO.

THE DEVIL: I'm weary of this: sending innocents to their deaths.
VERRIER: Perhaps I should have violated him first.
THE DEVIL: Oh Lord. Was I ever amused by this?

EXIT THE DEVIL AND VERRIER. ENTER CATHARINE LAMB AND JANE BECK.

JANE BECK: Come on, Kate, it's time for bed. The Prosecution has to sleep. We're on our way to winning.

CATHARINE LAMB: There are no certainties. He's got tricks we don't even know about yet. Who could have predicted he'd have that damn diary? And he can be seductive.

JANE BECK: I hadn't noticed.

CATHARINE LAMB: Oh?

JANE BECK: You always say: give it a chance, the world's good.

CATHARINE LAMB: It has to be better than good. Go to bed.

SHE PUTS HER ARMS AROUND JANE, AND KISSES HER, LIGHTLY BUT WITH MORE THAN SISTERLY CARE. FAR OFF, MILO MILO LETS OUT AN AGO-NIZED CRY.

JANE BECK: Did you hear that?

CATHARINE LAMB: A bird.

ENTER POPPER, AGITATED.

POPPER: That sounded like Milo Milo.

JANE BECK: Surely not.

POPPER: I could swear—Are you planning tactics?

JANE BECK: We're done.

POPPER: There's a note for you, by the way, from Macready. He's dead.

JANE BECK: Killed himself?

POPPER: Yes. How did you know? (*Hands Catharine the note*)

JANE BECK: I had a feeling.

CATHARINE LAMB: This makes no sense.

POPPER: The man was deranged. He was the second warrant-carrier to go: too bloody eager to get into Heaven.

JANE BECK: May I?

JANE BECK TAKES THE NOTE AND EXITS.

POPPER: There's a lot of venom in the air tonight.

CATHARINE LAMB: Do you wonder?

POPPER: Beautiful fireworks. Made me feel like a boy.

CATHARINE LAMB: I'm sure that was intended. He'd like us all reduced to children.

POPPER: You really hate him, don't you?

CATHARINE LAMB: No. Not hate. There are certain species that have lived underground for so long they've lost their senses, because they don't need them. Their eyes turn white over generations, their ears close up. They lose all their skin-color; just pale featureless things that squirm and speak softly in the dark. Would I hate such a thing? No. But I don't want to share a bed with it, either.

POPPER: There's been precious little evidence of interference; you won't convict on it. He's too passive.

CATHARINE LAMB: They also sin who only stand and wait.

POPPER: Not according to the law.

FAR OFF, MUSIC APPROACHING

POPPER: Now I do hear something.

THE MUSIC BECOMES LOUDER. THE DEVIL ENTERS WITH A NECKLACE OF CANS AROUND HIS NECK.

THE DEVIL: My, my. Such glum faces. Smile! Dawn soon. Another day, another chance to spit on me. I've been to see the Turkana. Have you met them? Extraordinary fellows. Outcasts. We had a lot in common. Too poor to have wives, they live in iron shacks at the top of the lake. Naked as babies, and all the time laughing at each other, every little misfortune, laughing. One fellow told me how he'd lost his foot and you know he found it so funny. Tears rolling down his face. I like them deeply. And look what a prize they gave me. (*He rattles his necklace.*)

ENTER TWO ACTORS, WITH A SMALL BOX. A LEG HANGS OUT OF IT.

POPPER: What's this?

CATHARINE LAMB: My God.

1ST ACTOR: We think it's Milo Milo, sir.

2ND ACTOR: Difficult to be sure.

1ST ACTOR: He's been taken by a crocodile.

POPPER: (*Peers into the box*) Is that his head?

1ST ACTOR: Some of it.

NAUSEATED, POPPER LOOKS AWAY.

THE DEVIL: Lesson number one: If we play with the Leviathan, we must expect to be bitten.

1ST ACTOR: Do we bury him?

POPPER: Not here.

2ND ACTOR: We can't just keep him—the heat.

POPPER: (*To The Devil*) One of your associates; would they . . . would they fly him home?

THE DEVIL: Of course. It's the least we could do. (*To Actors*) Find Verrier.

EXIT 1ST AND 2ND ACTORS WITH BOX.

THE DEVIL: Look, there's a little finger of gray poking over the horizon. Hallelujah.

EXIT THE DEVIL.

POPPER: He may have been foolish enough for it to have been an accident.

CATHARINE LAMB: But you doubt it.

POPPER NODS.

CATHARINE LAMB: I always say: give it a chance. The world's good.

EXIT POPPER AND KATE, IN OPPOSITE DIRECTIONS.

END OF ACT THREE.

Act 4

*AS THE COURT REASSEMBLES, AN ACTOR ENTERS
AND ADDRESSES THE AUDIENCE.*

ACTOR: Nothing reminds you more absolutely of your secret
crimes than being in Court. A terror comes upon you: the
finger that accuses might swing around and point at you.
One crime's already proved. The vicarious delight taken in
other people's misery: why else are you here in the first place?
Well, voyeurs, prepare for the best scenes: the crises, the
twists, the breakdowns, and, of course, the final judgment.

POPPER: This court is now in session. Mr. Kyle?

SAM KYLE: The defense calls Isobel Nider.

THE DEVIL: (*Alarmed*) No, Samuel.

POPPER: Is she here?

THE DEVIL: I don't want to see her.

POPPER: Your client seems distressed, Mr. Kyle.

SAM KYLE: A moment m'lord.

POPPER: Call Isobel Nider.

SAM KYLE: She'll help your case. Trust me.

*ENTER ISOBEL NIDER, A FIERCE, BRIGHT EYED
WOMAN. SHE STRIDES UP TO THE DEVIL. SAYS
NOTHING; JUST STARES AT HIM.*

THE DEVIL: (*Moved*) Isobel.

POPPER: Your witness, Mr. Kyle.

SAM KYLE: Are you Isobel Nider?

ISOBEL NIDER: Of course.

SAM KYLE: You were resident in Lucerne in 1505?

POPPER: Why's there another corpse giving evidence? When are
we going to see someone without soil in their hair?

SAM KYLE: M'lord: this witness is no stranger to courtrooms, dead or alive. You were tried as a witch, am I right?

THE DEVIL: Never tried.

ISOBEL NIDER: True. Never tried: I was saved from the trial.

SAM KYLE: And is your savior in court?

ISOBEL NIDER: Of course. (*She points to The Devil.*) There.

POPPER: The point's a little redundant, isn't it? The Devil saves the life of one of his own. So what?

ISOBEL NIDER: I was never a witch.

SAM KYLE: You were going to be tried, however.

ISOBEL NIDER: We'd been in prison God knows how long. They'd pricked us, cut us, filled us with water—

SAM KYLE: And had you all answered their questions?

ISOBEL NIDER: Would you, hanging by your thumbs? Barbara had accused her husband, but Therese was worse. She'd fingered her whole family. They'd all been arrested as Devil worshipers. They even exorcised the family dog, then burnt the mutt alive. Imagine, burning a dog as a witch. Oh they were strange times.

THE COURT DISAPPEARS. THE STAGE BECOMES A FILTHY PRISON CELL. BARBARA AND THERESE, TWO HALF-CRAZED VICTIMS, JOIN ISOBEL IN IT.

ISOBEL NIDER: We were like sick people who had grown used to our tumors. We no longer thought we suffered because we had forgotten what it was like to be without suffering.

BARBARA: You confessed a long while today, sweet.

THERESE: They poured water in my ears.

BARBARA: But you've got no family left to accuse.

ISOBEL NIDER: Let her alone.

BARBARA: I just want to know who she'd found to accuse. You didn't accuse me, did you, sweet?

THERESE: It must be May now. If we could only smell the flowers.

BARBARA: You did! You told them something about me.

ISOBEL NIDER: Did you?

THERESE: No.

BARBARA: What then?

ISOBEL NIDER: She accused her grandparents.

BARBARA: Her grandparents are dead.

ISOBEL NIDER: They'll dig them up and burn them.

BARBARA: Is nothing sacred?

ISOBEL NIDER: (*A fantasy*) There's only one safe place to be. In the air—

BARBARA: And how do I get into the air?

ISOBEL NIDER: Ash.

THERESE: (*Cries*) Oh God in Heaven.

BARBARA: (*To Isobel*) You can smile. They don't bruise you, do they? Because you give them what they want.

ISOBEL NIDER: What, a squeeze, a tit to suckle? Oh yes, they can have that.

THERESE: If they touch me I scream.

ISOBEL NIDER: We hear you, dearest.

BARBARA: Even when we tell them what they want to hear, they beat us.

ISOBEL NIDER: Because they enjoy it.

BARBARA: They don't beat you.

ISOBEL NIDER: I give them a pleasure greater than beating. I tell them what The Devil looks like, how he comes to me, what he does to me.

THERESE: You shouldn't say that.

ISOBEL NIDER: Why not?

BARBARA: Because the Evil One hears us.

ISOBEL NIDER: I hope he does.

THERESE: (*Frightened*) Isobel.

ISOBEL NIDER: I hope he's listening now.

THERESE: (*Dropping to her knees*) Christ be with me, Christ be within me, Christ before me, Christ behind me, Christ on my right hand, Christ on my left hand, Christ above me, Christ beneath me, Christ round about me.

ISOBEL NIDER: Listen to her. She's decimated her family and she prays like a virgin.

A SCREAM OFF.

ISOBEL NIDER: Another night.

BARBARA: That's a man.

THERESE: I don't want to hear.

ISOBEL NIDER: (*Covers Therese's ears.*) Shut it out then.

BARBARA: It's the charcoal-burner. I saw him brought in today. I'm going to go mad if he screams all night.

ISOBEL NIDER: He used to wash at the weir, sometimes, when I was there. Strip off shameless, and wash all the grime off. He'd pour a jug of water over his head and the dirt would run off his back and down his legs, 'til he was pink as a baby.

BARBARA: He's stopped.

ISOBEL NIDER: He was bound to be broken. Too good looking by half.

ISOBEL UNCOVERS THERESE'S EARS.

ISOBEL NIDER: She's asleep.

BARBARA: Bitch.

ISOBEL NIDER: Hush now.

BARBARA: Tomorrow, I'll recant.

ISOBEL NIDER: They'll break your fingers.

BARBARA: Let them.

ISOBEL NIDER: Tell them a story, like I do.

BARBARA: About what?

ISOBEL NIDER: The Synagogue of Satan: the Sabbath.

BARBARA: What makes you such an expert? Have you been to one?

ISOBEL NIDER: You stupid cow: there is no Sabbath, except in their heads. I tell them we eat babies, drink piss. I tell them we watch corpses raped by dogs, we shit on the Host. I tell them a goat with a prick of hot iron comes out the trees and we all kiss its rump, by the light of living children, buried in excrement up to their necks, with their heads on fire. And they believe it, every word. They cross themselves with every new abomination, and thank the Lord for bringing this poor monster into the light of His redemption.

BARBARA: And they never torture you?

ISOBEL NIDER: What for? They have trouble stopping me.

BARBARA: You'll be damned.

ISOBEL NIDER: I already am.

BARBARA: Why?

ISOBEL NIDER: They've made me into what they accuse me of. Every night, I burn seven hairs and pray. Pray to Satan. Pray he'll fill me up with new fictions. Pray he'll come for me—

BARBARA: Come here?

ISOBEL NIDER: —and take me away, into the air.
BARBARA: You bitch. You've damned us all.

THERESE WAKES UP.

THERESE: (*Terrified*) There's someone on the roof. So black the moon went out. Oh God!
ISOBEL NIDER: Hush.
THERESE: Now it's coming down stairs.

SCREAMS OFF.

BARBARA: Our Father—
ISOBEL NIDER: Who wert in Heaven, unhallowed be thy name—
BARBARA: Shut up!
ISOBEL NIDER: Thy Kingdom come, thy will be done, on earth as it is in Hell.

ENTER THE DEVIL, WITH BLOOD ON HIS HANDS. HE LOOKS LIKE A LOVER TONIGHT. DASHING AND HANDSOME.

ISOBEL NIDER: I knew you'd come.
BARBARA: This isn't The Devil. Ha! You've been duped. Look at him, he's an actor, or a dressmaker.
THE DEVIL: There are some casualties in the next room: are they to your satisfaction?
ISOBEL NIDER: The eyes?
THE DEVIL: Squeezed out.
ISOBEL NIDER: And the privates?
THE DEVIL: Torn off, testicle by testicle.
BARBARA: Who have you killed?
THE DEVIL: Look for yourself.

BARBARA DOESN'T MOVE.

ISOBEL NIDER: The priests. Our torturers.
THE DEVIL: God knows, they scarcely deserved it. Men of integrity, in their way. But you asked.
THERESE: You are The Devil.

THE DEVIL: Yes, Therese, I am The Devil, for my sins. I'm sorry not to be running around as a goat feeding on boiled boys, but she's the mother of those inventions, not me. And I adore her for it. Now, Therese, Barbara, the door is open: please go.

THERESE: There's somebody in the hall.

THE DEVIL: A young man they were trying to mutilate. A charcoal burner. He's catching his breath.

BARBARA: If we go, are we damned?

THE DEVIL: Why?

THERESE: You freed us: maybe our souls are forfeit.

THE DEVIL: God understands. It's your mothers, fathers, sisters and cousins who won't forgive you.

EXIT THERESE.

BARBARA: Isobel? Are you coming?

ISOBEL NIDER: Don't look for me in Heaven.

BARBARA: God have mercy.

EXIT BARBARA.

THE DEVIL: I should have killed her for that.

ISOBEL NIDER: Was it burning hair that brought you, or the praying?

THE DEVIL: Your testimonies brought me. Your descriptions are already notorious. You've set the seal on a history of infernal Sabbaths.

ISOBEL NIDER: It was you put the thoughts in me.

THE DEVIL: You're too modest. This was yours. Every word. I've simply come to pay my loving respects, and take you with me.

ISOBEL NIDER: Suppose I don't choose to go?

THE DEVIL: What perversity.

ISOBEL NIDER: That's why I prayed to you, out of perversity.

THE DEVIL: Don't I frighten you?

ISOBEL NIDER: There's nothing you can do I haven't already imagined.

THE DEVIL: Good, then you can teach me to remember myself. I need your guidance.

ISOBEL NIDER: Can you elevate me?

THE DEVIL: Queen? Pope?

ISOBEL NIDER: In the air?
THE DEVIL: Of course.
ISOBEL NIDER: Then take me up.
THE DEVIL: Why?
ISOBEL NIDER: Just take me, will you?

*ENTER ACTOR. ANOTHER FLIGHT BEGINS, THIS TIME
BY NIGHT. STARS GLITTER IN THE DARKNESS.*

ACTOR: Pinching the nape, so—
THE DEVIL: (*He pinches her nape.*) Count to three.
ISOBEL NIDER: You count.
THE DEVIL: One—
ACTOR: They take a steep step into the night.
THE DEVIL: Two—
ACTOR: To a dizzying height above the city.
THE DEVIL: Three—
ACTOR: And stoop on the air like hawks.
THE DEVIL: There. Happy?
ISOBEL NIDER: Wrap me up: I'm cold.
THE DEVIL: I never held anything so precious.
ISOBEL NIDER: You hold excrement. We both know that. Do you
    have the power to raise storms?
THE DEVIL: Of course.
ISOBEL NIDER: Then raise one. Bring it down from the moun-
    tains and destroy the city.
THE DEVIL: Why?
ISOBEL NIDER: For me. Do you need another reason?
THE DEVIL: You hate it that much?
ISOBEL NIDER: Just do it, if you have the power.
THE DEVIL: I have it.
ISOBEL NIDER: I want every living thing swept away.
THE DEVIL: Everything?
ISOBEL NIDER: To the lice on rats. Why are you hesitating?
THE DEVIL: I'm the Prince of the World.
ISOBEL NIDER: Prove it.
THE DEVIL: It's arbitrary.
ISOBEL NIDER: So are princes. Do it.
THE DEVIL: I'll fetch Belial to do it.
ISOBEL NIDER: Can't you legislate death yourself?

THE DEVIL: In my youth I loved destruction, as women love children.

ISOBEL NIDER: And now? Too old? Too weak?

THE DEVIL: We have to live in this cell, Isobel. If we shit in the corner, we'll smell it for a lifetime.

ISOBEL NIDER: I came to you in the last resort, looking for a companion. But you squirm with confusion like all the others.

THE DEVIL: If you are so wise, teach me.

ISOBEL NIDER: I'm too tired. Let me go.

THE DEVIL: We're a mile high.

ISOBEL NIDER: Let me drop, I tell you! I'm sick of weakness.

THE DEVIL: We can kill them another night.

ISOBEL NIDER: *Let me go!*

SHE BITES HIS HAND.

THE DEVIL: Ah! Isobel!

HE LETS HER GO. SHE SCREAMS AS SHE DROPS.

ACTOR: She falls like an angel.

THE DEVIL: Isobel!

ACTOR: And bursts like a bag on the road.

THE DEVIL: Isobel! Isobel!

ACTOR: She's dead.

THE DEVIL: I know. I see.

ACTOR: Pity, really: fierce woman.

LIGHT CREEPS BACK OVER THE SCENE. ENTER SAM KYLE.

SAM KYLE: So you lost her.

THE DEVIL: Yes.

ISOBEL NIDER: He could have kept me with some courage.

SAM KYLE: But he chose not to destroy the city.

ISOBEL NIDER: Yes.

SAM KYLE: Extraordinary: this creature, that my learned friend describes as malicious and murderous, will not raise his hand to destroy a city.

ENTER CATHARINE LAMB

CATHARINE LAMB: *(To The Devil)* You could have raised her from the dead. Why didn't you?

ISOBEL NIDER: I would have resisted him.

CATHARINE LAMB: Why?

ISOBEL NIDER: He was lost. Like all of you. I was better dead.

ENTER POPPER.

POPPER: Any further questions?

CATHARINE LAMB: No, m'lord. I . . . she . . . leaves me speechless.

POPPER: *(To Isobel)* Thank you; you're dismissed.

THE DEVIL: Isobel?

ISOBEL NIDER: I never said good bye to you. Maybe I thought you'd save me, at the last moment. Prove yourself. *(A beat).* Good bye.

EXIT ISOBEL NIDER. THE DEVIL COVERS HIS FACE.

CATHARINE LAMB: So what did you do?

THE DEVIL: *(After a moment.)* I . . . wandered Europe.

SAM KYLE: You were influential, I believe, at times.

THE DEVIL: In minor ways.

CATHARINE LAMB: Such as?

THE DEVIL: I was Grand Master of the Viennese Lodge of Freemasons for fifty years, doing good works.

CATHARINE LAMB: You met with magicians. Faust.

THE DEVIL: A common queer. He seduced a vice-roy of mine: Mephistophilis. They live in Rio, I think.

SAM KYLE: You dabbled in the Arts.

THE DEVIL: I was for a time with the Medicis.

SAM KYLE: You play the violin.

THE DEVIL: Not now. Music is all sadness. Except those Turkana drums and whistles. I like those.

CATHARINE LAMB: So you went back to Hell eventually?

THE DEVIL: Yes.

CATHARINE LAMB: Why?

THE DEVIL: To hide my head.

CATHARINE LAMB: Is that the entire reason?

THE DEVIL: Yes.

CATHARINE LAMB: Didn't you have a new project? A master-piece of engineering?

SAM KYLE: M'lord; the witness is being led.

THE DEVIL: I'm not a bull, Kyle. I only go where I want to go: let her ramble.

CATHARINE LAMB: You went into Hell to challenge God himself, isn't that correct?

THE DEVIL: She's so melodramatic.

CATHARINE LAMB: Not content to make a parody of the world, you wanted to copy humanity itself.

THE DEVIL: I made a doll, if that's what you're driving at.

CATHARINE LAMB: You confess to it then?

THE DEVIL: Confess? There's no guilt here; I'm an engineer. I'd read Descartes. One of his heretical papers especially, the "Traite L'Homme". In it, he makes the analogy between the physical body and a machine: the nerves are pipes, and so on. I myself had seen beautiful hydraulic automata in the royal gardens of Germany: the work of one Solomon de Caus. To a creature such as myself, rejected by all and sundry, what better solution than to construct a companion of my own, without will except my word? Twenty years, it took me, building from the marrow outwards.

CATHARINE LAMB: Easter.

THE DEVIL: Yes, I called him Easter, after the Resurrection.

CATHARINE LAMB: And was he perfect?

THE DEVIL: I thought so, for a time.

CATHARINE LAMB: And so you took him to show the world?

THE DEVIL: He was my pride.

CATHARINE LAMB: You went to Europe.

THE DEVIL: I was happy for a while. He was the ideal compan-ion. He never said no.

POPPER: Is he here? Do we get to see the doll?

CATHARINE LAMB: He's dead, m'lord.

POPPER: So what? Half the witnesses have been putrefying.

THE DEVIL: He's gone, Popper.

POPPER: We can fetch him. The court has the authority—

THE DEVIL: There's nothing to see! He's destroyed, knucklehead! Gone to itsy-bitsy pieces.

POPPER: How did that happen?

CATHARINE LAMB: I intend to go into that.

THE DEVIL: (*Vehemently*) You've got the instincts of a tape worm.

CATHARINE LAMB: This court is entitled to the truth.

THE DEVIL: Oh is it?

CATHARINE LAMB: Are you ashamed?

THE DEVIL: No. It's simply too painful.

POPPER: You do your case no good by obstruction.

CATHARINE LAMB: I can demand a retrial if—

THE DEVIL: (*To Lamb*) Damn you. What do you want me to say? That I murdered it? No: it had no life, so there was no murder. That I destroyed it? Yes, but it was mine to kill.

CATHARINE LAMB: You went to England?

THE DEVIL: Yes.

CATHARINE LAMB: Why?

THE DEVIL: Why does anyone go to England? Desperation.

POPPER: Answer the question.

THE SCENE CHANGES. ENTER AN ACTOR. THE NOISE OF A CROWD SWELLS AS THE COURT DISAPPEARS.

ACTOR: England. 1799. A yard behind an inn in Doncaster.

THE DEVIL: (*To audience.*) There'd been a bloody spectacle in England for many years. Spain had the Inquisition, France has its glorious revolution, but England, oh, England, it had the most barbaric, most poetic entertainment of all Europe. It was called prize-fighting; bare-fisted men, boxing each other in a ring.

ACTOR: Mendoza's won!

THE DEVIL: Of course he's won. Daniel Mendoza: born near Whitechapel, thirty three years ago. A small fellow, fearsomely bright.

ACTOR: They call him the Star of Israel.

THE DEVIL: He was the first to treat the sport as a science. He was a tactician, like David, bringing down men half his size again. Martin—the Bath Butcher, they called him—had gone down to Mendoza in '84 at Newmarket. Warr had fallen in '91. That was a rare fight: so much blood. I decided then, seeing that little Jew jubilant with his bloodied fists, that such a rebel, an emblem of natural wit, should be with me.

And Easter would bring him to me. I swore it. Go fetch
Mendoza here, please.

ACTOR: What's it worth?

THE DEVIL: I won't ask you to kiss me again.

EXIT ACTOR.

THE DEVIL: (*Calling*) Jack? Oh Jack?

*ENTER JACK EASTER WITH THE ACTOR. EASTER IS A
PERFECT SPECIMEN OF HEALTHY HUMANITY. PER-
HAPS HIS EYES ARE A LITTLE GLAZED AND HIS
MOTIONS VERY SLIGHTLY MECHANICAL, BUT
THESE ARE SMALL FLAWS. OTHERWISE, HE'S QUITE
AN ACHIEVEMENT.*

THE DEVIL: (*Presenting him to the Actor.*) Would you know this
creature from flesh and blood? Speak for them, Jack.

JACK EASTER: What shall I say?

THE DEVIL: Say the first thing that comes into your head.

JACK EASTER: Women.

THE DEVIL: Where did that thought spring from?

JACK EASTER: You built me, you should know.

THE DEVIL: Show them your teeth. Ivory. And the hair is horse-
hair: rooted in his copper skull thread by thread. I did it
myself.

ACTOR: Nice work.

*ENTER DANIEL AND MRS. MENDOZA. DANIEL IS
MUCH AS THE DEVIL DESCRIBED. WIRY, TENA-
CIOUS, SMUG. HE'S BRUISED AND SWEATY, HIS
HANDS STILL BANDAGED FROM THE MATCH. HIS
WIFE IS A SHARP-EYED VIRAGO.*

DANIEL MENDOZA: I was told somebody wanted to see me.

THE DEVIL: (*Warmly*) Daniel.

DANIEL MENDOZA: Do we know each other?

THE DEVIL: Not yet. My name is Maastern; I came across to see
you fight. You really are extraordinary. We have nothing so
beautiful in the Low Countries. Just tulips and dykes.

DANIEL MENDOZA: I'm pleased you enjoyed the match.

MRS. MENDOZA: It's the last Daniel's fighting.

THE DEVIL: Oh?

MRS. MENDOZA: He's thirty-three.

THE DEVIL: But healthy.

DANIEL MENDOZA: I'm tired. I'm *very* tired.

THE DEVIL: Brandy?

DANIEL MENDOZA: No cups.

THE DEVIL: Perhaps Mrs. Mendoza would fetch some?

DANIEL MENDOZA: Will you?

EXIT MRS. MENDOZA, SOMEWHAT RELUCTANTLY.

THE DEVIL: I'd like to introduce you to my boy, Jack Easter. He's a fighter too.

DANIEL MENDOZA: I can't shake hands, they're bruised.

THE DEVIL: He'd quite set his heart on sparring with you.

DANIEL MENDOZA: As my wife says; that was my last match.

THE DEVIL: The Star of Israel, extinguished so soon?

DANIEL MENDOZA: Your boy can find other opponents.

THE DEVIL: They're all thugs, with water-logged brains and gristle noses; not for Jack.

DANIEL MENDOZA: You don't look like the father of a prize fighter.

THE DEVIL: He's not my natural son. Besides, it's the sport of gentlemen.

DANIEL MENDOZA: I was born in Whitechapel.

THE DEVIL: There's some very fine property in Whitechapel. A match.

DANIEL MENDOZA: No.

THE DEVIL: I provide the purse.

DANIEL MENDOZA: I'm retired.

THE DEVIL: You've retired before. I offer twenty-thousand guineas.

DANIEL MENDOZA: (*Amazed*) Twenty-thousand? For a single match? Who are you?

THE DEVIL: Solvency.

DANIEL MENDOZA: One match?

THE DEVIL: One.

DANIEL MENDOZA: Here in Doncaster?

THE DEVIL: If you like.

DANIEL MENDOZA: I set the date.

THE DEVIL: I'm in no hurry.
DANIEL MENDOZA: And the purse to the winner.
THE DEVIL: Of course.
DANIEL MENDOZA: How fit's your boy?
THE DEVIL: Hit him.
DANIEL MENDOZA: Why's he staring at my hands?
THE DEVIL: He doesn't like blood.
DANIEL MENDOZA: A boxer who doesn't like blood? Ha!
THE DEVIL: He's a novice.
DANIEL MENDOZA: Is he?

> *DANIEL MENDOZA HITS JACK EASTER IN THE STOMACH.*

DANIEL MENDOZA: Ah! He's like iron.
THE DEVIL: Too tough for you?
DANIEL MENDOZA: I didn't say that.
THE DEVIL: You'll fight him then?
DANIEL MENDOZA: I'll fight him: just to put a flicker of life in his eye, I'll fight him. What's this?
THE DEVIL: A contract.
DANIEL MENDOZA: I can't sign: my hands are too sore.
THE DEVIL: Your mark'll do. A bloody palm.

> *THE DEVIL TAKES HOLD OF DANIEL'S WRIST.*

DANIEL MENDOZA: That hurts.

> *ENTER MRS. MENDOZA, AS THE CONTRACT IS "SIGNED."*

MRS. MENDOZA: Cups. What's this?
THE DEVIL: Daniel—
DANIEL MENDOZA: Just one last fight. Twenty-thousand guineas.
THE DEVIL: Against my boy here, Jack Easter.
MRS. MENDOZA: (*To Daniel, in a fury*) You promised: no more prize-fighting. (*To The Devil*) He's too old, he's too exhausted. You'll kill him.
THE DEVIL: Too late. The contract's signed.
MRS. MENDOZA: He can break it.

THE DEVIL: There's a clause should he rescind. Under the terms
of the contract he's liable—

DANIEL MENDOZA: I'll be there. (*To Mrs. Mendoza*) The boy's
afraid of blood. (*To Jack*) Drink?

JACK EASTER: No.

DANIEL MENDOZA: Afraid of brandy too?

THE DEVIL: To a fair and sporting match.

THEY DRINK. THE DEVIL AND DANIEL MENDOZA
STARE AT EACH OTHER.

DANIEL MENDOZA: This brandy's tasteless.

THE DEVIL: So it is.

DANIEL MENDOZA: It's more use to wash in. Why do you look
at me like that?

THE DEVIL: You sneer with every word.

DANIEL MENDOZA: It's the way my mouth's made.

THE DEVIL: Your eyes are always narrowed.

DANIEL MENDOZA: So?

THE DEVIL: You remind me of myself.

DANIEL MENDOZA: Then God help you.

THEY ALL EXIT. ENTER AN ACTOR.

ACTOR: The match was set for September: A warm month that
year. The yard behind the inn was full of spectators from the
early morning. Among the throng, the nobility.

ENTER THE DUKE OF YORK, A HORSE-FACED ASS,
WITH MARY ANN CLARKE, HIS PRIMPED AND PRET-
TIFIED MISTRESS.

ACTOR: The Duke of York.

DUKE OF YORK: Somebody call?

MARY ANN CLARKE: (*A whisper*) Hush, Freddy, you're incognito.

ACTOR: And his mistress: Mary Ann Clarke, an *actress*.

DUKE OF YORK: Where's Mendoza?

ACTOR: I haven't seen him this morning, sir.

DUKE OF YORK: Damn fine fighter. Saw him in Spring. You see
him? Damn fine. It was an education. These younger fighters

could learn a thing or two. Footwork. Speed. I gave him five guineas. I said to him; your boxer and your woman are both worth paying for. One to take a good hammering standing up, the other to take the same lying down, eh? There's the Prince of Wales! (*Calling*) Georgie, Georgie?

EXIT THE DUKE OF YORK.

ACTOR: What do you see in him?
MARY ANN CLARKE: La dolce vita.
ACTOR: Ah.

ENTER THE DEVIL.

THE DEVIL: Excuse me, aren't you Mary Ann Clarke?
MARY ANN CLARKE: Yes.
THE DEVIL: I'm thrilled. I saw your Desdemona: heart break-ing. I never hated the nigger so much in my life. Are you in company?
MARY ANN CLARKE: Freddy.
THE DEVIL: Oh, the Duke of York. Well, I saw him not a moment ago; shall we go find him? (*Glances at the Actor.*) This is no company for a woman of quality to keep. This fel-low kisses arses.

EXIT THE DEVIL AND MARY ANN CLARKE.

ACTOR: (*To audience*) You're damned if you do, you're damned if you don't.

ENTER JACK EASTER, SHADOW BOXING.

ACTOR: What are you doing?
JACK EASTER: Shadow boxing. One, two three. Box with me?
ACTOR: I'm out of shape. But look at you. Not a drop of sweat.
JACK EASTER: I never sweat.
ACTOR: What are your tactics?
JACK EASTER: Anything to bring him down.
ACTOR: The groin?
JACK EASTER: If necessary.

ACTOR: Don't you feel sorry for him? Poor circumcised little man.

JACK EASTER: I don't bruise, and I don't sympathize. If my maker tells me to bring him down, I obey.

ACTOR: When he loses, what's he forfeit?

JACK EASTER: I don't remember—

ACTOR: Going to Hell with you is he?

JACK EASTER: Could be.

ACTOR: At least he can sweat—

JACK EASTER: What did you say?

ACTOR: Nothing.

EXIT ACTOR. JACK SHADOW BOXES ON.

JACK EASTER: (*To himself*) One, two, one, two, he's nothing to me . . . he's nothing.

ENTER MRS. MENDOZA.

JACK EASTER: And she's nothing either, with her big Hebrew eyes. I don't see them. What he tells me, I obey (*To Mrs. Mendoza*) So you look at me as long as you like. I'm going to bring him down. (*To audience*) I have this feeling, sometimes, of being in a place I've never been. Do you know what I mean? (*Pause*) Never mind.

ENTER THE DEVIL. THE MURMUR OF THE SPECTATORS RISES THROUGH THE NEXT EXCHANGE.

THE DEVIL: Are you ready?

JACK EASTER: Yes.

THE DEVIL: The crowd's huge.

JACK EASTER: I don't care.

THE DEVIL: Don't break him down too fast: give them a little sport for their money. Play with him for a while; and when he connects, reel a little, give them a few cries of pain.

ENTER MARY ANN CLARKE.

MARY ANN CLARKE: (*Admiring*) Is this your boy?

THE DEVIL: It is. Jack: may I present Mary Ann Clarke?

MARY ANN CLARKE: The Prince of Wales has put money on you. (*She touches his chest. Smiles.*)

THE DEVIL: He's a wise man.

CHEERS ERUPT, OFF.

MARY ANN CLARKE: The champion's coming out!

THE DEVIL: They may boo you: they don't like upstarts. If they spit, don't spit back, just ignore it. And you break him, Easter, you hear me?

MARY ANN CLARKE: They're calling for your man.

THE DEVIL: Kiss me, boy.

MARY ANN CLARKE: Ready?

THE DEVIL: Kiss me.

*JACK KISSES THE DEVIL. ENTER MENDOZA, FOL-
LOWED BY MRS. MENDOZA, THE DUKE OF YORK,
MARY ANN CLARKE, SEVERAL CROWD MEMBERS,
AND AN ACTOR.*

ACTOR: Right lads: into the center please. Let's have a good match: no kicking or gouging. Shake hands.

JACK AND DANIEL SHAKE HANDS.

DANIEL MENDOZA: You're cold, boy.

ACTOR: And—fight!

*TO THE ACCOMPANIMENT OF SHOUTS OF ENCOUR-
AGEMENT, THE FIGHT STARTS. THE ACTOR KEEPS UP
A RUNNING COMMENTARY, WHICH SHOULD BE
LARGELY EXTEMPORISED TO MATCH THE ACTION.*

ACTOR: Mendoza's got the experience—he's nimble, but he tires more easily than he used to. Not as young as he was. The challenger takes a hiding there, to the head, classic Mendoza tactics, in and away before the new boy sees him. Doesn't seem to stir Easter much: he looks cool as a cucumber.

THE DEVIL: (*Troubled*) He doesn't look at me: see how he avoids my eye.

MRS. MENDOZA: Daniel! Daniel!

MARY ANN CLARKE: She's quite vicious when she gets going.

THE DEVIL: Most pacifists are.

ACTOR: The new boy's taking the blows, but they don't seem to be doing much damage.

MARY ANN CLARKE: Jack's not even fighting back.

THE DEVIL: I know what he's thinking: he's pitying the Jew. Fight, damn you!

JACK STRIKES AT DANIEL.

MARY ANN CLARKE: Oh! Mendoza's down!

MRS. MENDOZA: Daniel! Get up, Daniel! Fight!

THE DEVIL: Good boy! Grease is thicker than water, eh?

ACTOR: The crowd's in a frenzy. The champion's down, and he's not going to get up again.

MRS. MENDOZA: Get up, Daniel!

DUKE OF YORK: He tripped, that's all it was!

THE DEVIL: Never!

MRS. MENDOZA: Up, Daniel!

ACTOR: He tripped. That is the opinion of the Duke of York himself. It was a genuine accident.

THE DEVIL: It's just a matter of time.

ACTOR: End of the first round. Break, boys!

*THE FIGHTERS ARE PARTED. THEY GO TO BE TOWEL-
LED DOWN.*

DANIEL: He tripped me deliberately. Wanted to break my neck. You hear me Dutchman? Maastern: I'm talking to your boy. If he fights dirty, he'll get as good as he gives and better: so tell him to watch himself, got me?

ACTOR: Corner, Mendoza.

THE DEVIL: (*To Jack*) You did well, boy. Work him up to a good Yiddish fury, eh? Then floor him.

JACK EASTER: I didn't trip him.

THE DEVIL: So you say.

JACK EASTER: I didn't trip him.

THE DEVIL: Play him along a little while: the crowd's enjoying it.

ACTOR: Bottle-holders away. Second round. Round two.

DANIEL AND JACK COME TOGETHER AGAIN.

MARY ANN CLARKE: Mendoza's eye is swollen.
THE DEVIL: Everything expands before it pops. You watch.

THE FIGHTERS ENGAGE.

ACTOR: It's fiercer than ever now.
MRS. MENDOZA: Daniel's bleeding.
ACTOR: The new boy's come back with a vengeance.
THE DEVIL: Easter! Easter!
DUKE OF YORK: Mendoza! Break his bones!
MRS. MENDOZA: Daniel! Daniel!
ACTOR: The crowd's going wild!
THE DEVIL: Just a matter of time. Down, Israel, down! Put him
    down, boy!
ACTOR: It can't be long now. Wait!
THE DEVIL: Down!
ACTOR: The challenger's dropping his defence.
DUKE OF YORK: He's crying. You see that? Damnation! He's crying.
ACTOR: It's true.
THE DEVIL: No sympathy! Down! Down! Down! Down!
ACTOR: Mendoza's taking the advantage. He's giving him a ham-
    mering. Oh my God! This is slaughter!
THE DEVIL: Fight, damn you, fight!
MRS. MENDOZA: Kill him, Daniel! Kill him.
ACTOR: Why doesn't the kid fight back? He's reeling like a drunkard.
THE DEVIL: (*Furious*) Israel!

JACK GOES DOWN.

ACTOR: And he's down! He's down! The challenger's on the floor.
    His eyes are closed. He's not getting up. Give him air.

THE CROWD SURGES AROUND DANIEL.

MARY ANN CLARKE: Mendoza's won!
THE DEVIL: (*To Jack*) A hammering it is.

ACTOR: Ladies and Gentlemen! Daniel Mendoza is the winner.

*CHEERS. MARY ANN CLARKE AND MRS. MENDOZA
EMBRACE DANIEL.*

ACTOR: (*To The Devil, like a sports reporter*) Your boy's just gone
down in a sensational defeat. What are your feelings at this
moment as his manager?

*THE DEVIL GIVES THE ACTOR A SOUR GLANCE.
THE ACTOR RETREATS, CROSSING TO MENDOZA.*

ACTOR: Daniel. Daniel, incredible match, really incredible.
DANIEL: Thanks.
ACTOR: The whole thing suddenly seemed to go your way.
DANIEL: He was crying.
ACTOR: Incredible.
DANIEL: He'll do well, though—he's a strong boy—plenty of
time to improve.
ACTOR: Incredible. Thanks.

*EXIT DANIEL MENDOZA, MRS. MENDOZA, THE
DUKE OF YORK, AND MARY ANN CLARKE.*

ACTOR: (*To The Devil*) Any last words?

IGNORED, THE ACTOR EXITS.

THE DEVIL: (*To Jack*) Get up!

JACK GETS UP.

THE DEVIL: You sentimentalist. To lose your life for a little knot
of flesh like that.
JACK EASTER: You don't frighten me.
THE DEVIL: I don't intend to.
JACK EASTER: I'm out of myself.
THE DEVIL: Out of yourself. Ha! Why, Jack, and here was me
thinking there was a ghost in the machine.
JACK EASTER: Don't make fun of me.

THE DEVIL: I made you for my amusement. Allow me to be amused.

JACK EASTER: It'll hurt you less to listen now than to find out later.

THE DEVIL: Find out what?

JACK EASTER: I'm out of myself. Into another world.

THE DEVIL: Visions now, is it?

JACK EASTER: I've smelt this world before, without my nose; seen it without my eyes.

THE DEVIL: Apparently even your mechanical mind bypasses reason on occasion.

JACK EASTER: Until now, I never knew how to get there.

THE DEVIL: And now you do?

JACK EASTER: I do.

THE DEVIL: Perhaps I built my memories of Heaven into you.

JACK EASTER: This isn't your Heaven. It's in my substance.

THE DEVIL: The past, then. Childhood.

JACK EASTER: I had no childhood, as you well know.

THE DEVIL: You need an overhaul.

JACK EASTER: You're afraid.

THE DEVIL: Inferior engineering.

JACK EASTER: You're frightened because there's something you haven't taken account of; that makes me dream, that makes me bow my head to little Israel. You'll never be Prince of the World, you know that: because there's a mystery here you can't fathom. And if I dreamt it, who was never in a womb, who had no childhood, how much more certain is it that flesh has it in its head, this nostalgia? Can you explain, engineer? How is it an engine, mere mechanics, aches to hold in its works a half-remembered beauty?

THE DEVIL: Go to the orchard behind the inn. Wait for me there.

JACK EASTER: Yes.

THE DEVIL: There can be nothing between us now, you realize that? No plea for life? Wait. Kiss me.

EXIT JACK EASTER.

THE DEVIL: (*A sudden fury*) Kiss me, you cog-headed bastard. Kiss me!

ENTER DANIEL AND MRS. MENDOZA.

DANIEL: A fair decision?

MRS. MENDOZA: Of course it was fair.

THE DEVIL: Scrupulous.

MRS. MENDOZA: You won outright.

THE DEVIL: It was a good match, Israel. Here's an authorization: you may collect the money from my lawyer. He's in Oxford Street. Round the corner from Figg's gaming yard.

DANIEL: I'll find him.

MRS. MENDOZA: And the contract?

THE DEVIL: What about it?

MRS. MENDOZA: I'd like to keep it: for sentimental reasons.

THE DEVIL: Well, aren't you wise?

THE DEVIL GIVES HER THE CONTRACT.

MRS. MENDOZA: Your boy is sick, you know that.

DANIEL: Not now.

THE DEVIL: Sick?

MRS. MENDOZA: In the head.

THE DEVIL: In the head.

MRS. MENDOZA: He was at our window last night.

THE DEVIL: Was he?

MRS. MENDOZA: Watching us as we prepared for bed: Peeping on us.

DANIEL: Even when we were intimate.

THE DEVIL: You saw him clearly?

DANIEL: Mrs. Mendoza chanced to look up. He was at the window: tears pouring down his face.

MRS. MENDOZA: That's not savoury. He's sick in the head.

THE DEVIL: Then the head must be put right.

DANIEL: The boy's got a skill—but his co-ordination's bad.

MRS. MENDOZA: (*Taking hold of her husband's arm*) Daniel—

DANIEL: No bad feeling?

THE DEVIL: None.

DANIEL: Perhaps a re-match?

THE DEVIL: I don't think so.

DANIEL: Goodnight then. Mrs. Mendoza?

EXIT DANIEL.

MRS. MENDOZA: Shall I tell you what I think?

THE DEVIL: What's that?

MRS. MENDOZA: I think you're The Devil. No—don't say anything. If you are, every word you say is a lie, so I'll never
know. Not that I want to know.

EXIT MRS. MENDOZA.

THE DEVIL: They were to die in penury, of course, but I couldn't
take pleasure in that, not at the same time.

*EXIT THE DEVIL. NIGHT FALLS, INSTANTLY. ENTER
MARY ANN CLARKE, HER MELODRAMATIC SKILL IN
FULL FLOOD.*

MARY ANN CLARKE: Somebody help me!

ENTER ACTOR.

ACTOR: Don't shout so loud. Everybody's in bed.

MARY ANN CLARKE: There's been a murder.

ACTOR: Where?

MAR ANN CLARKEY: In the orchard. No, don't go—stay with
me.

ACTOR: I want to see.

EXIT ACTOR.

MARY ANN CLARKE: Where's Freddy? Freddy?

ENTER THE DUKE OF YORK.

MARY ANN CLARKE: Freddy! There you are.

DUKE OF YORK: The whole house is up.

MARY ANN CLARKE: Take me away.

DUKE OF YORK: Are you drunk?

MARY ANN CLARKE: We've got to get back to town, before I go
crazy.

DUKE OF YORK: Is this one of your scenes?

MARY ANN CLARKE: No.

DUKE OF YORK: Ophelia, or some such?

MARY ANN CLARKE: Christ, no! A murder, Freddy.

DUKE OF YORK: Where?

MARY ANN CLARKE: In the orchard behind the house. It's the boxer.

DUKE OF YORK: Mendoza?

MARY ANN CLARKE: The other one. The young one.

DUKE OF YORK: Maastern's boy.

MARY ANN CLARKE: I saw him from our window. He was just standing in amongst the trees.

DUKE OF YORK: Queer look on that one.

MARY ANN CLARKE: I waved.

DUKE OF YORK: Hussy.

MARY ANN CLARKE: He didn't see me. I thought he was ill. It was getting dark, and he was just standing there. So I went down. He was kneeling on the ground, had his shirt off from around his shoulders, all bare, with his arms outstretched, and holding two tree trunks, one in each hand.

DUKE OF YORK: Saying his prayers?

MARY ANN CLARKE: I was going to say something: then I saw the Dutchman, Maastern, coming up out of the mist, taking a running step towards the boy, with a two handed hammer. The boy didn't move. He just knelt there, wide, and let the hammer meet his head behind the ears. His neck split, his skull clove in, and sparks of blue fire leapt out. Pieces of his head: his teeth, one of his cheeks, flew off towards me: cut my arm. Silver, they were. Flesh on one side, silver on the other. I saw another blow before I ran. There was no more than a stump at his neck: his head was gone.

DUKE OF YORK: Damnedest thing.

ENTER THE DEVIL, WITH A PIECE OF JACK'S HEAD.

MARY ANN CLARKE: Jesus preserve us.

THE DEVIL: I thought I saw you running off.

DUKE OF YORK: (*Drawing his sword*) Don't get too close. Duke of York.

THE DEVIL: It had to be done.

DUKE OF YORK: Beat the fellow's block off?

THE DEVIL: He betrayed me. You understand. A general like yourself.

DUKE OF YORK: Touch perfunctory.

THE DEVIL: I made him what he was.

DUKE OF YORK: Was he to have no trial?

THE DEVIL: He was my flesh and blood.

DUKE OF YORK: Bad show.

THE DEVIL: He could have been a great fighter. His body was unscratched. It was this—

DUKE OF YORK: This?

THE DEVIL: His brain; what's left of it.

DUKE OF YORK: (*Peering at the mechanism*) Damnedest thing.

THE DEVIL: His sentimental, conscience-stricken, nostalgic little mind.

DUKE OF YORK: Weak in the head, eh?

THE DEVIL: Yes.

DUKE OF YORK: Out of his misery then.

THE DEVIL: You understand.

MARY ANN CLARKE: You brute.

THE DEVIL: Were I a brute, would I mourn?

MARY ANN CLARKE: (*Venomously*) I hope you burn in Hell.

EXIT MARY ANN CLARKE.

DUKE OF YORK: She doesn't know what she's saying.

THE DEVIL: I wish you health sir.

DUKE OF YORK: And to you sir.

THE DEVIL: And the company of mindless men.

THEY SHAKE HANDS.

DUKE OF YORK: Couldn't trouble you?

THE DEVIL: What?

DUKE OF YORK: The clockwork.

THE DEVIL: Why not?

HE HANDS THE PIECE OF JACK'S HEAD OVER.

DUKE OF YORK: (*Beaming*) Give it to the lady wife. On the mantelpiece or some such. Conversation piece.

EXIT THE DUKE OF YORK. THE LIGHTS RISE. THE

COURT BEGINS TO REAPPEAR.

THE DEVIL: I never made a man so happy so easily.

CATHARINE LAMB: Pitiful. After this fiasco, did you return to Hell?

THE DEVIL: Yes.

CATHARINE LAMB: For how long?

THE DEVIL: I intended to bury myself away forever. In 1812, I married Lilith. We had children.

POPPER: How many?

THE DEVIL: To date, six hundred and thirteen. All mortal.

POPPER: Thank God for that.

THE DEVIL: I wouldn't have my children live like me.

SAM KYLE: But you haven't stayed in Hell have you?

THE DEVIL: I made occasional visits to the world: but fewer and fewer.

CATHARINE LAMB: As you clearly have such deep-seated contempt for us, why do you come out of the earth at all?

THE DEVIL: It's not easy to completely forget your charges.

CATHARINE LAMB: So you still consider yourself the Prince of the World?

THE DEVIL: Until I'm delivered back to my father, yes.

CATHARINE LAMB: These last few decades, you've been more active than ever, surely?

THE DEVIL: (*Dismissively*) Flying visits.

CATHARINE LAMB: In Europe and America, we have account after account of appearances: the Pentagon, the Kremlin, a certain bunker in Berlin. This is high level influence.

THE DEVIL: There are, thankfully, parties who value my experience.

CATHARINE LAMB: I put it to you that you emerged at the beginning of this century to wipe out humanity. That since that time you've used every means at your disposal to encourage division and dissent.

THE DEVIL: You have no evidence of malice from me. Frustrated ambition, perhaps, resentment even, but nothing more.

SAM KYLE: Was it merely frustrated ambition that made you kill your own son?

THE DEVIL: Not that again. Leave it alone.

POPPER: Mr. Kyle, please remember that you're the defendant's Advocate. You're doing him a disservice.

CATHARINE LAMB: You felt cheated, isn't that right?

THE DEVIL: What of?

CATHARINE LAMB: The World.

THE DEVIL: I want to be home. Surely you understand that. Even you. Though I heard your mother would not have you at her deathbed.

CATHARINE LAMB: (*Ignoring this*) You felt vengeful.

THE DEVIL: No.

CATHARINE LAMB: You wanted us dust: because you couldn't have the power over us.

POPPER: Is that true?

THE DEVIL: No!

CATHARINE LAMB: I call your wife.

THE DEVIL: Lilith? She's here?

SAM KYLE: A wife cannot testify against her husband. That's the law.

POPPER: That's true.

CATHARINE LAMB: M'lord, this is no natural husband and wife.

THE DEVIL: We have children, a hearth—

LILITH: (*Off*) Too late.

ENTER LILITH, RESPLENDENT, IN BLACK.

POPPER: Wait!

THE DEVIL: Light of my life.

POPPER: This is the wife?

LILITH: I'm not his wife. I'm his concubine. Or I was.

POPPER: This is still unlawful. I think . . .

LILITH: Shut up, little man. I will have my say.

THE DEVIL: Why are you doing this?

LILITH: You think I don't know you? That woman.

POPPER: Who?

LILITH: (*Points to Jane*) Her!

CATHARINE LAMB: Jane?

POPPER: I'm lost.

LILITH: (*To Popper*) They look at each other: are you blind? My husband has been making love to one of his prosecutors for the last two days.

JANE BECK: There's nothing between us.

POPPER: Are you in alliance with the defendant?

JANE BECK: No.

POPPER: The wife can't testify. Remove her from the court.

LILITH: I demand to be heard.

POPPER: Will somebody *please* remove her?

SAM KYLE: Wait! As The Devil's Advocate, I move that the wife's testimony be heard. The defence has no objections.

THE DEVIL: I object.

SAM KYLE: I'm your lawyer. Sit down.

THE DEVIL: Kyle. I don't want her giving evidence.

SAM KYLE: Well I do. Maybe we need to hear your story from somebody close to you—

THE DEVIL: She's too cruel. Too petty.

SAM KYLE: (*Quietly*) Good. She'll humanize you. Make you look a little more human.

CATHARINE LAMB: Jane?

JANE BECK: What?

CATHARINE LAMB: Is what she says true?

JANE BECK: No. There was a misunderstanding last night, but I'm not in allegiance with him.

CATHARINE LAMB: Do you want to be?

JANE BECK: He's A monster: The Devil himself. Of course I want him.

THE DEVIL: (*To Sam*) After this, I'm dismissing you as my advocate.

SAM KYLE: Do that. Why did you choose me anyway?

THE DEVIL: Oh, little man, it's in your blood: Kneeling and kissing me. Kyle, you call yourself, so nobody will know; but I know.

SAM KYLE: I'm not ashamed.

THE DEVIL: You're a liar, Keipenhauer: Your blood's mine, like your father's, and your father's father.

SAM KYLE: Jesus: why am I so slow?

POPPER: So what does the defence want?

SAM KYLE: The wife testifies. Let's hear her.

POPPER: (*To Lilith*) Go on: before war breaks out.

LILITH: He was in Hell fifty years: and we lived together in peace.

THE DEVIL: Do you know how much you hurt me?

POPPER: Quiet.

LILITH: He was having a boil on his buttock lanced.

THE DEVIL: Oh, you remember every little detail, don't you?

POPPER: Silence!

LILITH: Verrier arrived. Poor deluded Verrier.

THE DEVIL: Now Verrier's the victim.

POPPER: I won't tell you again.

LILITH: He'd brought with him a book: and news from the world.

CATHARINE LAMB: What was this book?

LILITH: By Darwin: *The Origin of the Species*. His Satanic Majesty was most excited.

CATHARINE LAMB: And the news?

LILITH: Somebody had announced, in Europe, the death of God.

JANE BECK: Friedrich Nietzche.

THE DEVIL: The man was crazy, of course. Suspiciously devoted to his mother.

POPPER: The death of God?

LILITH: Lucifer was ecstatic. He danced; skipping on the spot and clapping his hands.

POPPER: Why?

CATHARINE LAMB: Did you believe that God was dead?

THE DEVIL: Of course not: But it was enough that humanity might believe it. Better yet they discovered their true heritage. (*To Sam*) I believe in tradition. Father to son, back beyond the apes.

LILITH: He said he had the opportunity now to tread the earth as its master.

THE DEVIL: And why not? With my experience, I'd be benevolent, rational—

LILITH: I said to him: aren't you happy here? And he said: how can I be happy, with a race of ambitious nits on my head?

THE DEVIL: Ambitious nits: did I say that? The woman has the memory of an elephant. And the thighs.

LILITH: I remember he took hold of Verrier and demanded the obscene kiss.

THE DEVIL: (*Furious*) Stop this, woman!

LILITH: He was smiling: I hadn't seen him smile like that before, or since.

THE DEVIL: Shut up! Shut up!

LILITH: A careful campaign, he said; and we can set the world on fire.

THE DEVIL: You lying bitch!

LILITH: It's true! You know it's true!

POPPER: Order! Order!

LILITH: He said that he'd hold a war.

THE DEVIL: I swear I'll beat your brains out!

POPPER: Silence!

THE DEVIL: (*Cold*) You say one more word . . .

CATHARINE LAMB: Go on.

LILITH: He said he'd hold a war, and it would be called The Twentieth Century . . .

SAM KYLE GRABS HOLD OF THE DEVIL, TO KEEP HIM FROM ATTACKING LILITH.

THE DEVIL: I never said that!

CATHARINE LAMB: You swear those are his words?

LILITH: I swear it.

CATHARINE LAMB: Thank you. No more questions.

POPPER: Kyle?

SAM KYLE: No.

POPPER: (*To Lilith*) You're dismissed.

THE DEVIL: You see, Jane? Everybody deserts me. I'm alone. (*To Sam*) Let go of me. I'm not going to do her any harm.

LILITH: Goodnight, light of my life.

EXIT LILITH.

CATHARINE LAMB: "I shall hold a war, to be called The Twentieth Century." With those words, the case for the prosecution rests, m'lord.

POPPER: Kyle?

SAM KYLE IS SITTING STARING BLANKLY, DEFEATED AND EXHAUSTED.

POPPER: Kyle?

SAM KYLE: That's not my name.

THE DEVIL: We have no more evidence to offer.

SAM KYLE: Oh yes we do. I've got a piece of evidence I'd like to give the court. My name isn't Kyle: it's Keipenhauer. My family is German. I've asked myself, these last two days, why I was chosen as The Devil's Advocate. After all, I'm not the greatest lawyer in the world. Well, it seems subservience to the Prince of the World runs in my family. A story my grandfather used to tell—so preposterous, nobody believed him, about how he met Lucifer—I want to tell it now.

POPPER: Is this relevant?

SAM KYLE: Oh yes, it's relevant. He was a soldier, my grandfather, in Russia at the end of the war. Just a common private, doing his common duty. A few weeks before the conflicts ended, he was in a forest near the Russian border when he met a man—

THE COURT RECEDES. A JOYLESS LIGHT FALLS THROUGH LEAVES. ENTER GEORG KEIPENHAUER, A YOUNG SOLDIER, WITH A BABY WRAPPED IN A BLOOD AND DIRT STAINED CLOTH, AND—FROM THE MURK BETWEEN THE TREES—THE DEVIL, WITH A BOOK AND PEN. GUNS CAN BE HEARD, NOT FAR OFF)

KEIPENHAUER: Are you Russian? There's a curfew—

THE DEVIL: I'm sorry?

KEIPENHAUER: Get back to your house. You want your head blown off?

THE DEVIL: I'm not a local man.

KEIPENHAUER: This is forbidden territory.

THE DEVIL: I'm a historian.

KEIPENHAUER: Just keep out of this forest.

THE DEVIL: What's your name?

KEIPENHAUER: Why?

THE DEVIL: Answer me.

KEIPENHAUER: (*Almost mesmerized*) Georg Keipenhauer.

THE DEVIL: I need some assistance from you.

KEIPENHAUER: I've no time. This child—

THE DEVIL: Dead?

KEIPENHAUER: Not quite. I found her amongst—why am I telling you this?

THE DEVIL: Could you just direct me to the mass graves? That is where you brought her from?

KEIPENHAUER: (*Nods*) They pile them up. Some of them are still breathing.

THE DEVIL: There have been atrocities, then? I thought I'd finished: but there's no rest for the wicked.

KEIPENHAUER: Finished?

THE DEVIL: I've taken it upon myself these last three years to chronicle the names of the casualties in Europe, especially the Jews. I've just come up from Dachau, thinking the work was done, and what do I find?

KEIPENHAUER: Why?

THE DEVIL: Why what?

KEIPENHAUER: Why chronicle the dead?

THE DEVIL: We've committed genocide, you and I, Germany: the least we can do is make an account. So I've been asking the dead their names before they go to dirt.

KEIPENHAUER: All the names?

THE DEVIL: As many as I can find.

KEIPENHAUER: You write them down?

THE DEVIL: Here.

KEIPENHAUER: Such a small book.

THE DEVIL: I have a neat hand. Germany, why do you look so unhappy? All the engineers of Hell couldn't conceive of this. I'm humbled. The teacher, taught. You've set the standard for a coming generation.

KEIPENHAUER: It wasn't me—

THE DEVIL: It never is, Germany, that's the trick of it. How shall we ever stop it, when we can't find the culprit? Owning up to evil takes the courage of an innocent: an unresolvable state of affairs. Do you want to give me the child?

KEIPENHAUER: What for?

THE DEVIL: Aren't you withdrawing? I heard artillery close. You don't want to be weighed down—

KEIPENHAUER: No, I'll take her.

THE DEVIL: What's her name?

KEIPENHAUER: I don't know.

THE DEVIL: For the records.

KEIPENHAUER: She isn't dead.

THE DEVIL: (*Reaching*) Give her to me.

KEIPENHAUER: (*Refusing*) She's not dead.

THE DEVIL: A little gestural, isn't it, looking after a single baby when somebody's laid her whole country to waste? Give her to me. You must save your spotless skin, Georg. No doubt you have a family of your own. Children, grandchildren. Give me the child and no bullet will touch you.

KEIPENHAUER: She's so small.

THE DEVIL: Dispossessed, Georg. She doesn't want life. She'll only resent you for it. Oh, everything's confusion isn't it? You don't know which way to turn. But between us we are architects of the solution. The world's ending, Georg. This is wise. There's no light to go by. There's only the engine demanding ceaselessly, ceaselessly demanding to continue. Relinquish the mite. No harm. Let her go. (*He takes the baby*) There. There. Which way are the graves?

KEIPENHAUER: Back along the path, to your left. Two hundred yards.

THE DEVIL: Thank you. You have my deepest respect and admiration. I'll always remember you. Please excuse me; I must take her into history.

EXIT THE DEVIL.

KEIPENHAUER: I let her go: to my shame I let him take the living child and bury her. Criminals I've known, always apparent; brutal men. I've showered with them. They were flesh enough. But this bland evil, so reasonable, so understanding. I never knew it. But it's The Devil himself.

EXIT GEORG KEIPENHAUER. THE COURT REAPPEARS.

SAM KYLE: The Devil himself. (*To The Devil*) That's why you chose me, isn't it? Because I was the son of the son of a man who'd served you, and you believe in history, in what's in the blood, in the great, squalid tradition.

POPPER: Is this the evidence?

SAM KYLE: What more do you want?

POPPER: Lamb?

CATHARINE LAMB: What more can I add, m'lord?

POPPER: What more indeed? Shall we move on to the summing up?

SAM KYLE: I refuse.

POPPER: Come on. We're so close to having this over and done with.

SAM KYLE: I call for a re-trial! I've gone along with this farce, and I shouldn't have done. He's a murderer, I know it! He's a rapist, he's responsible for more crimes than you'll see in a

thousand trials—
POPPER: Please, Kyle!
SAM KYLE: Keipenhauer, if you please.
POPPER: No re-trial. My heart wouldn't bear it.
JANE BECK: A recess, at least, m'lord.
CATHARINE LAMB: No, let's get to the finishing arguments.
JANE BECK: (*To Lamb*) A recess would give us time to talk.
CATHARINE LAMB: About what?
POPPER: A recess makes sense. But just a couple of minutes. I
    want us gone before dark. These crocodiles . . .

KYLE AND POPPER TALK TOGETHER IN WHISPERS.

CATHARINE LAMB: Why did you move for a recess?
JANE BECK: We've been so stupid.
CATHARINE LAMB: We should have pressed the home advantage
    while we had it.
JANE BECK: Macready left a message for us.
CATHARINE LAMB: I know, I read it. It was babble.
JANE BECK: You read the words, not the sense.
CATHARINE LAMB: Don't be so damned cryptic.
JANE BECK: Sleep: remember?—he told us he counted sheep
    going through the gates of Heaven so he could get to sleep.
    When he came back from Heaven, he hadn't slept. No more
    sheep, he said. Why? No shepherd, he said. Why?
CATHARINE LAMB: (*It's dawning on Lamb*) My Lord . . .
JANE BECK: Chomsky's dead too, remember. Slit his own throat.
CATHARINE LAMB: And Dante: accusing The Devil of keeping
    him out of Paradise.
JANE BECK: Nobody listens to him, he said.
CATHARINE LAMB: Nobody listens.
JANE BECK: We have to tell Popper. Kyle's right. The trial's void.
CATHARINE LAMB: No.
JANE BECK: But the whole point—
CATHARINE LAMB: The Devil wants to return to Heaven. Let
    him go.
JANE BECK: Catharine, the whole trial's a nonsense.
CATHARINE LAMB: (*To herself*) We have to lose. Give him the
    victory, and lock him away forever.
JANE BECK: Kate? That's not fair.

CATHARINE LAMB: Is he fair?

JANE BECK: You're no better than him if you trick him.

CATHARINE LAMB: So Lilith was telling the truth?

JANE BECK: Doesn't he fascinate you?

CATHARINE LAMB: He repulses me.

JANE BECK: You're being simpleminded.

CATHARINE LAMB: And you're behaving like an adolescent. God, if you want a father figure, take Popper.

JANE BECK: Damn Popper! Damn you! Damn all of you.

CATHARINE LAMB: He's got to you, hasn't he?

JANE BECK: Words are all you've got against him.

CATHARINE LAMB: More's the pity.

JANE BECK: He's more than words.

CATHARINE LAMB: Yes, he is. I said to Popper last night: he was like something you find under a rock, a soft voice that speaks to you in the dark. Well, he's not even that. He's a vacuum. He belongs where there's nothing. Nothing to nothing.

JANE BECK: I can tell Popper—

CATHARINE LAMB: Jane. No. I want him brought down.

POPPER: Attention, please. Mr. Kyle refused to continue as The Devil's Advocate. I have no choice but to call for a re-trial.

CATHARINE LAMB: Unless the defendant wants to act as his own advocate. We're so close to being done.

POPPER: Would you be happy with that?

CATHARINE LAMB: I'm not obstructive. And it would save the necessity of another trial.

POPPER: And the defendant?

THE DEVIL: I've never been very persuasive, but I'll try my best.

POPPER: Very well, this court is in session. Summaries, if you please. The case for the defense.

THE DEVIL: Ladies and gentleman: as well you know, denial is never as easy as assertion. To say no to the mirage is difficult, when one is thirsty, though to say yes will only prolong the agony. You're thirsty for a victim, and in this deluding heat, I look like your man, someone to hang your bad meat from, and say: that's the one! He's the cause! Now, I'm not spotless. I've been hungry, I've fed on power a little, flesh a little, drunk down unhappiness because it matched my mood, but ask yourself: is any crime deserving of ten thousand years of suffocation? You can give me air, which is joy:

don't envy it me. Put me back in Heaven, as justice demands. Or I will rage against confinement, and thrash in my pit until I bring down the world on my head. That's all.

THE DEVIL SITS DOWN.

POPPER: Most eloquent. The prosecution?

CATHARINE LAMB: First, m'lord, I'd like to say that Mr. Kyle's desertion leaves me aghast.

POPPER: Forget Kyle.

CATHARINE LAMB: I can't. I see his betrayal as the last of many described to us over the last two days. This creature came to us with a reputation so foul, that his name stood for depravity. But what have we found, when we look a little closer? That time and time again he is cheated by those he trusts, rejected by those he loves, and far from being the Great Manipulator, he's limped from one mincing failure to the next, crippled, loveless and defeated.

POPPER: I don't believe what I'm hearing.

THE DEVIL: (*To Jane*) Is this your influence?

JANE BECK: No.

CATHARINE LAMB: Can we convict him? Any more than we can kick a dog with its bowels out, dying in a gutter? Look at him—wounded, and out of his season. Doesn't he look, in his confusion, in his cowardice, and in the profundity of his misery, a little like us? Let him go to Heaven—and never come back.

CATHARINE LAMB SITS DOWN.

POPPER: This is most unorthodox. The Advocate starts giving us his family history. The Prosecutor decides she's got it all wrong. It's . . . bewildering. (*He rises; speaks to the dark air surrounding the stage*) Jury members . . . wherever you are out there . . . somebody's watching me, so it's either you or the crocodiles . . . let me point out that the rules of this court allow for no debate. Vote guilty or not guilty. The majority carries the day. Simple as that. If you want a little guidance, for what it's worth, let me say this: He's a mixed bag. So are we all. Even the best of us. I don't think we can doubt that he's done harm. Perhaps terrible harm. But he's also been cheated and betrayed. The question is: does he deserve paradise? Do any of us, come to that? (*A long beat. He ruminates, plainly troubled*) It's curious . . . watching him these couple of days, hearing the stories . . . to find a fallen angel so like ourselves. I don't find that very comforting, personally. I would have liked a little less humanity in him. But the similarity's no reason to punish him . . . (*His own confusions silence him. He stares out at us, perplexed*) Is it? (*Another long beat. Finally, he sits down*) My head hurts.

ENTER ACTOR.

POPPER: Has the jury decided?
ACTOR: Yes, m'lord, they have.
POPPER: Is the court assembled?
ACTOR: Yes, m'lord.
POPPER: Will the court rise? Read the decision.
ACTOR: In respect of the trial of Lucifer, also called Old Nick, also called the Evil One—
POPPER: Never mind the also calleds. Just get to the finale.
ACTOR: The jury finds the defendant . . . *not guilty.*

FROM EARTH, CHEERS.

CATHARINE LAMB: (*Smiles*) There is justice.
SAM KYLE: Why did you defend him?
CATHARINE LAMB: We all have our reasons.
POPPER: The defendant is now bound, under the rules of this assembly, to return into Heaven permanently. Do you agree so to do?
THE DEVIL: Of course. I would not overstay my welcome. It's not polite.
POPPER: And do you swear to never return to Earth?
CATHARINE LAMB: An oath isn't sufficient.
POPPER: If, having left us, he attempts a permanent return, his existence is forfeit. You understand that?
THE DEVIL: Yes. I understand perfectly.
SAM KYLE: (*To Catharine*) He's got what he wanted. Why weren't you swayed by the evidence?
POPPER: This court is dismissed. We can all go home.

THE DEVIL: Thank you all, and goodbye. My dear Jane, my Prosecutor, Catharine—thank you. Even you, Keipenhauer, Lucifer loves you. Remember that.

POPPER: I suppose we go home by truck, huh? No flying?

CATHARINE LAMB: I think the miracles are over for today.

POPPER: Then we should hurry. Kyle—could you organize the loading of the trucks?

KYLE EXITS.

THE DEVIL: Popper, my very best to your grandchildren. Especially Oscar. He's quite a boy. You should look in on him one night. Surprise him. For a twelve year old, he's got a way with a book of matches. (*To Catharine*) So sorry to have ruined your career, Lamb. If you weren't a lesbian, I'd suggest motherhood.

EXIT CATHARINE LAMB.

THE DEVIL: Your mind's closed, Jane. What are you thinking?

JANE BECK: Nothing.

THE DEVIL: You're struggling to keep something from me.

JANE BECK: No.

THE DEVIL: A declaration—?

JANE BECK: A minute here is a minute of neglected joy. Why don't you go?

THE DEVIL: At least a kiss—

ENTER VERRIER.

VERRIER: Your Majesty—

THE DEVIL: Live a short life, Jane. Come to me soon.

EXIT JANE BECK.

THE DEVIL: Verrier.

VERRIER: The hosts are assembled below us, lord. Principalities and dominations.

THE DEVIL: Are they really?

VERRIER: Are we ready to go?

THE DEVIL: No, Verrier. We shall not be going.

VERRIER: What?

THE DEVIL: Does a triumphant son return to the City of God trailing two hundred scabs? Would you wish that on me? I go alone.

VERRIER: Even me?

THE DEVIL: You remind me of my pain, Verrier.

VERRIER: Please—

THE DEVIL: Good night. Where I am gone, no one can follow. I'm there. You see me? In power. In glory.

EXIT THE DEVIL.

VERRIER: (*In anguish*) Come back!

IN THE EARTH, THE DEMONS HOWL.

VERRIER: Come back! . . . We won't be cheated! Come back!

ENTER CATHARINE LAMB.

CATHARINE LAMB: I warned you.

VERRIER: He left us here. Even me. Oh God . . . at least he could have put me out of my misery.

CATHARINE LAMB: Prepare yourself, Verrier. The story isn't quite finished. Give me the protection I'm going to need, and you may get the death you want.

VERRIER: What protection do you need? Against what?

A TERRIBLE HOWL RISES FROM THE GATHERING DARKNESS.

CATHARINE LAMB: I've tricked him, Verrier.

VERRIER: How? Is he out of Heaven?

ENTER POPPER, JANE BECK, AND SAM KYLE, ALL PANICKED.

CATHARINE LAMB: No, he's in Heaven.

POPPER: The whole sky's turned black.

JANE BECK: Kate, he'll kill us all.

CATHARINE LAMB: Verrier's here—
POPPER: Will somebody tell me what's going on?
CATHARINE LAMB: He wants a word with me, I think.
SAM KYLE: There's something coming out of the clouds—
POPPER: Christ help us—
SAM KYLE: There's nowhere to hide.

THE HOWL HAS RISEN TO A DEAFENING SCREAM.
ENTER THE DEVIL, NAKED FOR HEAVEN. HE
ATTACKS CATHARINE LAMB.

THE DEVIL: You vomiting crab-cunted bitch! You turd faced,
    pus-mouthed, putrid fucker! Scheming shit!
CATHARINE LAMB: Verrier!

VERRIER PULLS THE DEVIL OFF HER.

THE DEVIL: I'm too hot for you, Verrier! I'm burning! Let me go,
    or you burn too! I want this cunt—
POPPER: Why haven't you gone?
CATHARINE LAMB: You're bound to Heaven—
THE DEVIL: No!
CATHARINE LAMB: —Or you forfeit your life.
THE DEVIL: *She's cheated me!*
POPPER: You have to go back.
THE DEVIL: Let me go, Verrier! I'm too hot to hold!
CATHARINE LAMB: Go back where you belong, Satan.
THE DEVIL: You knew, didn't you?
SAM KYLE: Knew what?
CATHARINE LAMB: Yes, I knew. Macready told me.
POPPER: Knew what? What did she know?
THE DEVIL: The City of God's empty! Do you hear me? Let me
    go, Verrier. She's put me in Heaven, locked me away forever,
    and it's empty! That's why your miserable warrant carriers
    slit their Christian throats! *God has gone.* I'm alone! Verrier!
    Let me loose, or I burn you up!

VERRIER HOLDS ON. THE DEVIL FIGHTS HIM. VER-
RIER SCREAMS AND FALLS BACK, DEAD.

POPPER: You've killed him.

CATHARINE LAMB: It's what he wanted. (*To The Devil*) You can't help yourself now—giving gifts. You want to kill me, too? I don't mind so much.

THE DEVIL: Bitch! The others will come with me at least. (*He speaks to the Earth*) Carreau, Sonneillon, Procell, Belial! Do you hear me, angels? Come with me! I didn't mean what I said. Come with me.

SILENCE.

CATHARINE LAMB: A deafening hush. I should go, if I were you—they're not going to listen. And if you stay here, you may be hanged by the neck.

THE DEVIL: (*To Catharine*) I'll find some way to pain you. And it will be terrible.

CATHARINE LAMB: Your hand doesn't reach that far. Take another step, and you'll be wiped out—

THERE'S A MOMENT WHEN IT SEEMS THE DEVIL WILL RISK IT ANYWAY. THEN HE RETREATS. EXIT CATHARINE LAMB.

THE DEVIL: (*Whispered*) I'm not defeated. I'm strong. You can't throw me away.

POPPER: You have to go.

JANE BECK: I'm going too.

THE DEVIL: Jane?

POPPER: Are you crazy, woman?

JANE BECK: I want his company, and he needs mine.

POPPER: This is forever. Locked in Heaven. With *that.*

SAM KYLE: Don't touch him—he burned Verrier.

JANE BECK TAKES HOLD OF THE DEVIL.

JANE BECK: He's cold. It's all relative. I see that now.

THE DEVIL: Don't let them send me away, Jane. (*To the assembly*) You need me, for justification. What will you tell your children to keep them quiet? What will you hang your crimes on? There's no harm in me. No harm in all the world . . .

JANE BECK GENTLY COAXES HIM AWAY. THEY EXIT.

SAM KYLE: I've got to go back to the courts next Monday. Divorce cases, mostly.

POPPER: I'm not sure what she did was strictly lawful, you know. He may have grounds for another appeal.

SAM KYLE: (*Fingers to his lips*) Ssh. The point is . . . it was just.

POPPER: You're so old-fashioned. I like that.

EXIT POPPER. ENTER TWO ACTORS TO REMOVE VERRIER'S CORPSE.

SAM KYLE: Do you know how she worked it out?

ACTOR: Worked what out?

SAM KYLE: The trick.

ACTOR: Ask her.

ENTER CATHARINE LAMB. SHE IS PACKED AND READY TO GO.

ACTOR: He was just asking how you did it.

CATHARINE LAMB: Where's Jane?

ACTOR: Jane who?

EXIT ACTORS WITH BODY.

SAM KYLE: (*Delicately*) She's gone, Lamb.

CATHARINE LAMB: Oh?

SAM KYLE: She went with him.

CATHARINE LAMB: (*After a time*) Of course she did.

SAM KYLE: Are you upset?

CATHARINE LAMB: Real hurts go so deep you don't feel them for a while. Ask me in a week. I hope she's satisfied.

SAM KYLE: I think we ought to get going. I think I hear the crocodiles . . .

EXIT SAMUEL KYLE. ENTER AN ACTOR.

ACTOR: Finished?

CATHARINE LAMB: Finished.

ACTOR: (*Taking center stage for the final speech*) History always begins with a cry, and ends—

CATHARINE LAMB: Wait. What are you saying?

ACTOR: It's the wrap-up.

CATHARINE LAMB: Ends? History doesn't just end.

ACTOR: Well I have to say something.

CATHARINE LAMB: (*Insistent*) It doesn't end.

ACTOR: What should I say then?

CATHARINE LAMB: Whatever you like—you won't be shot for it.

ACTOR: I can't think. Wait!

CATHARINE LAMB EXITS, LEAVING THE ACTOR ALONE. HE IS UNCOMFORTABLE FOR A MOMENT. THEN HE EXTEMPORIZES.

ACTOR: Maybe history doesn't end. Maybe we go on. Sometimes this, sometimes that. What can I say? In one month, cold so your skin shrinks; in another month, fields of risen color, water-meadows filled with sky, new birds. On and on. World without end.

EXIT ACTOR.

THE PLAY ENDS.